Third Edition

· ·

MARKETING TODAY'S FASHION

Carol Stewart Mueller

Professor, Nassau Community College

Eleanor Lewit Smiley

Professor Emeritus, Nassau Community College

Prentice Hall Education, Career, & Technology
Englewood Cliffs, New Jersey 07632

In memory of Helena de Paola

• •

Library of Congress Cataloging-in-Publication Data

Mueller, Carol Stewart.
   Marketing today's fashion / Carol Stewart Mueller, Eleanor Lewit
Smiley. — 3rd ed.
      p. cm.
   Rev. ed. of: Marketing today's fashion / Helena de Paola. 2nd ed.
1986.
   Includes bibliographical references and index.
   ISBN 0-13-043001-3
   1. Fashion merchandising.   I. Smiley, Eleanor Lewit.
II. DePaola, Helena. Marketing today's fashion.   III. Title.
TT497.D46   1995
687'.068'8—dc20   94-17476
                                                            CIP

Acquisitions editors: Elizabeth Sugg and Priscilla McGeehon
Editorial/production supervision and
   interior design: Laura Cleveland, WordCrafters Editorial Services, Inc.
Cover design: Laura Ierardi
Buyer: Ed O'Dougherty
Marketing manager: Debbie Sunderland

© 1995, 1986, 1980 by Prentice-Hall, Inc.
A Simon & Schuster Company
Englewood Cliffs, NJ 07632

Printed in the United States of America
10 9 8 7 6 5 4 3 2 1

ISBN 0-13-043001-3

Prentice-Hall International (UK) Limited, *London*
Prentice-Hall of Australia Pty, Limited, *Sydney*
Prentice-Hall Canada Inc., *Toronto*
Prentice-Hall Hispanoamericana, S.A., *Mexico*
Prentice-Hall of India Private Limited, *New Delhi*
Prentice-Hall of Japan, Inc., *Tokyo*
Simon & Schuster Asia Pte. Ltd., *Singapore*
Editora Prentice-Hall do Brasil, Ltda., *Rio de Janeiro*

To Richard and Richard, Jr., for their patience and love

To Jerry for always being there for me

Contents

· ·

v

•••

WORLDWIDE INFLUENCES ON TODAY'S FASHION 69

Part Four

· ·

TODAY'S FASHION INDUSTRIES   223

Part Five

MERCHANDISING TODAY'S FASHION   327

Contents

Preface

· ·

The third edition of *Marketing Today's Fashion* retains the same practical, classroom-proven approach and purpose as the previous editions; that is, to provide the student with an in-depth understanding and appreciation of the dynamic and multidimensional nature of the fashion business.

The fashion industry—from the production of raw materials to the distribution of finished goods—accounts for an estimated one-third of the world's economy. In the United States, one out of every eight workers is employed in fashion or its allied fields. The buying and selling of fashion goods contribute billions of dollars to our gross domestic product. The fashion industry continues to offer a wide variety of exciting and financially rewarding career opportunities for those who are academically well prepared and who are willing to work hard.

In recent years, the marketing of fashion products and services has become increasingly difficult and highly competitive. Today's business is more uncertain and complex; therefore, students desiring a successful career in this field will have to be better prepared than ever. They will have to possess an awareness of current problems facing the industry and be able to offer several alternative solutions to them. They will need a full understanding of the environment and its impact on each of the various sectors within the fashion business. They will need to be able to analyze and understand the behavior of consumers and, of course, have the ability to predict the future accurately. These abilities are prerequisites to making sound marketing decisions, and this text is written to help the student acquire them.

Marketing Today's Fashion is intended for students enrolled in a one-semester, introductory/survey course in fashion merchandising or marketing. The text is suitable for use at either a two- or four-year college or business proprietary school and for the growing number of similar courses that are being taught in this field on the secondary level.

Structure

The book is divided into five parts, fifteen chapters, a bibliography, and a glossary. Each chapter begins with a set of Learning Objectives that familiarize the student with the important concepts discussed in the chapter. A new feature entitled Performance Outcome has been added to the beginning of each chapter to provide the student with a practical, behavioral application of the knowledge gleaned from reading the chapter. At the end of each chapter are several study aids: Terms to Remember, Highlights of the Chapter, Review Questions, and a Research and Projects section that provides the student with the opportunity to do creative, in-depth analyses of chapter topics. Items in Terms to Remember have been printed in bold face within the text of the chapter.

Industry Features and Fashion Features have been included as part of the text to spotlight outstanding people, places, things, and events that are a special part of the fashion industry. Thoughtful questions, which permit a student to go beyond the course content to creatively apply his or her experience and intellect to their resolution, are frequently offered in these sections. Career opportunities in the various sectors of the business have also been highlighted in this way.

Organization

The text is organized to give a logical and informative sequence to the presentation of the material. Part One provides the student with an understanding of fashion, its language, its movements, and its environment. Also included is an analysis of fashion's most important element—the consumer.

Part Two puts the information of the text into context with worldwide historical and economic changes occurring from the period of Louis XIV of France to the present. Students become aware that fashion is an international industry, and this global approach is one which every fashion apparel student should have.

The first two parts of the text set the stage for Part Three, which details the development and growth of the fashion industry in the United States. The historic and economic changes that occurred in this country shaped the fashion industry and provided the springboard for its present magnitude. This part of the text also emphasizes the importance of the primary markets. The fashion industry cannot exist without its raw materials.

Part Four presents all of the manufacturing aspects of the fashion apparel industry as a unit and gives the student a thorough understanding of what it takes to get a finished product into a retail store.

Once the students are aware of how fashion is produced, they then learn how it is merchandised. Retailers—who they are and how they operate—and their ancillary merchandising operations and methods of promotion are the subject of Part Five.

By organizing the book in this sequence, and especially by including the historical perspectives of the fashion industry, a twofold goal is achieved: first, a view of the past, present, and future provides the students with a keen understanding and appreciation of the business of fashion; second, the wide scope of the material gives the students an all-encompassing familiarity with other aspects of fashion. This equips them with additional authoritative knowledge of the subject, which is certain to help in their search for a successful career in the industry.

Acknowledgments

There are many people from business and academia who have made contributions to this book, and they are gratefully acknowledged throughout the body of the text. However, there are those who provided specific and invaluable assistance in putting this edition together and are therefore deserving of special mention. From Nassau Community College, Garden City, New York, Professor Constance Gottlieb offered valuable suggestions regarding the overall direction of the book and especially Chapters 1 and 2. Professor Patricia O'Beirne provided useful insights into the men's wear industry. Professor Barbara Blumberg Ostipikwo made important suggestions regarding the leading designers in the New York fashion world. Professor Harriet Strongin has been our mentor and inspiration for many years and encouraged us to produce this third edition. Jerome Ira Smiley, retired English Department Coordinator of the Sewanhaka Central District on Long Island in New York, offered learned guidance in language usage in order to make the text easily accessible to students on many different levels of education. Zelda Kessler carefully read the materials from a disinterested point of view to ensure that the text could be easily assimilated. Dr. Amy Louise Smiley of Washington College in Maryland also reviewed material in the text. Genevieve Jezick, a talented design student at Nassau Community College, drew the modern adaptations of Empire and Regency dress in Chapter 4.

Within the industry, gratitude is extended to Louis Kessler whose many years in the children's wear field added a special dimension to the chapter on the children's wear industry. Stanley Kaye, editor of *Kids Fashions*, sent us copies of his trade journals and information on the Larkin trade shows. Carol and Dick Jacobson of Ffany read the section on footwear in the accessories chapter and made valuable sug-

gestions. They also sent us a copy of the *Ffany Special Edition*—1993—
and allowed us to use the beautiful shoe illustrations from that journal. Harold Cohen of Empire Sales provided important information
about wholesaling apparel for men, women, and children. Alfred
Weiss, a newspaper writer who reports on trade shows in New York
City, provided us with innumerable valuable trade journals. Walter
Mankoff of the ILGWU Research Department provided information
about the imports of apparel. Barbara Fredericks, sweater designer,
provided information about the manufacture and design of knit goods.
We thank these people and others too numerous to mention for their
kind suggestions and input while writing this textbook.

Special mention must be made for the wonderful overall direction
offered by Priscilla McGeehon, our editor; Barbara Marttine, and Laura
Cleveland, our production editor.

Carol Stewart Mueller
Eleanor Lewit Smiley

Part One

UNDERSTANDING
TODAY'S FASHION

CHAPTER 1

The Meaning of Fashion

LEARNING OBJECTIVES

After reading this chapter, you should be able to:

- Give a specific, all-encompassing definition of what the word *fashion* means.
- Identify and explain the four areas of specialization in the fashion industry.
- Understand the framework in which the fashion business operates.
- Define the terms used as technical language or "jargon" by the fashion industry.

PERFORMANCE OUTCOME

After reading this chapter, you should be able to:

- Use the language of the fashion industry in the correct context and with the correct meanings.
- Be aware of the career opportunities and job descriptions in each of the four sectors of the fashion business.

Fashion. A complex word. Meaning glamour and excitement to many; creativity and business opportunity to a few. To some it suggests a world of fantasy—a world of designers, models, and expensive clothes. For these people "fashion" is often undefinable—something mysterious and illusive, something not really related to them.

But the word **fashion** can be clearly defined. It does have specific and concrete meanings. For something to be in fashion, it must be popular with a significant number of people. In order for that to happen, fashions must be copied or imitated so as to be available. What becomes fashion is a timely reflection or an artistic expression of a society and its values. Since we live in a rapidly changing world, what is in fashion is constantly revised and updated with new and innovative ideas.

Fashion also has an economic dimension. If something is in fashion, this means it sells. Determining exactly what will sell and make a profit has made fashion a marketing-oriented business. Since students should begin learning about fashion by defining it, each aspect about fashion is explained in the following section.

DEFINING FASHION

From an academic viewpoint, *Webster's New Collegiate Dictionary* defines *fashion* as "the prevailing style during a particular time."[1] The definition includes "the choice or usage (as in dressing, decorating, or living) generally accepted by those who regard themselves as up-to-date and sophisticated." In his book, *Economics of Fashion*, Dr. Paul Nystrom, a professor who was the first to apply economics to fashion, defines *fashion* as "nothing more or less than the prevailing style at any given time."[2]

These two definitions describe fashion in extremely general terms, referring to home furnishings, apparel, accessories, and even a style of behavior. Since these references are too broad for the purpose

[1]By permission. From *Webster's New Collegiate Dictionary*, 1976, by G. & C. Merriam Company, publishers of the Merriam-Webster dictionaries.

[2]Paul H. Nystrom, *Economics of Fashion* (New York: Ronald Press, 1928), p. 4.

3

of this text, the definition of fashion will be limited to the dress and personal decoration worn by men, women, and children. *Fashion,* then, is the prevailing style or styles in dress and accessories worn by a group of people at a particular time. It follows, "Whenever a style is accepted and worn by a sufficient number of people it is in fashion or becomes a fashion."[3] Simply stated, it is popular.

As this definition implies, different fashions can exist at the same time. Because we are a democratic society that values diversity, there is no single prevailing style. Different fashions exist simultaneously. What is popular on the college campus—jeans, tee-shirts, and sneakers—is not acceptable attire on Wall Street. While the young may follow fashion trends from the rock music world and MTV and wear the punk or grunge look, those over 40 may choose a conservative "Dress for Success" fashion look. Western wear—boots, bolos and cowboy hats—is popular in the West and Southwest, but not in the Northeast. What is standard garb for proms and weddings is certainly unfashionable for everyday casual wear. There is no one fashion look for everyone; what is popular varies with age, geography, occupation, and occasion.

Fashion Requires Imitation

For a fashion idea to be successful and popular, it must be copied. In the United States "success" means mass produced by manufacturers and mass purchased by consumers. Fashion involves producing and promoting new ideas and items that have widespread appeal. Imitation is so much a part of the fashion business, that manufacturers even have a word for it: *knockoff.* A knockoff is an adaptation or copy of an expensive original design. These originals are referred to as **high fashion.** Knockoffs are **mass fashion** items produced at a price point which makes them salable and affordable to a large number of people. The majority of fashion consumers wear knockoffs or mass fashion items, not high fashion designer originals.

Mass fashions are not copied "line for line," or exactly. High fashions created by designers in New York, Paris, or Milan inspire the general direction of mass fashion. For example, if the Paris runways show a long flowing silhouette, mass fashion producers interpret that look for their clientele.

Although fashion is an imitative process, it does not necessarily follow that everyone must look alike. Fashion is a general concept.

[3]Harriet T. McJimsey, *Art and Fashion in Clothing Selection* (Ames, Iowa: Iowa State University Press, 1973), p. 48.

Today the industry produces sufficient variations and interpretations of prevailing styles so that customers can choose apparel reflective of their own judgment and taste. However, this was not always the case.

Historically, fashion emulation followed a straight and narrow path. Royalty created fashions, which were then copied by the lower classes. French designers created looks, which were then closely copied by American manufacturers. Today, imitation is still the key to the process, but those who initiate fashion have changed. Ideas to be copied now come from anywhere and everywhere, as will be discussed later in the text.

Fashion Is Innovative

Just because imitation is a key element of fashion, this does not imply that fashion is repetitive or boring. In fact, even when fashions reflect a bygone era, there is no exact duplication of styles. That is, today's look evokes feelings and remembrances of the past, but the designs are totally new and original. For example, bell-bottom trousers were first worn by sailors as part of their Navy uniform. Men and women wore them again in the 1970s as part of the hippie fashion look. They were revived once more in the 1990s as fashion moved away from leggings and toward a softer more fluid silhouette. Each time bell bottoms were in fashion they looked new and fresh (see Figure 1–1).

Fashion innovation is an ongoing process because consumer wants and needs are unending and constantly changing. To meet this demand, the fashion industry updates its latest offerings with newer versions on a continuous basis. There is no ultimate design; there is always next season. In fact, the only constant about fashion is change. This constant alteration of what styles are fashionable and what styles are not has led to criticisms that charge fashion as an economic waste! Vance Packard, consumer advocate and author, charges that the fashion industry is based on the principle of "planned obsolescence." Packard coined this term and defines it as the deliberate outmoding of merchandise by the subsequent introduction of other products.[4]

In particular, Packard accuses the fashion industry of causing the obsolescence of fashion merchandise by eliminating its desirability. For example, a perfectly wearable pair of shoes goes out of fashion simply because the industry has introduced a "new look."

The reply to this criticism is simple: People become bored easily. Human beings have an insatiable appetite for new products, and the fashion industry responds to this basic need for variety and change.

[4]Vance Packard, *The Wastemakers*. Copyright © 1958. Reprinted by permission of the David McKay Company, Inc.

THE NEW GUARD.

The black leather policeman's coat. Andrew Marc's sleek offshoot of the motorcycle jacket, in a slightly longer silhouette. Soft English lambskin, imported for sizes S, M, L. (28-157) $740. Saks Fifth Avenue Collection, D/313.

Jet jewelry from Anne Klein Couture.
Button clip-on earrings. (28-159) $65.
Cross pin. (28-414) $65.
Designer Jewelry, D/416.

18

Ours exclusively. Fall's strong suit—
day-into-evening pants from
Constance Saunders. Black wool crepe romanced
by detachable ivory ruffle cuffs. Imported for
sizes 4 to 16. (28-158) $398.
Better Dressses, D/163.
Shoe featured on page 73.

Courtesy: Saks Fifth Avenue, New York

• • • • • • • • **FIGURE 1-1   This page from Saks Fifth Avenue Folio shows that bell-bottoms return to fashion again and again.**

Moreover, the industry is providing a very important and useful economic function: By directing raw materials into finished goods, it creates employment and revenues.

Fashion Is Art

Although fashion, as a business, depends on imitation to be financially successful, it is also an art. Those who create fashion use their talents to apply artistic principles of color, line, and design to their work. Customers putting together a wardrobe select garments that are aesthetically pleasing as well as practical. Therefore, the same qualities of beauty, creativity, and self-expression necessary to the work of a sculptor or painter are also essential elements in fashion. The medium of expression in apparel is cloth rather than marble or canvas.

Collections of apparel and accessories are housed in major museums both here and in Europe, adding legitimacy to the claim that fashion is art (see Table 1–1).

Designers, manufacturers, and retailers all consider visits to museums essential to, and routine in, their work. What transpires in the other mediums of art—painting, sculpture, and so forth—overlaps into the creative aspects of fashion.

· · · · · · · · **TABLE 1-1   Museums with Major Costume Collections**

Musée de la Mode Pavillion de Marsan Louvre, rue de Rivoli 75001 Paris, France	Centro Internazionale Arti e del Costume 3231 Palazzo Grassi 30124 Venice, Italy
Musée du Costume de la Ville de Paris 14 avenue New York 75001 Paris, France	Victoria and Albert Museum Brompton Road London S.W. 7, England
Costume Institute Metropolitan Museum of Art 5th Avenue and 82nd Street New York, NY 10028	Costume Institute McCord Museum 690 Sherbrooke Street W. Montreal, Canada
Costume Gallery Brooklyn Museum Eastern Parkway Brooklyn, NY 11238	Costume Gallery Los Angeles County Museum of Art 5905 Wilshire Boulevard Los Angeles, CA 90036

Fashion Is a Dimension of Time

Historically, fashions of the past have been identified regionally. Apparel worn by different groups was typically identified as Grecian, Roman, Egyptian, and so on. Today, designations that refer to places or nationality do not seem appropriate. Fashion apparel in the modern world is no longer a function of place but a function of *time*.

Fashion historian James Laver suggested that the "victory of time over place" occurred in the 1400s at the end of the Middle Ages.[5]

From then on it became easier to *date* a person than to determine his or her nationality. That is, by looking at apparel, one could more easily determine the period in history in which it was in fashion than the country in which it was worn. For example, by looking at Figure 1–2, it is apparent that this type of dress is a twentieth-century, post-World War II phenomenon. Certainly the look was not limited to one country, but rather was an accepted fashion worn by most of the modern world.

By introducing new styles of clothing, the fashion industry encourages change and emphasizes the future over the present and past.

Courtesy: Natalie Best for Copely Newspapers

• • • • • • • •   **FIGURE 1-2 Classic Levi's, worn by many women in today's modern world.**

[5]James Laver, *Modesty in Dress* (Boston: Houghton Mifflin, 1969), p. 3. Copyright © 1969 by James Laver. Used by permission.

These time zones become easily recognizable through apparel. If people are futuristic about their wardrobe, they are considered to be progressive and moving in the right direction. If they wear styles that are current, they are considered correct. However, if they wear outdated styles they may be subject to ridicule, scorn, and even considered backward in their thinking. In the words of Paul Nystrom, "To be out of fashion is, indeed, to be out of the world."[6]

Fashion Is Big Business

The acceptance of a prevailing style as a fashion automatically implies that consumers have *purchased* that particular garment or accessory. And since Americans purchase over $200 billion worth of fashion merchandise a year, fashion acceptance translates into big business. As in all businesses, the goal of those in fashion is to make a profit. And like other businesses that depend on the ultimate consumer for profit, the fashion industry has become marketing oriented.

No longer does the fashion industry dictate what customers should wear. Today, the successful process of marketing a garment or an accessory *begins* with the customer. *First* the customer is analyzed to evaluate his or her wants and needs. *Then* apparel designed to meet these wants and needs is produced and sold. This procedure is known as *fashion marketing* and can be defined as directing the flow of fashion goods from producer to consumer in order to profitably satisfy consumer wants and needs.

From the foregoing discussion a composite definition of *fashion* can be summarized as follows: *The acceptance and purchase by consumers of artistically designed apparel and accessories that are mass-produced and marketed by the fashion industry in a timely fashion in order to satisfy consumer wants and needs.*

••

THE FASHION INDUSTRY

Fashion doesn't just happen—someone is responsible for deciding which styles are presented to customers each season for their approval and purchase. That "someone" is not an individual, but rather a diverse group of professionals who make up the fashion industry. These individuals are categorized into four areas of specialization that operate conjunctively to market fashion apparel and accessories success-

[6]Paul H. Nystrom, *Economics of Fashion* (New York: Ronald Press, 1928), p. iii.

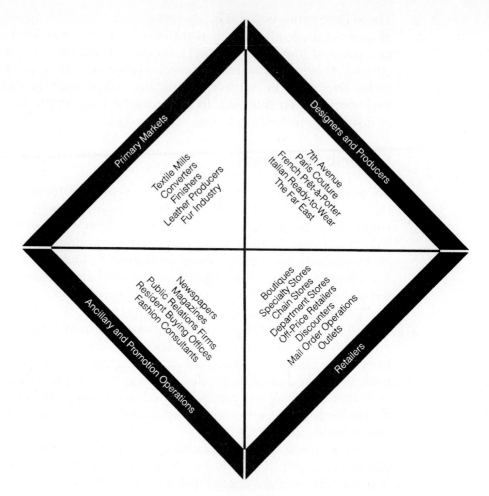

Primary Markets

Textile Mills
Converters
Finishers
Leather Producers
Fur Industry

Designers and Producers

7th Avenue
Paris Couture
French Prêt-à-Porter
Italian Ready-to-Wear
The Far East

Newspapers
Magazines
Public Relations Firms
Resident Buying Offices
Fashion Consultants

Boutiques
Specialty Stores
Chain Stores
Department Stores
Off-Price Retailers
Discounters
Mail Order Operations
Outlets

Ancillary and Promotion Operations

Retailers

•••••••• **FIGURE 1-3 The four areas of specialization in the fashion business.**

fully. They are the *primary markets, designers and producers, retailers,* and *ancillary and promotion operations* (see Figure 1–3).

The *primary markets* supply the raw materials of fashion—textiles, leather, and fur. Those who work in this sector are responsible for color and fabrication, which are the initial determinants of fashion direction. The *designers and producers* create and manufacture fashion merchandise in the United States and abroad. The most important fashion design centers are New York, Paris, and Milan. Major production centers are located in New York, Germany, and the Far East.

The *retailers* sell fashion goods through various types of outlets and are the direct link to the ultimate consumer. *Ancillary operations* communicate, analyze, and facilitate the fashion process of moving the goods from producer to consumer through the use of consumer and trade publications, newspapers, seminars, resident buying offices, and direct consultation.

Each area performs a unique but equally important aspect of the fashion marketing process. No one sector of the business operates independently; all facets of the business are totally interrelated. Therefore, when a customer buys a particular garment or accessory, it is the collective result of the whole fashion industry.

Because all the sectors of the business are so vital to fashion, each is individually explained and analyzed separately in later chapters. Also, career requirements and opportunities are covered in depth as they pertain to each.

However, it is important from the outset to see how multidimensional the fashion business is and how many different jobs exist within this exciting industry. The Industry Feature listing entry-level jobs in the fashion industry provides an overview of the business.

THE FRAMEWORK OF FASHION

Like all other businesses, fashion does not operate in a vacuum. The fashion industry, however, responds rather than initiates. What it responds to is the overall environment and the changes taking place in society. This external environment forms the framework in which fashion-marketing decisions are made.

The framework consists of four sectors: the social/psychological sector, the political/legal sector, the technological sector, and the economic sector (see Figure 1–4).

Social/Psychological Sector

The values, attitudes, and beliefs held by individuals and society at any given time form the basis of this sector. Culture, traditions, class structure, the role of various institutions, and the importance of different groups are sociological concerns that affect the overall direction fashion takes. Personality, aspirations, and the need for peer acceptance and recognition are the psychological influences that cause individuals to buy particular items of apparel and accessories. The way a society functions in terms of its structure, customs, and values provides the backdrop for fashion and fashion change. As social patterns undergo restructuring and re-evaluation, that change is often reflected in a corresponding change of dress. Some of the aspects of our society that have been the subject of recent radical change are class structure, changing lifestyles, the role of women, and a new ideology or value

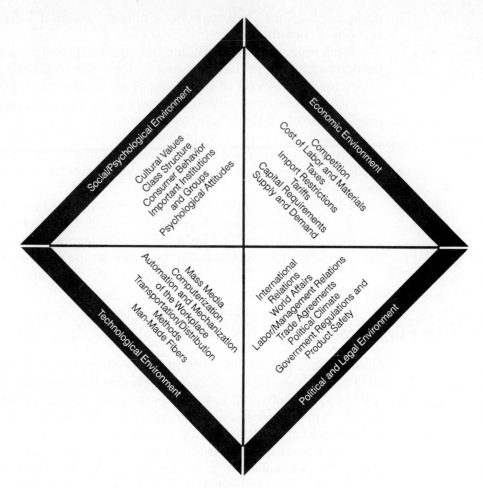

Social/Psychological Environment

Cultural Values
Class Structure
Consumer Behavior
Important Institutions
and Groups
Psychological Attitudes

Economic Environment

Competition
Cost of Labor and Materials
Taxes
Import Restrictions
Tariffs
Capital Requirements
Supply and Demand

Technological Environment

Mass Media
Computerization
Automation and Mechanization
of the Workplace
Transportation/Distribution
Methods
Man-Made Fibers

Political and Legal Environment

International
Relations
World Affairs
Labor/Management Relations
Trade Agreements
Political Climate
Government Regulations and
Product Safety

•••••••• FIGURE 1-4 **The framework of fashion.**

system. The way people think about themselves and their relationships with others is reflected in their choice of apparel. The kinds of activities people enjoy and participate in also require a certain way of dressing.

Class Structure

Over the past 200 years, the distinctions separating the upper, middle, and lower classes have blurred. With the redistribution of wealth, the middle class has emerged as the largest and most important group in terms of buying power and in the successful adoption of new fashion. This democratization has accelerated and increased the demand for fashion goods.

Entry-Level Jobs in the Fashion Industry

Primary Markets

textile artist	fabric technician
colorist	assistant converter
handweaver	quality control trainee
knit grapher	embroidery designer
silk screen artist	assistant stylist
assistant piece goods buyer	sales trainee
fabric librarian	

Design and Production

assistant designer	cutting assistant
sketcher	marker trainee
assistant patternmaker	showroom sales trainee
junior designer	production assistant
sketcher/stylist	costing engineer trainee
shipping clerk	road sales trainee

Retailing

assistant department manager	assistant buyer
executive trainee	display trainee
assistant to fashion director	assistant store manager

Ancillary Operations

mechanical artist	assistant art director
assistant photo stylist	assistant to fashion coordinator/ consultant
public relations assistant	
editorial trainee	junior copywriter
media sales trainee	resident buying office trainee
free-lance illustrator	distributor/planner trainee
assistant fashion editor	layout artist

It also means that the middle class needs avenues to express its acquired wealth. In the United States there are no means of acknowledging one's position in society by title, birth rights, or family names.

Possessions and purchases are the way to announce one's status in society. Items usually associated with the upper class—the right car or the right clothes—are the visible means of distinction. These items, known as *status symbols*, are the basis for evaluating one's rank in society.

Sociologist Thorstein Veblen in his famous book, *The Theory of the Leisure Class*, calls this concept "conspicuous consumption."[7] In summary, this means that a person wears certain clothes or purchases certain objects for the sake of improving his or her status in the eyes of others. These status symbols and their extravagant quality are a means by which the wearer communicates wealth and rank.

Although Veblen's book was written in the late 1800s, conspicuous consumption is still practiced today. In an article in *The New York Times Magazine*, columnist Russell Baker states, "In New York at least, males of the moneyed class announce their wealth through their shoes. On meeting a New York man, one instantly looks at his feet for the buckles of Gucci, which declare rich."[8]

The problem for the middle class is that Gucci shoes are very expensive. So are clothes designed by the world's great designers. For example, a dress created and made by Yves Saint Laurent can cost as much as $10,000. The fashion business has responded to this dilemma by creating what is known as "designer-label merchandise." These products—such as perfume, fashion accessories and mass produced clothing—carry the designer's name but are manufactured by private companies and are therefore less expensive. The designer gives permission to use his or her name through a "licensing agreement" that permits the manufacturer to label its products with the designer name in exchange for a fee or royalty. (Licensing will be discussed in depth later in the text.)

By purchasing designer-label goods, the middle class has access to upper-class status symbols but at affordable prices.

Changing Lifestyles

Over the past three decades, the way of life for most Americans has become "laid back." Formality has given way to a more relaxed lifestyle. For most people, formal dinner parties, strict rules of etiquette, and restrictive dress codes are exceptions in daily living. Many business firms across the country no longer obligate their employees to the

[7]Thorstein Veblen, *The Theory of the Leisure Class,* Mentor ed. (New York: New American Library of World Literature, 1963), p. 97.

[8]Russell Baker, "Talking Clothes," *The New York Times Magazine* (December 7, 1975), p. 6.

proverbial suit and tie as work attire. Restaurants and social establishments have changed their dress codes from jacket required to what prominent New Yorker Gerald E. McCarthy describes as "dignified casual."

For the fashion industry this has resulted in an increase in demand for sportswear for both men and women. In fact, sportswear represents the fastest growing category in terms of sales in womenswear and menswear. Comfortable and casual have become key designing concepts along with easy care, wrinkle free, and seasonless. People no longer want to fuss and bother when they dress for work or play.

The Role of Women

Since three-fourths of the fashion merchandise produced in this country is for women, the role of this group in society greatly affects the fashion business.

Today, women are being given greater responsibilities and freedom. As their experiences and roles become more diverse, their fashion tastes, needs, expenditures, and purchasing power change accordingly. For example, the number of working women in the United States has grown dramatically since 1950. Today, almost 70 percent of the women between the ages of 18 and 65 work outside the home. This has created a tremendous demand for additional clothing and a whole new category in women's wear called *career dressing* or *business attire.*

Although most groups in society have increased their leisure time, the working woman seems to have less now than ever before. Between work and family responsibilities, there is no time to browse, try on, or shop. The fashion industry has recognized this fact and has increased shop-at-home opportunities. Retailers and manufacturers send out direct-mail catalogs, have toll free 24-hour phone numbers, and have stepped up efforts to use shopping channels on TV. More and more upscale retailers such as Saks Fifth Avenue and designers such as Calvin Klein have made commitments to this new and exciting method of reaching their all-important female customers.

New Ideologies

The types of values that are important to a society at a given time directly influence taste and dress. Often, these prevailing values are embodied in persons who are admired, in groups who receive unusual amounts of attention and publicity, and in items or materials that are greatly sought after. These individuals, groups, and things in turn affect prevailing styles of behavior and dress.

The 1920s and its emancipation of women were symbolized by the bob haircut, a de-emphasis of the female shape, and shockingly short skirts. In the 1960s, the braless look and mini skirt were illustrative of women's new-found freedom. Women in the 1970s wore pant suits, which were as much a symbol of desired female equality as they were a symbol of casualness and comfort.

In the late 1960s, the fashion industry zeroed in on the "Woodstock generation," a term applied to those born during the baby-boom years following World War II. This 18- to 25-year-old age group was the largest and most influential age category at that time. Fashions were youthful, funky, and unconventional, reflecting the group's anti-Establishment values.

Today, it's the "over-40" market and senior citizens who are being catered to by most businesses, including fashion. Styles are conservative and more casual due in part to this group's age and lifestyle.

Sociologists and psychologists have done extensive research on role theory. For example, a man wears a variety of hats—such as father, husband, employee, sportsman, police officer—in order to function in society. To properly play each of these parts, different "uniforms" are worn. The fashion industry provides a varied selection of clothing and accessories to meet this demand for what might be termed "occasion dressing." When playing golf or going to work, a different outfit is worn for each assumed role.

Clothing becomes an accurate expression of personality—a visible, tangible extension of who we are and how we feel about ourselves. "You are what you wear—you wear what you are" may be an appropriate verbalization of this concept.

Finally a concern for causes and group identification has been replaced with individualism as a priority. People are more "into themselves," meaning self-indulgence is important. Personal needs such as one's health, nutrition, appearance, and overall well-being have become focal points for many individuals. One example of this phenomenon is the desire to be physically fit. This has resulted in large numbers of people becoming active participants in sports. Jogging suits, sweats, tennis outfits, swimwear, and leotards are but a few items of wearing apparel that have become extremely popular in response to this social phenomenon.

From these examples, it can be assumed that apparel expresses the predominant spirit and way of life of the times. "The dress of a nation reflects the core of beliefs of the nation and becomes a collective symbol of social identity."[9] In this sense, what we wear symbolizes

[9]Karlene Anspach, *The Why of Fashion* (Ames: Iowa State University Press, 1967), p. xiv.

both our individual and societal values and provides both psychological and sociological insight into people and their worlds.

The Political and Legal Sector

The climate of the country, be it liberal or conservative; the world situation and its effect on international trade; the implementation of quotas, tariffs, and government regulations as they pertain to business operations; product safety requirements; and employment standards directly affect the fashion industry's day-to-day operations. Even the president of the United States brings a particular lifestyle into focus that translates into what kinds of fashions are produced.

Within the political and legal environment, four major factors affect fashion: sumptuary laws, foreign policy, trade regulations, and the personalities of various political leaders.

Sumptuary Laws

A sumptuary law, also known as a sartorial rule, is traditionally defined as a law that prohibits lavish dress by regulating personal expenditures on extravagant and luxurious items. This has been expanded upon to include laws controlling nudity and behavior.

There have been and continue to be several motives behind the passage of sumptuary laws. These motives generally reflect prevailing *social*, *religious*, and/or *moral* beliefs of a given time.

Historically, most sumptuary laws were used to maintain class distinctions. For example, in previous centuries, French and English royalty decreed that only they could wear ermine, brocade, and other similar rich furs and fabrics. The idea was to keep the status quo and separation between the classes. Fashions changed very slowly under this system. During the Renaissance in Italy, which occurred in the fifteenth century, the rising middle class or merchant class acquired a great deal of wealth through commerce. These "merchant princes" began to emulate the ruling class in terms of their status symbols (as per the previous discussion of Veblen's conspicuous consumption concept). The end result was that the upper class had to continually find new status symbols and forms of dress to keep ahead of the new rich or "nouveau riche." In Europe, fashions began to change much more quickly. Entire industries of dress and decoration were created to meet the demands of both classes.

The correlation between the distribution of wealth and fashion change is explained by author Quentin Bell:

Fashionable changes can only occur when wealth is so distributed in a society as to allow more than one class to afford the luxury of sumptuous dress. There must, in addition to the ruling class, be a middle class, and this middle class must have the power, financial and political, to vie with that above it, to imitate its dress and defy its sumptuary laws.[10]

At other times, however, the laws were religious in nature. During the 1600s, the elders of the Puritan Church in Massachusetts preached against "love of fashion" and, through their influence, laws restricting opulent dress were passed.

Sumptuary laws were and continue to be used as well to uphold prevailing moral standards. During different periods in history, puritanical beliefs against nudity outlawed garments that exposed the arms, legs, and even the ankles.

Today, passage of sumptuary laws seems to be primarily motivated by the issue of *environmental control.* For example, laws have been enacted to prevent the use of furs and skins from animals considered to be in danger of extinction. It is illegal for any U.S. citizen to purchase apparel and accessories made from the cheetah, leopard, crocodile, or other animals listed by the government as endangered species.

Foreign Policy and Trade Regulations

The relationship between a country and the world community is another factor affecting fashion. When a country encourages travel, business expansion, and interdependence with other nations, that country is exposed to foreign fashion inspiration and foreign goods. With more ideas and materials at hand, the fashion creativity of that country expands.

The enactment of trade agreements among countries can also influence fashion. When a country encourages trade with nations by reducing tariffs and increasing quotas, these favorable conditions stimulate trade and increase the import of foreign-made goods. Today the United States imports more fashion apparel than it exports. This has negatively affected domestic garment manufacturers and textile producers. Going "off shore" in search of cheaper labor to make fashion goods has cost these industries thousands of jobs. At the same time, it has made less expensive and, in some cases, more creatively designed goods available to U.S. consumers. This and other issues concerning foreign policy and trade regulations will be discussed in detail in Chapter 6.

---

[10]Quentin Bell, *On Human Finery,* p. 113. Reprinted by permission of Schocken Books, Inc., New York. Copyright © 1976.

Political Leaders

A definite attitude toward fashion is established by those individuals who exert political power, particularly those who are in the White House. Each presidential term can be categorized by a different fashion look and atmosphere. To illustrate, while Jimmy Carter was president (1976 to 1980), he often appeared in casual clothes, popularizing the western look of plaid work shirts and jeans. This influence and type of apparel became the predominant theme in the consumer fashion marketplace with sales of jeans reaching all-time highs.

During the Reagan-Bush years and the glitzy eighties, there was a definite change toward more formal and sophisticated attire. Clothing became more elegant and extravagant, prompting the consumer to once again "dress up"—a natural byproduct of the tone established in the White House.

The 1990s ushered in a return to basics and a more casual presidential style embodied by Bill Clinton. Hillary Clinton popularized the first lady executive look by wearing tailored business attire and suits.

Perhaps, no first lady received as much fashion recognition in recent history as did Mrs. John F. Kennedy. In 1960, Jackie upgraded American fashion and gave it an international reputation. As first lady, she symbolized a new breed of fashion consumer—a well-spoken, well-educated young mother who loved clothes and wore them well! (See Fashion Feature—"The First Lady of Fashion.")

The Technological Sector

Perhaps one of the most visible influences on the fashion business is modern technology. Methods of production have been greatly altered and improved by the use of sophisticated technical equipment and machinery. Computers are now essential to all sectors of the industry. Newer and more rapid methods of transportation, distribution, and communication allow fashion to be publicized and delivered to the consumer with exceptional speed. Four areas of technological improvements directly relate to fashion. These are mass media, textile technology, newer methods of production, and newer methods of distributing fashion goods.

Mass Media

Before the 1800s, fashion information traveled very slowly. Fashion news took weeks and sometimes months to reach various cities and countries. As mass communication and transportation systems developed, the time span for disseminating information was dramatically shortened.

The First Lady of Fashion

The John F. Kennedy administration followed the eight-year presidency of Dwight Eisenhower. Mamie Eisenhower, although nicely dressed, was not a fashion plate during her husband's term of office.

When John F. Kennedy took office in 1960, he was the youngest person ever elected president of the United States. He and his wife, Jackie, brought a fresh, youthful sense of style into focus. Not only was Jackie Kennedy the first lady of the land, but she quickly became the first lady of fashion.

Her savvy look and self-confidence were enlarged by her bouffant hairdo. Her skirts were worn well above the knee. Her dresses were tailored and body skimming with relaxed waistlines. She did not wear fussy things such as lace, ruffles, or ribbons. Her accessories and how she wore them became legends.

She often appeared with sunglasses atop her head. She wore a three-strand pearl necklace inside a boat-necklined dress. Her handbags had longer straps, which allowed the bag to be tucked under an arm. She often wore short white gloves, and when she wore a hat, it was the famous "pillbox." She dethroned pointy toed, three-inch spike heels by wearing low-heeled, black patent leather, rounded-toe pumps with pilgrim buckles. Whatever Mrs. Kennedy chose to wear became instant fashion news.

It has been reported that Mrs. Kennedy lavishly spent money on her wardrobe. In the book *Jackie OH!* by Kitty Kelley, the author estimates Mrs. Kennedy spent in excess of $40,000 on clothes in the 16 months following her husband's election.[12] Although that is a large amount even by today's standards, it is impossible to estimate the financial impact Mrs. Kennedy had on the American fashion industry. However, one simply has to look at newspapers, magazines, and family photographs of the early 1960s to see that it was profound. The "Jackie Kennedy look" was ubiqitous (see Figure 1–5).

[12]Kitty Kelley, *Jackie OH!* (Secaucus, N.J.: Lyle Stuart Inc., 1978), p. 107.

Today, transcontinental messages are received within seconds of the time they were transmitted. Through satellite, visual pictures, and television, programs can be shown simultaneously throughout the world.

Technology has also increased the number of people that can be reached. Through readily available newspapers, magazines, television, and radio, an overwhelming number of Americans of all economic backgrounds are immediately informed of important national and world events.

Courtesy: UPI/Bettmann Newsphoto

• • • • • • • • • **FIGURE 1-5 The caption of this United Press International Telephoto of February 6, 1961, said Mrs. John F. Kennedy was wearing a gray suit and white hat when she visited a Paris museum.**

Because of its amazing scope and influence, television has generated its own fashions and fashion designers. They have moved off the screen and into the mainstream of American fashion. One example is the "MTV look," named for music television and those, like Madonna, who do music videos. Another example is Bob Mackie, who began his career in fashion as a costume designer. He dressed such personalities as Cher and Carol Burnett and now does a line of ready-to-wear clothing under his own label.

Because today's fashion news travels to so many so quickly, fashion trends are immediately absorbed. This rapid absorption often encourages fashion obsolescence, stimulating a demand for constant fashion change.

Textile Technology

By improving the utilitarian and fashion characteristics of textiles, and by introducing new production methods, new fashion looks can and often do appear. One such improvement that revolutionized certain areas of wearing apparel was the introduction of stretch fabrics. These fabrics immediately replaced the traditional ones in ski wear, hosiery, and intimate apparel. Machine double knits, bonded fabrics, spandex, and polyester that feels like silk are other excellent examples of innovative successes.

Improved Clothing Manufacturing Methods

Most steps in apparel production methods are mechanized and, in some cases, automated as well. New technological advances improving these methods have been and continue to be introduced. Sewing machines are now in use that are capable of sewing over 5,000 stitches a minute. New cutting techniques have been developed that are saving both time and money. Air-jet looms are replacing the slower shuttle ones used to weave cloth. CAD/CAM programs (computer-assisted design, and computer-assisted manufacturing) are revolutionizing production methods. Other advances include robotics, laser cutting, and UPC coding and scanning. With these improvements, a greater variety of less costly merchandise is produced.

Methods of Distribution

Having merchandise readily available for the consumer is an important element of the marketing process. This is particularly true for fashion goods since today's consumer, informed about new styles and fashion trends, wants those goods immediately.

Technology has played a major role in bringing goods quickly to the consumer. Because of the improved air, rail, and highway transportation systems, a manufacturer can ship goods rapidly and safely to retail customers throughout the country.

Merchants have also been able to meet consumer demand more efficiently by using computers for inventory control. Purchasing decisions can be made more accurately and quickly with these computerized systems. Improvements in the receiving and marking of merchandise have also speeded up the all-important process of getting the goods onto the selling floor.

The Economic Sector

Technological improvements such as the ones previously discussed can only occur in an economy that is highly developed and self-sufficient. Therefore, the economic condition of a country greatly affects not only the fashion industry but all aspects of consumer and industrial life. This sector deals with the fundamental laws of supply and demand; the competitive environment; the availability of resources and capital; and the costs of labor, materials, and of doing business. Pricing decisions, profitability, tax considerations, and consumer spending patterns are elements to be carefully monitored. There are, however, certain economic conditions that have a direct bearing on the rate of fashion change. These are the availability of resources, business expansion, consumer income, and the use of credit by the consumer.

Availability of Resources
In an economic context, resources are all the ingredients necessary to operate a successful business. In order to manufacture fashion merchandise, producers need raw materials, labor, production facilities, production equipment, and capital.

During its early development, America was most fortunate to have acquired an abundance of all the resources necessary to produce fashion merchandise. However, the present position of the industry is not invulnerable to losing one or more of these essential resources. For instance, skilled labor is in diminishing supply. Therefore, the industry must actively search for and train individuals who have the background and skills necessary to work in the fashion business. Furthermore, the industry must continue to replenish the other resources necessary for fashion production and update factories with the latest technological equipment.

Business Expansion
In today's economy, a business or an industry must grow to survive. In the fashion industry, part of that growth revolves around rapid style change and fashion evolution. In order to encourage change, larger and more efficient production facilities must be opened. More efficient, consumer-friendly retail outlets must emerge for the distribution of the finished goods.

Consumer Income
Important as it may be for consumers to desire new looks and styles, it is more important that they be able to afford them. Fashion change is directly associated with consumer income.

Fortunately, over the last 100 years, U.S. consumer income has generally been increasing. It has kept pace with and—over the long run—managed to outdistance inflation. This is especially true of the portion of the consumer income known as *discretionary* income. This type of income is the amount of money available to spend on luxury items and leisure time activities. Since the majority of fashion purchases are "luxury" items, not necessities, discretionary income has been available to buy them. However, should there be galloping inflation, recession, high unemployment, or depression—the rate of consumption of fashion goods would decline. For these reasons, consumer purchases of apparel and accessories have become an important economic indicator of the health of this country's economy.

Use of Consumer Credit

The rise in incomes and the dispersion of wealth have created the uniquely American phenomenon, consumer credit. Although other countries are introducing the "buy now–pay later" system, no country has extended consumer credit as has the United States.

Today, well over 60 percent of all department store sales are "charged." The customer does not have to have or save up the purchase price of a desired item. Instead, he or she can wear the merchandise literally before it is paid for and while it is still in fashion. With availability of credit, consumer purchasing power has increased tremendously, stimulating the demand for fashion goods.

THE CONSUMER

Since the fashion business is marketing oriented, the consumer is at the very "heart" of the decision-making process. Consumers are the pivotal point around which the business must operate. The consumer must remain the center of attention of a business if it is to succeed. Consumer wants and needs must be correctly anticipated and met if the fashion business is to have a strong "bottom line" (the term for making a profit). The approach to marketing is to begin the process with identifying and analyzing the customer. Then, design and distribute fashion merchandise that will appeal to, and satisfy, his or her fashion requirements. This concept will be further discussed in Chapter 3.

The four sectors of the fashion business—the primary markets, designers and producers, the retailers, and the ancillary operations—all must work together to deliver the fashion message and the fashion goods to their "target" consumer. At the same time that the industry is focused on the consumer, it must constantly monitor the external environment to keep pace with an ever-changing world. Figure 1–6 is a graphic representation of how these factors interrelate.

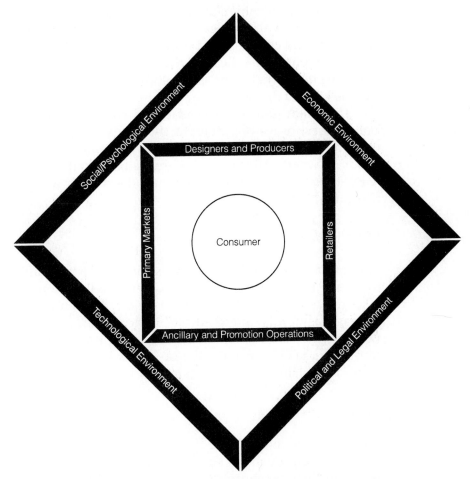

Designers and Producers

Primary Markets

Consumer

Retailers

Ancillary and Promotion Operations

Social/Psychological Environment

Economic Environment

Technological Environment

Political and Legal Environment

FIGURE 1-6   **The consumer is the center of the fashion industry's marketing efforts.**

THE LANGUAGE OF FASHION

As is true in any industry, the fashion business has a jargon or language all its own. Words and terms have specific technical meanings. Anyone learning the business of fashion must first become familiar with its special language.

High Fashion/Designer Fashion

When a look is introduced by the fashion business as the new trend it is usually very expensive and marketed to a small elite group of consumers. It is the fashion created by the world's leading designers in the fashion capitals of New York, Paris, and Milan. If garments are handmade and custom fitted using the finest fabric and workmanship, these garments are called *haute couture*. This term translates to "the finest needlework." Paris is the most important high fashion center for this kind of apparel.

If fashion goods are available to consumers in boutiques, specialty stores, or leading department stores and have notable designer or manufacturer names on the label, this merchandise is *prêt-à-porter* (ready-to-wear). All three cities are leading producers of high fashion ready-to-wear. They are joined by others such as Germany, Hong Kong, and Tokyo.

Mass Fashion

These fashions have the widest distribution base because they appeal to a large number of consumers. Often mass fashion imitates and revises the trends started with high fashion. As mentioned earlier, much of mass fashion is "knocked off" or copied from high fashion. Most people want to be in fashion, not ahead of it, which is the theme of most mass fashion firms. One of the most successful designers who views her business as mass fashion is Liz Claiborne.

Style

The term **style** refers to the characteristic inherent in a specific person, place, or thing. A singer sings in a particular style—rock, folk, or pop. Furniture may be chosen in many styles—among them Early American, French Provincial, or Contemporary. In apparel, the distinctive appearance of a garment through its shape, detail, and other visible design elements marks its style. This appearance immediately sets it apart from other styles.

Skirts are a style. Pants are also a style. But sometimes, certain characteristics are so pronounced within a large style classification that those characteristics develop into their own style. For example, bell-bottom pants and jeans are *styles* of pants. In essence, then, style refers to the visible characteristics of an item of wearing apparel. It does not refer to acceptance. It is incorrect to say that "pants are in style." Pants *are* a style. It is proper, however, to say that "pants are in fashion." *Fashion* refers to acceptance. *Style* refers to characteristics.

A style, though sometimes modified to conform to current fashion trends, basically remains the same. The shirtwaist is a style of dress that features a button-front closing, notched collar, and cuffed

• • • • • • • • **FIGURE 1-7 Variations of the shirtwaist dress—a basic style.**

sleeves. Details may vary throughout different periods of fashion (see Figure 1–7), but the basic characteristics that make up the shirtwaist style remain the same. The Empire style of the nineteenth century featured a high waistline placed directly under the bustline as its major characteristic. Today, any dress or coat featuring this high-placed waistline is identified as an Empire style.

Style, then, refers to the basic characteristics of an item of clothing. A style may grow or diminish in popularity throughout the years.

It may be modified slightly to conform to the current fashion trends. But a style remains a style, and its basic characteristics do not change.

In the fashion industry, the word *style* is also used by manufacturers and retailers in another way. A manufacturer gives each item produced a number for identification purposes. That item is then referred to as "style 00" or "style number 00." When store buyers order and reorder that particular item or design, they always refer to it as "style number 00." In this instance, the word *style* is not used in reference to the characteristics of an item. It is simply taking the place of the word *item*.

Design and Its Elements

A **design** is simply a unique version of a style. Though a shirtwaist is a style of dress, it can be interpreted in many ways. Variations such as silhouette, detail, trim, and fabric contribute to its overall appearance, creating different versions of a shirtwaist-style dress. Each version is called a *design*.

Silhouette, texture, color, detail, and *trim* are the basic elements of design. When one of these elements is changed, the original design is altered and takes on a different appearance, resulting in a new design.

Silhouette

The general outline or shape of a costume is its *silhouette*. There are three basic silhouettes. They are the straight or tubular line, the bell-shaped or curved, and the back fullness or bustle (see Figure 1–8). Throughout the history of fashion, all costumes have related to these three basic silhouettes.

Texture

The "hand" or feel of a fabric is called its *texture*. It is an important element in the total concept of a design. The texture of a fabric con-

FIGURE I-8   **Three basic silhouettes.**

Part One   Understanding Today's Fashion

tributes to appearance. For example, a rough, heavy tweed adds a casual dimension to a garment, whereas shiny satin gives it a formal feeling.

The texture of a fabric also contributes to performance. For example, tweed "tailors" well, taking naturally to precise sewing and pressing. On the other hand, satin "drapes" well, falling in soft folds. Texture also affects the quality of color. Light is absorbed by rough surfaces, and colors become muted, whereas light is reflected from smooth surfaces, making colors appear brilliant. Therefore, a tweed's texture causes tonalities that are soft and subtle, while color in satin, because of its smoothness, is rich and exciting. Both examples, the tweed and the satin, through their "eye" and "touch" appeal, demonstrate the important contribution texture makes to the ultimate purchase of the garment by the consumer.

Color

Color is a phenomenon of light that, in a visual sense, distinguishes one object from another. Because of its immediate impact, it can be the most important element in design. Each color seems to have its own emotional impact. The "cool" blues and greens are calming. Orange and red suggest excitement. And yellow, probably due to its identification with the bright sunshine, is considered a color of joy.

Color also has historical and cultural meanings. Purple has long been associated with royalty, white with brides, and black with mourners. These colors are certainly not relegated to be worn solely by these groups, but they, and other colors, continue to have well-known, traditional connotations.

In fashion, color preferences run in cycles. When pale colors have been popular, deeper shades begin to look "new." If color has been "hot"—bright and deep in its intensity—softer color interpretations seem to be a welcome change. These changes do not occur haphazardly. They evolve over a period of several seasons, with colors deepening or lightening in successive steps. These color changes are part of a color "cycle" forecasted nearly 18 to 24 months ahead of when the consumer buys the merchandise. Firms in the primary markets, trade associations, and the Color Association of the U.S. (CAUS) supply the fashion industry with these color projections. (This is further discussed in Chapter 9.)

Detail

The various components or parts within a silhouette are called its *detail*. These include collars, sleeves, shoulder treatments, waist treatments, and the length and width of skirts and pants. By changing any of these details, the design of a garment is transformed.

Changes can be made by altering the dimensions of a detail. Collars can be widened, narrowed, or removed. Sleeves can vary in shape and length. Waistlines can be placed anywhere between the bustline and the hips, or totally eliminated. And the dimensions of a skirt can be changed in a myriad of ways, including its length.

Trim

Trims are decorative additions that are not part of the construction of a garment. They include buttons, belts, buckles, stitching, embroidery, appliqués, beading, and edgings.

The type of trim used on a garment contributes a great deal to the overall appearance and characteristics of the design. A blouse immediately becomes "feminine" through the application of lace. Replace the lace with plain edging or remove it altogether and it has a "tailored" look.

The choice of trim is often governed by the other elements of a design. Heavy fabric and rough texture naturally dictate heavy buttons. An emphasis on the waistline often suggests an emphasis on belts. Like silhouette, texture, color, and detail, trim is an important tool in creating a design.

Accessories

Accessories are items that accompany a dress, suit, or other basic items of wearing apparel. Hats, gloves, jewelry, scarves, belts, handbags, hosiery, and shoes are all accessories. They serve to complement a garment and create a "total look."

Designers, stylists, and fashion coordinators work very closely with accessory makers. This close relationship automatically influences the trends within the accessory market. For instance, when the emphasis is on a narrow, defined waistline, belts are needed to point out that emphasis.

But belts become obsolete should the fashion trend veer toward a straight or tubular silhouette.

Classics

Styles or designs that remain in fashion year after year are known as **classics.** They are simple in design, and this simplicity ensures their popularity since they easily integrate into current fashion.

Though all classics are generally acceptable at all times, there are some that enjoy special acceptance. The Chanel suit is a perfect example (see Figure 1–9). Designed after World War II by the French

•••••••• **FIGURE 1-9 A classic—the Chanel suit.**

designer (Coco) Chanel, it features a simple cardigan jacket and a straight, slightly flared or pleated skirt. Throughout the years, some of its detail and trim has varied, but its silhouette has remained the same. It is just as wearable today as it was when Coco Chanel introduced it in 1954. And in some high fashion circles, an original Chanel suit takes preference over anything introduced into the current season.

The trench coat is another example of a classic. First worn by British soldiers fighting in the trenches during World War I, its popularity has existed for decades and will undoubtedly continue for many more.

Some other styles that are considered classics are the shirtwaist dress, the cardigan sweater, the navy pea jacket, and the blazer jacket. They require minor, if any, changes to acquire a contemporary appearance, thus earning the coveted label of "classic."

Fads

Though classics remain in fashion year after year, other styles or designs gain and lose their popularity within a brief period of time. These fashions are called **fads.**

Unlike classics, most fads are not simple in styling. Often they are extreme, causing people to tire of them quickly.

Fads occur more frequently when the economy is strong and consumer spending is up. When the economy is weak, consumers tend to buy merchandise that is "safe" and will be in fashion for more than a season.

Some examples of fads are the "punk/Elvira look," Nehru jackets, jellies (plastic shoes), leg warmers and hot pants.

Trends

The overall direction in which fashion moves is called a **trend.** It is the underlying theme that gives apparel and accessories unification. It is expressed through basic styling characteristics and through the elements of design. Several trends may exist at one time, each one experiencing various levels of acceptance. As a fashion gains popularity, it is called an *incoming trend;* as its popularity diminishes, it is called an *outgoing trend.*

Manufacturers and retailers capitalize on trend. Much of the success of their business is based upon their ability to recognize and predict current and future fashion trends. This prediction is called **fashion forecasting.**

.... TERMS TO REMEMBER

fashion   fashion marketing   the four areas of specialization in the fashion industry   the framework of fashion   high fashion   mass fashion style   accessories   design and its elements   classic   fad   trend   fashion forecasting

.... HIGHLIGHTS OF THE CHAPTER

- Fashion means a general acceptance of a prevailing style at a given time.
- Fashion is a business whose goal is to satisfy apparel and accessory wants and needs of consumers.
- Fashion is innovative. It constantly varies the selection of fashion goods offered to consumers.
- The fashion industry has been charged with using "planned obsolescence of desirability" in order to give customers a variety of goods.

- Fashion means imitation. Ideas must be copied, mass-produced, and mass-merchandised.
- Fashion is an art because it requires self-expression and creativity.
- Fashion is a dimension of time.
- The fashion industry consists of four areas of specialization: the primary markets, the designers and producers, the retailers, and the ancillary operations.
- The framework of fashion is made up of four sectors: the sociopsychological environment, the politico-legal environment, the technological environment, and the economic environment.
- Although the fashion business responds to changes taking place in the external environments, the consumer is at the "heart" or center of all its activities.
- Style is the distinctive appearance of a garment through its shape and design.
- The elements of design are silhouette, texture, color, detail, and trim.
- Accessories are items that complement a garment and create a "total look."
- Styles that remain in fashion are called *classics*.
- Fashions that are popular for a short period of time are called *fads*.
- Predicting incoming fashion trends is called *fashion forecasting*.

.... REVIEW QUESTIONS

1. Fashion means acceptance. Explain this concept.
2. Explain what is meant by "fashion means business."
3. What is planned obsolescence? How does it apply to the fashion industry?
4. Fashion means imitation, yet not all who are fashionable look alike. Why?
5. List and explain the four areas of specialization in the fashion industry.
6. Give an example of how the fashion business responds to a change in each of the four sectors of the external environment.
7. Define sumptuary laws. Give an example of a modern sumptuary law.
8. Mention some changes that have occurred in terms of leisure time, role of women, class structure, increased mobility, and changing ideologies. Show how each change has an impact on fashion.
9. Discuss the five elements of design, and give an example of each.
10. What is the difference between a classic and a fad? Give an example of each.
11. Define and give an example of an accessory.
12. What is fashion forecasting? Discuss an incoming trend.

.... RESEARCH AND PROJECTS

1. "Today the fashion business is marketing oriented, satisfying consumer wants and needs within the context of our present-day environment. Discuss the meaning and implications of this statement as it relates to each sector of the fashion industry.

2. Explain how fashion can be a business and an art at the same time. How is fashion innovative and yet so dependent on imitation?

3. Research a particular decade or fashion era, and identify and explain how the clothing of the period reflected the conditions existing in each of the four external environmental sectors.

4. Using the technical language and jargon found in this chapter, prepare your own fashion industry report and forecast for the upcoming fashion season.

5. Define the term *conspicuous consumption* and give specific examples of fashion apparel worn in your community that is regarded as a status symbol. What psychological needs are being filled for the wearer?

6. Research the current concerns, conditions, and problems affecting each of the four external environmental areas. After listing them, explain how they may affect the fashion business in terms of causing changes. (This can either be done in terms of a national or local perspective.)

7. Choose a garment from your wardrobe and give a detailed description of it using the five elements of design.

8. Select a job title from the Industry Focus that appeals to you. Go to your library and find the job description and job specifications in the *Dictionary of Occupational Titles* published by the U.S. Department of Labor. Prepare a summary of your findings.

9. Using the *Occupational Outlook Handbook,* also published by the U.S. Department of Labor and found in the reference section of your library, prepare a report about job opportunities and the industry projections for one of the four sectors of the fashion business that may interest you.

CHAPTER 2

The Why and How of Fashion

After reading this chapter, you should be able to:

- Identify and discuss four theories that explain how and why clothing began.
- Analyze fashion movements in terms of three processes.
- Explain the four stages of the fashion lifecycle.
- Cite the five principles that underlie fashion movements.
- Describe how basic styling characteristics and merchandise characteristics affect the life cycle of fashion goods.

.... PERFORMANCE OUTCOME

After reading this chapter, you should be able to:

- Analyze apparel in terms of how it satisfies the premises of the four theories explaining how and why clothing began.
- Evaluate merchandise in terms of where it is in the stages of the fashion life cycle.

T he successful marketing of merchandise—be it fashion or otherwise—is accomplished by satisfying the wants and needs of the customer. Therefore, analysis of the desires, ambitions, background, lifestyles, and underlying motives that govern the behavior of the customer is essential for a merchant in order to develop a marketing plan.

From this perspective, students of fashion marketing must familiarize themselves with the role that clothing and accessories play in the satisfaction of these human wants and needs. Why and how did wearing apparel originate? Why and how does it continue to be used? What purposes does it serve? The answers to these and other questions will be discussed in this chapter.

CLOTHING—HOW AND WHY IT BEGAN

From the earliest recordings of history, humans were never content with an unadorned, uncovered body. Instead they chose to put on themselves a variety of articles such as animal skins, leaves, and vegetable dyes. This crude form of dressing, still observable in primitive societies, has led many psychologists and anthropologists to conclude that clothing does serve to satisfy *basic* as well as *specific* human wants and needs. Simply stated, where there is human life there is some form of dress. Although this premise is generally accepted, a difference of opinion arises when further analysis of how and why clothing originated is undertaken.

Historically, three basic theories explaining the origins of clothing have been developed. Each theory contends that clothing satisfies a *single* human want or need. These theories are the **protection theory,** the **modesty theory,** and the **adornment theory.** Each offers plausible explanations for the origins and purpose of dress. But individually, each is inconclusive. Therefore, the **combined-need theory,** which is multidimensional and proposes that dress cannot be traced back to a single need but that it was devised to satisfy *several* human wants and needs at one time, is also presented.

The Protection Theory

Probably the simplest and most practical explanation for wearing clothes is the need for physical protection. Humans are relatively hairless and thin-skinned. Naked, they are quite defenseless against the elements, the environment, and other living creatures. Consequently, all humans need some type of shelter or protection.

In the beginning, caves, trees, huts, and so on provided this necessary coverture; but these were stationary. Clothing was an attempt to make protection portable. Animal skins were draped over the body to provide warmth and insulation. Leaves or bark were tied around the waist by males to protect otherwise exposed genitals. Bark and skins were wrapped around the feet to make walking more comfortable. Finally, since humans needed protection against their own species, they covered certain parts of their body, hoping to become more effective in battle.

Not all dressing was devised solely for physical protection. Some clothing was worn as "psychological armor" to provide humans with a defense against evil spirits. Certain articles of clothing and accessories were believed to have magical powers against demons and the "evil eye." Shells and other items were placed close to the sex organs in the belief that they would prevent "sterility and pain."[1]

Throughout history many articles of clothing have been devised for the purpose of protecting the wearer. Some examples are suits of armor, helmets, raincoats, and—the ultimate in protection—the spacesuit used by astronauts. However, one does not have to be a fashion or history expert to realize that even among the earliest civilizations articles of wearing apparel were not solely protective in design. This led to the development of the second explanation of the origin and purpose of clothing: that the human species was and is motivated to cover the body out of a sense of shame or modesty.

The Modesty Theory

Modesty is defined as behaving properly in dress, speech, or conduct. In all societies and with most people, a failure to do so results in feelings of personal shame. Shame is the underlying concept of the modesty theory.

The causes of this shame are open to speculation. There are two schools of thought. The first endorses the premise that humans are *born* with shame; the second proposes that people *learn* to be ashamed.

---

[1] James Laver, *Modesty in Dress* (Boston: Houghton Mifflin Company), p. 7. Copyright © 1969 by James Laver. Used by permission.

Proponents of being born with a sense of shame base their thinking on the Bible in the Book of Genesis. Adam and Eve ate the forbidden fruit from the tree of the knowledge of good and evil. This act made them aware of their nakedness, and they were ashamed. When the Lord discovered their disobedience, He punished them by expelling them from the Garden of Eden. The shame and guilt of Adam and Eve's original sin was then forevermore inherited by all human beings.

For centuries, inherent shame was universally accepted as the basis for modesty in dress. However, as the disciplines of psychology, sociology, and anthropology were developed, it became apparent that much about dress and behavior was left unexplained.

No evidence has been found to support the notion that humans are instinctively ashamed of their bodies or that guilt feelings pertain only to nakedness. In fact, there is much evidence to the contrary. For instance, along the Amazon River, the Botocudo tribe women are ashamed to be seen without wooden plugs in their earlobes and lower lip, but are unaffected if their breasts are exposed. Among the Australian aborigines, it is shameful to be seen eating, but perfectly all right to be seen naked.

In the Western world, there have been periods in history when it was considered "sinful" for a woman to expose her ankle or shoulder, while at other times it was socially acceptable for unmarried women to expose their breasts.

These examples lead to the conclusion that a sense of shame and modesty is not inborn, but is instead *learned*. It is governed by the customs, traditions, and mores of a culture or a society.

Therefore, modesty is the result of a socialization process; people are *taught* proper attire and dress. It is not an inherited trait. "A sense of modesty is," according to noted anthropologist E. A. Hoebel, "merely a habit, not an instinct."[2]

The Adornment Theory

The protection and modesty theories propose that humans initially covered their bodies for protection or because of a sense of shame. These two theories, however, do not explain a third phenomenon—the preoccupation with the beautification and adornment of the body.

The urge for self-adornment has always been compelling. Even before men and women discovered materials to fashion into some form of apparel, they enjoyed decorating their bodies. Noted fashion historian James Laver emphasized this point when he wrote that "a

[2]E. A. Hoebel, *Man in the Primitive World: An Introduction to Anthropology,* 2nd ed. (New York: McGraw-Hill, 1958), pp. 248–249.

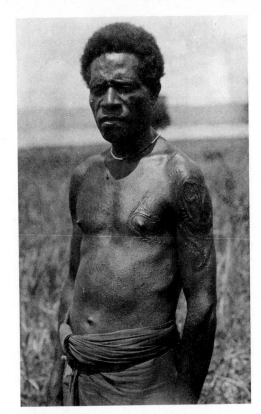

Courtesy: American Museum of Natural History, New York

• • • • • • • • **FIGURE 2-1 (a) Tattooed native of Nukahiwa. (b) A native with body scarring—cicatrization.**

delight in decoration was, of course, present even before clothes were invented."[3] Laver was referring to such uncanny techniques as body painting, tattooing, cicatrization, piercing, and body deformation—all devised by humans to achieve a desired self-image (see Figure 2–1).

Upon analyzing this preoccupation with beautification, many social scientists have come to the conclusion that *adornment* is the logical explanation for the origin of clothing. The original purpose of clothing, they claim, was to enhance one's *self-concept* and *self-image*. Humans want to call attention to themselves, thereby satisfying several conscious and unconscious ego needs. They list these needs as *self-beautification*, improving *sexual attractiveness*, and obtaining *social status*.

[3]James Laver, *Modesty in Dress* (Boston: Houghton Mifflin Company), p. 31. Copyright © 1969 by James Laver. Used by permission.

Self-Beautification

Although the definition of what is beautiful varies, aesthetic pursuits and a search for beauty are universal. By exposing some parts of the body and covering other parts, humans have been able to emphasize desirable physical qualities and hide their flaws. In doing so, the need for self-beautification is satisfied.

Sexual Attraction

Other sociologists feel that the need most satisfied by dress is that of *being sexually attractive*. Clothing has always played a role in erotic stimulation, and the poet Robert Burton observes, "The greatest provocations of lust are from our apparel."[4]

Different cultures consider different parts of the body sexually stimulating. Some cultures expose those parts of their bodies they find sexually exciting. Most cultures prefer to conceal the sexually stimulating portions of their bodies, considering complete nudity not nearly as alluring as suggestive concealment.

Social Status

Still a third group of scientists take the position that people are forever striving for social supremacy over other people. By wearing lavish, expensive clothing, the wealthy use dress as a means of conveying to others their social and economic superiority.

Similarly, the dress of primitive groups can also convey the rank and power of persons within those groups. Among Native Americans, for example, braves may wear one or two feathers in their hair but only their chief may wear an elaborate headpiece consisting of many beautiful feathers.

The conclusions of the adornment theory, then, are that human beings devised apparel as a means of beautifying their bodies, attracting a mate, or obtaining social acceptance and superiority.

The Combined-Need Theory

Upon reviewing the protection, modesty, and adornment theories, it is apparent that each contains intelligent, justifiable, but incomplete explanations for the origin of clothing. The combined-need theory accepts some of the premises of these theories and uses these concepts to develop the idea that *from the beginning,* clothing needs were *multidimensional.* Focusing on only one need to the exclusion of others seems incorrect. Clothing satisfies several needs concurrently.

[4]Quoted in Helen M. Evans, *Man The Designer* (New York: Macmillan, 1973), p. 305.

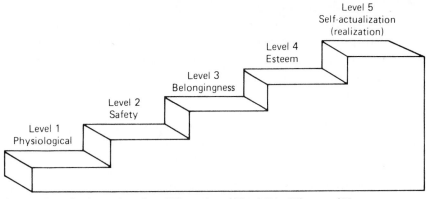

Source: Data for figure based on "Hierarchy of Needs" in "Theory of Human Motivation" from *Motivation and Personality,* 2nd ed., by Abraham H. Maslow. Copyright © 1970 by Abraham H. Maslow. By permission of Harper & Row, Publishers, Inc.

• • • • • • • •   **FIGURE 2-2   Maslow's Hierarchy of Needs.**

The combined-need theory borrows heavily from the work of psychologist A. H. Maslow. His theory, known as *the hierarchy of needs,* describes the human being as ever-wanting and whose behavior is determined by a priority of needs (see Figure 2–2).

For example, if climatic and environmental conditions are such that a person is in need of shelter and safety—levels one and two—then dressing will be practical and protective. It will be prompted by needs similar to those outlined in the protection theory. Since sex is also a first-level need, dressing might also incorporate the sexual attractiveness of the adornment theory.

After these basic needs are met, apparel will be chosen for reasons listed on level three. The choice of clothing will conform to that worn by peer groups, providing a person with a sense of belonging. The needs of this level are similar to the needs outlined in the modesty theory, where acceptance is an important motive.

Next, the wearer moves up to level four, where he or she can personalize his or her appearance. By doing so, the wearer enhances his or her self-esteem and gains prestige. This may be compared with the social status and beautification ego needs of the adornment theory.

It is difficult to determine the role clothing plays in satisfying self-actualization—Maslow's fifth and ultimate need. This is an internalized need dealing with maximizing one's potential in terms of creative ability. However, if clothing helps to satisfy lower level needs, then it allows a person to move upward and expand creatively within the highest level.

Today apparel does not perform merely one function. Nor does it satisfy one need. It appears to have had this multidimensional role from its inception. *Therefore, the origin of clothing seems most plausible if viewed as always having satisfied combined needs.* Fashion author Karlene Anspach summarizes several aspects of the combined-need theory as follows:

> *Theoretically, man's wants are unlimited. They vary among people and places, from time to time, but the urgency of wants does not appreciably diminish as more are filled. When man has satisfied his physical needs, his psychologically grounded desires take over. He demands high fashion clothing, foreign made cars, and original paintings rather than food for hunger or clothes for warmth.*[5]

HOW FASHION MOVES

Fashion is constantly changing, but those changes take place *within* fashion *movements. Fashion movements* pertain to the overall direction of fashion. For example, a trend toward longer skirt lengths or softer, more feminine clothes is a fashion movement. A movement of that type will last several years. Seasonal fashion changes—new colors, fabrics, styles, or trim—are expressed within that existing fashion movement.

Fashion movements do not occur in a haphazard or mysterious manner. In fact, by analyzing past fashion movements, one is able to see that most movements emerge with a predictable regularity and sometimes in a predictable sequence. For instance, a fashion movement toward softer, more feminine clothes may be safely predicted to follow an era of tailored, classic fashion.

This predictability is due to the fact that—regardless of the causes or the direction of a fashion movement—five basic principles underlie all fashion movement.

The Five Basic Principles That Underlie All Fashion Movement

1. Fashion Movements Are Evolutionary
Overall fashion does not move rapidly. It follows a progressive pattern in which change is introduced slowly, not radically.

---

[5]Karlene Anspach, *The Why of Fashion* (Ames: Iowa State University Press, 1967), p. 3.

An example of this phenomenon may be seen in the raising and lowering of skirt lengths. Hemlines literally inch their way up or down, depending on the fashion period. In recent history there has been one notable exception to this principle of the evolutionary movement of fashion. This unique event occurred in 1947 at the end of World War II. Because of the war and restrictions on the use of fabrics, fashion change had been at a standstill for several years. It had not continued along at its normal evolutionary pace. That year, French designer Christian Dior introduced his now famous "new look." It featured small waists, long, flowing skirts—a total departure from the austere, tailored, wartime garb worn by most women. Yet, even though the look was *revolutionary*, it was totally accepted (see Figure 2–3). Women were ready for it. The look was one they would have been wearing had the normal evolutionary process of fashion change been uninterrupted by the war. But unless such special circumstances occur again, it is correct to assume that Dior's "new look" will remain the only modern exception to this basic fashion principle.

FIGURE 2-3 Dior's "New Look," 1947.

The premise of this principle is best expressed by the following quote: "Fashion change is always gradual unless there is an abrupt dislocation of economic conditions or social values."[6]

2. Fashion Cycles Run to Extremes

This second principle deals with the lifespan of a fashion movement. Once a trend is set in motion, it will not end until an extreme interpretation of that trend is reached. French designer Paul Poiret is credited with best summarizing this thought by saying, "All fashions end in excess."

For example, in 1906, just prior to Poiret's emergence as an influential designer, women were crammed into wasp-waisted, corseted clothes that emphasized the bustline and derrière. When this fashion movement reached an uncomfortable extreme, Poiret introduced a relaxed look, eliminating corsets in favor of bras.

A more recent example of this principle is the mini skirt. When they could go no higher, skirts started on their way down until they covered and then passed the knees.

Be it silhouettes, skirt lengths, or overall fashion themes, a fashion movement must run its course, reaching an extreme before another can take its place.

Combining these first two principles, McJimsey further states, "Fashions change so gradually that as they move in one direction, one is scarcely aware of how much has occurred until an extreme has been reached."[7]

3. Fashion Repeats Itself

The third premise of all fashion movements is that looks repeat themselves. A good designer is constantly delving into the past for inspiration. A designer can revive past trends by studying his or her own and other designers' previous work and by reviewing historical costumes and art history. This is not to imply that designs are merely reused or recycled. Rather, the designer tries to capture the feeling and look of a previous era in a new and imaginative way. The period chosen for inspiration must have relevance to what is going on today. For example, the time to revive the 1920s flapper look of short skirts, short hair and a boyish figure de-emphasizing the female anatomy would be when women's rights or equality in society becomes a major issue as it did in the 1960s.

[6]Harriet T. McJimsey, *Art and Fashion in Clothing Selection* (Ames: Iowa State University Press, 1973), p. 25.

[7]Ibid., p. 59.

4. Fashion Change Never Ceases

Fashion change is and has been ongoing as long as fashion has existed. The reason for this is simple: There is no ultimate in design. Whatever look or style is currently being featured is not the final word.

This principle is the heart of the fashion business. No designer or manufacturer, no matter how perfect his or her work, would want to think of it as his or her last and ultimate design. Something past or current can always be improved upon, varied, or replaced.

At the same time, to a customer, something new is always more appealing. No customer, no matter how classic or perfect an item may be, would want to consider its design as final and irreplaceable. Therefore, to designer, manufacturer, and customer alike, there is no "ultimate," for this would imply the end of change. And without change, fashion and the business of fashion would cease.

Fortunately, fashion changes are continuously encouraged by the industry and the consumer alike. Because of that encouragement, fashion never stands still.

5. Repeat Time of Fashion is Decreasing

As previously discussed, the entire pace of life and change has increased. Today, events become "history" with amazing swiftness. Consequently, the length of time it takes for a fashion movement to be revived or to repeat itself is decreasing.

In terms of fashion, one excellent example of decreased repeat time is in the time it takes for the prevailing silhouette (the overall shape of apparel) to be replaced. Research shows that in the decades prior to 1947, a silhouette's life span was approximately 35 years. However, in post-World War II years, the silhouette has been changing on the average of every seven to ten years.

The fifth principle does not alter the first four principles of fashion movement. It simply implies that those principles must be viewed as functioning within a relatively shorter time span.

Analyzing Fashion Movements

To all involved in the profitable marketing of fashion, the reasons for analyzing the movement of fashion are twofold. First, it provides the ability to identify and determine the life span of current trends. Second, and more important, it provides the ability to identify and predict future trends. In the fashion business—where "wrong guesses" can be notoriously expensive—it is mandatory to be equipped with these abilities in order to be successful.

This thought was emphasized by Paul Nystrom when he wrote, "It would seem that a necessary step towards better merchandising of fashion goods would be to get more information about these fashion movements; in other words, to substitute facts for guesses, reasoning for hunches and a bit of science for the prevailing mystery regarding fashion."[8]

Predicting fashion correctly can and should be done within the context of the five general principles underlying all fashion movement. There are three other specific categories that provide more detailed information on the movement of fashion. These categories are the *adoption process*, the *fashion life cycle*, and *basic styling and merchandise characteristics*. By researching each category separately and then combining the results, the guesswork when analyzing fashion movement can be eliminated.

The Adoption Process

This category refers to the flow of fashion from one class or group to another. It explains with whom fashion originates and how it moves from acceptance by a few to acceptance by many. Understanding the adoption process is an important key to monitoring fashion movement correctly because it describes the sequence of acceptance for new fashion trends.

The oldest process of adoption has become known as **trickle-down.** Under this process, fashion originates with those at the top of a society and moves to the classes below. At first royalty unilaterally determined fashion for everyone. Then, the titled and noble class joined royalty as contributors to fashion trends. Still later, the entire group referred to as the upper class began and endorsed new fashions.

Today, social class structure is not as rigid as it once was. But this should not imply that the trickle-down process is not currently working. Yesterday's aristocrats and upper class—those with title and money—have been replaced by new arbiters of fashion: the **fashion elite.**

The fashion elite is composed of three groups: (1) the *creators*, (2) the *reporters*, and (3) the *wearers* of high fashion.

The *creators* of high fashion are the leading fashion designers of America and Europe. They create the fashion reported and worn by other members of the fashion elite.

The *reporters* of high fashion are, of course, the editors and publishers of leading fashion magazines and newspapers. This second group has the power to endorse and publicize those fashion trends it

[8]Nystrom, *Economics of Fashion* (New York: Ronald Press, 1928), p. 57.

deems most important. Consequently, they are powerful members of the fashion elite.

The *wearers* of high fashion, the third and last group, are usually moneyed people who can afford to indulge in expensive high fashion. Most have a built-in celebrity status as members of society or the sports, entertainment, and political worlds, but that in itself does not make them influential fashion arbiters. There are many celebrities who are not fashion leaders. The fashion leaders are those who display unusual, *news-making* fashion taste. Certainly Madonna fits this criterion.

The influence of these celebrities, however, exists only through and because of the attention and focus given to them by the media. Once the media have established the fashion credibility of the celebrities, this third group becomes the group of the fashion elite that *displays* what are considered important fashion looks.

Sometimes those at the top of society admire and subsequently copy fashion from the classes beneath them. This second adoption process has been labeled **bottom-up.** It is not a new process. Marie Antoinette, for example, though at the very top of society as Queen of France, loved the costumes worn by shepherdesses and had them copied for her own use.

One very important point must be made about the bottom-up process: Its movement seems to follow a distinct pattern from the lower class to the upper class or fashion elite, and then to the middle class. In other words, in order for a bottom-up fashion to gain the widespread acceptance of the majority, it must be legitimized by first gaining approval from those at the top. Some examples of the bottom-up movement include black leather motorcycle jackets, torn jeans, the punk look, the rap look, and even blue jeans, which were originally worn by miners and laborers.

Finally, the adoption process can be analyzed from a **horizontal** perspective. This approach recognizes that adoption of a fashion by individuals or groups with the same social status does not occur at the same rate. The acceptance of a look more often hinges on peer-group acceptance. A person who is a member of a particular group and who has popularity among its members initiates a look, which is in turn copied by his or her peers. These individuals are not part of the fashion elite as described earlier. Instead, they are friends, acquaintances, or group leaders of their own peers. They are, however, as influential as the fashion elite in getting their group interested in adopting a particular look.

In addition to following a social pattern, in this country fashion also follows a geographical one as it flows from group to group. Under this rule, looks are first accepted on the East and West Coasts. There, they are worn by people in major cities like New York and San Francisco. Fashion looks then spread to the suburbs and then they finally move to the Midwest. This cross-country trek applies to the adoption of all types of fashion whether it be trickle-down, horizontal, or bottom-up.

The Fashion Life Cycle

The movement of a fashion becomes even more understandable when it is translated graphically into a sales curve termed the **fashion life cycle.** All fashions, over time, pass through four stages: *introduction, growth, maturity,* and *decline* (see Figure 2–4). Each stage of the cycle is characterized by several distinct features.

In the *introduction* stage, the sale of a new fashion follows a gradual upward sloping pattern. Distribution of the goods is limited to those retailers who are innovative and whose customers desire the very latest looks.

The price of these goods is generally the highest in this first stage. This is attributable to expensive initial production costs and—because of possible consumer rejection—to the high degree of risk associated with innovative fashion. A high initial price tag thus becomes a common feature of this stage.

Trade publications and top high-fashion magazines feature introductory-stage fashions on their pages. This coverage and favorable commentary often give the necessary impetus to move the fashion into stage two, the *growth* stage.

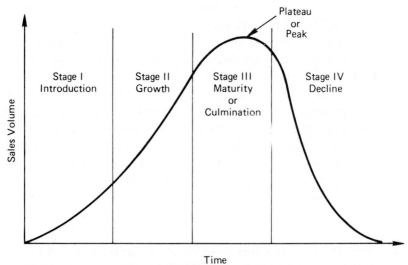

FIGURE 2-4 **The fashion life cycle.**

In the second phase, the fashion is popularized. Spurred by consumer interest and demand, manufacturers begin to copy the look to meet rapidly rising sales expectations. This in turn causes a decline in the selling price of the fashion, which serves to further stimulate sales during the growth stage. It also encourages increased distribution by retailers. All, including those retailers who initially were cautious, adopt the new fashion and mass-merchandise it. Thus, the sales during this period increase rapidly, and the look gains widespread acceptance. This acceptance is reported and confirmed by broad coverage from general readership publications, including the mass-market magazines.

By the time a fashion reaches the third stage, *maturity*, its sales potential is reached and a leveling off of volume occurs. This stage is characterized by a peak or plateau depending on how long the stabilization of sales continues. If customers do not repeat purchases of a look, then a peak will appear. If, however, customers buy various interpretations or collect several styles influenced by the current fashion look, a sales plateau will occur. How long a fashion remains in stage three depends on how quickly customers become bored with the look and desire to replace it with a new one.

When this occurs, the sales pattern for the current fashion will begin to show a sharp drop, entering into the *decline* stage, or step four. In this stage, price reductions, discounts, and markdowns abound as manufacturers and retailers alike try to move out their stock and reduce inventory levels. Virtually no production or reordering of the fashion occurs. A decreasing number of customers buy what remains of the stock, motivated mostly by the often exceptional "bargain" prices.

By the *decline* stage, all the media have literally abandoned the fashion. Like the manufacturers, retailers, and consumers, the media are already picking up on a new fashion that is entering the introductory stage. Thus, at any given point in time, several fashion looks can be depicted on the curve, as each moves along the stages of its own fashion life cycle.

Basic Styling Characteristics and Merchandise Characteristics

It was previously established that fashion movements refer to overall fashion trends and that these movements have a life cycle. Within the life cycle of these movements, however, shorter life cycles exist. These shorter life cycles belong to the **basic styling characteristics** of a fashion and to the **merchandise characteristics** used in expressing that fashion.

In a fashion trend, there are *four basic styling characteristics*. These are the silhouette, fashion look, body zone, and color and texture. As mentioned earlier, in determining the *silhouette* or shape of women's apparel, only three distinct forms emerge: the bell-shape, the tube, and the bustle or back fullness. All wearing apparel can be classified under one of these three silhouettes. Currently the fashion style of a silhouette lasts approximately seven to ten years.

Between the post-World War II period and today, only two silhouettes have recurred for daytime wear: the bell shape and the tube. It appears that modern lifestyles are not conducive to adding the back fullness of a bustle to garments except for evening and bridal wear.

Because there are only two basic silhouettes to choose from, designers have introduced four variations within the tubular silhouette (see Figure 2–5). The first variation is the *chemise*. It skims the body and does not have a defined waistline. The *trapeze* is triangular or A-lined, with the upper part of the silhouette closer fitting and with the bottom flared. The third variation is the *broad-shouldered look*. This appears to be an inverted triangle created by enlarging the proportion of the upper torso and curving closer to the lower part of the body. Finally, the *natural shape* defines the normal waistline and equalizes the upper and lower torso.

Fashion journalist James Brady claims that he can most graphically describe the predominant *fashion look* by using six terms. He maintains that fashion is either pretty or ugly; short or long; tight or loose. Under his theory, these six elements can be combined in various combinations to accurately describe the look of fashion.[9] It can be "pretty, long, and loose" or—for that matter—"ugly, short, and tight." Other fashion reporters may prefer to use more elaborate, "fashion"

1. Chemise Outline   2. Trapeze Outline   3. Broad-shoulder Outline   4. Natural-shape Outline

• • • • • • • •   **FIGURE 2-5   Variations of the tubular silhouette.**

[9]James Brady, *Super Chic* (Boston: Little, Brown, 1974), p. 49.

terms, but Mr. Brady's descriptive technique gets right to the point and seems to serve the purpose.

Fashion historian J. Flügel uncovered the fact that a current look emphasizes one particular part of the body at a time, making it a focal point, called a "shifting erogenous zone."

The emphasis is placed either on the breasts, waist, hips, buttocks, legs, arms, or on the overall circumference of the body. In order to analyze fashion movements correctly, it should be determined which part of the body is receiving current emphasis, since future fashion will focus attention upon a different part. For example, in the 1950s the emphasis was on the bustline. This spurred the sale of pointed and padded bras. The 1960s shifted the zone to the legs and the mini and micro-mini skirts were worn to show off that part of the body.

Color and *texture* are styling characteristics that generally complete their fashion life cycle in one season. Specific colors and textures from a given season will change in the next. The bright, lightweight fabrics of the summer, for example, will change to dark woolens in the fall.

However, there are broad color and texture trends that generally remain in fashion for one and sometimes as long as three or four years. Although new colors and textures are introduced each season, they are kept within these broad predominating trends.

Each type of fashion merchandise also has its own *merchandise characteristics*, which in turn have their own life cycle. The time span of these cycles varies, due to the unique characteristics of the merchandise.

For instance, *accessories* are a classification of goods that move through the fashion life cycle quickly. Merchandise such as jewelry, belts, and handbags, while keeping within the context of the current fashion trend, changes its dominant look from season to season. For example, if fashion emphasizes the "natural" look, handbags may be made of canvas for spring, straw for summer, and suede and leather for fall and winter.

Price also contributes to the short fashion life cycle of accessories. Accessory prices, in relative terms, are often lower than other types of fashion goods. Many customers find that they can vary and update their wardrobes frequently, but inexpensively, by purchasing new accessories.

On the other hand, *outerwear* has a much longer fashion life cycle. Purchases of such items as coats and capes can generally be postponed until there is a noticeable change in overall fashion, such as the rise or fall of hemlines. Drastic changes of this type usually take several seasons or even years to develop, thus lengthening outerwear's fashion life.

Other classifications of wearing apparel, from *sportswear* to *formal attire*, also exhibit variations in their fashion life cycles, and these are based on the styling characteristics previously mentioned.

By analyzing the movement of fashion from the perspective of the five general principles, as well as in terms of fashion life cycles as they pertain to general fashion trends and to styling and merchandise characteristics, a detailed picture emerges that removes most of the mystery and unpredictability from the movement of fashion.

,······ TERMS TO REMEMBER

protection theory   modesty theory   adornment theory   combined-need theory   trickle-down adoption process   bottom-up adoption process horizontal adoption process   fashion elite   fashion life cycle   basic styling and merchandise characteristics

······· HIGHLIGHTS OF THE CHAPTER

- Four theories explain the origin of clothes: the protection theory, the modesty theory, the adornment theory, and the combined-need theory.

- Five principles govern all fashion movement: fashion is evolutionary, cycles run to extremes, fashion never ceases, fashion repeats itself, and repeat time is decreasing.

- Fashion adoption moves in three directions: trickle-down, bottom-up, and horizontal.

- There are four phases to the fashion life cycle: introduction, growth, maturity, and decline.

- There are four basic styling characteristics: silhouette, fashion look, body zone, and color and texture.

- Specific types of merchandise have varying fashion life cycles.

······· REVIEW QUESTIONS

1. Cite the premise on which each of the four theories about the origins of clothes is based.

2. Show how fashion changes have recently been evolutionary, not revolutionary.

3. What does "fashion cycles run to extremes" mean?

4. Explain the concept of "fashion change never ceases."

5. Explain and give an example of how repeat time is decreasing for fashion change.

6. Define and give three examples of someone who is a member of the fashion elite (use one person for each category).

7. Give an illustration of bottom-up fashion.

8. What are the four variations of the tubular silhouette?

9. What are the specific pricing and promotional characteristics of fashion in each phase of the fashion life cycle?

10. How do accessories differ from outerwear in fashion movement?

.... RESEARCH AND PROJECTS

1. Assume you are helping a customer decide on an outfit to buy. Write a "sales script" incorporating the needs that could be satisfied based on the four theories about the origins of clothing if the customer were to purchase that outfit.

2. List those people who you think are today's fashion elite in the U.S. and the world.

3. Identify how fashion moves into your community. Using the society pages of your local newspaper, list the names of the people who are the fashion elite in your area.

4. Using a particular category of merchandise such as evening dresses or pants, find illustrations of that item in a variety of magazines and newspapers. Categorize the styles you have found in terms of their stage in the fashion life cycle.

5. Find at least two illustrative examples of each of the four variations of the tube silhouette. Which variation is currently the most popular in your opinion?

CHAPTER 3

···

Analyzing and Understanding Today's Consumer

After reading this chapter, you should be able to:

- Explain the four steps in consumer fashion research.
- Define *demographics* and *psychographics* and show how they are used in market segmentation.
- Describe the American fashion consumer of today in demographic and psychographic terms.

······· PERFORMANCE OUTCOME

After reading this chapter, you should be able to:

- Apply consumer fashion research techniques in order to identify a potential target market.
- Discuss the potential target market in terms of demographics and psychographics.
- Project how consumer attitudes directly affect the styling and design of fashion goods.

$$\bullet$$

Since the overall direction of the fashion industry is rooted in the wants and needs of the ultimate consumer, the success of those in the industry depends largely upon their ability to analyze consumers. This chapter begins by reviewing some of the methods and techniques of consumer research that help the fashion industry identify and anticipate the demands of its customers. It then describes demographics and psychographics and provides a profile of today's fashion consumer using those parameters.

In Chapter 1, *fashion marketing* was defined as directing the flow of fashion goods from producer to consumer in order to profitably satisfy consumer needs. A company that functions under this marketing concept plans its entire operation around the idea of satisfying the consumer. It begins by defining its customer and identifying the unfilled needs and desires that customer has. It then goes on to develop products and sales strategies that will cater to those needs and desires while yielding a profit for the company. A firm of this type is considered to be *marketing-oriented.* It produces the "right" products and distributes them in the "right" location, at the "right" price, and at the "right" time by using the consumer (its market) to help it define "right."

CONSUMER FASHION RESEARCH

In order to obtain detailed and specific consumer information, firms in the fashion industry cannot rely on casual observation or guesswork. Instead, they must turn to the structured, analytical, and formal approach, obtaining information rationally, honestly, and objectively. The best and most often used consumer research approach is based on the **scientific method.**

Following the guidelines of this method, consumer fashion research can be organized into four steps: (1) identify the potential market, (2) gather statistical data about the market and its profitability, (3) segment the market in terms of existing and potential needs, and (4) determine and develop products that will best satisfy those needs, testing the products on a sample group before distributing them to the potential market.

Identifying the Potential Market

The term *market* can have many meanings, all of which connote a gathering of people for the purpose of exchanging goods and services. Specifically, the market for fashion goods may be defined as a group of people who have the money and the desire to purchase fashion merchandise. These people may be identified and described by using two kinds of data: *demographic* and *psychographic*.

Demographics is the use of statistics to describe people. Some of the most common ways to describe a population demographically are through breakdowns of age, income, location, occupation, and so on. The information is categorized numerically, making use of the principles of statistics. For example, "In 1990, the median age of the U.S. population was 32.8 years" is a statistic that means that of all the people living in the United States, 50 percent were older than 32 years and 8 months and 50 percent were younger.

Since the definition of a market for fashion goods includes the desires or motivations of people, additional data about their psychological concerns are needed. The kind of statistical data that evaluate a person's attitudes, values, and beliefs as they affect behavior is called **psychographics.** Less exact than demographics, psychographics tries to measure how a person's lifestyle influences his or her attitude toward a certain product, affects his or her evaluation of the product, and contributes to his or her purchasing decisions.

Although obtaining this kind of consumer information is difficult and prediction methods are complex, it is generally agreed that understanding and analyzing the consumer is incomplete without psychographic data.

Gathering Data

Basically, data gathering for any kind of research is done in three ways: (1) by *observation* of the subject; (2) by a *survey* of the subject (through face-to-face, telephone, or mail interviews); and (3) by *conducting experiments* with the subject. These experiments take place under controlled scale-model circumstances set up by the researcher.

The information obtained through any of these three data-gathering techniques is labeled either primary or secondary data. **Primary data** are collected firsthand and have not previously been available to the researcher from any other source.

Primary data are very specific and detailed and thus somewhat limited in application, as well as rather expensive to obtain. **Secondary data,** on the other hand, are readily available from material that has been gathered and published by others. It is often free or inexpensive and can be obtained from such suppliers as the U.S. government, magazines, periodicals, industry trade associations, and year-end company reports; or it can be purchased from marketing research firms, computer companies, or advertising agencies at nominal cost. Secondary data usually offer general information and are lacking in certain particulars needed for sound decision making. Therefore, most companies gathering consumer data use both kinds—primary and secondary. Customarily, they begin by culling needed information from secondary data sources. If the information they require is unavailable or if they need more detailed information, they then revert to gathering primary data.

Segmenting the Market

Once a firm has collected and categorized demographic and psychographic data on the total fashion market, an analysis of that data begins. Hopefully, the analysis will reveal "submarkets" consisting of groups of people with similar characteristics, financial means, and motivations who are potential users of the fashion producer's product or service. Each of these submarkets or market segments is called a firm's **target market.**

Upon identifying its target market, a fashion firm will make a further analysis into the characteristics of that market, looking for answers to several key questions. For example, does the target market have similar or different psychographic and demographic characteristics from the overall fashion market? Is the target market going to increase or decrease in size during the next several years? The more a firm knows about its target market, the easier it is to identify and profitably cater to the needs of that market. Should a firm choose to satisfy more than one target market, it does so by simply diversifying and setting up a separate organizational division to market the new line.

Elizabeth, by Liz Claiborne, is an example of how this was done successfully. Through its research, the company discovered that by the late 1980s 40 percent of the females in the United States wore size 14 or larger. Many of these women worked in businesses requiring a professional wardrobe. The fashion industry had all but ignored this customer both at the manufacturing and retail level. Once the potential for this market was identified, Liz Claiborne and other designers began developing a line specifically aimed at the large-size career women. In turn, major department stores and chains have added a women's department catering to the size 14 to 26 customer.

Product Development and Testing

After a product is developed, the last step in the research process is to test a target market's reaction to that product. There are several ways to test a product; the methods vary with each type of business. For instance, apparel manufacturers may produce sample runs—small quantities of specific styles—and do checkouts by placing them with select retailers for careful monitoring of consumer reaction and sales. Textile firms may survey their apparel manufacturer accounts by sending them fabric samples for their reaction. And magazines may conduct surveys to obtain feedback from their readers on newly advertised products.

Regardless of the method a firm uses in its testing, the critical testing factor is the selection of a sample group of users that is truly representative of a firm's target market. Those surveyed and analyzed must be an exact, albeit miniature, duplicate of the target market. The closer a sample group comes to accurately representing a target market, the more accurate are the test results. Careful selection of a sample group, therefore, is the most important factor during the testing phase of market research.

The idea of "know your customer" is not new to the fashion industry, but much of the consumer research of the past was informal and perhaps subjective. Today—especially since the emergence of the giant textile, apparel, publishing, and retail companies—many firms have full-time consumer research and product development programs that use sophisticated and elaborate computer systems to precisely and objectively get to "know their customer."

· ·

PROFILING THE AMERICAN FASHION CONSUMER

We can now examine how demographic and psychographic data on the American consumer are utilized by the fashion industry to develop fashion products and services for its consumer.

Demographic Characteristics

Population Size
Past experience has made the fashion industry keenly aware of the effect changes in the size of the population can have on its business. For instance, the clothing demands of the great waves of immigrants

who came to this country during the late 1800s literally built the foundation of America's ready-to-wear industry. Subsequent population increases such as the post-World War II baby boom created tremendous business for maternity and children's wear firms.

During the 1960s and 1970s, population growth conspicuously slowed down, making these years known as the "zero population growth period." The era is characterized by the lowest recorded birth rate in the country's history.

In the 1980s, the United States experienced a "baby boomlet." This was caused by the large number of women in their 20s and 30s who decided to have children. These babies, born into double-income households, dramatically affected the children's wear market (see Chapter 12).

Today, the U.S. population continues to grow at a slow pace. In 1990, there were approximately 244 million Americans.

Most demographers agree that the slowdown will continue and that in the year 2030, U.S. population growth will stop at about 250 million. Aware of this projection, the fashion industry no longer expects population expansion to be an important determining factor in the future of its business.

Population Age

Lower birth rates and increased life expectancy have also affected the average *age* of the country's population. In 1976, the population's median age was 28 years, 9 months. By 2000, the median age is expected to jump to 36 years, 9 months. In the year 2030, it will reach 40 years, 8 months (see Figure 3–1).

This "graying" of America has occurred rapidly since 1970. By 2050, people over age 65 will outnumber those under age 18. The over-65 group will make up nearly 24 percent of our population by the year 2080. Today, this group represents only about 13 percent of the population (see Figure 3–2). These figures project two important market trends: the emergence of larger "mature" (over 55) "senior citizen" markets; and the decline of the "youth" market.

Because of these trends, the fashion industry has recognized that the majority of its future business will come from increasingly older groups. Some manufacturers have begun to rethink the sizing of their garments and are cutting them fuller for the mature figure type. Eliminating long back zippers and replacing difficult closures with velcro are just some of the ways the industry is responding to this trend.

Location

What people wear and how they buy are very much affected by *where* they live. It is therefore extremely important for the fashion industry

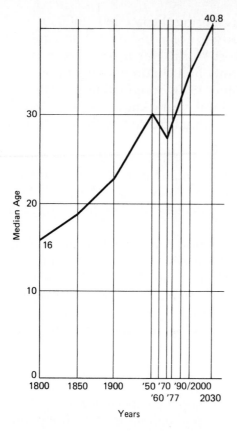

FIGURE 3-1   How America matures: Median age, at which half the population is younger, half older.

to know exactly how the American population is distributed through-out the country.

Americans are not, of course, evenly divided among the 50 states. In fact, nearly half of the present population is located in 10 states. But Americans have become an increasingly mobile group, and the country's population is very much on the move. In the 1990s, substantial population shifts are expected to take place, drastically increasing the number of people in some states while decreasing the number of people in other states.

Presently, the greatest population growth is in the South and Southeast. Known as the Sunbelt region, this area is attracting people from the older and colder Northeast. Its population is expected to continue to increase at a tremendous rate (see Figure 3–3).

Within the states, there have been other profound population shifts. Both rural areas and central cities have been losing their popu-

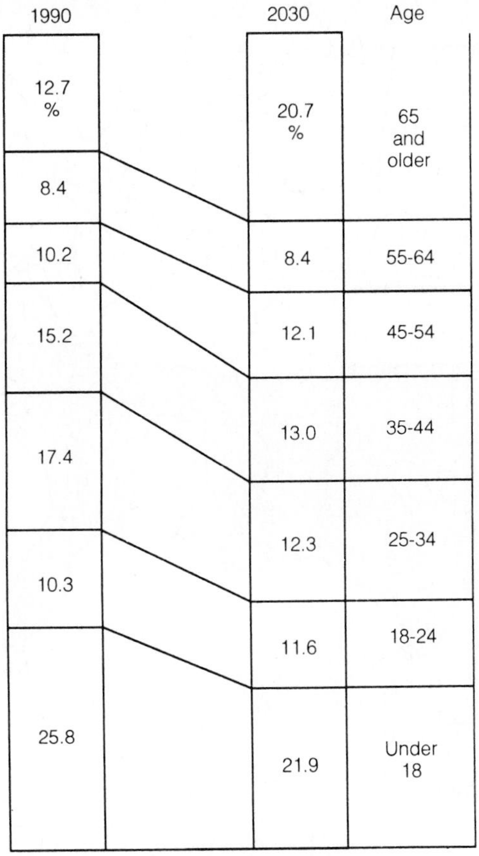

1990	2030	Age
12.7 %	20.7 %	65 and older
8.4		
10.2	8.4	55-64
15.2	12.1	45-54
17.4	13.0	35-44
10.3	12.3	25-34
	11.6	18-24
25.8	21.9	Under 18

Source: U.S Bureau of the Census

• • • • • • • • **FIGURE 3-2 Age distribution of total U.S. population.**

lations to suburban areas. Most of these areas are within commuting distance to jobs in the inner cities and are often referred to as the "urban sprawl."

As Americans change their location from city to suburb, north to south, even state to state, they automatically change their lifestyle. The more drastic the move, the more drastic the change in their clothing needs, their tastes, and their buying patterns. In order to successfully service the needs of a mobile population, the fashion industry studies population shifts and plans its marketing strategies accordingly. Manufacturers, for instance, translate a population increase in the Sunbelt into an increase in their production and sale of warm-weather clothes, while retailers see the shift to the suburbs as a signal

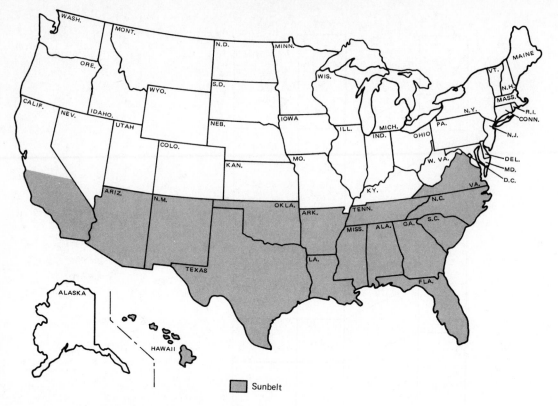

FIGURE 3-3 Sunbelt states

for them to open store branches to meet their moving customers' needs.

By closely monitoring these and other trends in population shifts, the fashion industry has much better opportunities to keep existing markets and capitalize on new ones.

Education

The average amount of education an American receives increases every year. In 1960, for instance, all Americans over the age of 25 had an average of 10 years of education. By 1990, that average had gone up to 12 years, with nearly 21 percent of the population completing 4 years of college. The trend toward higher education continues, not only for recent high school graduates, but for women and older adults as well, and these educational achievements have made the United States the most educated country in the world.

Presently, clothing expenditures represent between 6 and 8 percent of a consumer's disposable income (amount of money left after taxes to spend on necessities and luxuries). Since, in most cases, the motivation toward higher education is "a better paying job," to the fashion industry a better educated consumer represents a more affluent consumer, one who has more money for clothing expenditures. The industry cannot overlook the fact that a better-educated consumer is also a more discriminating one, however, and it has been increasing both the quality and the appeal of its fashion merchandise in order to meet the high demands of the better educated consumer.

Occupation

Perhaps the most significant result of America's higher educational achievement has been the tremendous changes that have taken place in the country's labor market since 1950.

Two major changes have occurred. The first involves a shift from blue-collar to white-collar jobs. The number of blue-collar jobs requiring manual or physical labor has decreased, while the number of white-collar jobs requiring technical skills and specialized services has increased.

The second change pertains to an increase in the number of women who work. Today, women make up 49 percent of the U.S. work force. They are performing all kinds of jobs, from laborers to corporate executives. Many are career-oriented, remaining on the job for longer periods of time and refusing to drop out after marriage or while raising a family.

Both these occupational changes in America's population have directly affected the fashion-buying habits of the consumer and the fashion offerings of the industry. As the number of both male and female white-collar workers increases, the demand for suitable "on-the-job" apparel intensifies, expanding the industry's production of men's and women's tailored business clothing.

Purchasing Power

The **purchasing power** of a consumer is determined by three factors: personal income, accumulated or net worth, and available consumer credit. Today, Americans have more purchasing power than they have ever had. But over the years, the percentage of that purchasing power used to buy apparel has decreased.

Most fashion firms define their competitors as those who produce similar goods. There are other firms, however, that believe that in order to capture a large share of the American dollar, the fashion industry will have to redefine its competition and vie with those outside the industry for the consumer's discretionary dollar (the amount spent on luxury items). Apparel, long classified as a necessity, must be presented as a "necessary luxury," upgraded through promotion so it is considered an exciting and important part of "the good life."

Psychographic Characteristics

As previously defined, psychographic data reflect a person's attitudes, values, and beliefs. An analysis of these data can reveal how those attitudes, values, and beliefs will influence a person's purchases.

Attitudes Toward Personal Spending

Purchasing power may enable the consumer to buy goods, but the attitude of a consumer toward spending actually determines whether or not that consumer will buy those goods. That attitude is governed

Applying Market Segmentation

Using people's lifestyles, attitudes, and beliefs to help determine the products that should be manufactured is not yet a widespread practice in the fashion industry. Some have hesitated to try market segmentation because they feel it is too difficult, too inaccurate, or even not necessary.

However, a most successful application of market segmentation was undertaken by Warner Slimwear, a division of Warnaco, Inc., and it proved how valuable market segmentation can be.

The company was interested in producing a new line of bras. Unsure of the type of customer it could most profitably service, it undertook an extensive marketing research program. It obtained both demographic and psychographic information which, when analyzed, revealed a variety of attitudes and preferences in reference to bras.

The research revealed five distinct target markets, as follows: (1) conservative, (2) fashionable, (3) brand conscious, (4) outgoing, and (5) home/price oriented. Further research enabled Warner to evaluate the size and financial potential of each segment on a national scale. They uncovered that the most profitable segments were: (2) fashionable, (3) brand conscious, and (4) outgoing. Thus, the company was able to eliminate segments 1 and 5 as unprofitable markets. It was already catering to segments 2 and 3, so segment 4 became the focus of its attention.

As a result, a sheer stretch bra named "Starkers" was specifically designed for and marketed to this segment. Reorders were three times the normal level. Both Warnaco and participating retailers enjoyed additional profits. In their estimation, segmenting the market for the development of salable fashion goods is possible, sometimes necessary, and certainly profitable.

by two factors: a consumer's past economic experience and the current economic conditions or affluence of the country.

Remember the Great Depression of the 1930s? Those over 65 years of age do, and those difficult times have greatly influenced the attitude of that age group toward personal spending. Conservative and cautious, many reject credit or impulse buying and consider job security and financial solvency ("a little something in the bank") most important. For the younger, under 65 age group, these considerations are not so important. Raised in an affluent society, they consider credit and free spending a way of life, and they place relatively little importance on savings and job security.

The condition of the country's economy, however, can alter the established spending attitudes of both groups. When the U.S. economic system is healthy, both jobs and goods are plentiful. America appears to be a "land of plenty." Under those conditions, the older generation is encouraged to relax its normally cautious attitudes and increase spending. Should the economy slow down, making jobs and goods scarce and expensive, the free-spending younger generation tightens up its purse strings and becomes more concerned with the stability of a job.

From a fashion marketing perspective, a positive attitude on the part of the consumer toward personal spending is absolutely essential. If consumer confidence is shaken, even slightly, fashion purchases are among the first to be curtailed. The use of psychographic surveys on consumer confidence allows the fashion industry to monitor any changes in the attitude of the consumer that might have a subsequent effect on consumer spending.

Attitudes Toward Materialism

Americans have always used appearance, possessions, and purchases as expressions of affluence and to improve their status in the eyes of others (Thorstein Veblen's conspicuous consumption theory). During the 1960s there was much talk about a trend toward "antimaterialism," but in reality the trend was not against materialism as much as it was against the old, established "status symbols." Materialism continued to exist; only the symbols changed. Obvious signs of wealth became unpopular and distasteful and were rejected in favor of understated possessions. When the 1980s gave way to the 1990s, the fashion world abandoned the glitz and glamour of the Bush-Reagan years. Looks such as "grunge," "waif," and "hip-hop"—all up from street fashion—became popular. People's attitudes toward waste and recycling were reflected in their apparel.

Attitudes Toward Marriage and the Family

Getting married has remained one of the most treasured rituals in our society. Ninety percent of all adults have married, or will marry, at least once in their lives. Of course, there have been some changes. Most notably, couples are waiting until their mid-20s or even longer before saying "I do." Because they are older and making more money, they are spending more on the ceremony including their wedding attire. Even in situations where one partner is divorced (i.e., Elizabeth Taylor), remarriages are often grander than the previous ones.

Attitudes toward children have also changed. The preference toward large families has disappeared, and most couples now consider one or two children "ideal."

Women continue to work after their children are born. The working mother is a significant trend that is expected to remain a part of the lifestyle of American families. Also, because working wives and mothers are pressed for time, shopping is no longer a leisurely process. There has been an increase in catalog shopping, and in-home shopping via cable TV is certain to become even more important in the near future.

These changes in the attitude toward marriage and family have been reflected throughout different segments of the fashion industry. The bridal market, while remaining strong, has changed its styling to cater to a more sophisticated and older clientele. A delay in marriage and children for working women has caused the industry to increase its production of suitable "nine-to-five" business clothes. And since the social values of a society are always reflected in the fashion trends of its apparel, the liberalized attitudes toward marriage and the family have created an equally permissive attitude on the part of both the consumer and the industry toward choice of dress.

Attitudes Toward the Quality of Life

As people become better educated, make more money, and have more leisure time, they expect more from life. Their pursuit of the "good life" increases. They take a greater interest in music, theater, dance, and other cultural arts; they develop a keener appreciation for quality and beauty; and, in general, they seem to show a deeper appreciation of the finer things in life. This appreciation extends to food, entertainment, and of course, clothes.

Clothing, as described in Chapter 2, serves many purposes. In addition to offering protection and comfort, it serves as a tool for expressing one's affluence, personality, and taste. For those who have developed keen fashion tastes, clothes serve as a personal statement.

As more and more Americans improve their lifestyle, the fashion industry has been increasingly pressed to produce finer fashion products that will satisfy both basic needs and aesthetic tastes. As a result, most current fashion reflects an improvement in quality and taste, adding enormously to the overall quality of the American lifestyle.

Attitudes Toward the Importance of Self
When people begin to upgrade the quality of their lifestyle, it is natural for them to become much more introspective, to concentrate on themselves. Self-understanding and self-beautification become prime objectives. The success of countless how-to books offering advice on improving one's emotional, sexual, and physical state is directly related to the increasing interest people have been taking in themselves.

Psychographic surveys that reveal how consumers are satisfying their search for self-improvement are important to the fashion industry. For instance, efforts toward physical self-improvement have resulted in a growing preoccupation with jogging and tennis, as well as a surge in the popularity of health and beauty spas. As survey data inform them of these trends, manufacturers are able to provide the consumer with sportswear that is suitable for these activities.

Demographic and psychographic characteristics of the U.S. population are constantly changing. In order to correctly identify consumers and their needs, consumer research must be continuously updated through an ongoing, uninterrupted process. Only the most accurate data can help the fashion industry properly profile and evaluate the American consumer so that it may provide them with the "right" product at the "right" place, price, and time.

.... TERMS TO REMEMBER

scientific method   demographics   psychographics   segmenting the market   primary data   secondary data   target market   purchasing power

.... HIGHLIGHTS OF THE CHAPTER

- Being marketing-oriented means using a marketing concept that begins with defining the customer and identifying unfulfilled needs.

- To learn about the consumer, consumer fashion research is done using the principles of the scientific method.

- The market for fashion goods is defined in terms of both demographic and psychographic characteristics.

- Demographics is the use of statistics to describe a population.

- Psychographics refers to describing people's attitudes, values and beliefs as they affect behavior.

- Demographic and psychographic data are gathered by observation, survey, or conducting experiments.

- The data are analyzed to determine potential market segments or target markets.

- The final step in the consumer research process is testing.

- The American fashion consumer is changing demographically in terms of population size, age, and location; educational achievement; occupation; and purchasing power.

- The American fashion consumer may be described psychographically in terms of attitudes toward affluence, materialism, marriage and the family, the quality of life, and the importance of self.

······· REVIEW QUESTIONS

1. List the four steps of organization used to obtain consumer fashion research.

2. What are demographics? Give four demographic characteristics the fashion industry can use to identify a market.

3. Define the term *psychographics*. Give four psychographic characteristics the fashion industry can use to identify a market.

4. List three ways to gather data for fashion consumer research.

5. What is a firm's "target market?"

6. What is happening to the size, age, and location of the U.S. population? Specifically, how will the fashion industry be affected?

7. How do education and occupation influence consumer spending for fashion merchandise?

8. What is meant by the term *purchasing power?* What has happened to the amount spent on fashion goods since 1950?

9. How does consumer confidence affect consumer spending for fashion goods?

10. How have changes in marriage and the family affected fashion?

······· RESEARCH AND PROJECTS

1. Probably the most significant changes in American life have taken place in the institution of marriage, the family, and the role of the wife. Elaborate on this statement.

2. "Americans are very much into themselves and have become too materialistic!" React to this statement by giving your personal opinion and examples from the chapter.

3. Research what family life was like in the 1950s. What was the role of women in society? What were the prevalent attitudes toward marriage and the family? How did so much change so quickly? What changes in these areas can we expect in the future?

4. Describe the lifestyle of the mature and senior citizen markets, using demographic and psychographic terminology. Assume you were going to market a line of apparel or accessories to this group. Explain your product's features in terms of appealing to these groups.

5. Find copies of fashion magazines from the 1950s, 1960s, 1970s, and 1980s. Study the editorial pages of these publications and cite the differences that appear in terms of the target market. (Describe each briefly in terms of demographic and psychographic characteristics.) Pay attention to the models and the copy used for describing the clothing and accessories for assistance with this assignment.

Part Two

··

WORLDWIDE INFLUENCES ON TODAY'S FASHION

········ In Part One we learned about the meaning of fashion, how it changes, and what the future holds in store for the fashion industry. In the second section of this text, we explore the historical influences and developments that shaped the origins of this fledgling industry. From these beginnings we see how the creative genius of a handful of people contributed to a new way of thinking about clothing.

CHAPTER 4

The Origins of Modern Fashion

.... LEARNING OBJECTIVES

After reading this chapter, you should be able to:

- Explain where and how modern fashion design began.
- Understand France's early impact on fashion.
- Recognize the names and achievements of the great fashion designers and fashion personalities of the past.
- Describe the evolution of European fashion history from the time of Louis XIV to the 1960s.

.... PERFORMANCE OUTCOME

After reading this chapter, you should be able to:

- Recognize elements of style in current fashion that originated with the earliest fashion designers.
- Attribute the source of beautiful design in clothing found in works of art created during this period to the appropriate designer.
- Select a unique element that made each of the designer "greats" famous.

From the loincloth to the bikini, from Joseph's coat of many colors to minks that have been ranched over many generations to achieve the perfect hue—how did we get from there to here? How did the simple shops of tailors and dressmakers become the great fashion industry of today? The road was trod by men and women who led in establishing new ways of adorning the body to enhance its beauty and to make a statement. These, then, are the "Pied Pipers of Fashion." They led and the world followed.

FRANCE—THE FIRST FASHION CENTER

Until the thirteenth century, the fashions of each country differed from one another. Dress was a form of national costume, and consequently an international fashion influence did not exist.

During the late 1200s, France emerged as an important European center of culture and learning. Although its reputation grew steadily for the next 400 years, it was during the reign of Louis XIV, which began in 1661, that France's worldwide reputation peaked. Under Louis XIV (the Sun King), the expansion of cultural achievement was encouraged as part of his scheme to politically dominate the Western world.

Louis XIV's ambitious plans included the building of a magnificent palace in Versailles, a suburb of Paris. The palace served as his home, military headquarters, and as the social and political center of France. Sparing no expense, the palace was landscaped and decorated with the finest furnishings and art. The splendor of Versailles became legendary and served as a showcase of luxury and the "fashionable" life. Likewise, the elaborate clothing preferences of Louis and his court were widely copied by other royalty and the wealthy throughout Europe (see Figure 4–1).

To meet the growing interest in and need for beautiful fabrics, tapestries, and ribbons, Louis established textile production in Lyons and a lace works in Alençon. This was the beginning of France's fashion industry and marked its start as the fashion capital of the world.

FIGURE 4-I   Louis XIV—The Sun King

ESTABLISHING FASHION LEADERSHIP

The First Fashion Leaders

During the next century, the monarchs who succeeded Louis XIV and the women of their royal courts continued to encourage and support the French fashion industry. One of the most famous was Madame de Pompadour (see Figure 4–2). As mistress of Louis XV, she assumed an important political role, dressed extravagantly, and was a noted fashion leader of her time. Probably the most influential fashion leader of the century was Marie Antoinette. As wife of Louis XVI, she was Queen of France until her execution in 1793.

•••••••• **FIGURE 4-2 Madame de Pompadour—fashion leader.**

Because of her absolute passion for clothes, Marie Antoinette was known as the "queen of fashion." Her huge and lavish wardrobe occupied three of the palace's large rooms. Unfortunately, her clothes were so important to her that she refused to flee France without them. Traveling with several huge wardrobe trunks, she was easily spotted and arrested by the revolutionists. Her attachment to her clothes literally cost her her head!

The First "Name" Fashion Designer

The clothes of the rich and titled were made in shops owned by former dressmakers and tailors whose outstanding ability and good taste enabled them to direct the design and construction of the lavish garments demanded. They were called *couturiers* and received little personal recognition.

Chapter 4   The Origins of Modern Fashion

FIGURE 4-3   Rose Bertin—the first "Minister of Fashion."

But during the 1770s, a talented *couturière* named **Rose Bertin** became famous for her flair for choosing flattering fabrics, colors, and trims for her aristocratic customers (see Figure 4–3). Her fame brought her to the attention of Queen Marie Antoinette, then a shy and uncertain 16-year-old. Under Bertin's guidance, the young queen was transformed into France's leading fashion personality.

One of Bertin's great achievements was to persuade Queen Marie to simplify her elaborate dress by adding more practical wool and cotton costumes, similar to those worn by shepherdesses. These imitations of lower class apparel delighted the queen. They became immensely popular with her court and are an early example of a *bottom-up* fashion. Another well-remembered Bertin innovation was the elaborate hairdos and wigs that so typify the late 1700s (see Figure 4–4).

Bertin also counted foreign royalty among her clients, and she sent exquisitely dressed "**fashion dolls**" as far away as Russia and Turkey for the approval of her titled clientele. As a salute to her genius, the French government honored her with the official title "Minister of Fashion."

The French Revolution forced Bertin to flee France, but she returned in 1800 and reestablished her business. Unfortunately, she

When the rest of the world began to copy French fashion, news and illustrations of the latest styles were eagerly sought. However, in the late 1700s, fashion magazines and newspapers did not exist. Women relied on word of mouth and a unique means of communicating the latest fashions—fashion dolls.

Fashion dolls were approximately 18 inches high and had cloth bodies and china heads and hands. French dressmakers dressed them in exact replicas of the latest fashions—from the most elaborate Bertin hairdo to the tiniest miniature accessory.

The dolls originally circulated within France, but as French fashion influence spread, they were sold abroad. After the styles were copied and the dolls became outmoded, they were given to children as playthings, and very few, if any, of the eighteenth-century fashion dolls now exist. In the early 1800s the introduction of the fashion magazine replaced the need for these unique fashion dolls.

In the 1920s and 1930s in Europe and in the United States, it was fashionable to have replicas of fashion dolls displayed on benches and couches in the front parlors of homes. Today, a new variety of fashion doll is marketed for collectors (see Figure 4–5 and Color Plate 10).

never regained the prominence she enjoyed under Marie Antoinette, and she died in obscurity in 1813. Although her fashion credits are many, Rose Bertin is remembered as the first person to gain recognition from the public as a famous "name" designer.

Early Trend-Setters

The Empire Look

After the French Revolution, the French fashion industry fell apart. The ostentatious fashions of Louis XVI and Marie Antoinette (see Figure 4–6) were banned. Robespierre's "Reign of Terror" was characterized by fashions inspired by the Revolution and the bourgeoisie. Clothes became plain and peasantlike. Gone were the magnificent jewelry, perfumes, cosmetics, laces, silks, and brocades. In their place were somber wool coats, pantaloons, and stiff collars for men and drab-colored straight dresses with aprons for women (see Figure 4–7).

Many believe that menswear has never recovered from this drastic turning point in fashion. The transformation from opulent to subdued is a legacy found in menswear, even today. The trend toward plainer attire was further enhanced by the regime of Napoleon Bonaparte I. He assumed power in France in 1795, ushering in the Direc-

• • • • • • • • FIGURE 4-4 Elaborate hairdressings made popular by Marie Antoinette in the 1780s were created by the world's first designer—France's Rose Bertin.

Courtesy: Fortunoff, New York

• • • • • • • • FIGURE 4-5 These costumed bisque dolls of today are direct descendants of Rose Bertin's Fashion dolls.

FIGURE 4-6 Typical costume worn during Marie Antoinette's time, just prior to the French Revolution.

toire period. L. H. Leroy was chosen to design clothes for Napoleon's wife, Josephine. In the spirit of this new politically free atmosphere, he chose to follow the ancient classical style of the Greeks.

It was appropriately named the "**Empire look**" (see Figure 4–8). For about 25 years, it remained the accepted fashion of Europe and America, helping France once again to establish itself as the fashion leader of the world.

The low-cut, tiny sleeved white dresses were made of very sheer fabric, worn over flesh-colored body suits called maillots. Once on, the dresses were often dampened so that they would hold their pleating by clinging to the body. This practice caused many a wearer to become ill and some even to die of pneumonia. Thus, at the height of

FIGURE 4-7 Typical French dress after the Revolution.

its popularity, the look caused great concern as women were literally "dying" to be in fashion.

Once Napoleon assumed power and crowned himself emperor, he insisted that his court resume wearing beautiful clothing made of elegant fabrics.

The fashion scene now shifts to England where tailors of men's clothing began to assume great importance.

The Dandy of Them All—Beau Brummel

Although there was no one fashion look in menswear, those of wealth and leisure remained fascinated with dress. Therefore, a variety of styles emerged. In England, those who were loyal to the use of lace,

FIGURE 4-8 (a) Simple, high-waisted styles, called Empire gowns and patterned after ancient Greek costumes, flourished in France's post-Revolutionary early 1800s.

feathers, and elegant fabrics were grouped by their preferences. Names such as "Beaus," "Spivs," and "Macaronis" were used. The Macaronis—who were partial to rosettes and feathers—became immortalized in the old chant: "Yankee doodle went to London, riding on a pony, stuck a feather in his cap and called it Macaroni."

But the most influential group of the time was the "Dandies." Their undisputed leader was Beau Brummel. Educated at Eton and Oxford, he was a master at the social graces and traveled in high cir-

FIGURE 4-8 (b) A modern adaptation of Empire clothing.

cles. He was a gentleman of leisure, and his occupation was dressing to perfection. He was the "prince of good grooming" and the "prime minister of taste" from 1796 to 1816 (see Figure 4–9).

These so-called titles were given to Beau Brummel because of the extraordinary manner in which he bathed and clothed himself. His wardrobe was spotless and without wrinkles. He bathed three times a day—an unheard-of practice. He was such a perfectionist that it was said he employed two different glovers—one to fit the hand and the other to fit the fingers. It took nearly two hours to correctly tie his cravat to his satisfaction and the shine on his boots was attained by using champagne as polish. Beau Brummel was greatly admired and emulated by the upper class.

FIGURE 4-9 Beau Brummel

Brummel was eventually noticed by the Prince of Wales, Regent and future King of England. The Prince was so impressed with Brummel that he invited him to join the royal regiment. Thus Brummel had direct access to the Prince and advised him on how to dress in the proper Dandy manner. The Prince abandoned his foppish attire and became the picture of male elegance, wearing skin-tight, below-the-knee trousers; boots; a tail coat in either blue or black; and a cravat, meticulously tied. British tailors were hard pressed to meet the demand for similar garments desired by all those who could afford to dress in the Regency manner. Figure 4–10 illustrates a current adaptation of the Dandy look.

All of this fashion power and influence made Brummel overconfident. When he openly criticized the tailoring of a coat worn by the Prince Regent, he fell out of grace and into debt. To avoid his many

FIGURE 4-10 **A modern-day adaption by of the Beau Brummel Dandy.**

creditors, Brummel fled to France, where he died in 1840 penniless and unnoticed. However, the Dandy style continued to be the fashion, and British tailors prospered as the demand for superior fit and handiwork grew.

Savile Row and Henry Poole

One such tailor who became quite wealthy because of his fashion know-how and excellent handiwork was **Henry Poole.** His London shop, located on Savile Row, supplied young English aristocrats with outstanding wardrobes. Sometimes, instead of payment, Poole would accept invitations to important social functions. At one such event, he met Louis Napoleon, the French Prince in exile after the downfall of Napoleon I. Louis needed money to wage a campaign to be reinstated to power in France. Poole graciously gave him $50,000 for this undertaking. When Napoleon III was elected ruler of France and formed the Second Empire, Poole was named official Court tailor. British tailoring ruled supreme. The Emperor of France was dressed by the tailor of Savile Row, making that street synonymous with the finest in men's fashion. Although France re-emerged as the center for women's fashions, Britain retained, even until today, the distinction of being the fashion capital of menswear.

ESTABLISHING *HAUTE COUTURE*

Charles Frederick Worth—Beginning the French Couture

Henry Poole was not the only Englishman to do well in the Second French Empire. **Charles Frederick Worth,** the founder of the French couture, was also a British tailor who became the Court's official fashion designer for the Empress Eugenie. Worth, often called the "father of the French couture," learned about the fashion business at the early age of 11 when, forced to help support his family, Worth acquired sales ability and tailoring skills in various London shops. At the age of 20, he decided to go to Paris, becoming a salesperson in a ladies' dress shop. There, he met his wife and began designing clothes for her. Worth's designs caught the attention of the shop's customers and this led to a successful partnership in the business. In 1860, Worth opened his own establishment, the House of Worth.

Because his creations were in such demand, Worth chose to dress only clientele with the "right" social status and rejected customers who would not do "justice" to his designs. As a way of having his designs worn to the French Court, he dressed Princess Pauline von Metternich, wife of the Austrian ambassador. When the Empress saw the dresses worn by the Princess, she immediately sent for Worth, and he was named the imperial dressmaker.

Unlike his predecessors, Rose Bertin and L. H. Leroy, Worth was a dictatorial designer. He did not accept advice from his clients. He considered himself a supreme artist on matters of fashion design. He created complete outfits, not just dresses. And his final word was graciously accepted by those who were privileged enough to be dressed by such a magnificent creator. This change from dressmaker to designer established a precedent followed by French couture today and earned Worth his title—"father of the French couture."

Among the many other Worth "firsts" was his decision not to advertise. Instead, each season he prepared hand-colored portfolios for each of his customers. Another idea he is credited with, and which he started by dressing his wife, was the use of live mannequins (models) to display his creations. Worth was also the first to select and supply fabrics for a design. Previously, customers supplied their own.

The House of Worth is credited with setting the major fashion trends of the middle to late 1800s. The most famous of these was the crinoline. By using a cagelike device made from whale bone to hold out the nearly four yards of fabric, Worth created some of the largest gowns ever worn (see Figure 4–11). Eugenie so loved the enormous skirts that she became known as "Empress Crinoline." This fashion was so popular that it even influenced architecture. Doorways were widened to allow the women to move from one room to another.

Following the fashion rule of excess, the bell silhouette reached its extreme interpretation with this look. Realizing this, Worth intro-

• • • • • • • FIGURE 4-11 **Worth achieved a sweeping effect in his designs of the 1850s.**

duced a gradual change. Skirts started to appear oval, extending toward the back. Eventually, Worth made the front of the skirt straight, and the bustle was born. The "swan bend" stance and the desired 18-inch waistline were achieved by a tightly laced corset. Once again the health of women was affected by the dictates of fashion. The overtightened waists and the fainting spells that followed became a way of life for women. By the 1870s, women everywhere had adopted the bustle and abandoned the crinoline. Truly, Worth's influence was profound; he was called the first fashion dictator of modern times. His needlework was the very finest, thus the phrase *haute couture* was created.

After Worth's death in 1895, the House of Worth was operated by his heirs; and although dressmaking activities stopped in 1930, the famous Worth fragrances are still successfully marketed today and proudly worn by connoisseurs.

. . . .

PAST DESIGNING GREATS OF THE FRENCH COUTURE

After Worth opened his couture house in 1860, others followed his lead. Between the turn of the century and the 1960s, France remained the undisputed mecca of fashion design. Among the many well-known French designers, several emerged as "greats." Most of these designers were revolutionaries, rejecting the accepted fashion standards for their own radical new ones. The remaining "greats" can be classified as traditionalists. Their innovations were more subtle, introducing gradual but nevertheless influential fashion changes.

The French Revolutionists

These fashion revolutionaries were designers who were tuned into the quickened pace of the twentieth century. Their greatness came from their ability to recognize the changing needs of women and to translate them into fashion.

Paul Poiret

When this designer opened his salon in 1904, women were uncomfortably poured into S-shaped corsets that emphasized their bustline and derrière. **Paul Poiret** considered this form of dress not only unhealthy, but passé. He felt it was time to "free the body" from this "swan" shape, and he introduced a simple tubular silhouette and replaced the hideous corsets with his new invention—the brassière.

Poiret's revolutionary design concepts and campaign against the corset were welcomed by free-thinking women everywhere. Until 1914 he was, as he called himself, "king of fashion."

Poiret's clothes were exotic with oriental overtones. One of his most famous shapes consisted of a "lampshade" tunic with a circular *wired* hem worn over a narrow skirt (see Figure 4–12).

Many of Poiret's friends were artists. By asking them to paint his collections, he was instrumental in elevating fashion illustration to an art form. Poiret also encouraged his friends to design fabrics, and several of the ones he used are outstanding examples of classic Art Deco,

FIGURE 4-12 Poiret's famous tunic of 1912 was stiffened with hoops for its "lampshade" effect.

which was popular at that time. He not only lectured about fashion design, he also founded a School of Decorative Arts called *Martine*.

Although Poiret is credited with freeing the female body, he did not continue to evolve this trend. Instead, he introduced the "hobble skirt," so named because the wearer was unable to walk normally. Poiret's exotic fashions became hopelessly out of step with the times, and the great designer's influence quickly diminished.

The period after World War I was an important one in the women's liberation movement. All over the Western world women were fighting for equality and the right to vote. One means of expressing this new freedom was through appearance and dress. Curls, frills, and flounces were out. Short haircuts, tubular flat-chested silhouettes, and *simplification in design* were in.

Gabrielle (Coco) Chanel

The most powerful personality behind this new look was **Coco Chanel.** From the beginning of her career in 1909, Chanel rejected Poiret's elaborate designs, maintaining that *couturiers* were not "artists"; they were "furnishers." She believed women should dress *simply* and *comfortably.*

The first time she put her theories into practice was during World War I. French women could not successfully take over the jobs of the fighting men and still wear ornate fashions and hobble skirts. In her small shop, Chanel offered an alternative style of dress: men's pullover sweaters, sailor jackets, and straight skirts. The new "working costume" was a success, and so was Chanel.

Chanel was often inspired by the everyday clothes worn by working people around her, borrowing from a mechanic's blouse, a ditchdigger's scarf, and the white collar and cuffs of a waitress for ideas.

The first designer to use wool jersey in women's wear, Chanel revolutionized the textile industry. Originally, the fabric had been produced for use in men's underwear, but men found it too "scratchy." However, the jersey appealed to Chanel, who found it perfect for the kind of comfortable and understated apparel she had in mind.

She was also the first to make costume jewelry socially acceptable. Previously, imitation jewelry was called "paste" and was worn with embarrassment. She popularized the use of "fake" jewels by lavishly using rope upon rope of imitation pearls and other fake stones to enhance her simple, understated clothes. The simplicity of her designs made them easy to copy in the factory, and she is credited with being the designer who had the greatest effect on the early development of American mass production.

Until her retirement in 1939, Chanel was one of the world's most influential prewar designers. Her retirement was not permanent, how-

FIGURE 4-13 Mademoiselle Gabrielle "Coco" Chanel, the great French couturière, photographed in the drawing room of her salon in the late 1950s.

ever. In 1953, she was prompted into a comeback by her distaste for postwar fashions. In opposition to the cinch-waisted, full-skirted styles being presented by Dior and other designers, she reintroduced her *simple, comfortable* shapes (see Figure 4–13). By 1959, her famous Chanel suit had become the "uniform" of well-dressed women everywhere. Original Chanel suits are still worn with pride by women of means and good taste.

Chanel died in 1971 at the age of 88, but under the talented designer Karl Lagerfeld, her business continues producing clothes that reflect the classic look of Chanel. The famous numbered Chanel fragrances also continue to be produced, including the legendary No. 5, named by Chanel for her lucky number. Most fashion authorities agree that Coco Chanel was the century's most "influential and revolutionary designer because she brought simplicity and freedom to women's clothes."[1] Figure 4–14 is a modern adaptation of a Chanel suit by Rodier of Paris.

[1]Bernard Roshco, *The Rag Race* (New York: Funk and Wagnalls, 1963), p. 210.

Courtesy: Rodier, Paris

•••••••• **FIGURE 4-14 A current adaptation of the Chanel look.**

Besides Chanel, there were two other important designers who had a revolutionary impact on the fashions of the 1920s and 1930s. They were Madeline Vionnet and Elsa Schiaparelli.

Vionnet
The design concept of Madeline Vionnet was quite different from that of Chanel. It was revolutionary; her greatest contribution was her invention of intricate bias cuts (fabric cut on the diagonal of the grain line). She also believed in retaining the natural lines of the body and rejected corsets, padding, or stiffening that might distort the anatomy.

Vionnet was in business several years before her bias cut made her famous in 1922, and she continued to design until 1939. Born in 1877, Vionnet was in her late 90s when she died in 1975. Although Vionnet's dressmaking techniques differed from those of Chanel, both introduced a contemporary approach to fashion.

Elsa Schiaparelli

While Chanel and Vionnet designed easy, soft clothes, this designer's look was quite different. Elsa Schiaparelli was an Italian who began her Paris career in the early 1930s by knitting beautiful sweaters. Her subsequent couture collections seemed to mirror the chaotic times. She used unusual and shocking colors: "shocking pink" was her invention. She introduced "mad" prints, buttons, and accessories; and an upturned shoe became one of her most famous hat designs. She was the designer for those who advocated "hard chic," who wished to be "shocking," and as such became quite successful. Current designers use a combination of color in all kinds of clothing, but especially in sportswear. Figure 4–15 (and Color Plate 6) shows a competitive bathing suit. The color plate appears at the front of the book.

Schiaparelli is also credited with introducing the **boutique** into the couture business. She decided to sell some of her unusual accessories, sweaters, and other, less-expensive items of clothing in a corner of her salon. After the war, her boutique concept was copied by other French *couturiers*.

At the start of World War II, Schiaparelli closed her business. She never returned to fashion but continued to enjoy a successful perfume business. Elsa Schiaparelli died in 1973 at the age of 83.

During and immediately after World War II, the influence of the Paris couture was interrupted and fashion remained unchanged. But by 1947, the Paris couture was on its way to recovery. That fall, Christian Dior introduced the "New Look" in his first collection. Instantly the dress of women all over the world was revolutionized, and Paris' position as the world center of high fashion was restored.

Christian Dior

The "New Look" (see Figure 4–16) that **Christian Dior** presented was a radical departure from the existing silhouette. He eliminated shoulder pads, cinched the waist, and—unhampered by former wartime cloth restrictions—widened and lengthened the skirt.

The initial reaction was explosive and controversial, but women welcomed its luxurious feminine look; eventually, the New Look was overwhelmingly accepted.

COMPETITION-LYCRA

Courtesy: Ocean Pool Company, Commack, New York.

FIGURE 4-15 A modern adaptation of Schiaparelli's unusual combination of colors—this time in a bathing suit designed for competitive swimmers.

Christian Dior died in 1957 at the age of 53, 10 years after he started his business. In those 10 years, he developed his organization into one of international scope. After his death, designer Yves Saint Laurent took over the firm's designing duties, but after a few seasons, he was called to serve in the French military. Marc Bohan became the firm's design director and under him it has continued to produce luxurious, beautiful clothes. In 1989, Bohan was replaced by Italian-born

• • • • • • • • **FIGURE 4-16 Christian Dior's revolutionary "New Look" of 1947 made him the leading designer of the post-World War II years.**

Gianfranco Ferre, who has added new life and interest to the House of Dior.

Although Christian Dior's revolutionary "New Look" made him the most famous postwar designer, fashion authorities agree that, until the youth revolution of the 1960s, the designer who had the most overall influence on postwar fashion was Christobal Balenciaga.

Christobal Balenciaga

Unlike Dior, **Christobal Balenciaga**'s clothes were understated and tailored, relying on cut and shape for design. Through the use of interfacings and linings, his sculptured shapes were built into his clothes.

His concern for shape and form led him to introduce new shapes, earning him the name "prophet of silhouette." One of his most influential silhouettes was the 1957 chemise. Its tubular shape was the forerunner of the popular straight "shift" of the late 1950s and early 1960s.

The rest of the couture was tremendously influenced by the work of the man they called "the master," and they followed his lead. Because of that influence, he is credited with creating the major trends of the 1950s and 1960s (see Figure 4–17).

To Balenciaga, fashion and elegance were inseparable. Disillusioned with the new young revolution in clothes, he retired in 1968. He died in Spain, his birthplace, in 1972 at the age of 77.

The French Traditionalists

While the revolutionists dramatically influenced fashion direction, other designers earned their reputations as excellent interpreters of the trends. Their commitment to *haute couture,* that is, the finest needlework, made them important contributors to the French domination of fashion.

- *Madame Paquin,* named the "queen of Paris fashion," was the first woman to establish a couture house and to be elected president of the *Chambre Syndicale de la Couture Parisienne*—the parent organization that directs those who are members of the Haute Couture group.

- *Jeanne Lanvin* was the first *couturière* to make children's wear. Her "mother-daughter" outfits were very successful. She was also known for her luxurious embroideries and perfumes, My Sin and Arpège.

- *Jean Patou* created beautiful sportswear and tennis outfits. He began the tradition of giving gala parties after the collections were shown.

- *Captain Edward Molyneux* was born in Ireland and gained a reputation in Paris for his fine tailoring and elegant classic designs.

- *Lucien Lelong* was a master of the technical aspects of garment construction. Lelong is credited with saving the French couture organization from Nazi control during World War II.

- *Nina Ricci* had great success with her boutique and accessories. Her perfume, L'Air du Temps, remains very popular today as does her couture house.

- *Pierre Balmain* was a co-designer with Dior in the Lucien Lelong House. His expert ability to construct garments came from his early training as an architect. He once stated, "Dress making is the architecture of movement."

- *Jacques Heim* revolutionized swimwear by introducing the draped suit and shocked Paris with the bikini in 1945.

- *Jacques Fath* was one of French couture's most flamboyant designers. He loved strong colors and youthful looks. He was also a master showman, putting on glamorous fashion shows and elegant parties.

- *Mainbocher* (born Main Rousseau Bocher and contracted his name to Mainbocher when he became a *couturier* in 1929) was the "American in Paris," editor of the French *Vogue* magazine, and self-made *couturier.* He was known for his timeless and understated but totally original designs. His credits include the beaded evening sweater, the dinner suit, short evening dresses, and the sleeveless suit blouse. His most celebrated client was the Duchess of Windsor. After the outbreak of the war, Mainbocher came to America and continued his couture business. He became the only "name" designer in the United States whose business was devoted exclusively to making custom-made clothes, and though he greatly influenced Seventh Avenue fashion, he never produced ready-to-wear clothing. Mainbocher retired to France in 1971, where he died five years later at the age of 85.

The Costume Institute of the Metropolitan Museum of Art

· · · · · · · · · · ·
FASHION FEATURE
· · · · · · · · · · ·

One of the great collections of costumes in the world can be found in the United States at the Metropolitan Museum of Art in New York City. Evolving from a concept in 1937 as a resource for authentic costume design for the theater, the Museum of Costume Art moved to the Metropolitan as a wing in the 1940s and became a department in 1959.

Over the years, the Institute has grown to become an inspiration to fashion designers, scholars, and students from all over the world. It houses a collection of more than 60,000 costumes and accessories representing clothing worn over a 500-year period from five continents of the world. The department includes exhibition and office space, a conservation facility for the collection, and areas for storage and study. In addition, the Irene Lewisohn Costume Reference Library houses more than 110,000 books on costume and textiles, fashion plates, photographs, and clippings. It is named for the original founder of the Museum of Costume Art.

In the early 1970s, Diana Vreeland, former fashion editor for *Harper's Bazaar* and editor-in-chief of *Vogue,* joined the Costume Institute as Special Consultant. Under her aegis, marvelous exhibitions including The World of Balenciaga, Hollywood Design, The Glory of Russian Costume, and Vanity Fair were presented to museum goers to great acclaim.

Since that time, the Institute has undergone a complete reorganization. It now offers ongoing exhibitions in more than 5,000 square feet of space with a climate and lighting system that enables viewers to inspect the offerings in an environment that includes panoramic displays as well as intimate spaces. Original mannequins were developed for the new galleries to display body types and attitudes of different eras; hairstyles have been carefully researched for each costume that is exhibited.

The Costume Institute plans to prepare training programs and teaching materials for teachers. Students are invited to come with their classes to inspect the new facilities and to examine both the exhibitions and the areas of the Institute which are behind the scenes. Reservations must be made well in advance. Lectures and activities are held frequently and the Museum should be telephoned for the calendar of events.

Problem Solving

1. The new Costume Institute at the Metropolitan Museum of Art in New York City offers an outstanding opportunity to people in many fields of study all over the world. What is the best way to utilize the Institute if you are pursuing the following fashion careers?
   a. fashion writer and critic
   b. visual merchandiser
   c. apparel designer
   d. store buyer
   e. museum curator
   f. fashion illustrator
   g. store public relations
   h. fashion advertising
2. Which other fields of study can be enhanced by a visit to the Costume Institute? Name five fields.

······· TERMS TO REMEMBER

fashion dolls **boutique** **Empire look** **Rose Bertin** **Beau Brummel**
Henry Poole **Charles Frederick Worth** **Paul Poiret** **Coco Chanel**
Christian Dior **Christobal Balenciaga**

······· HIGHLIGHTS OF THE CHAPTER

- The world's first fashion center was France. It was established by King Louis XIV in the middle 1600s as part of his scheme to culturally and politically dominate the Western world.

- During the following centuries, French women of the royal courts became the world's first fashion leaders. They encouraged and supported the French fashion industry, maintaining France's reputation as the fashion capital of the world.

- Rose Bertin, French dressmaker to Marie Antoinette during the late 1700s, was the first "name" designer. But it was Charles Frederick Worth, an Englishman, who is the "father of the French couture." The House of Worth—opened in 1860—set the pattern for future couture houses.

- Beau Brummel and Henry Poole are responsible for making London the fashion center for menswear.

- Paul Poiret and Coco Chanel, designers during the first 30 years of the 1900s, were two revolutionaries of the French couture. Both "freed the body" from restricting clothes and undergarments, reflecting the new "equality and freedom for women" of the early 1900s.

- The great designers are those who reflect the spirit of the times. Because of the simplicity and freedom of her clothes, Coco Chanel is considered the greatest designer of the first half of the twentieth century.

- Christian Dior's "New Look" of 1947 restored France as the arbiter of women's fashion after World War II.

- Christobal Balenciaga was considered "the master" at cut and shape. He set the major trends of the 1950s and early 1960s.

.... REVIEW QUESTIONS

1. Why did King Louis XIV develop France's fashion industry? Where was his palace located, and how did it help France's fashion reputation?

2. Name the first French fashion leaders and describe their position in French history.

3. How did Rose Bertin become France's first "name" designer?

4. What were fashion dolls; how did Bertin utilize them?

5. When and how did the Empire look originate?

6. Who was Beau Brummel? Who was Henry Poole? What are their contributions to fashion?

7. Describe how Charles Frederick Worth began his career. Mention some Worth "firsts."

8. Who were the French fashion revolutionists of the early 1900s? Why was each considered so?

9. Name the great postwar French designer who revolutionized fashion. Describe the look that made him famous.

10. What qualities are associated with Christobal Balenciaga's designs?

11. What do we mean when we call some designers revolutionaries? What do we mean by a radical fashion standard?

.... RESEARCH AND PROJECTS

1. Explain why France, rather than another country, became the world's fashion center.

2. Menswear changed dramatically in appearance after the French Revolution. Cite the reasons why, by whom, where, and how this occurred.

3. Using texts on the history of costumes and art, research the lifestyle, fashions, and times of either King Louis XIV, XV, or XVI.

4. Select a French revolutionist designer discussed in this chapter, and show how his or her designs reflected the external environment and how they differed from their predecessors.

5. Because the work of Paul Poiret, Coco Chanel, Christian Dior, and Christobal Balenciaga was so profound, their influence in terms of design remains apparent even today. Using current magazines and newspapers, locate fashions that are in the manner of each designer.

CHAPTER 5

··

European Design Centers

······· LEARNING OBJECTIVES

After reading this chapter, you should be able to:

- Identify the European fashion centers.
- Understand how the French couture business operates and evaluate its relative importance in fashion.
- Identify the greatest of the European ready-to-wear and couture designers.
- Describe the rise of the European ready-to-wear designers and elaborate on their impact on the status of the European couture.

······· PERFORMANCE OUTCOME

After reading this chapter, you should be able to:

- Compare and contrast the workings and designer objectives of the couture and ready-to-wear industries in Europe.
- Locate important cities for couture and ready-to-wear fashion direction and inspiration.
- Identify the various trade associations in each country and explain what functions they perform.

· ·

M ost European designers work in Paris, helping to maintain that city's 300-year-old fashion reputation. Others work in Milan, Rome, and London. Together—along with the great talent on Seventh Avenue—these designers set the pace of fashion throughout the world.

· ·

THE COUTURE

France

France has long been synonymous with the best—albeit, at times, the most outrageous—in fashion. For generations Paris has been a center of fashion creativity, providing the world with its main source of fashion inspiration. Several factors have contributed toward shaping France into a world fashion leader, and all are related to the historic support and encouragement of the industry by the French government *and* its people. From the time of Louis XIV, the French have considered fashion a creative art as well as one of the country's important industries. The government considers designers as major contributors to the economy, while the people—men and women alike—regard them as gifted artists and shower them with recognition and affection.

Because of this support, designers work under ideal conditions. Small specialized industries are part of this tradition. The finest trims, embroideries, and other materials are available to, and often developed for, the designer.

One of the first steps France took toward developing a fashion industry was to establish textile centers. Today, these centers provide designers with what are generally conceded to be the finest fabrics in the world. French textile manufacturers are both willing and able to cooperate fully with designers. They gladly develop new colors and textures to specifications, running off short lengths of cloth for experimental purposes.

All these agreeable and supportive conditions have served to develop and maintain Paris's reputation as the fashion center; one which, for over a century, has housed the world's most accomplished creator and expressionist of fashion—the **couturier.**

99

Operation of the Paris Couture

Literally translated, **couturier** (masculine) and *couturière* (feminine) are the French words for "dressmaker," while **haute couture** translates into "the finest sewing." In France, however, these terms have a broader meaning. They refer to the designers and firms who create and sell the finest, *high-fashion, custom-made* apparel. A *custom-made* item is one that is made to the measurements of the individual customer. The making of custom apparel is a lengthy and expensive process. For example, a suit may cost $25,000 and an evening gown may be as much as $100,000.

It begins with a presentation of a *collection* of original designs. The designs are sewn in workrooms by seamstresses called **midinettes,** who are supervised by a *première*. Each design is called a *model*. The models of the collection are presented to the press and potential customers during a runway show called an *opening* or **showing. Mannequins**—the French word for live models—are used. A house *directrice* supervises the mannequins, the showings, and the salespeople or **vendeuses.** After seeing a collection at a showing, clients have the models of their choice made to order—on a one-at-a-time basis—with each garment fitted and made to conform to individual size specifications.

Couture openings take place twice a year. The spring-summer collections are shown in the latter part of January; the fall-winter collections are presented in July. It is at these showings that the new French couture fashion trends emerge.

The collections are first presented to a mixed but, to the couture, important group. It includes the wealthy private customers, who number under 1,000 but provide the couture with 75 percent of its business, the press, and customers who are part of the fashion industry. There are three types of customers in this latter group:

1. American and European ready-to-wear manufacturers, who purchase models for use as a source of inspiration when designing their own lines.

2. American and European retail store buyers, who purchase models for the express purpose of selling lower priced, ready-to-wear copies or adaptations in their own countries.

3. Paper pattern manufacturers, who purchase models or models made in muslin (*toiles*) to reproduce into paper patterns for the home sewer.

Several weeks after the initial showings, private clients are invited to view the collections and make their selections.

All private clients and members of the press are admitted free, but manufacturers and retailers are charged a fee. The fee may consist of a **caution**—the French word for deposit—or it may take the form of a required *minimum* purchase. The size of the *caution* depends on the importance of the couture house and can range anywhere from $1,000 to $5,000. The amount of the *caution,* however, is deductible from the cost of subsequent purchases. In the event a customer does not make a purchase, the caution is kept by the couture house as an admission fee. When a *minimum* purchase is specified, it generally consists of a requirement to buy a certain number of models or paper patterns.

Chambre Syndicale de la Couture Parisienne

There are many designers and custom dressmakers in Paris, but only a few are officially recognized as *haute couturiers.* To earn that distinction, a designer must meet specific qualifications as set down by the **Chambre Syndicale de la Couture Parisienne,** the trade organization of the Paris couture.

The Chambre Syndicale de la Couture was organized in 1868 by Gaston Worth, the son of Charles Worth. He recognized the need to curtail competition and coordinate the activities of the growing French industry. Throughout the years, the members have changed and grown, and the Chambre has changed accordingly. For example, in 1936, the Chambre's policy was reorganized to strengthen the professional unity of its members against threatening political conditions. During World War II that solidarity was successfully tested when Hitler began making plans to move the couture industry to Berlin. Lucien Lelong, then the president of the Chambre, succeeded in convincing German officials that the French couture could not operate outside of France. Remarkably, many couture houses continued to operate on a very limited basis during the German occupation, serving as training grounds for such postwar greats as Christian Dior. Today, the basic function of the organization continues to be based on its original premise of representing the couture in all labor, legal, and business matters.

The average membership of the Chambre Syndicale usually numbers between 20 and 25 *couturiers.* Only a handful of members, however, become world famous. Acceptance by the Chambre is considered prestigious and advantageous, but not all qualified couture houses wish to become members (see the Industry Feature on the Chambre). For example, Coco Chanel and Christobal Balenciaga never joined. Nevertheless, members and nonmembers alike regard the guidelines set by the Chambre as acceptable requirements for the establishment of a couture house.

Chambre Syndicale de la Couture Parisienne

Requirements for Membership in the Chambre Syndicale
The following requirements must be fulfilled to join the Chambre

1. A formal written request must be presented by the couture house to the organization.
2. Workrooms must be established in Paris with a minimum of 20 workers. Workmanship must be in the highest French tradition and, whenever possible, done by hand.
3. Each house must offer a collection designed by the designer or a member of his or her staff.
4. The clothes must be custom made and individually fitted to each client.
5. Sketches must be made by the house designer only.
6. A design must remain as it appeared in the original collection—it may never be changed to suit a client.
7. No work may be done by outside workrooms except for such specialized crafts as embroidery.
8. Each house must agree to show at least 75 models on live mannequins at the dates in January and July established by the Chambre Syndicale.
9. Three mannequins must be employed by the house year round.

Duties and Responsibilities of the Chambre Syndicale de la Couture Parisienne

1. Schedule and coordinate dates and times of couture openings for both visiting buyers and the press.
2. Issue invitations and press cards for openings.
3. Arrange shipping dates so that all models are sent to manufacturers and retailers on the same date—about 30 days after the showing.
4. Set official release date of press photos and sketches to coincide with introduction of ready-to-wear copies in stores. Date is usually about six weeks after the showing.
5. Regulate copying conditions. Under current rules, manufacturers and retailers who purchase original models may sell copies in their own country, but they may not sell paper patterns of a model to other manufacturers or to pattern companies. Though copying

L'École de la Chambre Syndicale de la Couture

In 1930, the Chambre founded a school to train French youth for the couture. Today, it is considered Europe's leading fashion school. One of its students was the great Yves Saint Laurent.

To accommodate foreign students, the school has an international division that has traditionally attracted many young Americans; the talented designer Geoffrey Beene is one of its best known alumni.

Business Organization of the Couture. Couture houses are usually founded by a designer and are known by the founder's name. The houses of Saint Laurent, Cardin, Chanel, and Dior are examples. In the event of the death of the designer, the firms usually continue to function, employing a successor to fulfill the designer's responsibilities. Inevitably, the work and name of the successor become widely recognized but as in the case of Karl Lagerfeld, designer for the House of Chanel, the firm almost always retains the name of its celebrated founder.

Although all couture houses are founded by designers, most designers begin with outside financial help and guidance provided by entering into partnerships. A classic example is that of designer Yves Saint Laurent. When he opened his house in 1963, he was backed by an American businessman from Georgia and by the American cosmetic firm Charles of the Ritz.

Once successful, some Paris couture houses also enter into conglomerates similar to those described under the business arrangements of American designers. The great House of Lanvin, for instance, became part of a conglomerate headed by Squibb Pharmaceuticals in 1971.

Other Activities of the Couture. The Paris couture designs for the ultra-rich woman who demands the newest and the best in fashion, materials, and workmanship. Because garments are made one by one, by hand, and require several customer fittings, the labor costs for couture are astronomical. Fabrics can cost as much as $300 per yard. Then there is the cost of the twice yearly openings that often runs into hundreds of thousands of dollars. Sales of couture clothing total between $50 and $60 million annually. All of this results in *haute couture* being a money-losing business. To survive, the couture designers have expanded their operations into other fashion-related activities.

The first of these activities was the *boutique*. Introduced by Schiaparelli in the 1920s, postwar designers recognized the value of this concept. Today, designer boutiques sell exquisite accessories and ready-to-wear designed by the *couturier* or member of the staff and bearing the designer's coveted label.

Perhaps the most unusual means of expansion has been the entrance of the *couturier* into the designing of **prêt-à-porter**—ready-to-wear—apparel. This step was taken during the late 1960s and early 1970s to meet the new and formidable competition of both American and foreign ready-to-wear designers. By 1977, all members of the couture but two produced *prêt-à-porter.* The exceptions were the House of Chanel and Mme. Alix Grès, then president of the Chambre Syndicale. But in March of that year, Chanel's house introduced its first ready-to-wear collection, and Grès joined in the ready-to-wear business in 1979.

The most obvious distribution method for *prêt-à-porter* was via designer boutiques. In the late 1960s, early 1970s, many designers did just that. In addition, designers such as Yves Saint Laurent, Valentino, and Givenchy began to franchise their boutique operations. Under a franchise agreement, an independent retailer sells the designer's products in a joint venture. The designer sets the rules of distribution and the retailer manages the store and shares in the profits of the operation.

In addition to their boutique products, most designers now market goods under extremely profitable licensing agreements. Like their American counterparts, through licensing, French designers have given their names to a wide variety of products that are sold internationally. The first designer to license his name was Christian Dior. In 1950 his name appeared on a line of men's ties. Today, the most widely licensed designer is Pierre Cardin. He holds over 800 agreements on every kind of product from home fashions to restaurants. Licensing generates billions of dollars for all designers. In just one product area—fragrances—the Chambre reports it yields over $1.2 billion to French designers.

The Current Status of the Paris Couture. In the fashion industry, there are differences of opinion on the influence today's Paris couture wields over world fashion. The controversy began in the 1960s, focusing on the *haute couture* versus American and European *ready-to-wear*. Ready-to-wear designers were producing fashion that was more contemporary and that reflected that turbulent era's life styles. Over the years, these designers grew to be as influential as the couture, and as a result of their strong competition, the couture lost much of its dictatorial punch.

Today, this situation persists. The Paris couture has not regained the authoritarian power it once held. Some consider it hopelessly out of date, producing clothes that have no relationship to what's happening to women today. Others point to the fact that it is unprofitable. The initial production costs of presenting a couture collection can run as high as $4 million. Subsequent sales do not return this initial investment, and couture houses must make up their losses from the profits of their boutiques, *prêt-à-porter*, fragrances, and licensed products.

Nevertheless, the couture does serve a purpose, one that is more important than providing a monied clientele with made-to-order clothes. Several byproducts of the couture compensate for its shortcomings and validate its existence. First, pro-couture forces maintain that the couture is indispensable as a *laboratory for ideas*. Couture designers agree. With unlimited access to the finest materials and workmanship, the *couturiers* argue that they can uninhibitedly experiment on developing fashion trends.

Second, the *couturiers* point to the invaluable *publicity* and *prestige* they receive from their *haute couture* and credit it with spurring the sales of other products sold under their label. They insist that the losses of their couture collections are easily made up through the additional sales of the other goods.

Third, the French government is convinced that the couture helps to *stimulate all French fashion business and trade*. The collections draw members of the fashion industry from all over the world. These visits add additional foreign dollars to the French economy through *cautions, minimums,* and other purchases. The couture is a national treasure, a source of pride and prestige for France. It is therefore likely that the government would do all in its power to maintain the couture, should such assistance be required.

Finally, French *haute couture* has an unfaltering commitment to perfection. The quality of workmanship has remained unequaled. Couture clothes are still the ultimate. And although one season's designs may be blasé or uninspiring, the next may be brilliant. In this respect, French couture has withstood the test of time. The showings are a "must-see" and continue to affect the course of all fashion.

THE GREAT HAUTE COUTURIERS

Of course what makes French couture great is the creative brilliance of its members. Nearly two dozen couture houses belong to the Chambre Syndicale de la Couture Parisienne (see Table 5–1), but only a few produce collections that make an international impact.

Today's Major Couture Houses

The House of Saint Laurent
5 Avenue Marceau, 75116, Paris

The most famous and influential of these important few is Yves Saint Laurent. Saint Laurent began his work with the French couture in 1954 at the age of 17 as an assistant designer to Christian Dior. When Dior suddenly died in 1959, Saint Laurent, then only 21, succeeded Dior.

His first collection featured a new shaped dress, the A-line or "Trapeze look" and was an immediate success. Parisians demonstrated in the streets because Saint Laurent had saved the House of Dior and the French couture.

The success of Saint Laurent at Dior was short-lived. In 1960, his collections were badly received because they were too radical and "beat." Turtlenecks and black leather jackets were not liked by the Dior clientele. That same year, Saint Laurent was drafted into the French

TABLE 5-1   Couture Houses in Operation Today*

Pierre Balmain (Oscar de la Renta)	Ted Lapidus
Pierre Cardin	Serge Lepage
Carven	Hanae Mori
Chanel (Karl Lagerfeld)	Jean Patou
André Courrèges	Paco Rabanne
Dior (Gianfranco Ferre)	Nina Ricci
Louis Feraud	Yves Saint Laurent
Hubert de Givenchy	Jean-Louis Scherrer
Mme. Alix Grès	Per Spook
Hermes (Gérard Pipart)	Torrente
Lanvin (Claude Montana)	Emanuel Ungaro
Guy Laroche	Philippe Venet
Christian Lacroix	

*House designer is named in parentheses. Houses are listed by names of their founders.

•••••••• **FIGURE 5-1   Saint Laurent's famous "Russian Peasant Look" greatly influenced fashion in the late 1970s.**

Army. He suffered a nervous breakdown, and as a result, Marc Bohan was named head designer at Dior. Backed by American capital and in partnership with Pierre Berge, an art entrepreneur, Saint Laurent finally opened his own house in 1962. From the beginning he was successful, introducing visionary styles that became part of fashion for years afterward. The Rajah coat, the "Safari look," the Mondrian dress, the Peacoat, and the "Russian Peasant look" (see Figure 5–1) have been some of his most influential innovations.

In 1966, Saint Laurent began to do *prêt-à-porter* collections in addition to his couture work. His *prêt* fashions are sold in the nearly 200 Rive Gauche Boutiques located in cities throughout the world.

Saint Laurent's youth has made him extremely sensitive to young tastes, and he has never hesitated in accepting their influence. Today, Yves Saint Laurent is unquestionably the most influential and trend-setting *couturier* in the world.

The House of Chanel
31 Rue Cambon, 75008, Paris

However, Saint Laurent is not without challenge. Karl Lagerfeld, named house designer for Chanel in 1983, has been outstanding in terms of talent and creativity. He has been compared as an equal to Saint Laurent.

Lagerfeld's previous association was with Chloe, the firm that pioneered couture-quality *prêt-à-porter.* Besides being with Chloe for nearly 20 years, the German-born Lagerfeld also has been designing furs for the Italian firm of Fendi for more than 20 years. Through these endeavors he has come to be a highly respected and recognized name designer. Most observers agree that Lagerfeld's position as house designer for Chanel has added a positive competitive boost to *haute couture.*

The House of Dior
30 Avenue Montaigne, 75008, Paris

An immensely successful couture house is the House of Dior. A huge worldwide organization, it is often called the "General Motors of the French couture." In addition to the couture house in Paris, it has branches in New York and other major cities and sells fragrances, cosmetics, accessories, luggage, menswear, and home furnishings under its prestigious Dior label.

Christian Dior became famous in 1947 for his "New Look." Unfortunately, he died suddenly a short 10 years later. That left two young apprentices, Marc Bohan and Yves Saint Laurent, in charge. When Saint Laurent decided to leave, Marc Bohan became the house designer. He remained at Dior until 1989, when Gianfranco Ferre of Italy was hired to replace him. Ferre has been extremely successful in designing fashion that reflects the trends while satisfying the elegant customers of Dior.

The House of Hanae Mori
17–19 Avenue Montaigne, 75008, Paris

Hanae Mori, a Japanese designer who is based in Tokyo, has long been a participant in French couture. She is best known by her insignia— the butterfly that often appears on her beautiful long, flowing chiffon gowns. Her other classic designs include knitted tunics worn over black satin pants.

The House of Cardin
27 Avenue Marigny, 75008, Paris

One of the most diversified designers in France is Pierre Cardin. He began his first couture house in 1950, designing traditional fashion. By 1960, however, he was introducing design and business concepts that were to make him a fashion revolutionist and an industry tycoon.

The list of Cardin firsts is enormous. He was the first to sell ready-to-wear and custom clothes under one roof. In 1960, he became the first *couturier* to present men's clothes. He dressed men in "space age" fashion—another innovation—and by designing similar jumpsuits, goggles, and other "astronaut" fashions for women, he was one of the first to present the prophetic "unisex" trend.

Today, the famous Cardin label and his recognizable monogram are found on 150 different products sold in over 70 countries. He also has more than 800 wholesale licenses, making his estimated income well over $1 billion a year.

In addition to clothing for men, women, and children, Cardin markets everything from candy to wine. His goods are produced in South Africa, Russia, Japan, Australia, India, throughout Europe, and in the United States.

For over a quarter of a century, the extraordinary accomplishments of this designer have made him one of the industry's most progressive and influential forces.

The House of Givenchy
3 Avenue George V, 75008, Paris

Another great *couturier* is Hubert de Givenchy. Urged by Balenciaga, Givenchy started his couture house in 1951. His clothes were classic and immaculately tailored, similar to Balenciaga's. During the "elegant fashion" period of the 1950s and early 1960s, he joined Balenciaga and Dior as the "trio" who dressed the most famous women of the world, including Jacqueline Kennedy Onassis.

Today, in keeping with the current spirit, Givenchy designs softer, younger clothes. He owns a worldwide chain of boutiques and, like most *couturiers,* produces a variety of products under his label.

The House of Ungaro
2 Avenue Montaigne, 75008, Paris

Another designer who came into prominence in the 1960s is Italian-born Emanuel Ungaro. Like Courrèges, he is best known for his space-age fashions. He also worked under Balenciaga and for a short period of time was in partnership with Courrèges. In 1965, he opened his own couture house. Today Ungaro is considered a master at draping fabrics into beautiful, sexy clothing.

The House of Grès
19 Rue de la Paix, 75002, Paris
Mention must be made of a designer who is not easily copied and thereby is unable to influence mass fashion. Nevertheless, Mme. Alix Grès is one of the truly great Paris *couturières*. Mme. Grès has become famous for intricately cut and draped dresses. She became a designer in the late 1920s after studying sculpture and deciding to "sculpt through fabrics."

An independent woman, Mme. Grès opened her couture house in 1942 during the Nazi occupation, only to have it closed by the Germans when she defiantly presented her collection in France's colors of red, white, and blue. Her designs have always been considered elegantly low-keyed, and her silk jersey evening gowns are her trademark. Although Mme. Grès sold her house to Bernard Tapie in 1984, she continues as couture designer and also oversees the ready-to-wear operations.

The House of Courrèges
Probably the most unique modern "revolutionary" is designer André Courrèges. For 11 years he worked as an assistant to Balenciaga, learning immaculate tailoring from "the master." He struck out on his own in 1961, but continued to design Balenciaga-influenced fashion. In 1963, however, he departed radically from that traditional look to introduce a revolutionary new concept in modern clothes.

All his life Courrèges had been interested in architecture. Utilizing his tailoring talents, he designed structured, "architectural" mini-skirted dresses and pant suits using only antiseptic white, pastels, and tattersall checked fabrics. Accessorized by white helmets and short white boots, the Courrèges look became a part of the youth fashion revolution of the mid-1960s (see Figure 5–2).

Fashion, however, moved on to other things. Today, Courrèges is still successfully selling in three apparel divisions: Prototypes (couture), Couture Future (expensive ready-to-wear), and Hyperbole (inexpensive). In the mid-1970s, he opened Courrèges retail boutiques for women in New York and other cities and began to produce apparel for men.

FIGURE 5-2 The Courrèges look of the mid-1960s.
Giorgio Armani

House of La Croix
73 Rue du Faubourg-Saint Honoré, 75008, Paris
One of the newest couture houses to open was the House of La Croix. However, Christian La Croix is no newcomer to the couture. He first worked at Hermes and then in 1981 he became the house designer for Jean Patou. In the 1980s, he was credited with adding great excitement to the couture and the entire fashion industry with his "pouf" dresses and extravagant costume looks. In 1987, financier Bernard Arnault backed La Croix in opening his own couture house.

Other European Couture

Although most of the world's couture designers are drawn to the legendary atmosphere of Paris, there are a few *couturiers* of importance in other European cities, most notably in Madrid, London, and Rome. No city has achieved the recognition of Paris, and particularly in London, the emergence of ready-to-wear has all but caused the demise of *haute couture* there. Still, Madrid has couture shows twice a year that feature such designers as Pertegaz, Pedro Rovira, and Carmen Mir under the direction of the Alta Costura—the Spanish equivalent of the Chambre Syndicale.

Prior to World War II, the British had a prestigious couture, which dressed English royalty and society. Almost all of those couture houses are now gone. The only two of note remaining are Norman Hartnell and Hardy Amies. Hartnell opened his business in 1928 and dressed several members of the Royal family until his death in 1979. Marc Bohan, formerly of the House of Dior, has been hired to revive the Hartnell couture business.

Hardy Amies has also had a long-running relationship with Queen Elizabeth and the Royal family. He holds the title of dressmaker to the Queen and provides her with much of her wardrobe.

Since the English couture has virtually disappeared, today's fashion impact of London is concentrated in women's ready-to-wear and in the menswear produced by England's highly talented men's fashion designers. These designers are discussed in the next section of this chapter.

As in France, the people and government of Italy have long supported their fashion industries, and when the Italian couture was formed after World War II, it too received strong government endorsement and support. Today, the government continues this practice by generously subsidizing any financial losses of its couture. It justifies this extraordinary expenditure by pointing to the Italian couture as "the research sector of the clothing industry" and "a vital part of the economy."[1]

Rome is Italy's couture center. Most couture designers work there, although a growing number prefer Milan, Florence, and other cities of the north, especially since Milan has become, after New York and Paris, the world's third ready-to-wear fashion center.

Italy's counterpart of the French Chambre Syndicale is *Camera Nazionale della Moda*. It is organized and functions like the Chambre. The Italian collections are shown just prior to those in Paris, allowing foreign buyers to cover all the European collections in one trip.

[1]Eleanor Lambert, *World of Fashion* (New York: R. R. Bowker Company, 1976), p. 141.

The reputation of the Italian couture was made by producing fashion distinctively different from the French. Italian fashion was and is much more colorful, tailored, and very sportswear oriented. As a result, many of our past sportswear trends have come from Italy including the skinny capri pants of the 1950s and the wide-legged "palazzo pajamas" introduced in the 1960s. In all there are approximately a dozen couture houses in operation in Rome today.

Valentino is Italy's best-known *couturier.* He began his business in 1960 in Rome, producing understated, softly tailored fashions that were primarily in stark white or brown and white. The popularity of his work with Jacqueline Kennedy Onassis, Elizabeth Taylor, and other celebrated clients has brought him international fame. Valentino now works in Paris.

Other Italian couture designers include Andre Laug, Mila Schon, Irene Galitzine, Renato Balestra, Raffaella Curiel, Odicini, and Carlo Tivioli.

EUROPEAN READY-TO-WEAR

As stated earlier, the importance of European ready-to-wear emerged in the 1960s. It was during this time that the French couture, unable to dictate fashion, lost ground to the new breed of designers working in Paris and New York. Ready-to-wear collections began to set fashion directions and pace, making the couture no longer the only source of fashion inspiration.

Today, the couture *and* the ready-to-wear showings are both considered essential to view by those who predict and interpret fashion trends. One source has not replaced the other, but fashion inspiration now comes from several sources and cities.

France

Historically, *prêt-à-porter* consisted of high-priced, well-made, but traditionally styled goods with little fashion impact. For the most part, they carried unknown manufacturer labels.

When couture designers joined in the production of *prêt-à-porter,* women the world over discovered that they could obtain a French designer label by visiting their local department store or designer boutique. The prestige and exports of the French ready-to-wear clothing industry grew.

While *prêt-à-porter* clothing is accessible and more reasonably priced than couture, it is not inexpensive. Prices can range anywhere from several hundred dollars to several thousand dollars, depending on the item and the designer who created it. *Prêt-à-porter* clothing is not one of a kind or custom fitted. It is mass produced and uses standard sizing. It can be bought immediately by the customer because it is sold "off the rack" in department stores and specialty stores. It is available locally to the customer. She does not have to go to Paris to buy and be fitted for her garments as is the case with couture clothing.

In 1975, the fashion leadership of French *prêt-à-porter* designers was finally recognized by the French fashion industry. That year, the Chambre Syndicale—formerly restricted to couture—formed the *Chambre Syndicale du Prêt-à-Porter des Couturiers et des Créateurs de Mode.* It was organized by Pierre Berge, Saint Laurent's business administrator, and it represents designers in the French ready-to-wear industry.

Designers who work exclusively in *prêt-à-porter* and are acknowledged by the Chambre Syndicale are referred to as *créateurs.* There are a total of 44 members in the Chambre Syndicale; 24 are *créateurs* and the remaining 20 are the couturiers who produce both *haute couture* and *prêt-à-porter* (see Fashion Feature—Important Prêt-à-Porter Designers). In 1988, Patrick Kelly of Mississippi was the first American given créateur status. Unfortunately, his brilliant career ended with his death just two years later.

Today, Oscar de la Renta (Dominican by birth but an American designer) shows his collections at the *prêt* openings. It is likely that other American designers who wish to have a global presence will do the same.

The Chambre Syndicale du Prêt-à-Porter schedules and coordinates the openings of the *prêt* collections each March and October. These openings have become as important, and receive as much media coverage and industry attention, as the couture shows in January and July. The *prêt* shows are held at the "Forum des Halles," located in central Paris. They are attended by thousands of people from around the world.

Soon after recognizing *prêt-à-porter* as an important aspect of French fashion, the Chambre added a third division to its organization to include the menswear industry. It formed the *Chambre Syndicale de la Mode Masculine.* This division stages semi-annual menswear shows held in Paris in February and September. The shows, called "Salon de l'Habillement Masculin," or SEHM, feature the collections of Europe's leading menswear designers.

To coordinate the three branches of the Chambre Syndicale's activities, a parent organization, the *Fédération Française de la Couture,* was formed. Its purpose is to promote France as the creative center of world fashion.

During the same weeks the designers are showing their *prêt-à-porter* collections in Paris, the more than 1,200 French apparel manu-

Important *Prêt-à-Porter* Designers

Besides the French couture designers who also do ready-to-wear collections, the following are important Paris based *prêt-à-porter* designers:

Azzedine Alaïa

Beretta

Dorothée Bis

Cacharel

Jean-Charles de Castelbajac

Jean Paul Gaultier (unusual hand knits and tapestry-like designs)

Philippe Guilbourge (designer for Chloe)

Kenzo (Takada) (Japanese-born designer known for easy witty styling)

Emanuelle Khanh (a former couture model who was a *prêt-à-porter* [ready-to-wear] pioneer)

Karl Lagerfeld (now designs under his own label)

Claude Montana (known for wide-shouldered "menswear look" women's clothes)

Thierry Mugler

Guy Paulin

Gerard Penneroux (for Christian Dior)

Sonia Rykiel

Angelo Tarlazzi

Chantal Thomass

Kansai Yamamoto (also Japanese and important to the "Androgynous look")

Yohji Yamamoto

facturers stage an exhibition/trade show called Salon du Prêt-à-Porter Féminin in Porte de Versailles. These manufacturers are collectively represented by their own trade association, the Fédération Française du Prêt à Porter Féminin, which oversees the industry and coordinates the trade shows. These manufacturers, such as Girbaud and Naf Naf, produce over $3 billion in annual sales. The clothing is designed to appeal to a wide audience of fashion forward customers who cannot or do not want to pay couture or *prêt-à-porter* prices for their apparel.

The Fédération Française de la Couture and the Fédération Française du Prêt-à-Porter Féminin focus most of their promotional efforts within the geographical boundaries of France. In order to promote French fashion internationally, the French government has formed another trade association, the Fédération Française des Industries de L'Habillement. The purpose of this organization is to increase world consumption of French fashion goods. To this end, it organizes the participation of French designers and producers in international trade shows in such places as Dusseldorf, Tokyo, and Milan. It also supports a permanent office in New York City called the French Fashion and Textile Center.

The French government strongly supports the fashion industries because they are an extremely important contributor to the French economy. The couture, *prêt-à-porter,* and French manufacturers collectively make fashion France's second most important industry.

Italy

The second most important European ready-to-wear fashion center is Milan, Italy. Ready-to-wear in Italian is *moda pronta.* For years, Italy has enjoyed an excellent reputation for its fine leather goods and beautiful fabrics. Its couture achieved international status during the 1950s and 1960s. Ferragamo and the Gucci name have become synonymous with excellence in leather.

But it was not until the mid-1970s that Milan emerged as an important trend-setting center for women's *moda pronta.* There were two reasons for this occurrence. The first was the talents of the young avant garde designers. Their creative use of leather and fabric, combined with fine tailoring and workmanship, were just the right combination necessary to interpret the classic sportswear look of the time. Second, the Italian Fashion Industry Association (the *Associazione Italiana Industriali Abbigliamento e Moglieria*) organized and scheduled the ready-to-wear showings (*Milanovendamoda*) into two seasonal events just a week prior to the *prêt-à-porter* openings in Paris. These carefully planned events take place in late March for the fall-winter showings and early October for the spring-summer collections. Table 5–2 lists those designers of importance who participate in Milan's ready-to-wear shows. Not all of the designers are Italian, and some do not sell their collections under their own labels.

· · · · · · · · **TABLE 5-2 Important Italian Ready-to-Wear Designers and Manufacturers**

Giorgio Armani	Gianni Versace
Basile	Krizia (Mariuccia Mandelli)
Laura Biagotti	Luciano Soprani
Byblos (Keith Varty and Alan Cleaver)	Mario Valentino
Complice (Muriel Grateau)	Max Mara
Dolce e Gabanna	Missoni
Fendi (Karl Lagerfeld)	Franco Moschino
Genny (Donatella Girombelli)	Romeo Gigli
Gianfranco Ferre	

Giorgio Armani

Perhaps no name is more widely recognized in Italian ready-to-wear than Giorgio Armani. His reputation for beautifully tailored, elegantly understated apparel for both men and women is worldwide. The cut and workmanship of his clothes are considered to be the standard by which all others are measured when it comes to the most fashionable office attire.

Armani was born in 1934, near Milan, Italy. His original goal was to become a doctor but he was unhappy in school. He began his fashion career doing window displays. Eventually, he became an assistant menswear buyer for Rinascente, a fashionable department store in Milan. After learning the retail and merchandising side of menswear, his next position was with the design firm of Nino Cerruti. There, he learned about fabrics and apparel production.

By 1974, Armani felt confident enough to produce his own menswear line with the help of his partner, Sergio Galeotti. This undertaking was a resounding success. The following year, Armani decided the time was right to add a line of career clothing for women. This, too, proved to be overwhelmingly successful.

In the late 1980s, Armani added a popular-priced line of ready-to-wear under the Mani label. His A/X Armani Exchange and Emporio Boutiques are located around the world. He has a variety of licenses for accessory products, and in 1992 he launched Gio, a $300 per ounce perfume. Today, the Armani empire is valued at more than $250 million. Armani's creativity and financial success as a designer certainly rank him at the top of the world's most influential designer list.

Italy's fashion reputation has been further enhanced by manufacturers such as Benneton and GFT (Gruppo Fenanziario Tessile). Benneton is a vertical company that is famous for its beautiful knitted sweaters and sportswear, as well as its retail operations located around the world.

GFT is a clothing manufacturer of excellent quality that has licensing agreements with such famous designers as Dior, Valentino, and Armani. It produces designer label merchandise which is also distributed worldwide.

As in France, the fashion industries of Italy are extremely important to its economy. Italian goods are in great demand in Europe, especially in Germany and France. These countries are Italy's number one and number two markets. Of course the United States is a major consumer of Italian fashion goods, in fact it ranks as Italy's number three customer (see Industry feature—Giorgio Armani).

England

Before the 1960s, British ready-to-wear was like the French *prêt-à-por-ter*, traditionally styled with little fashion impact. In the early 1960s, young Londoners began to break with tradition in everything from music to fashion. Their fashion preferences consisted of clothes in outrageous colors with hand-me-down, handmade appearance. The clothes were a revolutionary departure from the elegant fashion of the couture, but to the young, the "Mod look" (see Figure 5–3) had an enormous appeal.

FIGURE 5-3 The "Mod Look" of the 1960s.

The trend toward this avant garde way of dressing was first expressed by a young Chelsea shopkeeper, Mary Quant. Dissatisfied with the clothes supplied by her manufacturers, she began to suggest changes to them that reflected her tastes and those of her contemporaries. Soon, other young people began to design and sell their interpretation of the "Mod look," and for the first time, designers who made popular-priced ready-to-wear began to receive recognition in England. The trend for young, "kicky" fashion spread to France and the United States. By the mid-1960s, "mod" was the magic word.

After the "youth kick" of the 1960s ended, British influence in women's wear also diminished. However, a revival occurred in the 1980s. In part, this was due to the worldwide attention given to the wedding of Prince Charles and Princess Diana. Lady Diana, known for her elaborate wardrobe, became a strong proponent of the British fashion industry by wearing the designs of the many talented British designers. The British fashion industry also received official support and recognition from the British Board of Trade and from Prime Minister Margaret Thatcher. And, as in the 1960s, British youth and various music groups popularized a new fashion look—the "Street Scene

· · · · · · · · **TABLE 5-3   Some Important Leading British Designers**

Laura Ashley (her son Nick is the firm's womenswear designer)	Jean Muir (known for her elegantly controlled classic styles. She also achieved recognition during the 1960s.)
Sheridan Barnett	
John Bates	
Caroline Charles	Bruce Oldfield (known for feminine evening wear)
Jasper Conran	Maxfield Parrish
Wendy Dagworthy	Arabella Pollen
David and Elizabeth Emanuel (designers of Princess Diana's wedding dress)	Anthony Price
	Zandra Rhodes (known since the 1960s for her beautifully designed fabrics and outlandish appearance. Often her hair is dyed shocking pink or other unusual colors.)
Katherine Hamnett (known for her message-bearing T-shirts)	
David Holah (designs for Body Map label along with Stevie Stewart)	
	Stevie Stewart (designs for Body Map label along with David Holah)
Betty Jackson	
Roland Klein	Chrissie Walsh

look." Fluorescent colors, Mohawk hair styles, and lots of leather were a part of this avant garde, "Punk-inspired" trend for the young.

These factors, in turn, spurred the talents of British designers, who, with the assistance of the British government, staged British Fashion Weeks twice yearly and revitalized the London fashion influence. Today, the British Fashion Weeks, held in March (or early April) and October (or late September), are attended by major store buyers, designers, and manufacturers from around the world. Table 5–3 lists some important British designers and, when applicable, their specialties.

####### TERMS TO REMEMBER

**couturier   haute couture   caution   minimum   model   mannequin
showing   Chambre Syndicale de la Couture Parisienne   midinette
vendeuse   prêt-à-porter**

####### HIGHLIGHTS OF THE CHAPTER

- The three most important European fashion centers are in France, Italy, and England—of which Paris, Milan, and London are the leaders.

- The French *haute couture* is composed of designers who produce custom-made clothes. They are represented by the *Chambre Syndicale de la Couture Parisienne* in all labor, legal, and business matters. To become a member, couture houses must meet rigid guidelines set by the Chambre.

- Although the couture business is not profitable, it is maintained through the profits of its licensing and ready-to-wear operations. Nevertheless, French designers insist that the couture serves a purpose as a laboratory for ideas and as a source of stimulation through its publicity and prestige.

- Italy has several couture houses, but the fashion reputation of Italy today is centered around its ready-to-wear producers.

- European ready-to-wear has grown tremendously in the past decade. The French ready-to-wear designers are the most avante garde and therefore the most famous. Designers in Milan and London also influence world fashion.

####### REVIEW QUESTIONS

1. Describe some of the conditions that have made Paris a centuries-old fashion center.

2. Define and describe the meaning of *haute couture*. How does a couture house function? Who are its customers?

3. What is a *caution*? A *minimum*?

4. Give the background and function of the *Chambre Syndicale de la Couture Parisienne*.

5. How many members does it average, and what are the requirements for membership?

6. What other business activities do couture houses run to maintain a profitable business? Describe them.

7. What arguments do pro-couture forces give for the continuation of French couture?

8. Name today's great Paris designers and describe their work and influence.

9. Name some famous Italian and British designers and describe what they are best known for.

10. In your opinion, who are the most influential French, Italian, and English ready-to-wear designers of today? Why?

.... RESEARCH AND PROJECTS

1. Although the French couture produces so few clothes a year compared with the ready-to-wear industry, it has been able to maintain a position of world influence in fashion. Explain what factors make this possible.

2. The Italian fashion industry has assumed a position of design influence in today's fashion world. Why, when, and how did this occur?

3. London has periodically been a force in fashion. What years were London's best, and what particular fashion trends began there? What is London's current position regarding fashion design influence?

4. Choose one of the *haute couture* designers listed in Table 5–1. Prepare a biography about this person including examples of his or her work, licensing arrangements, and design philosophies. Be sure to separate his or her work in terms of couture and *prêt-à-porter* collections.

5. Using current fashion publications, compare the fashion stories from Paris, Milan, and London for the upcoming fashion season. What similarities do you find, and what differences are apparent?

6. So many European designers have their own boutiques either as separate stores or in department stores. How many of these are located in your area? Which, in your opinion, are the most successful? Why?

CHAPTER 6

Other Foreign Producers— Import Buying and Sourcing

After reading this chapter, you should be able to:

- Describe the ready-to-wear industries of other foreign countries and identify the countries whose industries are most successful.
- Elaborate on why imports have been able to compete so effectively with American producers.
- Have some insight into how the United States can ultimately solve some of its fashion import problems.

······· **PERFORMANCE OUTCOME**

After reading this chapter, you should be able to:

- Follow with understanding the recent worldwide events affecting the future of imported and exported merchandise.
- Appreciate the reservations that the labor movement and the ecologists have concerning the North American Free Trade Agreement.
- Weigh the effect of the General Agreement on Tariffs and Trade.
- Understand the fear of the countries that benefit from the Caribbean Basin Initiative as the North American Free Trade Agreement evolves.
- Recognize the changes that American fashion producers are effecting in order to become more competitive with foreign producers.

T he technique of mass-producing clothing was developed in the United States, undergoing its most rapid rate of growth and refinement in the first half of this century. Foreign mass-production of clothing was minimal. Ready-to-wear was basically an American phenomenon.

After World War II, however, foreign governments began to rebuild their economies by offering financial as well as moral support to their industries, particularly those that could produce goods for export. Aware of the wide global market for fashion goods, governments gave special encouragement and subsidies to fashion firms and designers. In addition, U.S. manufacturers themselves provided technological aid to both America's allies and its enemies of World War II. Due to these reconstruction efforts, the second half of this century has witnessed the emergence of ready-to-wear industries on a global scale.

OTHER EUROPEAN FASHION PRODUCING CENTERS

Besides France, Italy, and England, there are other European countries that contribute fashion goods to the American marketplace. Although these other fashion centers do not have "name designers" to any great extent, they each supply specialty items on which their fashion reputation is built.

Germany

The international textile fair, **Interstoff,** is held in Frankfurt two times a year. This is an important part of the fashion scene. Designers and retailers from all over the world attend to view fashion trends in fabrics and colors. The **Igedo,** held in Dusseldorf, is Europe's largest fashion fair for women's ready-to-wear apparel and accessories. The fair is held in September of each year and often in the spring and offers an opportunity for 2,500 exhibitors from all over the world to show their lines to international buyers. Both vendors and buyers from the United States have a strong presence at the fair because Germany is

Europe's largest clothing producer. More than two-thirds of the clothing produced by the members of the **European Union (EU)** are produced in Germany.

Spain

Spain's exports are primarily leather goods. Although Spain sells some moderately priced knitwear, the majority of the fashion goods it exports to the United States are made of leather and suede. Jackets and coats for men and women, handbags, gloves, small leather goods, and shoes are beautifully hand-produced by Spanish artisans. It is these products that draw foreign buyers to the handbag fair in Barcelona and the annual leather fair held in Madrid each January. Spain is high on the list of shoe suppliers to the United States, and nearly 75 percent of Spain's shoe production is bought by U.S. merchants.

Spain has an association known as **Cámara de la Moda Española,** headquartered in Madrid, to assist women's and children's ready-to-wear producers and to organize the trade shows held in March and October. There is also a Spanish couture that consists of approximately 20 designers, who are represented by the **Alta Costura** located in Madrid. It has couture showings in January and July, just prior to the French couture's shows. However, to date, Spain's fashion influence remains with its leather producers and leather goods.

Scandinavia

The Scandinavian countries are Sweden, Norway, Finland, and Denmark. Grouped together geographically, they all work with the same basic materials of wool, fur, leather, synthetic fabrics, gold, and silver, and because of its international ambience, they use the city of Copenhagen as their central fashion market. Twice a year, usually in March and September, Scandinavian Fashion Weeks are held in the **Bella Centret,** Copenhagen's location for its fashion fairs. Permanent showrooms are located in the Scandinavia Fashion Center also in the city. Two menswear fairs are held here, usually in September and February. The trade organization that oversees these events is the Scandinavian Clothing Council headquartered in Copenhagen.

Although there is a great deal of cooperation and similarity among Scandinavia's countries, each has a fashion reputation for different goods. Finland produces the most exciting and original fashions. Marimekko, a firm that makes the clothing and products for the home that are so popular in America, is in Finland. Finland's fashion industry is a major contributor to the country's economy, and textiles and clothing represent the country's third largest export.

Sweden is known for its "young" fashions. In fact, it claims to have introduced the string bikini in 1973. Favored Swedish imports are jacquard wool sweaters, knitted separates, leather and suede coats, sportswear for men and women, and rainwear.

Norway also produces a wide range of moderately priced clothing for men, women, and children. Outerwear is a very popular export item to the United States.

Denmark produces very highly styled, expensive clothes. Many of its designers create on a wide scale, also designing avant garde jewelry, silverware, kitchenware, and other products for the home. Because of their high price and styling, Denmark exports fewer fashion goods to America than do the other countries.

Other European Countries

Austria, Portugal, and Switzerland are other European countries that export their fashion goods to the United States. The amount and type of merchandise received from each of these countries vary.

Austria's specialty is toggle-buttoned, loden cloth coats for men, women, and children. Portugal excels in hand-embroidered cottons (dresses for infants and blouses for women) from its famed Madeira Island.

Switzerland—whose fabric firms like Stehli Silks have an international reputation—sends the United States the finest in textiles. And from the Bally Shoe Company comes the shoe many men and women consider to be the best in the world. Of course, Swiss watches are legendary.

Rumania and Poland have healthy clothing industries.

MIDDLE EASTERN AND INDIAN FASHION PRODUCERS

Israel

Israel is one of the most exciting of the post-World War II fashion centers. This small country has been able to develop an internationally respected and recognized apparel industry. Today, the manufacture of apparel is Israel's second largest industry, with an accompanying textile industry ranking third.

Much of this success is due to the fact that the Israelis patterned their industry after America's textile and ready-to-wear operations. To teach the fashion business, Israel has even opened Shankar College.

Israel's initial success began with its production of knitwear and leather fashions in the early 1960s. Leather makers like Beged-Or pioneered the export market by offering men's and women's beautiful leather and suede jackets and coats, while knitwear manufacturers supplied exquisite hand knits. Both caught the eye of American store buyers and began to sell.

Swimwear is also an important Israeli fashion item. Leah Gottlieb, sometimes called the "matriarch of the maillot," is the power behind Gottex Industries, probably the most prestigious swimwear producer in the world (see Figure 6–1).

Courtesy: Gottex of Israel

FIGURE 6-1 Gottex bathing suit.

There is strong government support of the fashion industry through the Israel Company for Fair and Exhibitions, which aggressively promotes Israeli fashions throughout the world. For example, twice a year Israeli Fashion Weeks, known as **Isra Moda,** are held in New York and in London to showcase the Israeli designers and manufacturers. Through these efforts, Israel has emerged as an up-and-coming center for fashion and design.

India

In the 1970s the fashion trend toward natural fibers and textures stimulated a demand for gauze and madras cottons. That demand was met by India's cottage industries. Clothes for men, women, and children were exported to the United States on a large scale, contributing to an enormous growth in India's textile and apparel industries. Today, there is less demand for this apparel, and the apparel industry is not fully developed. Because of its internal problems, the government has been unable to assist with the industrialization of the nation.

. . . .

FAR EASTERN FASHION PRODUCERS

The world's largest apparel and textile producers are located in the Far East. The largest, China, is followed by Japan, Hong Kong, Taiwan, South Korea, Sri Lanka, and the Philippines. Most of the merchandise from this part of the world is **produced to specifications** and provides the **private label** merchandise of the world's largest stores. It is also the source of apparel sold under national-brand designer labels and can be glorious products of world-famous designers as well as inexpensive merchandise found in discount and off-price stores.

China

The impact and scope of China's fashion industry can be felt in every kind of retail store in the United States. China is one of the world's largest textile producers. It has the trained labor, raw material, and machinery to produce every grade of silk for the global market. In addition, labor costs are low, and American producers have been helpful with teaching the newest techniques for the production of apparel and accessories. Other Far Eastern countries are using the inexpensive resources of China to produce their upgraded products or components of products at a lower cost.

China's trade fair is held in Guangzhou (Canton) each year, and more and more American buyers are invited to come. In addition, the country's first international fashion fair, Chic '93, proved to be a big success. Shanghai is leading the way for the promotion of Chinese products for export. Its Fashion Design Institute teaches new design ideas and tailoring methods. Fashion models are being trained as well in the techniques of modeling in shows that promote Chinese fashions.

One of China's most important exports is footwear. Indeed, it is difficult to find low-end footwear that is not made in China in the discount stores in the United States.

Japan

After World War II, a devastated and defeated Japan began to rebuild its industries and—with the help of the United States—transformed itself into the third largest producing nation in the world.

One of Japan's great industrial successes is its clothing industry. It is built around the manufacture of ready-made, Western-styled clothing for men, women, and children. The majority of the firms that deal with the United States serve as contractors for large American manufacturers and retailers.

The "Made in Japan" label once stood for inferior, cheap goods; but, over the years, the Japanese have upgraded their standards so that their export products—from automobiles to clothing—are no longer stigmatized.

The Japanese also appreciate top-quality Western fashion for themselves. Since the mid-1970s, Japanese stores have been successfully selling Japanese-produced clothes of Anne Klein, Oscar de la Renta, Bill Blass, Calvin Klein, and other American designers to Japanese fashion-conscious women.

It is therefore not surprising that Japanese designers have become known to the American fashion consumer. Names such as Yohji Yamamoto, Kansai Yamamoto, Issey Miyake, Rei Kawakubo of Comme des Garçons, Kenzo, and Hanae Mori are in the forefront of creative and inspired design today. Most of these designers work out of Paris, but some also maintain workshops and showrooms in Tokyo and New York City.

Hanae Mori is probably the best known Japanese designer in the world. With locations in both Japan and Paris, her clothing has had a strong fashion impact among Parisians and globally. She is noted for the lovely handwork that is an integral part of her designs. From time to time her Japanese heritage makes a strong statement in the evening wear of her Paris showings as she uses the fabrics, colors, and prints of her background. She is the preferred designer of the royalty and upper-class industrialists in her native land.

Hong Kong

Soon to be reunited with the People's Republic of China, Hong Kong under British rule has developed into one of the largest exporters of apparel in the world. Hong Kong's past reputation had been built upon its cheap imitation of Western fashion. In 1960 that changed. The **Multifiber Arrangement** with the European Union established severe import quotas on the amount of goods entering the United States. This affected Hong Kong's five most popular exports—tee-shirts, trousers, blouses, and knitted shirts and sweaters. To compensate, Hong Kong's manufacturers wisely turned to the production of garments and the use of fabrics not restricted by **quotas** or trade agreements. Today, Hong Kong is concentrating on changing its reputation from making **knock-offs** and low-end budget merchandise to making fashion.

To publicize its new image, the top clothing firms have formed the Hong Kong Development Council. As part of its sales promotion efforts, the Council stages spectacular fashion presentations in Hong Kong, Los Angeles, New York, and other cities throughout the world. Reaction to the fashions shown has been excellent.

Hong Kong also has a group of talented and creative designers who are achieving world recognition. Hannah Pang, a top leather designer who produces clothes for Giorgio Armani and Calvin Klein, to name just two, has established a separate line under her own label. Other designers include Eddie Lau; Patricia Chong; Bobbie Tu; Jenny Lewis, who is British; and Diane Freis, an American, whose lines are carried by Saks Fifth Avenue and Neiman Marcus.

Hong Kong has demonstrated it has the talent and capacity to create fashion. With many retail buyers going to Japan and the Far East, Hong Kong stands a very good chance of keeping its largest industry intact by promoting high-quality, up-to-date fashion apparel.

Taiwan, South Korea, the Philippines, and Vietnam

As in Japan and Hong Kong, most of the clothing produced for export in these countries is for Western consumption. Labels with these countries of origin are now widely seen on medium- and low-priced goods sold in American stores.

Most of the firms in the clothing industry of these countries function with some type of foreign help or advice. Many are either owned, co-owned, or supervised by foreigners who provide technical know-how. It is not uncommon for foreign brand-name companies to maintain branch factories or to have licensing agreements with native manufacturers. American retailers also utilize the service of these native firms for their competitively low-priced private-label merchandise.

The spectacular success of these countries has been due to low-quality goods and cheap labor. However, other Far East neighboring countries like Indonesia and Malaysia, which have lower labor costs, are now placing their competitively priced goods on the world market. It is also expected that exports from Vietnam will gradually develop since trade relations have now been normalized with the United States.

As a consequence, Taiwanese and South Korean manufacturers are also beginning to **trade up.** They feel the future is in the production of better quality goods and that they must now compete with the more sophisticated styling and workmanship of Japan and Hong Kong in order to remain in business.

OTHER IMPORTANT FOREIGN EXPORTERS TO THE UNITED STATES

Mexico

Since Mexico is just south of the United States, many of its factories are located close to the border, and the quality of its products and components of products can be better controlled than ever before. Mexico also has a large pool of cheap labor that can be trained to produce products to specifications. Frequently, apparel products pass back and forth across the border, with plants on both sides supplying different components. With the passage of the **North American Free Trade Agreement (NAFTA),** all **tariffs** applied to merchandise from either Mexico or Canada will gradually be phased out.

Canada

At one time, the Canadian fashion industry was of no real significance to the United States. However, in 1967 with the help of the Canadian government, the fashion industry came to life with the advent of fine designers such as Alfred Sung and Pat McDonagh, and the fashion

Courtesy: Revillon, New York.

••••••••   **FIGURE 6-2   Canada is famous for its fur industry.**

scholarship international marketing program which promotes Canadian fashion around the world.

Today, Canada's unsurpassable leathers, outerwear, active sportswear, accessories, and other ready-to-wear for men, women, and children are enthusiastically purchased by American department stores.

Montreal and Toronto are the two major fashion centers, and it is here that the trade shows are held. Winnipeg is famous for its outerwear and fur show which is the largest show of its kind in North America. Canadian furs are retailed by many institutions in the United States (see Figure 6–2 and Color Plate 5). Montreal is the city in which most of the designers and manufacturers in Canada are located.

The Caribbean Basin

Section 807, also known as the **Caribbean Basin Initiative,** is the reason for the tremendous growth of apparel production in Central

America and the islands of the Caribbean. Only the value added to the apparel from these countries is tariffed, making the merchandise less expensive and faster to import than garments from the Far East. However, there are difficulties with lack of stability in many of these governments, lack of training of the labor force, and lack of equipment for garment production. In spite of these difficulties, many American manufacturers are exporting their cut-to-pattern and uncut textiles to these nations for sewing and finishing.

South America

In recent years, Brazil has been able to develop a huge leather goods industry with major emphasis on shoe production. The cattle herds of the Brazilian pampas provide an abundant supply of hides, while strong antistrike government restrictions give the industry cheap labor. Assured of raw materials and cheap labor, astute Brazilians have built a shoe industry that is one of the largest exporters of shoes to the United States. Other Brazilian leather exports—handbags and belts—are also prevalent in the American retail market.

In addition to Brazil, Argentina, Colombia, and Uruguay supply leather products to the U.S. market. Each country specializes in a particular price line of merchandise, with Colombia known for inexpensive items, Brazil and Uruguay for moderately priced lines, and Argentina for better quality goods. Brazil is also an important center for moderately priced sportswear, while Colombia has a concentration of popular-priced menswear producers. Textile production of cotton and wool is increasing in these countries, making South America another source of relatively inexpensive fabrics. Since South American labor, although not highly skilled, is abundant, it becomes clear that these countries can and will become important sources of supply of moderately priced, medium-quality, high-volume fashion goods.

• •

WHY IMPORTS?

Today, more than 50 percent of the clothing sold in the United States is made abroad. For women's garments, the percentage is higher; for men's and children's apparel, the percentage is lower. Since America is the pioneer and acknowledged world expert of ready-to-wear, why have wholesalers and retailers turned away from goods made at home to purchase those of other countries? Why do companies like Calvin Klein go to Hong Kong to have their clothes produced? The answers are simple: lower price, good quality handwork, fashion mystique, and the possibility of gaining exclusive rights for merchandise and sourcing off-shore.

Lower Price

One of the prime reasons for buying foreign goods is *price*. American wholesalers and retailers have discovered that, despite the need to supervise foreign production and despite extra shipping costs, most imported goods are still very much lower in cost than those made in the United States.

The low price of imports is primarily due to cheap foreign labor. In determining the price of a garment, labor is usually the most costly ingredient. When labor costs are cut, the price of goods comes down. It is therefore understandable why fashion goods produced outside the United States are so much less expensive than those manufactured by U.S. labor. In some countries, costs are brought down even further by the subsidies of their governments. Many foreign governments provide "rebates" in the form of discounts—some as high as 20 percent—to Americans and other outside buyers.

Also, an important void is filled in the shopping marketplace. Many U.S. manufacturers have traded up and no longer produce low-end or budget lines. Discount stores and mass-merchandisers can be hard pressed to find domestic merchandise to sell at bargain price points. By buying foreign goods, quality may be compromised, but inexpensive price offerings can at least be provided to cost-conscious shoppers.

Workmanship

Fine handwork, a tradition in Europe and the Far East, is scarce in the United States, and that which is available is costly. The more **labor intensive** a garment is, the more likely it will be imported. Although lured by price, many of the better U.S. manufacturers and retailers are also turning to imports because of the fine workmanship in foreign products. Skills such as embroidery, hand finishing, beading, and hand knitting are areas in which U.S. labor lacks expertise. The desire to acquire a craft such as shoemaking is not popular here. Italy, on the other hand, where the finest shoes are made, fosters the development of young shoemakers through the guild system of labor.

Fashion Mystique

A search for new, varied merchandise, and—most importantly—fashion that is fresh and quite different from our own are the important reasons why retailers send their buyers and executives abroad. Europe continues to be where most fashion trends originate. However, as the Far East increases its skill in interpreting and directing new trends, it has begun to exert a fashion leadership of its own. The fashion mystique of foreign-made merchandise has always had a sense of glamour and prestige for Americans. People enjoy the exotic and somewhat unfamiliar influences that come from around the world. "Getting it abroad" has always conjured up an image of sophistication. Therefore, merchants shop outside the United States to find items that fulfill the consumer need for status and for the unusual.

Exclusive Rights for Merchandise

In this same vein, retailers want to offer their customers unique, incomparable merchandise. "Made exclusively for . . ." carries with it a fashion sense as well as an opportunity to price these items without considering competition. Fashion retailers aggressively seek sources of supplies that will allow them to build an exclusive fashion reputation. U.S. manufacturers are often too volume oriented to provide an exclusive right to just one retailer. On the other hand, foreign producers of textiles and other items of fashion apparel are willing and able to enter into these exclusive rights on merchandise. Because they do not function on such a mass scale, foreign producers provide made-to-order goods to the retailer's specifications, and private store labels play a major role in this category of goods.

In many cases, exclusive merchandise is highly unusual and trendy. American manufacturers work with such large quantities of orders that their styling philosophies are conservative and popular rather than innovative and risky. For these reasons, American buyers often seek out small foreign manufacturers to help them project fashion leadership.

Reduction of Capital Expenditures

Many foreign producers are willing to take the risk of setting up their factories and equipment without the contribution of money by American manufacturers. In this way, manufacturers in the United States can expand their production without investing great sums of money. In times of economic slowdown, this is an important factor as American manufacturers turn to **sourcing** off-shore rather than their own production.

APPAREL PRODUCTION IN THE UNITED STATES

Some manufacturers in the United States, such as The Limited, Gap, and Esprit, prefer sourcing domestically. They cite difficulties with quality control as a major problem with imports. This is because proper supervision is not always possible. Returns of unsuitable merchandise are extremely difficult when it comes from Asia. Sometimes foreign banks limit the amount of letters of credit used in international trade, thus forcing manufacturers to maintain large amounts of capital overseas. In addition, domestic contractors can provide apparel with a shorter lead time on a guaranteed delivery date. Allen B. Schwartz (ABS USA) attributes the monumental growth of his company to his ability to deliver within two to four weeks items that are fashion forward and good value.

Many American manufacturers are using **CAD** (computer-aided design) and **CAM** (computer-aided manufacturing) in an effort to further automate the apparel industry. Items that are less labor intensive are less expensive to manufacture in this country. In addition, there is a good pool of skilled immigrant labor from Hong Kong, South Korea, and Taiwan presently in this country that is willing to work for minimum wages.

Some contractors who have had facilities off-shore are returning to the United States and are resuming operations in Manhattan, Maine, and North Carolina. They feel that there is an uncertain political environment at the present time in many countries, especially in Hong Kong. They have found that labor costs in the Asian countries are rising and workmanship is deteriorating. The complexities of shipping according to quota and fiber are becoming increasingly difficult. The changes that will gradually be implemented as a result of the GATT agreement discussed below may contribute additional confusion.

IMPACT OF IMPORTS ON AMERICAN INDUSTRY

After World War II, as part of an effort to rebuild their countries, the U.S. government encouraged European and Japanese businesspeople to study American clothing and textile manufacturing methods. At that point, the United States was the largest and most advanced producer of ready-to-wear in the world. American manufacturers saw no reason not to help them.

Unfortunately, once familiar with how America styled and made clothing, some of the foreign visitors made it clear that they would now try to market their exports in this country. Aware that cheap foreign labor would enable these countries to produce lower priced comparable goods, American manufacturers quickly withdrew their offers of further technical assistance. In later years, however, many American technicians were hired by foreign firms and—by the late 1950s—most countries in Europe and the Far East had developed clothing industries capable of producing apparel for themselves and for export.

Today, the exports of these countries have made a tremendous impact on America's textile and apparel industries. With more than 50 percent of the nation's clothing and 78 percent of its shoes imported, the number of manufacturers and workers in the American fashion industries has dramatically dwindled.

Unable to compete with low-priced foreign goods, many manufacturers have fled from unionized Seventh Avenue to nonunionized importing operations in places like Hong Kong, Taiwan, and South Korea. Others have simply gone out of business.

Adding to the difficulties is the increase in operating costs for America's textile industry as it meets government requirements for pollution control.

Disturbed by the decline of the American textile and apparel industries, American manufacturers and organized labor jointly stepped up their efforts to slow down the flow of imports. Unfortunately, although the president has agreed to help these beleaguered industries, there has not been much success in banning imports via quotas and tariffs. The reason is that the overall import-export picture is not as bleak as it is for shoes, apparel, and textiles. Also, since these industries comprise only about 20 percent of the manufacturing output of the United States, they do not command a great degree of concern when put in the context of the balance of trade picture.

THE UNITED STATES IN A GLOBAL MARKET

Many agreements have been negotiated among countries that produce fashion apparel in order to protect and nourish their industries. Where the government sees no threat to its industries, it has exempted these countries from paying tariffs on goods imported into the United States. For example, there are no tariffs demanded on goods imported into this country from the members of the EU. These member countries have living standards and wages comparable to those of the

United States and there is, therefore, no threat to the industries here from cheap labor.

The MFA

The **Multifiber Textile Arrangements Act** provides for bilateral agreements with the countries involved to control the amount of apparel and textile imports entering the United States. They are called bilateral because each country involved has enacted a separate agreement directly related to the domestic industry in the United States. The agreements are for specific numbers of kinds of garments entering and fibers used, based upon past shipping experience. When the United States government feels that American labor and industries would be harmed by "disruptive imports," quotas are set as limits. These quotas are changed as the need arises.

It is for this reason that territories such as Hong Kong started to produce **high-end** merchandise. The quota represented numbers, not value of merchandise, and it became possible to ship the same number of products and increase profits at the same time by manufacturing products of greater value than before.

However, the MFA will gradually be phased out over a fifteen-year period because of the implementation of the new NAFTA and GATT agreements discussed below.

The Caribbean Basin Initiative

There has been a great increase in the amount of trade between the United States and the countries of Central America and the Caribbean Basin. This is due to the implementation of Section 807, also known as the Caribbean Basin Initiative. It provides for the importation of merchandise from these areas with tariffs applied only to those components of the garments that have been added in these countries. In this way, these countries have been able to compete successfully with the countries of Asia since shipping costs and tariffs are so much lower. Indeed, according to the International Trade Commission, 35 percent of the total domestic textile and apparel exports have been to the countries of the Caribbean. When the exports arrive, they are sewn and finished and returned to the United States for distribution.

Many of the countries of the Caribbean are now seeking free trade agreements with the United States similar to the NAFTA. They are fearful that United States trade with Mexico will strongly undermine the newly developed apparel industry in the Caribbean and Central America.

GATT

The United States is a member of the world trade body, **General Agreement on Tariffs and Trade,** which is headquartered in Geneva, Switzerland. The function of this organization is to give meaning and perspective to all aspects of international trade among its members. Seven years of trade negotiations were completed in December 1993 by its 117 member nations. Under the agreement, tariffs are cut by about one-third on international trade of major industries. Retailers in the United States who depend heavily upon imports from the Orient expect to lower the cost of goods to the consumer by about $46 million a year as a result of the reduction and phasing out of tariffs and quotas. Many retailers in the United States are dependent upon these low cost goods as part of their private label lines of fashion merchandise.

The manufacturers of fashion merchandise in the United States as well as the unions which represent their workers are concerned that the gradual reduction of tariffs and quotas provided for in the GATT agreement and the additional NAFTA agreement discussed below, will mark the end of the industry in the United States as we have known it.

The textile industry, which has been heavily protected by tariffs and quotas will also be adversely affected. Tariffs will be reduced gradually over a period of ten to fifteen years and quotas will also be gradually eliminated.

Despite these drawbacks to the fashion industry, the president and his advisors feel that an open world trading system will reinforce economic growth globally and ultimately provide a better life for the citizens of the United States as a result of new, more open export markets in 116 countries and an estimated increase in new business of $200 billion. It is expected that Congress will approve the new GATT accord in July 1995.

The name of the body which will administer the new GATT agreement is called the World Trade Organization.

GATT meets regularly in various host countries around the world. Although it is only an advisory organization, its opinions are considered to have a great deal of weight because so many trading nations are members and agree to abide by its decisions. Because

GATT's emphasis is on world relations, the decisions reached are generally unbiased toward any one country and in the best interest of all.

NAFTA

The North American Free Trade Agreement stipulates that the borders among the United States, Canada, and Mexico will be open and there will be no quotas or tariffs among these nations. The existing quotas and tariffs will gradually be phased out. The fashion apparel industries are fearful that this agreement will undercut the fragile apparel industries in the United States and raise the level of imported merchandise into this country at the expense of American industries and jobs. The Caribbean countries with their new fashion industries made possible by Section 807 are fearful that they will be unable to compete with Mexico as well. Environmentalists in this country are fearful that in an effort to maintain lower costs, Mexico will contribute a greater share of pollution to the Western Hemisphere and the world. However, President William Clinton has pledged to do whatever he can to protect American labor and the environment. The president's newest goal is to work for an agreement similar to the NAFTA among all the nations of the Western Hemisphere.

The accord was passed by Congress in November 1993, and some parts of the treaty are already in effect. Other parts of the treaty will be implemented in five, ten, or fifteen years. While the fashion apparel industries may be adversely affected by the agreement, other industries such as banking, advertising, and trucking will be positively affected, contributing to the economic well-being of North America.

The Global Picture

Many different groups are working in their own way to provide world order in a fragmented structure. The MFT multilateral approach seems to conflict with the GATT agreements which are worldwide, and those, in turn, seem to conflict with the regional agreements such as the European Free Trade Agreement of the European Community and the North American Free Trade Agreement. Add these to the traditional United Nations International Monetary Fund and World Bank and you have what seems to be diverse missions. This is not necessarily true. The future stability of the world will rest upon all of these kinds of agreements working together harmoniously to produce understanding and cooperation.

Is the United States the Watchdog of the World?

In recent years we have seen United Nations intervention, spurred on by the United States, in countries where civil strife has caused starvation, murder, and destruction of natural resources. Members of the armed forces have lost their lives, and the citizens of the United States have footed the bill in spite of an insurmountable national debt.

In some cases, the delicate ecological balance of the planet has been jeopardized by the despoilment of the world's natural resources by countries that try to industrialize as quickly and inexpensively as possible in order to effectively compete in a global market. The rain forests of Brazil, which provide oxygen, are disappearing in order to make room for cultivation. Chemicals are carelessly disposed of in the rivers and streams of many countries because it costs a lot of money to dispose of these chemicals properly. Noxious fumes are emitted into the air, creating respiratory problems among the inhabitants of industrial cities.

What is the responsibility of the United States to the preservation of the ecological balance of the world? During the presidential terms of Ronald Reagan and George Bush, we witnessed the sale of national forests and wetlands to spur industrial growth. What is more important—the preservation of jobs or the preservation of our national resources? Do preservation of jobs and natural resources have to be mutually exclusive? How should we deal with those cycles of economic slowdown when employment levels are low?

The U.S. fashion apparel industry must also come to terms with its responsibility to the good and welfare of the world. Rumors that are unconfirmed, but probably true, claim that prison labor in China is used to produce products that are shipped to the United States. Because prisoners do not earn wages, the cost of the merchandise is low. Other workers in impoverished countries earn a few cents an hour for the labor they perform on different items shipped here. In some cases, there are no child labor laws, and conditions in the factories are brutal. Even in this country nonunion sweatshops are springing up in areas in which illegal aliens live. Working conditions are poor and wages are low.

How can we, as enlightened citizens, deal with all of these problems that seem to exist everywhere we turn? If we import fashion apparel from countries that offer cheap labor, we provide inexpensive merchandise for our stores and keep inflation rates down. If we do not import from these countries, the poorest members of those societies will not have even their low wages in order to survive. The cost of preserving the fragile ecology is high. If we import from countries that pollute and thus keep the prices down, we benefit with low-priced merchandise; if not, retail prices rise and many people will not be able to buy affordable clothing. If we buy all of our apparel from countries that exploit their labor and their resources, we destroy our own industries and undermine our own economy. People who do not work do not pay taxes, and government services such as police and fire will be eroded.

Problem Solving

People in different stages of life look at these problems in different ways. What we do to earn a living will also reflect upon how we feel about these problems. The United States is a pluralistic society—a kaleidoscope of religions, ethnicity, and races. What would your point of view be regarding the import of goods from the EU, the Caribbean, Mexico, Canada, and the Far East if you were:

1. A student majoring in fashion merchandising.
2. A retailer opening your first boutique, after borrowing and saving money for five years.
3. A buyer for a department store chain.
4. A discount store owner.
5. A retiree.
6. Unemployed with no savings and a young family.
7. The president of the United States.

● ●

MAINTAINING THE FASHION APPAREL INDUSTRY IN THE UNITED STATES

As discussed throughout this section, competing against foreign-made goods is an especially critical problem facing all those in the textile-apparel complex of industries. In summarizing possible solutions, it seems essential for U.S. fashion producers to work collectively to gain increased American consumer support. More important, the fashion industry—with the help of the government—must not react to the threat of foreign imports but must actively increase the demand for high-quality, beautifully styled, "made in the U.S.A." merchandise in the expanding consumer markets around the world.

It is especially important that the fashion industries demand and secure the help of the government in ways other than quotas and tariffs as a result of the passing of the new international trade agreements. In fact, the government has already provided assistance in the shoe industry. To help it become more competitive, the assistance includes supplying technological and financial help to increase and improve production, to develop new markets, and to improve marketing

Sing out for the union label!

Look for the union label
when you are buying a coat,
dress or blouse.
Remember somewhere
our union's sewing,
our wages going
to feed the kids
and run the house.
We work hard,
but who's complaining?
Thanks to the ILG
we're paying our way.
So always look for the union label,
it says we're able
to make it in the U.S.A.

International Ladies' Garment Workers' Union, AFL-CIO, 22 W. 38th Street, New York, New York 10018

Courtesy: International Ladies' Garment Workers' Union, New York

FIGURE 6-3

techniques. The results are already beginning to show. The high-end lines of American-made footwear are improving their sales and are developing export business.

Meanwhile, the industry is also trying to help itself. Labor and management, with the help of New York State and New York City funding, have organized the Garment Industry Development Corporation. The GIDC helps New York firms export their products by providing them with marketing information. It also provides training to update the skills of workers in the apparel industries. Another labor-management organization is called the Council for American Fashion. Its main efforts are directed at promoting the women's apparel industry.

American manufacturers are "trading-up" and turning to the production of better goods, an area offering the least amount of foreign competition. They are also looking to enlarge their fashion exports to other countries. And in a strong advertising campaign, American labor has joined the fight against importers by urging the public to "buy American." The International Ladies' Garment Workers' Union uses the media to get its message across, spending part of its multimillion-dollar effort on television commercials, which have popularized the union theme song, "Look for the Union Label" (see Figure 6–3). The retailing arm of the fashion industry is also working to help improve the import-export picture. The Crafted with Pride in the U.S.A. Council, Inc. works with the retailers such as Mercantile Stores, Wal-Mart, Hills, Venture, and Sears. These stores are featuring clothing that is manufactured in the U.S.A.

.... TERMS TO REMEMBER

German trade fairs   Bella Centret   Isra Moda   exclusive rights for
merchandise   MFA   GATT   European Union (EU)   Cámera de la Moda
Española   Alta Costura   production to specifications   private label
trading up   tariffs   labor intensive   sourcing   CAD   CAM   quotas
low-end merchandise   Section 807—The Caribbean Basin Initiative
North American Free Trade Agreement (NAFTA)   low-end and high-end
merchandise

.... HIGHLIGHTS OF THE CHAPTER

- Before World War II, foreign countries did not have thriving ready-to-wear industries. Their mass production of clothing began as a result of the postwar reconstruction efforts of the United States and their own governments.

- Germany, Scandinavia, and most other European countries produce fashion products, but by comparison with those of France and Italy, the quantity of their fashion exports to the United States is small. The majority of exports from each country reflects its raw materials, culture, and technology.

- India and Israel are the two greatest producers and exporters of clothing in the Middle East; while China, Japan, Hong Kong, Taiwan, South Korea, Sri Lanka, and the Philippine Islands are the leading ready-to-wear-producing nations in the Far East.

- Imports of wearing apparel have become a grave problem for the United States' fashion industries in recent years. Currently, this country is importing more than one-half of its apparel needs. Because of high labor costs and a dwindling supply of skilled workers, it is difficult for American clothing producers to compete with the cheaper imports.

- With the sweeping changes that will be taking place in the next five, ten, and fifteen years as a result of the NAFTA and GATT agreements, all the arms of the fashion industries from the primary markets to the retail stores must find ways to increase their competitive stances globally. No industry will be able to survive without a global presence.

.... REVIEW QUESTIONS

1. In what ways does Germany contribute to today's fashion industry?

2. Besides Italy, what other countries are important producers of leather goods?

3. What special fashion goods are produced by the Scandinavian countries?

4. Why are the nations that are profiting from the Caribbean Basin Initiative fearful of the NAFTA?

5. What has been the basis for Israel's ready-to-wear success? How do the apparel industries of Israel and India differ?

6. What kind of ready-to-wear is produced in Japan? In China, Hong Kong, Taiwan, and South Korea? How are these countries trying to stay competitive in the world market?

7. What is meant by the terms *fashion mystique* and *exclusive rights* as they pertain to fashion merchandise?

8. What is the current status of exports to this country from Canada and South America?

9. Explain the MFA. How does GATT function? What is its purpose?

10. Why are some contractors formerly located in the Far East returning to the United States?

.... RESEARCH AND PROJECTS

1. Germany, Spain, Scandinavia, Israel, and India all contribute to America's fashion marketplace. Give examples of products from each country.

2. There are several valid reasons why imports have grown in popularity with the American consumer. What are they?

3. Select a particular line of merchandise—women's wear or shoes, for example. Using government and industry reports available in your school library, research the specific impact imports have had on these American products. What future projections are being made with regard to imports of this particular item?

4. Assume you are making a presentation to U.S. government officials advocating help for the ailing fashion industries. What suggestions can you make to help the manufacturers and retailers? Whom can you enlist to support your position? Which arm of the fashion industry has the least to lose and the most to gain from the NAFTA and GATT accords? Why?

Part Three

....

MARKETING TODAY'S FASHION IN THE UNITED STATES

In Part Two we learned about the inception of fashion design in Europe and the myriad of events and people who influenced the changes that led to modern European fashion. From these beginnings we will see the parallel developments that occurred in the United States and the explosion of the American fashion scene upon the world.

CHAPTER 7

The Birth and Growth of the American Fashion Industry

.... LEARNING OBJECTIVES

After reading this chapter, you should be able to:

- Understand that colonial America was a primary market supplying England with raw materials.
- Recognize how the country's early textile industry provided the foundation of America's great fashion industry.
- Grasp the significance of how mechanization of the early fashion industries was responsible for the initial economic expansion and industrialization of the United States.
- Tell how ready-made clothing was first introduced in the United States.
- Explain why the sewing machine had a great impact on the American ready-to-wear industry.
- Describe the development and growth of the country's ready-to-wear industry and its colorful New York City Garment Center.

.... PERFORMANCE OUTCOME

After reading this chapter, you should be able to:

- Compare the strategic New York City retail locations of Brooks Brothers from the years 1857 to 1970 to the current flagship store on 39th Street and Fifth Avenue.
- Visualize the first American mechanized cotton spinning machine.
- Compare a women's apparel catalog presentation circa 1880 with a current catalog from any major retail store.
- Contact the International Ladies' Garment Workers' Union for more information about its development, its growth, and the reasons for its current decline in membership and importance.

When we see films about the earliest European colonizers of this country and visit historical places of interest such as Colonial Williamsburg in Virginia and Old Sturbridge Village in Massachusetts, it is sometimes difficult to see the connection between those earliest beginnings of households using the wool from their sheep to create yarn, weave cloth, and sew garments, to our megafactories which use computerized techniques to produce brilliant arrays of apparel for the populations of this country and the world.

It is amazing how the development of the apparel industry parallels the economic and political development of the segments of the United States that were once colonies of England, Holland, Spain, and France. At first, the colonists subsisted in a primitive manner, supplying most of their needs from the abundant raw materials that surrounded them. "Pop Goes the Weasel," an American classic folk song, is based upon the spinning of the fibers into yarn that would be woven into cloth. The Homecloth Period, the years from 1640 until the American Revolution, were so called because the settlers had to develop the techniques for making the fabrics and the clothing they wore. Not all the colonists who came to this country were penniless. Some brought with them furniture from Europe and beautiful textiles that were used to make clothing and draperies. We will see how industries grew and developed into valuable assets that could be used for trade with the European nations.

After winning political freedom, the country sought to obtain economic independence from England by concentrating much of its resources on the development of a textile industry. As America grew, it established more than economic autonomy. The birth of the textile industry also marked the beginning of its Industrial Revolution, changing the country from a land of agriculture into a nation of manufacturers.

Equipped with the know-how of producing unlimited amounts of piece goods, America was in an excellent position to mechanize its production of wearing apparel. By the middle of the 1800s, because of technological developments such as the invention of the sewing machine and the fortuitous, coincidental rise in our immigrant population, America's now famous "factory-made" clothing industry automatically and logically evolved.

FROM A PRIMARY MARKET TO AN INDEPENDENT NATION

From the beginning, the reasons for exploring and colonizing the New World in the 1600s were to find new riches and raw materials and to enlarge the geographic and political sphere of influence of the European domains. The colonies took on the role of a primary market supplying raw materials such as wool, indigo for dyes, tobacco, fish and whale byproducts, and lumber and furs to the mother countries. Of all the products, the most lucrative was fur. It prompted the establishment of companies such as the Dutch West India Company and the Hudson Bay Company, both of which were granted charters to explore and extract the fur riches in the New World.

Many of the fur trading posts developed into major cities such as Chicago, St. Louis, and New Orleans. Even the motive for buying Manhattan Island from the Indians for $24 worth of beads and trinkets was to give the Dutch a port from which the furs could be shipped back to Europe quickly and without interference.

The New World also provided Europe with a market for finished products. Goods such as fine fabrics and manufactured products were shipped and sold to America. This relationship made the establishment of factories unnecessary in the colonies. Other goods, not available to the colonists but needed by them, were made at home. Leather was cured and tanned and made into shoes. Wool and flax were spun into yarn, woven into cloth, and sewn into garments by the woman of the house. These activities became known as the *home industries,* and the hand-made, crude cloth was referred to as **homecloth.**

As the colonists continued to expand their trading activities, some manufacturing began to emerge. Shipbuilding facilities, sawmills, gristmills, and fulling mills used to smooth and dye homecloth were constructed. This expansion was not well received by England, and to counter the growth of the colonies, Parliament passed acts and levied taxes to restrict trade and curtail industrial development. But these impositions served to strengthen the colonists' determination for economic expansion and independence. A boycott of British-made goods was begun. This, in turn, resulted in a significant number of patriotic protest statements. For instance, the 1768 Harvard graduating class wore suits made of homespun cloth to their commencement, and a year later, Yale graduates did the same. As political and economic relations between England and the colonies continued to deteriorate, England became even more adamant about curtailing the rights of the colonists.

Eventually this hostility led to the writing of the Declaration of Independence and the Revolution, which began in 1776 and continued until 1783.

· ·

FROM THE POLITICAL REVOLUTION TO THE INDUSTRIAL REVOLUTION

When the war ended in 1783, the newly formed United States of America found itself with a myriad of problems, not the least of which was acquiring manufactured goods, especially clothing. Since there was little industry, and trade was not re-established with England and other foreign countries, the nation continued to depend on the home industries for its needs. During the war, American women devoted all their time and efforts toward the production of clothing for the people and the militia. Records and diaries of these small wartime enterprises exist today. Among these amazing reports are statistics indicating that over 13,000 wool winter overcoats were produced for Revolutionary soldiers by the home industries. Peacetime demands became, by comparison, relatively simple, and women gladly undertook the job of continuing to provide the country's clothing needs until trade could be resumed and prized imports were again available.

When trade with England resumed, however, it was more beneficial to England than it was to the United States. The textile products of England's mechanized industry were not only cheaper, they were also of better quality. America's home industries had neither the machinery nor the skilled labor necessary to produce and export comparable goods. To compete with England both domestically and in the world market, America would have to get both.

Samuel Slater—Father of American Manufacturing

Unfortunately for America, England was determined to keep her superior position in the world's textile market and forbade the export of textile machinery as well as the emigration of any person knowledgeable in the construction or running of these machines. The American government, hoping to acquire such information, offered rewards to anyone able to produce any of these inventions. A 1789 Philadelphia newspaper account of one of these rewards found its way to England where it was read by a young man named **Samuel Slater.**

For seven years the 21-year-old Slater had been an apprentice in a cotton mill in Darby, England, where he learned to run Richard Arkwright's cotton spinning machine. Eager to strike out on his own, but aware that his extensive textile experience could prevent him from leaving England, he left for New York without notifying anyone.

Shortly after his arrival, he heard of a Rhode Island man who was looking for an engineer-inventor. Moses Brown was so impressed with Slater that he offered him all the profits if he would come to Pawtucket, Rhode Island, and perfect Brown's machinery. But Slater found the machinery so inadequate that he duplicated the Arkwright cotton spinning machine he knew so well (see Figure 7–1), relying totally upon his remarkable memory. Samuel Slater completed his spinning device in 1790, introducing the first successful manufacturing machinery into the United States. This accomplishment earned him the title "Father of American Manufacturing."

Although the spinning machine was a great step forward, there were still other areas in the production of cloth that had to be mechanized.

Source: *The Copp Family Textiles*, published by the Smithsonian Institution Press, p. 58.

•••••••• **FIGURE 7-1 Samuel Slater built a version of England's cotton spinning machine totally from memory.**

Eli Whitney—Inventor of the Cotton Gin

In 1793, the introduction of the cotton gin made it possible to separate cotton from its seed quickly and efficiently. The invention had a great impact on the economy of the entire country. New England replaced expensive imported cotton with the much cheaper cotton of the South. The South, meanwhile, became immensely wealthy as it expanded its cotton agriculture and its exports.

With an unlimited supply of cotton and with the machines to spin it, the next device America needed for mechanizing its textile industry was the power loom.

Francis Cabot Lowell—Manufacturing Innovator

In the early 1800s, a Bostonian, **Francis Cabot Lowell,** traveled throughout England and Scotland studying all phases of textile manufacturing. Like Slater, Lowell had a remarkable memory and was able to duplicate the construction of British power looms and manufacturing methods. Working with Paul Moody, a skilled mechanic, he succeeded in erecting an *improved* version of the English power loom. By 1814, his mill in Waltham, Massachusetts, became the first American factory to process cotton from its raw state to finished cloth entirely by machine.

Building the First Mills

America's conversion to machines gave it the first of the three key elements it needed to mechanize its textile industry. The other two, power and labor, would prove to be readily available.

Water was the power used to run the machines, and once again, it was Samuel Slater who showed America how to harness that power. He built the first mechanized mill in Pawtucket, Rhode Island, using the power supplied by the running water of a nearby river. Soon mills were being built—mainly by Slater's former employees—wherever rivers ran.

Mills continued to be built throughout the 1800s, interrupted only by the Civil War. Some of the early ones are still in existence today. The well-known Wamsutta Mills began to manufacture cloth in Massachusetts in 1847.

The history of most mills parallels that of Slater's and Lowell's. They were built by men who saw a future in the production of textiles, for themselves and for the country.

Labor in the Factories

As Samuel Slater and Francis Lowell opened their mills, they patterned their production techniques after those in the English mills. In time, they began to change some of these techniques, introducing new ones that satisfied their special needs.

When the first mills were built, America's population was relatively small. The leading occupation was agriculture, which engaged the family as a unit. When Slater began to gather his labor force from the surrounding rural areas, the New England farms had become increasingly difficult to cultivate. Slater was able to use these unfavorable conditions to his advantage, offering these families work at his mill.

The workers were often recruited through local newspaper advertisements. The ads called for families with "five or six children" and for "widows with children." They offered Sunday School "to improve the mind." Those who responded were generally poor people with little hope for the future—but the ads seemed to offer them assurance of, at the very least, food and lodging.

By the mid-1830s, over half of the mill workers were families working under Slater's Rhode Island system of manufacturing—the *family type*. The other half were employed under the method developed by Francis Lowell—popularly known as the *boarding house* type.

When power looms were introduced into the mills by Lowell, he deliberately avoided instituting the "family type" method of employment. His business as well as his humane instincts rejected the premise of child labor, with its permanent village of poor families. He wanted able and intelligent adults to run his large power looms.

Most of Lowell's mills employed young women between the ages of 18 and 22 who lived in boarding houses near the mills. In contrast to the other mill villages with their congregation of poor families, Lowell's factory towns were pleasant places, consisting of groups of well-kept boarding houses filled with young women who were pleased with the opportunity to be employed.

The operating success of the Waltham system, however, was not due solely to its "boarding house" system of labor, but to three other innovative factors. First, the owners made sure to maintain working capital. Second, they combined all operations in one plant. And third, they limited themselves to producing one type of cloth.

Both the Waltham and the Rhode Island systems of manufacturing were important in establishing the mechanization of the textile industry.

GROWTH OF THE COTTON
AND WOOL INDUSTRIES

Before machines, America's "textile industry" (composed of home manufacturers) produced fabrics made primarily of wool and of linen. After its conversion to machinery, the industry expanded to include cotton. Almost immediately, cheaper cotton replaced linen in many areas of wearing apparel and home furnishings—decreasing the production of linen substantially. Cotton and wool became the major fibers of the newly mechanized textile industry.

King Cotton

The establishment of Samuel Slater's mill in Pawtucket and the invention of the cotton gin occurred within two years of each other. New England went into the business of manufacturing cotton cloth, while the South went into the business of supplying raw cotton. Its fertile land and the huge world market for raw cotton were two of the inducements that contributed to the South's decision, but the greatest factor of all was slavery.

The economic advantages of slavery promised to make the South rich. Cultivating the cotton fields required little training of the slaves. If the South converted to factories, it would have taken considerable time and effort to train the slaves.

As the cotton industry flourished so did the slave trade. In time, the South would discover the immeasurable damage that slavery caused to all involved. In addition to the grievous suffering of the slaves, it also impaired the industrial and social development of the South.

After the Civil War, the South was economically ruined. There was no industry. All manufactured goods had to be imported from Europe or the North. Though the South returned to the cultivation of cotton, leading Southerners stressed the need to become self-sufficient and urged the establishment of cotton mills. Northern and English textile machine manufacturers also encouraged Southern textile manufacture and invested large sums of capital in the new firms.

The Wool Mills

Copying the successful manufacturing methods of the established cotton industry, wool mills began to grow in size and multiply in number.

By 1840 there were 1,420 wool mills in the United States. Originally, 90 percent of these mills were established in New England and the middle states, but as the West opened up, they moved with the pioneers. By 1870, over half the wool mills were in other areas of the country.

The mills produced fabrics that best suited America's needs, an approach particularly helpful to the growing number of menswear manufacturers. Though most fine woolens were imported, the manufacturers were able to rely upon the domestic mills for adequate supplies of good medium-quality wool fabrics.

By 1870, American sheep could supply all the quality raw wool the industry needed, and its factories could function independently, performing all the steps required to transform greasy raw wool into handsome finished fabric.

So much of the political and economic background of America is directly related to the textile industry that their history becomes inseparable. The manufacture of cloth was America's first industry, and it gave the country economic independence. As the American textile industry grew, it stimulated and developed many other industries and areas of commerce in the United States. Today, it is considered the largest and most advanced in the world and continues to contribute enormously toward the strength and stability of the American economy.

THE FIRST READY-MADES

By the 1800s, textile production and cotton growing were major industries in America. They greatly contributed to this country's successful Industrial Revolution. However, with ever-increasing capacities for output of manufactured goods, it was only natural for the country to begin to seek new markets in which to sell these products. This, in turn, led to a boom in overseas trade via the mighty U.S. clipper ships—the fastest ships afloat.

These glorious ships could cross the Atlantic in a mere 13 days, and by 1845, 52 ships were making the voyage on a regular basis. In addition, large numbers of these ships were making the journey around Cape Horn to San Francisco and on to the Orient.

At the same time, U.S. fishing and whaling industries were at their peak. Demand for whale bone used in corsets and in hoop skirts was followed by a demand for whale and sperm oil used for making candles. In 1846, there were approximately 736 American whaling ships employing over 70,000 men and boys. It is therefore not surpris-

The Birth of Blue Jeans

During the Gold Rush of 1894, one of the many who hoped to strike it rich was a young immigrant named Levi Strauss. In 1850 he headed west with little except a roll of tenting sailcloth as insurance against California's much publicized housing shortage. Strauss was unsuccessful in his search for gold, but he did find miners who were desperately in need of work clothes. Resourcefully, he turned his roll of tent canvas into work pants and began the first and most famous blue jeans business in the world.

After experimenting with sailcloth and duck, Strauss imported a French cotton that was stronger and far more suitable for work pants. Called *serge de Nîmes*, it was shortened to *de Nîmes*, which, in turn, was Americanized into *denim*. Joined by double stitching and rivets, denim gave jeans one of its most prominent style characteristics. Each of those characteristics was introduced by Strauss for strictly utilitarian purposes: denim for strength and double stitching and rivets for re-enforcement at points of wear.

Women began to wear jeans in the 1930s after discovering their comfort for horseback riding and other active sports. During the 1940s, teenagers adopted jeans, and their popularity with this age group continued to increase, becoming—during the youth revolution of the 1960s—an anti-establishment symbol. At that time, jeans also became a bottom-up fashion, embroidered, jeweled, and otherwise embellished by high-priced manufacturers for their older, affluent, high-fashion customers.

Today, jeans are an integral part of just about everyone's wardrobe. The fact that they still exist is proof of the value of Levi Strauss's marketing concept. In the 1800s, he stitched up blue cotton denim pants to fill a consumer need and created a classic.

ing that the first large-scale demand for clothing came from these sailors, who in most cases were unmarried and did not have anyone to sew for them.

Since New Bedford, Massachusetts, was the country's largest whaling port, it became the location of the first outlets to sell ready-made clothing. Visiting sailors, mostly men without wives and permanent homes, depended upon the city's tailors to outfit them with their sailing clothes.

Unfortunately, the length of a sailor's leave was short. To eliminate the normally long wait that accompanied made-to-order clothes, tailors began to make and stock simple shirts, trousers, and coats for the sailors.

Shops catering to sailors became known as **slop shops,** a reference to the ill-fitting, poor quality of the clothes.

There were, however, some shops that offered imported ready-mades of a quality superior to those sold in "slop shops," and by mid-century, "off-the-rack" men's and boys' ready-to-wear clothes had gained some measure of respectability.

Other manufacturers and dealers of sailors' clothing soon emerged throughout the Boston and New York areas. The most famous of these is Brooks Brothers, the well-known men's clothier and the nation's oldest clothing store (see Figure 7–2). Founded in 1818 as a tailor shop by Henry Sands Brooks, Brooks Brothers began to produce sailors' ready-mades in 1830. Today, Brooks Brothers has expanded its operations and is owned by the English company, Marks and Spencer.

Courtesy: Brooks Brothers

• • • • • • • • **FIGURE 7-2 Broadway and Grand Street, 1857—1970.**

In the 1840s, ready-made clothing for slaves was introduced. In the past, slaves had always made their own clothes, but with the cotton boom, the southern plantation owners needed their labor on the fields. From 1840 until the beginning of the Civil War in 1861, the manufacture of slave clothing was a large, profitable business. The next large demand for ready-mades occurred in 1849 when men headed west for the California gold mines.

Once the stigma of ready-mades eased, the early manufacturers of sailor, worker, and slave clothing converted part or all of their production to the new ready-to-wear for men and boys. As these suppliers joined the custom tailors in the business of producing menswear, they established America's ready-to-wear industry. Many expanded their retail business to include the wholesale market. On the other hand, some who entered the industry as wholesalers expanded into retailing, thus beginning the policy known as dual distribution. **Dual distribution** refers to the sale of goods by a manufacturer at both the wholesale and retail level.

With the increased production of ready-mades, more American men were offered a desirable, cheaper alternative to expensive custom-made clothing, and the popularity and demand for men's ready-made clothing grew.

Much of this demand was due to America's increased immigration. As the population grew, ready-made clothing seemed to be the only way to meet growing clothing needs. New production techniques could produce several ready-mades in the time it took to prepare a single custom garment. Instead of "one at a time," garments were cut several at a time. Construction was farmed out to sewing **contractors** by the tailors and owners of the shops. In turn, the contracting firms utilized the sewing services of farm wives—a technique long employed by the Army.

Machines Enter the Factory

When the sewing machine was brought into the factory in 1852, the production of clothing was revolutionized: A seamstress machine-stitched a man's shirt in 1 hour and 15 minutes, a job that normally took almost 15 hours to perform by hand. Brooks Brothers produced a coat in three days instead of six. Hoop and crinoline makers eliminated hand sewing problems, radically speeding up production. And manufacturers of women's cloaks slashed retail prices as the new machines substantially reduced operating costs.

Elias Howe and the Sewing Machine

By the early 1800s, most of the processes used in the production of clothing had been mechanized. The one exception was sewing.

Intrigued with mechanization, many Americans had devoted much time and effort toward the invention of a sewing machine. All tried to imitate hand sewing by using a single thread. In 1834, Walter Hunt built a device that formed an interlock stitch with *two* threads but, unable to perfect the device, Hunt abandoned it.

Ten years later, a young mechanic named **Elias Howe, Jr.,** became obsessed with the same double-thread principle, and after two years of hard work developed a machine that was similar but superior to Hunt's (see Figure 7–3).

On September 10, 1846, Howe was granted a patent. Unfortunately, Howe was unable to sell his machine; it was vehemently rejected by tailors, who feared that it would somehow cut into their business.

Discouraged, Howe sent his invention to England, where it was purchased by a "William Thomas, Corset Maker." Thomas promised to obtain an English patent for Howe, making an oral agreement to give Howe three pounds for each machine that was sold. But the corset maker never kept his word. Though he made over $1 million on Howe's invention, his sewing machine had been copied and manufactured by others in America and was successfully sold. One of its enterprising marketers was **Isaac M. Singer,** the founder of the Singer Sewing Machine Company. In 1854, a desperate and destitute Howe sued Singer and two other firms for patent infringement; the courts decided in favor of Howe's patent and Howe was finally recognized as the original inventor of the sewing machine (see Figure 7–4).

A financial agreement was made whereby Howe allowed Singer and the others to continue manufacturing the machine. Howe died 13 years later at the age of 49, but between his legal victory and his death, his invention earned him over $2 million in royalties.

With Howe's sewing machine, America now had all the ingredients necessary for the establishment of a mechanized ready-to-wear industry.

GROWING PAINS OF THE INDUSTRY, 1860s–1880s

Prior to ready-mades, size was not a problem since everything was made to order (cut from the measurements of the individual and fitted directly on the body). With the introduction of ready-mades, however, sizing became an issue.

TABLE 7-1   American Inventions That Mechanized the Garment Industry

1874	Machine makes pleats and ruffles.
1877	Machine stitches bone stays into corsets.
1883	Machine stitches, cuts, and trims in one operation.
1891	Machine produces zig-zag stitch.
1892	Electrical round-knife cutting machine—based on circular saw premise—cuts six layers of cloth at one time.
1893	Electrical vertical-knife cutting machine cuts 40 layers of cloth at one time.
1897	Electrical vertical-knife cutting machine improved to cut up to 100 layers or 1½ inches of cloth at one time.
1899	Machine automatically stitches and cuts buttonholes.
1914	Pressing machine invented.

Sizing the Men

The first attempt to standardize sizes of menswear was made by the United States Army Clothing Establishment, organized in 1812 to provide soldiers with uniforms. The clothing was cut from patterns developed by a master tailor, but the few sizes could not properly fit

Courtesy: Smithsonian Institution

FIGURE 7-3   Elias Howe's sewing machine, 1845.

Courtesy: Smithsonian Institution

••••••• **FIGURE 7-4 Isaac M. Singer's adaptation of the Howe sewing machine.**

10,000 men, and uniforms in the first half of the 1800s were either too short, too long, too tight, or too loose.

During the Civil War, over a million chest and height measurements were taken for uniforms. After the war, these measurements plus those acquired from other studies enabled manufacturers to develop and perfect accurate patterns.

By the 1870s, men could purchase ready-made suits off the rack and be assured of a relatively good fit simply by giving their chest measurements.

Sizing the Women

After the introduction of machine sewing in the factories of the 1850s, the manufacture of men's clothing quickly became an important part of the economy. It was not until 1860, however, that the United States officially recognized the manufacture of women's clothing.

That year, the Eighth Census of the United States contained a report on the "women's clothing industry." It listed 188 establishments employing 5,739 people and producing a total of over $7 million worth of goods. All these companies produced cloaks, mantillas, or crinolines—simply because they came in one size and fit almost all women.

The art of *grading* patterns for women (duplicating a style in various sizes) had not yet developed into the sophisticated science it had become in the men's industry. Manufacturers were still unable to produce well-fitting women's merchandise in a variety of sizes.

In 1863, Ebenezer Butterick, the founder of the Butterick Pattern Company, developed a concept for grading patterns. To introduce the patterns to the public, Butterick published *The Metropolitan* (later called *The Delineator*), a magazine illustrating the latest styles. Women were able to purchase the paper patterns by mail or at their favorite shop. The Butterick pattern quickly became a major fashion innovation as well as a technical one. Fashions that were once too difficult and complicated for cutting and sewing at home were now available to the home sewer. Ready-made manufacturers also began to use Butterick's concepts for the purpose of developing and evolving patterns of their own.

The Growth of Women's Wear

After patternmaking was developed, women's dresses began to appear on ready-to-wear racks. At first they were inexpensive, to meet the demands of the immigrant women. As manufacturers improved upon their patternmaking and sewing techniques, and fit was perfected, the ready-made stigma began to diminish. Soon, they were "trading-up," producing merchandise for the growing fashion-conscious middle class. By the 1880s, B. Altman and Company of New York and other prestigious shops and department stores were advertising "Ladies' Dresses (ready-made)" in their catalogs (see Figure 7–5).

ESTABLISHING MASS PRODUCTION

Division of Labor

Makers of the first ready-mades, eager to produce in quantity but pressed for skilled labor, used the limited talents of the local women to sew the simpler items, while tailors produced the complicated ones. This innovative procedure became known as the **division of labor**, and it proved to be a highly efficient method of production.

When the sewing machine was introduced, production steps were divided even further. Workers were trained to sew on just one part of the garment—a collar or a cuff—in a technique called **specialization.** In the 1880s, the **task system** became another method of divid-

Courtesy: Smithsonian Institution

•••••••• **FIGURE 7-5** **One of the first women's ready-to-wear ads, circa 1800s.**

ing labor using a team of workers—baster, operator, finisher, and presser—to work on each garment.

The Producers

Manufacturers
The first manufacturers began as retailers, and the background of most was similar. The majority were German and Austrian Jews who, after emigrating to America, gravitated toward the same business they knew in their homeland. Gradually, they expanded their retail operations into manufacturing.

The manufacturers of high-priced, quality women's coats were motivated by a concern for quality rather than cost and preferred to use expert workers under the slower "task system." But with manufacturers of medium-priced goods such as men's shirts, for example, cost was the most important consideration. By having as many as 30 workers handle one shirt under the "specialization method," they could produce a profitable, moderately priced, quality product.

The majority of manufacturers had large plants for their manufacturing and selling operations. The designing, sample making, cutting, sewing, pressing, and selling of a garment took place under one roof. This type of operation was known as an **inside shop** and, until the 1880s, most manufacturers operated in this manner.

Jobbers and Contractors
In time, many plants found it profitable to farm out some of the sewing and pressing. A plant of this type became known as a **jobber.** It gave those tasks to one or more *contractors*, paying them a specific amount for work done on each garment. Because the work performed for the jobber by the contractor was done outside the premises, the contractor's factory was known as an **outside shop.**

The choice between an inside or an outside shop by a manufacturer was often governed by quality considerations as well as profit. To control quality, high-priced goods were generally made in an inside shop. Medium-priced goods were usually produced with the help of an outside shop.

Between 1880 and 1890, contractors became a dominant force in the industry. Most were Russian and Polish Jewish immigrants, and, although some were located in a number of large Eastern cities, the majority were in New York's lower East Side.

The term *jobber* was also used to identify firms that distributed the lines of several manufacturers. This type of jobber emerged when Eastern manufacturers found it difficult to reach the many small retailers who were cropping up throughout the expanding country.

These firms—or jobbers—carried large assortments from several manufacturers, and with a "one-stop" seasonal buying trip, local merchants could adequately replenish their stocks.

As transportation improved, manufacturers were able to service retailers directly, and many of these jobbers disappeared. At the present time, some do exist in the fashion industry, but they usually deal with low-priced goods.

THE WORKERS AND THE SWEATSHOPS

The great waves of immigrants who came to America during the late 1800s and early 1900s provided workers for the clothing industry. Russian and Polish Jews contributed the most to the industry's development. Entire families, including women and children, went to work in the needle trades.

The Italians arrived about the turn of the century, but in their case, it was mainly their women who, with their dressmaking skills, entered the industry.

Like most immigrants, all of these people were intent on bettering themselves and were willing to work hard and put in long hours. Unfortunately, their willingness to sacrifice was shamefully capitalized upon.

The term **sweatshop** originated in England and was first used in America during the early 1800s when the production of sailor clothing began. It referred to the slop shop dealers who gave out work to local women, making a profit on their labor or "sweat." As the industry grew, it was then applied to contractors.

The working conditions of the contracting shops were awful, and *sweatshop* soon took on the added connotation as any place of business with unsanitary conditions, excessively long hours, and extremely low pay.

Many of the contractors set up shop without much capital. They rented dilapidated lofts and used the front room for the sewing factory and the rest of the flat for living quarters.

As many people as possible were crowded into these filthy tenements, and their unsanitary conditions became breeding grounds for tuberculosis and other diseases.

Wages and working hours were just as appalling. The average paycheck was $3 a week for a ten-hour, six-day work week. During the busy season, the work week was stretched even further, and employers would force their workers to come in by posting warning signs (see Figure 7–6) threatening them with a loss of their jobs. These con-

Courtesy: International Ladies' Garment Workers' Union, New York

•••••••• **FIGURE 7-6   A notice to workers from management announcing the seven-day work week.**

The Triangle Fire

•••••••••••
**INDUSTRY
FEATURE**
•••••••••••
The **Triangle Shirtwaist Company** was the industry's largest manufacturer of women's shirtwaist tops. The company was located on the eighth, ninth, and tenth floors of the Asch Building (next to what is now New York University in Greenwich Village).

It employed 500 workers, most of them young women who worked crowded together on the eighth floor, surrounded by cardboard boxes of flammable cloth clippings. To prevent the workers from stealing a shirtwaist or sneaking out before closing time, all the doors leading to the stairwells were kept locked.

On the afternoon of March 25, 1911, eyewitnesses told of seeing smoke coming out of the eighth floor. Then they saw that one after another, bolts of dark cloth were being thrown out of the windows. As they approached the building to inspect the fallen bundles, they saw that the bundles were not cloth. They were young women.

The fire began in one of the cloth-filled boxes, and in minutes the smoke and flames had spread to the ninth and tenth floors above. Unable to open the bolted doors, the girls ran to the fire escapes and elevators. The fire escapes collapsed from overloading, hurtling bodies to the courtyard below. The elevators were filled immediately by people on the top floor and bypassed the floors below. Though firemen arrived within minutes, their ladders were useless; the ladders could not reach to the eighth floor.

Some girls, immediately overcome by smoke, were found still sitting at their machines—charred. The others, trying to escape the flames, jumped to their death. A newspaper reporter at the scene described the tragedy in his column:

"Thud—dead! Thud—dead! Thud—dead! I call them that because the sound and the thought of death came to me each time at the same instant."[1]

A half hour after it started, the fire was out. In that half hour, 146 died—mostly girls—with 124 of them jumping to their death.

The two owners of the company escaped unharmed. They were indicted on charges of first- and second-degree manslaughter and brought to trial. Both were acquitted. The shock of the acquittal created public outrage and a cry for reform.

A special factory investigating commission was formed in June 1911. Inspectors were sent into factories, tenements, and shops—anywhere sweatshop conditions existed. Their findings publicized the horror of the sweatshop and led to corrective legislation.

The site of this now infamous fire is commemorated by the following plaque:

Triangle Fire

On this site, 146 workers lost their lives in the Triangle Shirtwaist Company fire on March 25, 1911. Out of their martyrdom came new concepts of social responsibility and labor legislation that have helped make American working conditions the finest in the world.

International Ladies' Garment Workers' Union
March 25, 1961

ditions not only existed in the outside shops of contractors, but in the inside factories as well.

The Unions

Appalling working conditions in the clothing industry prompted the workers to organize. On June 3, 1900, 11 delegates from 7 small locals met in New York, representing less than 2,000 cloakmakers. They established the now great **International Ladies' Garment Workers' Union**—the ILGWU. By 1910, the union had won many important reforms and much recognition for itself. The other union of the industry—the **Amalgamated Clothing Workers**—was formed in 1914, representing men's clothing workers.

[1]Leon Stein, *The Triangle Fire* (Philadelphia: J. B. Lippincott Company, © 1962), p. 19.

The reforms achieved by these unions had a profound effect on the sweatshop worker. In 1924, Dr. Louis Levine wrote that the immigrant "had been transformed into an industrial citizen who begins a new and constructed struggle for the democratization of his workshop and for the Americanization of his home."[2] This transformation spurred the workers to seek other goals, and "these unions were the *first* in the American labor movement to bring economic experts into the service of labor, to organize departments of research and investigation, to carry on special educational activities." He credited "their spectacular struggle for a living wage and for constitutionalism in the industry"[3] as a factor toward awakening the "social consciousness" of America to the plight of the working person—an awakening that was to influence the entire labor movement of the country.

Today, these unions are praised and respected by all for their early progressive policies.

THE INDUSTRY BLOSSOMS

After the 1880s, the industry grew at an incredibly fast pace. Three factors contributed to its growth: *immigration, economic depressions,* and *simplification* in women's clothes.

Immigration, described earlier in this chapter, spurred the development of the clothing industry by providing the industry with its main source of workers, while adding to the demand for all types of wearing apparel.

Economic depressions helped the industry by converting men to ready-mades when they found that quality comparable to that in custom-made clothing was available at half the cost. The depression of 1873 also gave birth to a new industry: "pants makers." To economize, men bought ready-made pants for their contrasting custom jackets.

Because of the elaborate styling in women's apparel, women's wear developed at a much slower pace. It was only after the 1890s, when the *simplification* of women's fashion began, that mass-produced clothing for women was successful.

The item most responsible for popularizing women's wear was the shirtwaist top. It was introduced in 1891 to be worn under suits. Working women found that by having several of these tops, they could add to the versatility of a few suits. In time, the suit jacket was discarded for the "shirtwaist and skirt."

[2]Louis Levine, *The Women's Garment Workers* (New York: B. W. Heubsch, 1924), Preface.
[3]Ibid., Preface, p. ix.

Courtesy: Smithsonian Institution

•••••••• **FIGURE 7-7   Example of Charles Dana Gibson's illustrations of the famous "Gibson" waistline.**

••••••• FIGURE 7-8 In 1911, dress manufacturers
who were born as blouse makers switched to
making one-piece shirtwaist dresses.

The shirtwaist fashion was immortalized by **Charles Dana Gibson,** the creator of the "Gibson girl." A popular illustrator, Gibson painted beautiful young women who were dressed in a shirtwaist and skirt. In time, the tops came to be called "Gibson waists" (see Figure 7–7).

For 20 years—from 1892 to 1912—the shirtwaist costume was the uniform of American women.

In 1911, as an outgrowth of the shirtwaist top fashion, the **shirtwaist dress** (see Figure 7–8) was introduced. At that time, there were no dress manufacturers, only those who produced separates, suits, and coats. As business slowed down, blouse manufacturers switched to the one-piece shirtwaist dress, and dress manufacturers were born.

FIGURE 7-9 **The simple styling of the flapper dress was very suitable for mass production.**

By the 1920s, women's clothing had changed radically from the small waists and respectable ankle-length skirts of the prewar period to the emancipated "Flapper look" of the 1920s (see Figure 7–9).

Thus, the simplification of fashion was complete. Astute manufacturers welcomed the change, well aware of the important relationship between simple styling and mass production.

By 1929, 3,500 dress manufacturers had joined the industry, and sales rose to $900 million. Eighty percent of all American ready-to-wear manufacturers were in New York City, and the majority of them had moved to the industry's present location in midtown Manhattan, establishing the world-famous "Garment Center" along the now-famous Seventh Avenue. In less than 40 years—from 1890 to 1929—the colorful, exciting wearing apparel industry of today had blossomed.

The Museum of American Textile History

. . . .
**FASHION
FEATURE**
. . . .

Located at 800 Massachusetts Avenue in Andover, Massachusetts, the Museum of American Textile History contains the world's largest collection of machinery, tools, textiles, prints, photographs, and documents relating to the history of textile production in the United States. The museum's offerings date from 1810 through 1970 and provide an opportunity for students and practitioners in the fashion apparel industries to see in a graphic way the changes that occurred from the earliest beginnings of the industry to today's multifaceted giant complexes that offer livelihood and attractive clothing at reasonable prices to the citizens of this country.

In the collection can be found approximately five million textile swatches, many with good color and finish retention. This is a marvelous source of inspiration for textile designers and fashion designers alike who find ideas from the earliest plaids and prints in cloths woven in this country, both pre- and post-Industrial Revolution.

For those students who are interested in the history and development of the mill towns, the museum collection documents the growth, the machinery used in each phase of development, the people who operated the mills, and the corporations and labor associations that provided the capital and the organization of the workers. The library has printed matter, paintings, glass plate negatives (see Figure 7–10), stereocards, maps, and trade cards that span the European and North American textile industries from the sixteenth century to the present time.

In addition, there is a textile conservation center that strives to preserve historic textiles from other eras. If an object is too large or too fragile to be shipped, the staff members will visit the site of the textile and prescribe remedial treatment. This is an international resource for museums whose collections need restoring or preserving.

Most of the museum's collection of pre-industrial tools is hidden from view as are most of the tools used after the Industrial Revolution. This is because the current quarters of the museum cannot accommodate the enormous collection. In the not too distant future, the museum will move to Lowell, Massachusetts, often described as the birthplace of the Industrial Revolution in this country, just adjacent to Lowell's National Historical Park, which features restored canals and factories. The Museum of American Textile History will be the largest indoor history museum in New England. The exhibits will illustrate all of the aspects of textile production at different stages of our history. There will also be a fulling mill with a water wheel, a weaving shed, a nineteenth-century clothier's shop, and a small working factory of the 1950s.

The objects displayed will enable scholars, designers, writers, filmmakers, historians, curators, and many other professionals to do with great facility the kind of research necessary in their fields.

Courtesy: Museum of American Textile History, North Andover, Massachusetts.

•••••••• **FIGURE 7-10 The earliest known daguerreotype of a woman at a loom, circa 1850.**

Problem Solving

1. You are a buyer for fashion apparel in a prestigious department store chain in the United States. How could you use the information and exhibits in The Museum of American Textile History to increase the sale of the merchandise you offer in your stores? Describe five different ways.

2. Which fields other than those mentioned in the Fashion Feature might you be employed in where you could benefit from a visit to the museum. Name five fields and describe how this information could benefit you in this occupation.

The information in the Fashion Feature comes from *The Campaign for the Museum of American Textile History*, published by the museum.

Samuel Slater   Eli Whitney   Francis Cabot Lowell   Elias Howe   dual distribution   contractors   jobbers   inside shops   outside shops specialization or piece work   task system   sweatshop   slop shop Triangle Shirtwaist Company fire   International Ladies' Garment Workers' Union   Amalgamated Clothing Workers Union   homecloth   Isaac M. Singer   division of labor   shirtwaist dress   Charles Dana Gibson

.... HIGHLIGHTS OF THE CHAPTER

- So much of the political and economic background of America is directly related to the textile industry that their histories become inseparable. The manufacture of cloth was America's first industry, and it gave the country economic independence.

- Aware of the success of the mechanized English textile industry, America tried to copy its machinery and manufacturing methods.

- The father of American manufacturing is Samuel Slater, who, in 1790, built a replica of the Arkwright spinning machine that was used to spin cotton yarn.

- The most revolutionary American invention was Eli Whitney's cotton gin. Invented in 1793, it quickly removed the cotton seed, making the cotton usable for American mills.

- The power loom, built in America in 1814 by Francis Cabot Lowell, provided the final device in the mechanization of textiles.

- The first ready-made clothing to be produced in America was made in the 1830s and 1840s for sailors, slaves, soldiers, and laborers.

- Denim blue jeans were devised by Levi Strauss, an immigrant-peddler who outfitted miners with work pants during the 1849 California Gold Rush.

- The sewing machine was invented in 1844 and patented in 1846 by Elias Howe; in the 1850s the sewing machine transformed the clothing industry from a hand industry into a mechanized one.

- The sweatshop was a clothing factory with unsanitary conditions, long hours, and low pay. The fire at the Triangle Shirtwaist Factory sweatshop on March 25, 1911, killed 146 people. It shocked the country into passing reform legislation for the abolishment of sweatshop conditions.

- The International Ladies' Garment Workers' Union and the Amalgamated Clothing Workers Union, founded in 1900 and 1914, respectively, launched improvements in the wage and working conditions of the industry.

- The period between 1870 and 1920 marked the establishment of America's ready-to-wear industry. Immigration, economic depressions, and the simplification of women's clothing were the three factors that spurred the development and establishment of the industry.

.... REVIEW QUESTIONS

1. What were the most important factors needed to industrialize America's textiles?

2. Who was Samuel Slater? Why was he important to the development of the American textile industry?

3. Describe America's most famous invention for the cotton industry. What effect did it have on America's textile industry?

4. What machine did Francis Lowell introduce to America? What did it do?

5. Name and describe the two labor systems used in the mills. Who were their originators?

6. Where, when, and for whom were the first ready-made clothes made? Why did middle-class men reject them?

7. How did blue jeans originate?

8. After the invention of the sewing machine, what were the other ingredients America had that made the development of a mechanized clothing industry successful?

9. What were the first ready-made items produced in women's wear? What prevented early manufacturers from expanding into other areas of women's wear? How and when were those problems resolved?

10. What is one of the requisites for mass production? What was the first sized, ready-made item for women to be mass-produced and sold in volume? Why was it so successful?

.... RESEARCH AND PROJECTS

1. Why was the demand for the first ready-mades in the form of menswear and not women's wear?

2. In order to make ready-made clothing, an abundant supply of fabric, labor, and machinery is needed. In order to make fabric, an abundant supply of fiber, labor, and machinery is needed. Explain how these statements pertain to the development of America's fashion industry.

3. Research the changing styles of clothes worn by Americans during the Colonial period, the Revolutionary period, and the post-Revolutionary period up to the 1830s. Describe the garments using the five elements of design as discussed in Chapter 1.

4. Describe the working conditions of a typical sweatshop as they existed in the garment and textile industries in the early 1900s. Use materials and texts that deal with the origins of labor unions—particularly the ILGWU and the ACWUA—to help you.

5. Locate illustrations from old catalogs and newspaper advertisements published between 1880 and 1920 of the various garments offered for sale as ready-to-wear for men and women.

CHAPTER 8

···

American Design

······· LEARNING OBJECTIVES

After reading this chapter, you should be able to:

- Trace the development of American fashion design.
- Identify the three American influences on fashion and explain how each elevated American design.
- Be familiar with the names of past American designing greats and their specialties.
- Understand the post-World War II circumstances that elevated American designers to a position of world influence and leadership.

······· PERFORMANCE OUTCOME

After reading this chapter, you should be able to:

- Follow the newspaper reports on showings of new collections with greater understanding.
- Recognize the names of rising stars of American design.
- Appreciate the contribution of American designers to the fashion apparel industry.

In the previous chapter, we saw how America acquired the technology to develop the textile and garment industries. With these production facilities in place, the next issue to confront American producers was what styles should be made. Since, for centuries, France was considered the source of design inspiration, it naturally became the focus for American garment makers. They merely took French designs and copied them, continuing France's undisputed supremacy in fashion design leadership.

However, world events and circumstances during the first half of the twentieth century caused considerable changes in the lives of Americans. These, in turn, drastically affected the French position of design leadership. America found, perhaps to its amazement, that what the French couture designers could no longer provide in the form of style inspiration was readily available on America's own shores. More important, there were individuals who were capable of creating and designing fashion and who, up until this time, had been ignored because of the dictatorial power of French couture.

THE EARLY 1900s

As the twentieth century began, America found itself in a progressive period. The standard of living was rising, levels of education were increasing, labor unions had reformed the workplace, and mass production was making a whole new array of products available to the average consumer. The automobile was within the means of the middle class, thanks to Henry Ford, who adapted the mechanization and specialization techniques used in the textile and garment industries to the production of cars.

In addition, there was an ever-increasing public accessibility to the goods via the "grand emporiums" and specialty stores, which were springing up in most major urban centers across the country. Chain stores such as Woolworth's were also making fashion goods and other kinds of products readily available. If, however, one lived too far out of town to shop in these stores, one could shop by catalog. Sears, J. C. Penney, and Montgomery Ward brought all sorts of merchandise, including a wide variety of ready-to-wear, right into the home using the U.S. mail.

It seemed that even the outbreak of World War I and the United States' brief involvement in it from April 1917 to November 1918 did not dampen the positive spirit and feeling of optimism that pervaded the land. Then, with the war over and the passage of women's suffrage, the 1920s began with a partylike atmosphere, even though Prohibition was in effect.

The American fashion industry had no problem keeping up with the ever-increasing demands for fashion apparel and accessories. Short flapper dresses and blue serge suits all in the same basic style were easy items to mass-produce. Unfortunately, Americans overindulged in all this prosperity. They were completely unprepared when the good life came to an abrupt halt in October 1929. The stock market crash and the Great Depression that followed were the worst economic disasters ever experienced by this country.

Yet, out of the depths of depression came a new sense of patriotism and firm commitment to make America stronger than ever, both economically and industrially. There was also a turning away from things foreign. We became political isolationists. These circumstances and attitudes fostered three distinct and unmistakably American influences on fashion: (1) the Hollywood influence of the 1930s; (2) a new type of apparel called *sportswear;* and (3) extraordinary American off-the-rack clothing, referred to as *couture-ready-to-wear.* Each of these three influences was led by a particular designer who is credited with having a permanent effect on American fashion. They are Adrian, Claire McCardell, and Norman Norell, respectively.

· ·

THE 1930s—HOLLYWOOD'S INFLUENCE ON DESIGN AND ADRIAN

As the new decade began, America and most of Europe were in the height of economic depression and chaos. The rate of unemployment was over 25 percent, and more than 1,400 banks had failed, leaving depositors penniless and without recourse. Franklin Roosevelt assumed office in March 1932 and began his New Deal, which unleashed a wave of social legislation aimed at getting the country back on its feet.

Naturally, the textile and garment industries were affected by the Depression, but their response to their problems was quite clever. Manufacturers created the "no-price" look—a basic, simply styled outfit consisting of a skirt (or trousers), a blouse (or shirt), and a sweater.

Each item could be purchased separately as needed, costing between $2 and $3 per item. Colors were neutral. The silhouette was tubular, since this required less fabric and therefore was less costly to produce and sell.

These clothes quite accurately reflected the mentality of the people—somber and resourceful. There was little frivolity and happiness to be found either at home or at work. Therefore, movies became the place to dream and fantasize or to escape briefly from one's troubles.

America's supremacy for making motion pictures had already been established prior to World War I. With the discovery of recording sound on tape made by General Electric in 1926, Hollywood's "talking" movies became a source of entertainment and wonder for the entire world.

The "stars" who played leading roles in the new "talkies" were so admired that they were considered by many to be living idols. Whatever these stars said, did, and wore was instant news so that the costumes of these personalities completely overshadowed the not-so-glamorous looks coming out of Paris at the time. Soon people began to ask, "Who is responsible for the magnificent wardrobes of these stars?" The answer was Gilbert Adrian, a man who used only one name in his professional career—**Adrian.**

Adrian

This talented and influential designer began his career as a costume designer for the Broadway stage. Adrian's first famous client was Rudolph Valentino, who encouraged him to move to Hollywood. Once there, Adrian worked for Cecil B. DeMille and then signed with MGM studios. At MGM, Adrian dressed the most famous leading ladies of the screen: Norma Shearer, Greta Garbo, Joan Crawford, and Jean Harlow. The costumes in which these women appeared were quickly copied by Seventh Avenue and sold to a most eager American public. Hollywood was *the* source of fashion during the 1930s, and Adrian was totally responsible!

In 1939, Adrian married actress Janet Gaynor. When his wife became pregnant, Adrian designed maternity smocks and straight skirts for her. After the couple was photographed for *Vogue* magazine, Adrian's designs completely transformed the entire maternity clothes market.

By the 1940s, Adrian was designing the costumes of nearly every major star in Hollywood. Actresses such as Greer Garson, Katharine Hepburn, Lana Turner, and Judy Garland all wore clothes by Adrian. As Dorothy in the *Wizard of Oz*, Judy Garland's costumes, including the famous red shoes, were all Adrian's creations.

68A-F

Courtesy: Neiman Marcus, Dallas, Texas

•••••••• **PLATE 1 This cashmere ensemble by Donna Karan appeared in the Neiman Marcus 1993 Christmas catalog.**

(a) Surprisingly modern is this example of seventeenth-century shoes from the Vivegane Museum in Italy.

(b) From the Museum of Footwear in Elda, Spain, are two winning entries in a competition for young designers to create shoes in the tradition of Spain.

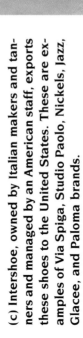

(c) Intershoe, owned by Italian makers and tanners and managed by an American staff, exports these shoes to the United States. These are examples of Via Spiga, Studio Paolo, Nickels, Jazz, Glacee, and Paloma brands.

Courtesy: Fashion Footwear Association of New York. From the FFANY Special Edition 1993.

•••••••• PLATE 2   Yesterday, today, and tomorrow.

COACH

AN AMERICAN LEGACY

Courtesy: Coach Leatherware Company, New York

· · · · · · · · · **PLATE 3 Quality leather handbags by companies such as Coach are manufactured in the United States.**

Courtesy: Ross-Simons, Cranston, Rhode Island

· · · · · · · · · **PLATE 4 Consumers may purchase fine, bridge, and costume jewelry by means of a catalog or store visit. This is an example of private-label fine jewelry from a recent catalog.**

COMPETITION-LYCRA

Courtesy: Ocean Pool Company, Commack, New York.

PLATE 6 A modern adaptation of Schiaparelli's unusual combination of colors—this time in a bathing suit designed for competitive swimmers.

Courtesy: Revillon, New York

PLATE 5 Canada is famous for its fur industry.

Courtesy: Liz Claiborne, Inc.

PLATE 7 Claiborne Menswear

Courtesy: Biobottoms, Petaluma, California

PLATE 9 A successful, ecology-minded mail order catalog, Biobottoms, offers infants', children's, boys', and girls' wear.

Courtesy: D.A.Y. Kids Sportswear Inc., New York

PLATE 8 This photograph is part of an advertisement that appeared in *Kids Fashions*, a trade journal of the children's wear industry.

Courtesy: Fortunoff, New York

• • • • • • • • **PLATE 10 These costumed bisque dolls of today are direct descendants of Rose Bertin's Fashion dolls.**

Courtesy: Sawgrass Mills, Sunrise, Florida

• • • • • • • • **PLATE 11 Interior of Sawgrass Mills in Sunrise, Florida—a unique enclosed factory and retail outlet mall.**

Rue de Faubourg-Saint Honoré, Paris

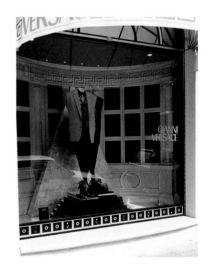

At this time, Hollywood was undergoing major changes in movie production techniques and budgeting. Unhappy with these changes, Adrian left the costume business and opened his own ready-to-wear and custom-made clothes operation. The firm was called Adrian, Ltd., and was located in California. During those years, Paris was occupied by the Germans because of World War II, and American designs were the only fashions of note. Adrian, therefore, gained in reputation and, because of good press coverage, his collections were a huge success. His "little black dress," tailored suits, and beaded evening dresses were copied by every Seventh Avenue manufacturer and sold to those who could not afford an original Adrian. The broad-shouldered look was so popular that it even bore his name—the "Adrian silhouette."

When World War II ended, Dior's "New Look" was introduced in 1947, and Adrian's influence lost its trend-setting impact. In 1952, Adrian suffered a heart attack, and as a result, Adrian, Ltd., closed its doors. After several years in retirement, Adrian again returned to designing for the Broadway stage. His last creations, made before his death in 1959, were for the award-winning musical *Camelot*.

Hollywood's influence on fashion and Adrian's contribution to it were the world's first acknowledgment of this nation's creative fashion abilities. Adrian should, therefore, be thought of as an American pioneer, blazing the way toward an appreciation and recognition of America's ability to design and create fashion.

The Sportswear Influence and Claire McCardell

Although Adrian was the first American "name" designer to achieve international recognition, original American designs were being produced as far back as the late 1800s in the form of *sportswear*. The first example of American sportswear is traceable to an early female rebel—**Amelia Jenkins Bloomer.** Tired of the restrictive crinolines of the 1850s, she devised a "walking suit" that featured harem-type pants (see Figure 8–1). The fashion and her *Rational Dress Campaign* were ridiculed and rejected, but they marked the introduction of pants for Western women. Thirty years later, Amelia's "bloomers" were accepted as an alternative to skirts while cycling or participating in other sports.

By the 1930s, sportswear had come to be identified as an exclusively "American" phenomenon. Paris ignored both its design and its manufacture. But the farsighted people in the American industry did not. One of the first to recognize and promote sportswear and its influence on a developing American look was Dorothy Shaver, who, in 1945, became president of Lord & Taylor. As early as 1932, she launched a campaign heralding American designers. It was a radical

• • • • • • • • **FIGURE 8-1 First Western "pants," introduced by Amelia Jenkins Bloomer in 1850.**

departure from the tradition that all fashion came from France. Some
of those early American talents were Tom Brigance, Claire Potter, Vera
Maxwell, and Elizabeth Hawes. But the most outstanding and visionary **sportswear** designer of the period was Claire McCardell.

Claire McCardell

Thought by many to be the most brilliant of American designers,
Claire McCardell was the one most responsible for developing an
American look. The ideas and concepts she introduced between the
beginning of her career in the 1930s and her death in 1958 have become
fashion and marketing classics. The success of this designer was par-
tially the result of World War II, which was raging in Europe. Paris
was occupied by Hitler's troops, and the French couture had ceased
to function. America was thrust into the war by the surprise bombing
of Pearl Harbor in 1941. The average woman, hard at work in a factory,

became known as "Rosie the Riveter" because she performed manual tasks while the men were engaged in combat.

Hollywood was still creating glamorous clothes, but there was a void in terms of practical, easy-to-wear apparel for the woman on the go. After the war, even though women quickly gave up their jobs, they still found themselves in need of clothing to meet new demands: being suburban housewives and mothers with more physically active lifestyles.

One of Claire McCardell's first marketing innovations was coordinated separates. At first the stores were afraid of "leftover" tops or skirts and would not adopt her coordinates concept. Today, it is the backbone of the sportswear market.

In the 1940s and 1950s, she conceived what we now call the "total look," accessorizing her dresses with matching caps, hats, and shoes. This prompted her partner, Adolf Klein, to pioneer the concept of "designer licensing" by having accessory manufacturers make and sell the accessories under the McCardell label.

Her designs were as original as her marketing theories, and she may be compared with Chanel in terms of design philosophy. Both advocated simplicity and comfort; both respected and followed the natural lines of the body, rejecting rigid construction or padding; and both were utilitarian in their approach. A button must button and a tie must tie.

Her design innovations—some of which have become classics—include the dirndl skirt, the "monastic" bias-cut tent dress, hardware closings (grommets, rivets, and so on), shoestring ties, ballet slippers for streetwear, and unlined bathing suits. She was equally original with fabrics and began the then-unorthodox use of wool tweeds and cotton for evening wear and mattress ticking for a town suit. She was the first to revive colonial calico and popularize wool jersey, anticipating the later popularity of both cottons and knits. Her clothes were totally American in character: easy to wear and easy to mass-produce. They were also so timeless that they could be and are, in fact, being worn today.

In her book *What Shall I Wear?* McCardell verbalized what her clothes had been expressing all along:

> We [designers] specialize in what we like best, in what we do best, and what satisfies us most deeply. For me it's America—it looks and feels like America. It's freedom, it's democracy, it's casualness, it's good health. Clothes can say all that.[1]

---

[1]Claire McCardell, *What Shall I Wear?* (New York: Simon & Schuster, 1956), p. 156.

• • • • • • • • **FIGURE 8-2 Claire McCardell—cover girl.**

The clothes of Claire McCardell did.

Because Claire McCardell's contributions to the American fashion
industry were so profound, she was selected by *Time* magazine to be
one of its "cover personalities," a rare honor for a fashion designer
(see Figure 8–2).

THE INFLUENCE OF AMERICAN COUTURE READY-TO-WEAR AND NORMAN NORELL

Although Adrian was recognized for his creative costuming and
McCardell was known for the American look in sportswear, fashion
design in the traditional sense returned to being dominated by Paris
in 1947 with Christian Dior's "New Look." Fashions that were pro-

duced by American ready-to-wear manufacturers were primarily successful in the moderately priced lines. Ready-to-wear lacked originality and quality. That is, until Norman Norell created his magnificent "off-the-rack" couture ready-to-wear.

Norman Norell

In 1941, Norell joined with Anthony Traina to produce a two-name label collection, Traina-Norell. Their collection was immediately recognized as being original, elegant, and creative, as well as expensive for off-the-rack clothing. More important, it was a demonstration of American design talent in the ready-to-wear medium. Norell bridged the gap between *haute couture* (custom-made clothes) and high-quality, **high-fashion ready-to-wear.**

It was apparent very early in their partnership that Norell was the design genius behind the Traina-Norell label. However, Norell did not have his own name label until the death of Traina in 1960. In 1943, the first Coty American Fashion Critic's Award was presented. The winner was Norman Norell. He again won this honor in 1951, and in 1956 he was elected into the Coty Hall of Fame.

In 1968, the first American designer-named perfume was successfully launched. Norell perfume, made by Revlon, continues to be a popular fragrance today (see Figure 8–3).

Courtesy: Norman Norell Perfumes, New York

••••••• **FIGURE 8-3 Norman Norell—dean of American designers.**

The most popular of Norell's daytime dresses was the chemise, which was made of wool jersey and simply designed. His evening wear was elaborate and usually covered with sequins. He was a perfectionist, paying very close attention to every detail. A Norell design always evoked a sense of elegance and originality.

Norell's career spanned five decades. It began in 1928 with the firm of Hattie Carnegie and ended with his death in 1972 while he was working on a retrospective showing of his work for the Metropolitan Museum of Art. The Norell legacy to American fashion goes beyond any one design or trend he may have helped set. What he gave to the entire industry was a sense of prestige and confidence. Because he was such a master at tailoring and designing, he broke the stranglehold Paris had on fashion. His talents elevated American ready-to-wear to a level on a par with *haute couture* designs. His name gave respectability to clothes bearing the American label, thereby establishing once and for all the industry's creative credibility. Certainly the title "dean of American fashion designers" belongs to Norman Norell.

AMERICAN DESIGN RISES TO THE TOP

By the 1950s the reputation of American design and the American look were firmly established as fashion forces. However, primarily because of Dior's "New Look" of 1947, the collective power of French couture regained its position as the strongest overall fashion influence and dominated fashion throughout the decade.

In order for American design to surpass or even match French couture in terms of influence, it would have to develop its own following of clientele. At the same time, French couture would have to lose its world prestige. Neither seemed likely, that is, until the 1960s.

The 1960s did indeed change everything. This country had just elected its youngest and first Roman Catholic president—John F. Kennedy. The Beatles introduced a whole new kind of sound onto the music scene. And most important of all, a new generation called the *baby boomers*—those born just after World War II—was beginning to exert its strong and unconventional influences.

It was the start of the "youth kick," a time of psychedelics and fashions designed for and by the young. The most influential designer of the time was an upbeat English woman by the name of Mary Quant. She introduced the "Mod look," which has as its most important fashion element the miniskirt (see Figure 8–4).

FIGURE 8-4 **The miniskirt and youth kick look of the 1960s by Mary Quant.**

Ready-to-Wear Takes the Lead

Although some remained faithful to the Paris couture during this period, many—particularly the younger clients—did not. Stung by its new competition, Parisian couture began to pick up the "youth kick." Pea coats, granny dresses, and jeans were translated into couture versions. These were perfect examples of "bottom-up" fashions, a term defined in Chapter 2. Others, including André Courrèges and Emanuel Ungaro, introduced their own revolutionary looks.

But the energetic concepts of young ready-to-wear designers continued to exert a powerful influence on fashion trends. Most of the designs revolved around unorthodox looks that seemed to best express the turbulent times. And American designers of ready-to-wear fashions such as Bill Blass, Rudi Gernreich, and Oscar de la Renta were now leading the way.

To meet the competition from these American designers on equal terms, Paris couture entered the ready-to-wear business in the late 1960s. At that point, most of the better French ready-to-wear exports, its **prêt-à-porter,** were limited to high-quality, but conservatively styled, fashion. The aim of the couture was to compete against Seventh Avenue for worldwide ready-to-wear dollars, but their entrance into that market *helped* rather than hurt American designers.

To begin with, the French couture stimulated interest in *all* designer labels. One of their natural selling points was their names. The prestige of the French label—a Saint Laurent or Cardin—was and is enormous. These designers took advantage of the fact by extensively promoting their labels. Their most ingenious method of publicity was to use their names or initials as a status symbol, integrating either one into the overall design of their wearing apparel in a print or as a monogram.

American designers quickly joined the "status name" game and began to get equal publicity. The interest of the fashion customer in designer fashions was successfully and extensively stimulated.

The entrance of the French couture into ready-to-wear also served to democratize the caste system of designers. Formerly, these French designers were producing the most expensive clothes in the world— the *haute couture*. That fact alone automatically gave them a heady status. Though they continued that part of their business, they were now into a new game. French designers' ready-to-wear operations automatically shifted them to the level of the top American designers. To the consumer, all designer names provided an equal amount of prestige. A Bill Blass and a Pierre Cardin necktie were equally desirable; it was taste that determined the sale.

The Final Rejection of French Trends

Paris tried to continue to introduce revolutionary trends, but the concepts were rejected by the American consumer. The most significant of these rejections was the midi or maxi skirt, which Paris showed in 1970 (see Figure 8–5). Many American manufacturers and retailers backed the calf-length midi—hailing it as a welcome and timely change from the then-popular thigh-high miniskirt. Unfortunately, American women refused to buy it, and both manufacturers and retailers lost a tremendous amount of money that season. That financial catastrophe cost the Paris couture most of the remaining influence it had with America's fashion industry. On the other hand, the acceptance of American designers continued to grow. They were increasingly in tune with the kind of clothing contemporary men and women preferred. Their collections gained worldwide popularity, their names worldwide recognition. Customers in Europe, Japan, and the United States began to consider the American designer label as prestigious as that of the French *couturier*.

FIGURE 8-5 **The midi look, introduced by the Paris couture in 1970, was overwhelmingly rejected by the American consumer.**

A Return to the Classics in the 1970s

After a particularly turbulent period, fashion reacted by reverting to the other extreme. In the 1970s, fashion simmered down; the classic look of American sportswear took over. Both the French couture and Seventh Avenue designers projected the new quiet look (see Figure 8–6). Unfortunately for the couture, it was competing with what America did best—classic, tailored clothes. Pants, shirts, blazers, and sweaters were part of the new trend, and it was now quite evident that the line of any top American designer could easily compete with the French couture.

Reporting on the acceptance of American fashion, the March 22, 1976, *Time* magazine cover story printed the following:

FIGURE 8-6 In the early 1970s, fashion turned to the classics, a look Seventh Avenue designers did best. For the first time, America—not Europe—was setting the pace.

After more than a century of obeisance to Europe's high priests of couture, American designers have won worldwide respect as creative interpreters of a way of life—and style. It is a rebellion and an achievement which has been building since World War II. But it has, in the eclectic fashion world of 1976, undeniably come of age and attained a new level of élan and confidence.[2]

[2]Reprinted by permission from *Time*, The Weekly Newsmagazine; Copyright, Time Inc. (March 22, 1976), p. 62.

The 1980s—Paris and New York Offer Their Own Specialties

With the liberation of fashion that occurred in the 1960s and 1970s, fashion design now had more than one source. The French couture re-established itself as an influence, mainly in terms of dressy dresses and evening wear. At the same time, American influence remained superior in the categories of sportswear and daytime attire. Of course, on both sides of the Atlantic, there were designers who excelled in opposite categories. However, the overall consensus was that Paris and New York had different specialties and that each did its own superbly.

But Paris and New York were not alone in influencing the direction of world fashion in the 1980s. Milan, Italy, established itself as a major design center. It offered still a different dimension to fashion—that of expert fabrication and tailoring. It did this, not at the expense of New York and Paris, but rather in conjunction with them.

THE COTY AMERICAN FASHION CRITICS' AWARDS

Until 1985, the "Oscar" of the fashion industry was the **Coty Fashion Critics' Award.** This famous award for excellence in fashion design was conceived in 1942 by publicist Eleanor Lambert under the sponsorship of the international cosmetic and fragrance firm, Coty, Inc. Although publicity for the Coty name certainly must have been a consideration, the prime purpose of the awards was to encourage the development of the fashion industry during World War II by focusing upon the creativity and originality of the American designer.

There were several types of Coty Awards. The most famous was the original Coty Fashion Critics' Award, also known as the "Winnie." It was given to the American designer of women's wear who, in the opinion of the judges, had made an extraordinary contribution to the direction of that year's contemporary fashion design. A second prize, the Coty Special Award, was given to those who excelled in a specialized area of the industry. Stephen Burrows, for instance, was given a Special Award in 1974 for his creative treatment of lingerie and loungewear. Until 1968, the awards were given exclusively to those who produced women's fashions, but the innovative changes in menswear design during the 1960s prompted the introduction of the Coty Menswear Fashion Award. Designers who received any of these awards more than once were presented with the Coty Repeat Award. On winning their third Repeat Award, talented designers entered the prestigious Coty's Hall of Fame. This honor was considered to be the highest accolade in American fashion.

In June of 1985, Pfizer, Coty's parent company, decided to discontinue the awards. This was not a surprise considering the problems and controversies surrounding the awards in recent years. One issue that led to the demise of the awards was Coty's decision in 1979 to introduce a line of cosmetics entitled "The Coty Awards Collection." This infuriated that year's top award winners—Halston and Calvin Klein—because they, like many designers, had their own cosmetic lines. They viewed Coty as their competition and refused to accept the awards. This incident precipitated another problem for the awards—dwindling attendance at the annual awards banquet. Without the top names in attendance, interest in the event waned. Finally, in January 1985, the **Council of Fashion Designers of America,** an organization created to protect the interests of American couture ready-to-wear designers, staged its own awards and fund-raising banquet. It completely outdid the Coty Awards and the company's decision to discontinue the awards was reached six months later. Those having won a "Winnie" and those who aspired to that honor will remember the Coty Award as a prime source of inspiration in America's struggle to become a world fashion power.

The Current Status of American Design

American design continues to grow in importance in the 1990s. Young men and women are urged to develop their talents in colleges such as Nassau Community College and the Fashion Institute of Technology. As a result, there has been an explosion of new ideas and new young innovators on the fashion scene. Fashion writers from *Vogue, Harper's Bazaar, Women's Wear Daily,* and especially Carrie Donovan (recently retired) and Bernadine Morris of *The New York Times* write enthusiastically about all the events and offerings of the American designers.

The Council of Fashion Designers of America celebrates itself by presenting awards in the 1990s for the greatest achievements of the year. Lifetime Achievement Awards have been presented to Ralph Lauren for having changed the direction of American fashion and Pauline Trigère, who has created beautiful designs for more than 50 years. Designers such as Karl Lagerfeld from Paris and Giorgio Armani from Milan participate in the festivities and present awards. Gianni Versace was presented with the Council's first International Award, and Donna Karan was presented with the Men's Wear Award. Marc Jacobs for Perry Ellis received the award as the Designer of the Year. Stars of stage, screen, and television are on hand to applaud the creative talents of so many fine artists. The gala event is held at the New York State Theater in Lincoln Center in New York City each February. Hearst Magazines, publishers of *Harper's Bazaar*, is the sponsor of the event.

On a sad note, there have been a number of tragic deaths from AIDS. The rising stars of designers such as Perry Ellis and Willie Smith have fallen, and the fashion industry stands together to mourn those who have died.

·
LICENSING—AN ADDED BENEFIT

As American designers gained in reputation and became more popular, an important offshoot of their success was their use of the time-honored practice of licensing. **Licensing** is an agreement between a designer and a manufacturer whereby the manufacturer pays the designer a fee or royalties for the use of his or her name on a product. The amount of money paid the designer varies according to the input of the designer and the merchandise, but a typical fee is 10 percent of the retail price. The design of a product is usually created by, but sometimes merely approved by, the designer. However, actual production and distribution of the merchandise are the responsibilities of the manufacturer. In these licensing agreements, the designer is called the licenser and the manufacturer the licensee.

By far, the most licensed name in fashion is Pierre Cardin. To his credit are more than 540 licenses, which have a combined sales volume of over $1 billion a year. Royalties to the designer are between $35 and $50 million annually. In addition to his retail operations, Ralph Lauren has successfully licensed fragrances, luggage, handbags, belts, scarves, sunglasses, hats, quilts, pillows, and all manner of home furnishings.

The type of product carrying the designer's name can be anything from pantyhose (Donna Karan) to sunglasses (Gloria Vanderbilt). However, the types of products that seem to be the most successfully franchised are fragrances. For instance, it is well known that the perfume sales of Chanel No. 5 made Coco Chanel a millionairess; and that the Joy fragrances bring in the main revenues of the French couture house, Jean Patou, Inc. Today, American designers have joined the profitable fragrance market with perfumes such as Obsession (by Calvin Klein), Claiborne (by Liz Claiborne), Blazer (by Anne Klein), Norell (by Norman Norell), and Halston (by Halston). Some have also introduced men's fragrances: Grey Flannel by Beene and Blass's Bill

Blass are two of these earliest entries. Safari for Men is a fragrance for men by Ralph Lauren.

In the late 1960s, many designers entered into licensing via the accessory market when fashion's "total look" became the dominant trend and designers decided to create their own accessories for their clothes. By the early 1970s, accessories with designer names and initials had become status symbols.

Today designer-labeled accessories are a big business. Manufacturers of accessories produce a wide array of designer merchandise through a substantial and ever-increasing number of licensing agreements.

INTERNATIONAL BUSINESS ARRANGEMENTS

As distances between lands and people decrease, opportunities for designers to become multinational in their business arrangements increase. Licensing agreements of American designers are no longer exclusively with American manufacturers. The ever-improving status of American designers abroad has made agreements with manufacturers in Europe and Japan profitable ventures. Likewise, designers from other countries have found it worthwhile to license in the United States. Some designers are also establishing sales, manufacturing, and distribution centers throughout the world.

TODAY'S TOP AMERICAN DESIGNERS

When Hattie Carnegie manufactured her first line of ready-to-wear in 1928, she also became the first American designer to have her name on a fashion label. Fifty years ago, she was one of the few *authentic* designers in the country. Most of the others were really copyists, people who interpreted French fashions. *Today, there are more professional designers in the United States than in any other country*, and their originality equals and sometimes surpasses that of any designer in the world.

Oscar de la Renta, who trained in Paris but became one of the established greats in New York, has returned to Paris to design *haute couture*. He is the first American designer to do so since Mainbocher, who concluded his *haute couture* designing in 1940. Oscar de la Renta is now the chief designer for the House of Balmain and will also be designing *prêt-à-porter* for this prestigious fashion organization.

Bob Mackie, one of the established great designers, is unusual in that he designs for the stage, the screen, and television. He counts many famous actors and actresses as his customers, and his home base is not Seventh Avenue in New York City, but Hollywood, California.

The following women's wear designers are those currently in the limelight as major business and creative forces in the American fashion industry. (Major menswear designers are included in Chapter 13.) Though the work of each is highly individual, the designers seem to share several characteristics. Based on these characteristics, they have been divided into three groups: the young innovators, the tycoons, and the established greats. It is important to note that opportunities in this country for succeeding in the business of fashion design are excellent. Because of this, the following lists could change overnight to include the name of a brilliant, but as yet unknown, designer.

The Young Innovators

Originality and youth are the characteristics the following designers have in common. Each has his or her own design philosophy, and each projects his or her own distinctive look. Having gained recognition within the last ten years, they represent the newest designing talent in the industry.

Victor Alfaro
Pamela Dennis
Mark Eisen
Gordon Henderson
Marc Jacobs
Gemma Kahng
Stephen Sprouse
Todd Oldham

Byron Lars
Isaac Mizrahi
Kenneth Richard
Christian Francis
    Roth
Ronaldus Shamask
Anna Sui
Richard Tyler (for
    Anne Klein)

The Tycoons

The following people share a design and business philosophy that may be characterized as purely American. Their clothes, casually elegant by day and softly romantic by night, typify the "American look." Their enormous business success meanwhile typifies American "business savvy." Their high-priced clothes are bought by affluent high-fashion customers, while their sportswear-oriented, less expensive

Donna Karan—An Established Great

• • • • • • • • • • •

FASHION FEATURE

• • • • • • • • • • •

Courtesy: Donna Karan, New York

The fastest growing designer in the apparel industry, Donna Karan employs 750 people in 17 floors of two buildings. In addition to her signature lines of women's and men's wear, she markets her ever-popular bridge line, DKNY for men, women, and children. Add to that intimate apparel co-licensed with Wacoal America; a beauty company that begins with her own perfume designed for her by her husband, Steven Weiss; and her pantyhose collection licensed with Sara Lee. The result is a creative, talented woman sparkling with energy and drive, always thinking of new concepts and new dimensions for her business.

Donna Karan's signature color is black. She feels that people have to be really comfortable in their clothing and yet have to have a "put together" look. Every woman must have a black skirt and hose as well as a black body suit—boots are important, and lots of black cashmere. Gold jewelry is another must for the perfect effect.

Ms. Karan insists on hands-on involvement with every item that comes out of her workrooms: from concept meetings, to sketches, to the selection of models and music for her shows, to the advertising and marketing of her products. She keeps in close touch with her partners and licensees.

Her father died when she was three, and she learned to be independent early in life as her mother modeled and sold in the apparel industry. Because she was not academically inclined, Hewlett High School encouraged her artistic talent, and upon graduation, she entered the Parson's School of Design. After her first year she was offered a position with Anne Klein, along with a classmate of hers from Parson's, Louis Dell'Ollio. After nine months she was fired. She was having a difficult time trying to make a decision about marrying Mark Karan and was insecure about her talent and her ability. After she married, she worked for a sportswear designer who taught her marketing. Then, feeling more secure, she talked herself back into Anne Klein. Anne Klein died three days after Donna gave birth to her daughter, Gabby. Tomio Taki, a Japanese textile magnate who had bought a 50 percent interest in the firm, named her as successor. After nine years, a divorce, a remarriage to Steven Weiss, a sculptor, she decided to go out on her own.

Mr. Taki and his partner, Frank Mori, invested $3 million in her new company. After a successful partnership, Donna Karan felt ready to restructure her company to make expansion of her product lines easier. History is being made everyday with her exciting and growing company.

Problem Solving

1. What do you think were Donna Karan's most important personality traits that contributed to her success?
2. To be successful, a designer must create an image that is unique. What does she do in order to foster that image?
3. Why is it that television anchors such as Diane Sawyer and Barbara Walters and actresses such as Candace Bergen, as she appears on "Murphy Brown," wear Donna Karan clothing?

lines appeal to those looking for a young and casual approach to fashion.

Jennifer George

Louis Dell'Ollio

Norma Kamali

Betsey Johnson

Gloria Sachs

Michael Kors

Carol Little

Linda Allard (Ellen Tracy)

Michael Volbrecht

The Established Greats

Most of the following designers began as "young innovators" in the post-World War II period. Like their counterparts of today, they were singled out because of their originality. They have been able to remain on top because of an extraordinary ability to interpret current fashion and retain their own unmistakable looks. They are known for high prices as well as high fashion; their customers include those celebrities and other wealthy people who appreciate and can pay for the best in fashion.

Arnold Scaasi

Adolfo

Geoffrey Beene

Bill Blass

Oscar de la Renta

Mary McFadden

Calvin Klein

Donna Karan

Carolina Herrera

Liz Claiborne

James Galanos

Ralph Lauren

Bob Mackie

Pauline Trigère

Adrienne Vitadini

.... TERMS TO REMEMBER

Adrian   sportswear influence   Amelia Jenkins Bloomer   Claire McCardell   couture ready-to-wear   Norman Norell   licensing agreements Coty American Fashion Critics' Award   Council of Fashion Designers of America   prêt-à-porter.

.... HIGHLIGHTS OF THE CHAPTER

- American fashion design emerged as a major influence because of Hollywood and Adrian, Claire McCardell's sportswear, and the outstanding couture ready-to-wear of Norman Norell.

- The "youth kick" of the 1960s revolutionized fashion, causing Paris to lose its dictatorial influence on fashion design.

- In the early 1970s, the classic look of American sportswear became dominant. The trend served to make American designers as important as the French.

- To compete with American designers, most couture designers began to produce ready-to-wear. Their entrance into mass production added prestige to ready-made clothing and helped rather than hurt the American designers.

- Today Seventh Avenue designers are considered world fashion leaders, and their labels are as prestigious as those of the French.

- Designer "names" are big business. Royalties can be made through licensing

agreements in which designer labels appear on products for a share of the profits.

- American designers have now expanded their business internationally, lending their name to merchandise that is produced and sold in foreign countries. Some are also establishing sales, manufacturing, and distribution branches throughout the world.

- The great American designers may be divided into three categories—the young innovators, the tycoons, and the established greats. All types are major business and creative forces in the American fashion industry of today.

- To pay tribute to these American designers whose work is considered exceptional, the Coty American Fashion Critics' Award was presented each fall from 1942 to 1985. Today, awards are presented by the Council of Fashion Designers of America.

.... REVIEW QUESTIONS

1. Describe the Hollywood influence on fashion in the 1930s.

2. What innovation did Amelia Bloomer introduce?

3. Explain the concepts of fashion and marketing introduced by Claire McCardell.

4. Give a summary of McCardell's definition of the "American look."

5. What was Norman Norell's contribution to American fashion?

6. What was the "youth kick" of the 1960s, and who were some of its originators?

7. How did this fashion development affect the position of American designers in terms of fashion influence?

8. What fashion trend in the 1970s helped American designers?

9. How did the French couture hope to compete with America?

10. In your opinion, what is the current status of American designers? Do you consider them as creative as the French? Why?

.... RESEARCH AND PROJECTS

1. The decades of the 1920s, 1930s, 1940s, and 1950s are remembered as having distinct socioeconomic themes and therefore special fashion needs. Describe two of these periods including the popular styles each had.

2. The 1960s were probably the most traumatic period in the twentieth century. What made this so, and how was fashion affected?

3. By using the old movies of the 1930s, elaborate on Adrian's contribution to American fashion. Mention particular stars and any looks they were responsible for.

4. Claire McCardell's sportswear is classic and timeless. Locate examples of her work from design books and compare them to the sportswear being featured today. Elaborate on the similarities and differences you find.

5. Using current magazines and newspapers, find what today could be termed as examples of a truly "American look." What makes these clothes different from those of Paris and Milan?

6. Choose a designer listed in one of the sections Young Innovators, Tycoons, or Established Greats. Research and prepare a biography of your designer complete with illustrations of his or her work. (You may be able to obtain information directly from the designer's New York office by writing for a press kit.)

7. On your next visit to your favorite department or specialty store, be sure to visit such departments as cosmetics, accessories, and home furnishings. Make note of how many products sold in these departments are designer-labeled merchandise, indicating that the designer and manufacturer have established a licensing agreement.

CHAPTER 9

....

The Role of the Primary Markets

······· LEARNING OBJECTIVES

After reading this chapter, you should be able to:

- Identify the three segments of the primary markets.
- Cite the products and services each primary market provides for the fashion industry.
- Discuss the role each primary market plays in deciding what kind of fashion merchandise will be produced.

······· PERFORMANCE OUTCOME

After reading this chapter, you should be able to:

- Differentiate between natural and synthetic fabrics.
- Locate the major production and marketing centers for each sector of the primary markets.
- Describe the role each of the sectors of the primary market plays in determining fashion direction.

In order to produce goods, one must begin with raw materials. In the fashion business, those who supply the raw materials—textiles, leather, and furs—are known collectively as **primary markets.** They are so called because their activities comprise the first steps in the production of fashion goods.

THE TEXTILE INDUSTRY

Of the three industries that comprise the primary markets, textiles is the largest. Within the realm of this vast industry are four levels, each dealing with a distinct phase of textile production. These are *fiber production, yarn production, fabric construction,* and *fabric finishing.* Some companies specialize in only one phase, while others handle as many as all four phases.

Fiber Production

A *fiber* is a natural or synthetic hairlike filament. It provides texture and substance to yarns and fabrics and is literally what goods are made of.

Natural fibers come from either an animal or plant. Included are cotton, wool, linen, and silk. **Synthetic fibers** are manufactured and are either cellulosic (byproducts of wood and cotton) or noncellulosic (made chemically).

Of the natural fibers, *cotton* is the most widely produced. In the United States it is grown primarily in two regions: the Southeast and the Southwest. Local farmers sell their crops to wholesalers, who in turn move the goods to such central markets as New Orleans, Dallas, Houston, or Memphis for national and international distribution. Egypt, Brazil, China, and the CIS are other recognized world cotton producers.

The United States also produces a substantial amount of *wool.* Sheep farmers, located in the Rocky Mountain states of Colorado and Utah, are the leading wool producers. However, 27 states, including Alaska, also contribute to U.S. wool production. Like cotton farmers, sheep farmers sell wool locally to wholesalers, who then sell it in the central wool market in Boston. Wool is also produced in large quantities by the United Kingdom countries of Australia, New Zealand, and Scotland and by Argentina and South Africa.

Linen is a fiber that comes from the flax plant. Since the Colonial period, the United States has produced flax crops each year. Today, however, the demand for the oil of the plant is greater than the demand for the fiber. Therefore, the United States has to import nearly all the linen used in apparel production from countries such as Belgium and Ireland. Fabrics made purely of linen are consequently expensive.

The same basic criticisms can be applied to *silk*. All the silk used in apparel is now imported into the United States, making it very expensive. Silk is also a delicate fiber, and it requires considerable care.

In previous years, attempts were made to bring natural silk production to the United States, but all efforts proved to be unsuccessful. The fiber is produced by the silkworm, which needs a special diet and climatic conditions to survive. Today, China, Italy, and Japan account for the world's major production of this fiber.

Both silk and linen fibers have had a decline in usage because of the so-called miracle fibers, the synthetics. In fact, it was the search for "artificial silk" that prompted the research and eventual discovery of the first cellulosic synthetic fiber, *rayon*.

The first noncellulosic fiber to be produced chemically was *nylon*. Its discovery in 1938 led to the development of an entire group of synthetics known as *polymers*, such as *polyesters, acrylics*, and the stretch fiber *spandex*. Probably these fibers are better known by their registered trade names rather than by their generic names. For example, Dacron polyester, Orlon acrylic, Qiana nylon, and Lycra spandex are Du Pont trade names. Fortrel polyester is a Celanese Corporation trade name, and Acrilan acrylic is owned by Monsanto.

The majority of synthetic fibers used here are made in the United States. They are produced in large chemical plants located in 12 states, most of which are on the East Coast.

Yarn Production

Once the fibers are acquired, they must be spun into long strands called *yarn*. Many synthetic fibers emerge as long filaments and, unless blended with natural fibers, do not necessarily have to be spun. Since the use of blends of natural and synthetic fibers has dramatically increased, however, most large synthetic fiber producers now produce yarn as well. Today, this is a highly automated phase of textile production (see Figure 9–1).

Courtesy: Burlington Industries

• • • • • • • • **FIGURE 9-1** **Air-jet open-end spinning equipment produces yarns at high speeds.**

Fabric Construction

The next phase of textile production is the actual making of the fabric. There are several methods that can be used. The yarns can either be woven, knitted, bonded, felted, laminated, crocheted, or braided. Most fabrics made today are either woven or knitted (see Figure 9–2).

Once the fabric is made, it is called **greige goods,** a term used to connote unfinished fabric. As mentioned before, some companies also go on to finish their goods. Those that do not sell the greige goods to a **converter,** who then makes them into finished goods.

Fabric Finishing

It is at this phase of production that the fabrics are transformed. The dull, unfinished fabrics are treated to any of a variety of steps that

Courtesy: Burlington Industries

**FIGURE 9-2 High-speed shuttleless looms provide
better quality and higher productivity.**

beautify their appearance and improve their salability. This procedure
is called *fabric finishing,* and a few of the many finishing processes include *bleaching, smoothing, shearing, brushing,* or *embossing.*

It is also at this stage that fabrics are *dyed* and *printed.* Although
some fabrics may be *yarn dyed* (meaning the yarns are dyed before the
fabric is made), most goods are *piece dyed,* because it is the most economical of all the methods.

The printing of fabric is done by using one of four methods: hand
printing, machine printing, heat transferring, and (the newest) jet
printing. The choice of printing method, therefore, is influenced by
the type of pattern or design desired for a fabric.

The finishing process can also enhance the fabric's performance.
For instance, cotton can be *sized* to give it body. Wool and cottons can
be *preshrunk* to prevent excessive shrinking when cleaned. Other fabrics may be made *crease resistant, wash-and-wear, colorfast,* or *permanent
press* simply by applying the proper finishing techniques.

Finally, the finishing process can also provide protection. Such finishes as *waterproofing, flame* or *fire retardation,* and *mildew and rot repellency* can be applied to fabrics to make them safe and durable.

Characteristics of the Textile Industry

From the beginning of fiber production to the completion of finished goods, the textile industry plays an important part in the U.S. economy. It provides jobs for over 600,000 workers in 2,500 plants, which represents 5 percent of all production employment. The industry output at wholesale equals $69 billion.

Location of the Industry
In the search for cheaper labor and to be closer to resources, U.S. textile production has shifted from the Northeast to the South. Currently 93 percent of all cotton fiber and fabric and 85 percent of all synthetic fibers are produced below the Mason-Dixon line. States that are leading producers of textiles (including the few in the Northeast) are North and South Carolina, Georgia, Tennessee, Alabama, Pennsylvania, New Jersey, and New York.

A Change in Raw Materials
Another important shift has been in the kind of raw materials produced. Natural fibers have been replaced by synthetics. In less than half a century, the growth of synthetics has been astounding. For example, in 1930 the fiber market was divided as follows: 95 percent natural and 5 percent synthetic. By 1950, synthetics were beginning to rise. The market was approximately 80 percent natural and 20 percent synthetic. In 1970, there was a complete reversal: 56 percent of all fibers produced were synthetics. Today, synthetic fiber production accounts for a 63 percent share of the market.

The Structure of the Industry
The textile industry has also been transformed from a highly fragmented, highly specialized operation into an industry dominated by giants who are **vertically integrated.** This means that a company handles all four steps in the production of textiles within its own divisions. They (1) process the fiber, (2) spin the yarn, (3) make the cloth, and (4) finish the cloth.

Today the bulk of the 2,500 textile firms are small, doing less than $50 million each in sales a year. However, the top mills (Table 9–1) generate nearly 30 percent of the industry's sales and most of these

•••••••• **TABLE 9-1 Major U.S. Textile Mills in Terms of Sales Volume**

Burlington	Fieldcrest/Cannon
Milliken	West Point Pepperell
Springs Industries	Guilford Mills

are vertically integrated. (See Industry Feature on Burlington Industries.)

Like other sectors of the economy, major mergers, acquisitions, and consolidations took place in the 1980s. Fiber production sales are also dominated by giants. Chemical companies such as Du Pont, Celanese, Monsanto, Eastman Kodak, and Phillips Petroleum are the leaders.

The entire structure of the textile industry has moved from being production oriented to being more marketing oriented, with an increased emphasis on the ultimate consumer via **derived demand** advertising and stimulation. In previous years, the target for promotion and sales was those intermediaries who directly bought fibers, yarns, and unfinished and finished goods. Fiber producers and mills were concerned with their immediate customers, not their ultimate users. This meant that, prior to the 1960s, consumers did not know one brand name of fiber from another, nor were they familiar with the names of firms responsible for producing the goods used in their clothing.

In order to gain consumer confidence and acceptance of new fibers and fabrics, as well as to establish loyalty to brand names, large chemical companies began aggressive ad campaigns aimed at the ultimate consumer. They sponsored cooperative ads with apparel manufacturers, exposing the consumer to the virtues of the fiber and fabric as well as those of the garment. The consumer would then buy garments made of a particular fiber or fabric, thereby increasing the demand for either one in a secondary or derived manner (see Figure 9–3).

Thus, those in the textile business have become more than just weavers, knitters, chemists, or finishers. Companies in this industry have incorporated into their business the entire marketing concept of expanding old markets and creating new ones.

Labor and Import Problems
The industry has been faced with two major problems—rising labor costs and increased competition from inexpensive imported goods.

Profile of a Giant: Burlington Industries

With sales in excess of $3.2 billion, Burlington Industries is one of the world's largest producers of textiles and related products. The company does everything from researching and developing new fibers; to producing fabric for apparel and industrial use; to making finished products such as hosiery, carpets, and sheets. Besides its own brands, it markets its products through licensing agreements with Vera, Anne Klein, Oleg Cassini, John Weitz, and Levi Strauss, to name some examples.

Burlington was founded in 1923 by J. Spencer Love in Burlington, North Carolina. Corporate headquarters is still in North Carolina, but this huge firm also operates 135 plants in 14 states and abroad and maintains over 30 research divisions. The company's merchandising and marketing activities are centered in New York City at Burlington House.

Listed below are Burlington's domestic divisions.

Apparel Products Divisions	*Industry Products Divisions*
Burlington Knit Fabrics	Burlington Glass Fabrics Company
Burlington Men's Wear	Burlington Industrial Fabrics Company
Burlington Retail Fabrics Company	Burlington Ribbon Mills
Burlington Winmoor	Goodall Vinyl Fabrics
Burlington Woolens	
Burlington Worsted	
Galey and Lord	*Hosiery Divisions*
Klopman Mills	Burlington Hosiery Company
Burlington Greige Sales Company	Burlington Socks

Yarns Divisions	*Other*
Atwater Throwing Company	Burlington Management Services Company
Burlington Yarn Company	Burlington Export Company
Madison Throwing Company	Burlington Trading Company

Although certain phases of it are automated, textile production remains a labor-intensive industry. This means a large number of employees is necessary to operate machinery and equipment.

Pay scales and benefits are low in comparison to other U.S. industries. However, companies have had to gradually increase employee remunerations due in part to organizing campaigns by the

Courtesy: Du Pont Co.

• • • • • • • • **FIGURE 9-3 An example of cooperative advertising between a manufacturer of fibers and a fashion apparel producer.**

Amalgamated Clothing and Textile Workers Union. Still, less than 10 percent of the workers in this industry are unionized, making these gains modest at best.

Even though textile workers are not highly paid by U.S. standards, they are when compared with foreign labor. This has resulted in imports from places such as Japan, Hong Kong, Taiwan, and South Korea to amount to more than $6.5 billion annually. There has been a major loss of textile jobs (over 200,000 since 1980) and a decline in demand for American-made fabrics.

To combat these problems, U.S. producers are investing over $1.5 billion in new equipment designed to speed up and automate production. Robotics, computer-assisted design (CAD), and computer-assisted manufacturing (CAM) methods are being incorporated into existing production methods in order to become more competitive in the world marketplace.

A program of "Quick Response" (QR) has also been developed by the textile industry to reduce the time needed to supply manufacturers with desired fabric. The program uses bar codes and scanners to stock and restock orders in a matter of weeks instead of the months required by imported goods. This has increased the demand for domestic goods considerably.

The "Crafted with Pride in the U.S.A." council was formed in 1984 to promote the use of American-made goods including textiles to the ultimate consumer and the other sectors of the fashion industry.

In addition, efforts are being made to increase U.S. exports which are currently valued at approximately $4 billion annually. The United States is already the number one world supplier of cotton, synthetic yarns, and mohair.

Marketing Activities of the Textile Industry

Consumer Advertising and Promotion

As previously mentioned, two successful marketing activities carried on by the textile industry have been consumer advertising and promotion. Not only are these done on an individual basis (as in "Qiana by Du Pont," for example), but fiber promotion is often done collectively as well.

One such cooperative group is the Man-Made Fiber Producers Association. This organization seeks to inform consumers about the virtues of all synthetic fibers, regardless of which company makes them.

Among the natural fiber growers and producers, trade associations also exist. They help by compiling and disseminating fiber and fabric information to their members and consumers alike. Two such associations are the American Wool Council in Colorado and the National Cotton Council of America in Tennessee.

In addition to these trade groups, advertising and promotional activities are conducted by special organizations for their producers. Cotton Incorporated is headquartered in New York and specializes in promoting cotton to all members of the industry, as well as directly to the consumer. Monies to run Cotton Incorporated come from a bale assessment fee collected by the Cotton Board, a division of the U.S. Department of Agriculture. Another group functioning in basically the same manner for its fiber producers is the Wool Bureau, Inc.

The Wool Bureau, Inc., established in New York in 1949, is a branch of the International Wool Secretariat headquartered in London. Like Cotton Incorporated, the Wool Bureau promotes wool use through advertising to the consumer. Garments that bear the "Woolmark" label must meet Bureau standards of performance (see Figure 9–4). The Bureau also assists manufacturers and retailers as well. The International Wool Secretariat has branches in 33 countries, A Wool Men's Wear Fashion office in London, and a Women's Wear Fashion office in Paris. This organization works to increase the consumption of wool, develops new products and processes for wool, does marketing research, and coordinates marketing activities for wool and wool products. There are no charges for the services provided by the Secretariat. The organization is supported by sheep growers in major wool-producing nations around the world.

Services to the Trade

Besides advertising, textile producers perform various other marketing services, especially for the trade. Most large companies and trade organizations maintain extensive **fabric libraries.** These libraries do not contain any books. Instead, they display swatches of fabrics that

PURE WOOL

The sewn-in Woolmark label is your assurance of quality-tested fabrics made of the world's best...Pure Wool.

Woolmark™ Courtesy of The Wool Bureau

• • • • • • • • FIGURE 9-4 **The popular woolmark used to promote garments made from 100 percent wool.**

are currently in production or are slated for production in the upcoming seasons. Designers, manufacturers, retailers, fashion editors, and consultants use these libraries as sources of inspiration and to gather information about future fabric and color trends. Textile companies and associations also sponsor fashion shows and fashion seminars for the trade. Garments used in the shows are usually described in terms of fiber, fabric, and apparel manufacturer.

Fabric libraries are also maintained of historic plaids, prints, and weaves. These libraries are found in museums and fabric houses such as Forstmann Woolens.

Trade Shows

Trade shows are an important means of promoting textiles both at home and abroad. Many U.S. manufacturers participate in the industry's largest show, **Interstoff.** This event is held twice a year in March and September in Frankfurt, Germany. It is attended by thousands of designers, manufacturers, and retailers who wish to gain an early insight into future fabric and fashion trends.

A second important show is **Première Vision.** It takes place in Paris during the months of March and October. Smaller shows include Ideacomo in Como, Italy; Texitalia in Milan; and Canton Trade Fair in China. The two major U.S. shows are held in New York; they are the New York Fabric Show and the Knitting Yarn Fair.

Projections made at these shows are usually 18 to 24 months ahead of consumption. Because textile firms work so far ahead of the rest of the fashion industry, they are a primary indicator of fashion direction.

Fabric Innovations

In the last few decades, the textile industry has assumed a much larger role in steering the direction of fashion. The introduction of so many new and innovative fibers and fabrics has often resulted in the development of a major fashion trend.

The trend toward the "natural" fabrics of cotton, wool, linen, or silk—in real or cheaper, synthetic versions—is a more recent example of how fabric can provide the major fashion interest in apparel while silhouette and detail remain secondary. Today, as the inventiveness and influence of the textile industry grow, it becomes even more impossible to separate the fashion direction of the apparel industry from the developments and decisions of the textile producers. Both factions—the textile producers and the apparel makers—work extremely closely in order to successfully market fashion goods.

Research and Planning

Because fashion and textiles are so vital to each other, the textile producers keenly recognize the importance of extensive marketing research. Though research is naturally conducted for the development of new fibers, fabrics, and methods of fabric construction and finishing, it also encompasses areas of consumer research, the development of new outlets for distribution, introducing cheaper and better methods of production, and increasing the effectiveness of promotion and advertising.

The long-range planning of the textile industry also involves color development. The Color Association of the United States (CAUS), located in New York, researches and promotes new colors for the industry, disseminating important color trends to all members of the trade. Internationally, Intercolor and International Color Authority (ICA) research trends and present them to the trade twice a year in Europe.

Consumer Information and Protection

The textile industry has begun to take the initiative in the areas of consumer information and protection. In previous years, the information provided pertained mainly to the fiber content and finish of fabrics and was government imposed. For example, in 1939 the Wool Products and Labeling Act was passed requiring disclosure of fiber content. Then, in 1954, the Flammable Fabrics Act was passed, banning certain fabrics from U.S. markets. In 1973, the Federal Trade Commission amended this act. Fabrics used in certain types of wearing apparel such as children's sleepwear and home furnishings had to meet U.S. government standards regarding flammability.

Another federal act, the Care Labeling of Textile Wearing Apparel, was also put into effect by the FTC. Under this law, manufacturers must provide specific details regarding the washing and/or dry cleaning methods to be used by the consumer in caring for the garment or accessory.

Today, the industry itself is constantly testing and improving the safety and quality of its products. Some companies have gone far beyond minimum government standards. For example, in 1962 Monsanto introduced its "wear-dated" guarantee. In addition to covering its fiber and fabric for one year, Monsanto also guarantees zippers, seams, color fastness, shrink resistance—in fact, everything pertaining to an item. If the customer is not satisfied, he or she may write to Monsanto for a refund or replacement.

Many companies in the industry maintain full-time customer relations staffs to handle inquiries and complaints, and most take a

Careers in the Primary Markets

FASHION
FEATURE

Most career opportunities in textiles, leather, and fur require specific technical skill as well as general fashion knowledge. However, opportunities do exist in these industries for those who have basic marketing or business backgrounds and who are willing to learn the specific aspects of a particular company's product line. These positions would most likely be in the sales, advertising, public relations, marketing research, personnel, and accounting areas.

Fashion careers in the primary markets include the following:

Textile designer. This job requires artistic ability as well as a thorough knowledge of textiles and their properties. It requires an educational or business background in fashion, which the textile designer needs to correctly evaluate overall fashion trends.

Fabric stylist. Working closely with the textile designer, the fabric stylist revises or adapts existing fabric designs for a new seasonal line. The same basic knowledge and skills of a textile designer are required of the stylist. In some companies, this position serves as an apprenticeship to the job of designer. Other companies, however, consider the position of fabric stylist equally important, especially if they deal in mass fashion goods.

Fabric librarian. This individual is responsible for preparing and maintaining the fabric library. He or she enters the fiber and fabric descriptions that accompany each swatch. The job also involves communicating with those in the trade who seek information on the properties and colors of the firm's fabrics.

Color stylist. Generally employed by fiber or yarn producers, the color stylist needs a knowledge of textiles and chemistry. He or she is responsible for obtaining the best method of dyeing fillers or yarns and must help in selecting the tints, tones, and shades of color that are being used that season.

Fashion director or researcher. Most leather and textile firms have a position that requires an ability to scout the fashion markets and spot upcoming fashion and marketing trends. Sometimes the individuals holding this position must travel to and report on trends in the United States, Europe, and the Far East. Their findings and their recommendations guide the company in its decisions concerning its future fashion and marketing trends. This job may also involve fashion coordination, staging fashion shows and exhibits for the trade, and working with members of the industry as well as consumer or educational groups.

Usually, if the company is large, this work is carried on by more than one individual. In this case, there are several staff or supportive positions that provide excellent training and exposure to the overall business of fashion.

strong position, guaranteeing the performance standards of their products.

Another offshoot of consumerism has been the concern for environmental protection. Spurred by government action, the textile industry is now researching and developing new methods of operation that are nonpolluting, conserve energy, and reduce waste. Overall, the public's concern for the environment and resource allocation has become an important concern of the textile industry as well.

THE LEATHER INDUSTRY

Another vital sector of the primary markets is the leather industry. Like textile production, producing leather has long been a part of the American heritage.

In recent years, the leather industry has become more fashion oriented. Though leather has always been used for fashion accessories, today it is also very important in apparel. This increasing use of leather has strengthened even further the bond of cooperation between leather producers and the fashion industry.

The Product

Leather is a natural byproduct of slaughtered animals. Around the world, animals such as cattle and sheep are raised for multipurposes. In addition to providing a source of food, they supply a variety of byproducts, including leather.

The raw materials termed *hides* come from large animals—mainly cows, steers, or horses. *Skins* come from smaller animals such as sheep, goats, calves, and pigs.

Leather has distinct pattern characteristics that differentiate one leather from another. These differences are found in its *grain*. The leather also has unique physical properties that are associated with individual types of leathers. For example, calfskin and sheepskin are soft and supple and are preferred for items requiring those qualities such as shoe uppers and gloves. On the other hand, leather from steers is thicker and more durable and therefore suitable for shoe soles or luggage. The dominant type of raw material used by the leather industry comes from cattle because it is in abundant supply. The second most available raw material used for leather making is sheepskin.

Once the skins and hides are obtained from the animals, they must immediately be *cured* if they are going to become leather. This treatment is an important first step affecting the quality of the finished product. There are a variety of other steps, such as soaking and unhairing, that the skins and hides go through before they are ready for the *tanning* step, the actual converting of skins and hides into leather. Once this process is complete, the leather is ready for *coloring.* Today, leathers can be dyed in a wide array of colors thanks to the modern technology developed by the industry. Next, the leather is finished, measured, and graded in terms of quality. All in all, there are 19 steps in the process of making leather.

The entire process is usually completed in four weeks, making leather production slow in comparison to textile production. It is for this reason that those producing leather begin 18 to 24 months in advance of the sale of the finished product. Because they must work so far in advance, fashion researchers and coordinators who are affiliated with tanneries must also be able to forecast far into the fashion future. Since leather houses are then the first to project color and texture trends, those in other fields of the fashion industry use the leather fashion experts as a primary source of information for future fashion trends.

Characteristics of the Leather Industry

In the United States, the production of leather is primarily done in approximately 200 tanneries and finishing plants in the northeastern and north central states. Industry shipments total over $2 billion annually, and production statistics include the tanning of over 18 million hides and 17 million skins a year.

Leather is used in the production of wearing apparel (coats, skirts, pants, and jackets) as well as accessories such as gloves, luggage, handbags, and small personal leather goods. A portion of the leather also goes into the industrial sector for use in furniture and car interiors.

Labor and Import Problems

Like the textile industry, the leather industry is facing increased labor costs and the competition of imported goods. Finished goods containing leather are also being imported at ever-increasing rates, further decreasing the demand for U.S. leather. These changes are partly due to a shifting of production facilities from the United States and Europe to the developing nations of Asia and South America. Traditionally, these areas have simply been suppliers of raw hides; now they are establishing tanning and finishing facilities at a rapid pace.

Competition has also come from those engaged in producing leather lookalikes. Vinyls, plastics, and even textiles that simulate leather have been used in increasing amounts, especially in mass-merchandised apparel and accessories.

Structure of the Leather Industry

Basically, tanneries are small, with most employing under 100 workers. They are generally located in close proximity to slaughtering houses; in some instances, they are even subsidiaries of them. For example, the largest tanner, the A. C. Lawrence Leather Company, is a division of Swift's and Company. Most companies maintain marketing operations in New York City to better service the fashion industry and, at the same time, to feel its pulse.

Three kinds of tanning operations exist today. The first type is the *regular tannery*, which buys skins and hides and sells finished leather. These operations dominate the industry. The second type of operation is the *converter*. Hides and skins are bought by these companies, but they do not engage in the actual tanning process. Instead, a converter uses a *contract tannery*, which does the tanning to the converter's specifications. The converter company then sells the finished goods to its customers. The industry is also highly specialized. That is, tanneries work on only one type of hide. If they tan sheepskin, they probably do not handle cowhide.

Marketing Activities of the Leather Industry

Like textile producers, tanners are becoming more and more marketing oriented in their operations. They have discovered the importance of advertising and promotion and, in combination with leather product manufacturers, spend millions of dollars each year advertising their products.

Marketing research naturally includes better and faster ways of completing the curing and tanning processes. But it has also been expanded to include research on consumers all over the world. Innovative uses for natural leather products, as in wearing apparel, have been researched and promoted by individual companies as well as by the industry trade association Leather Industries of America, formerly known as the Tanners Council of America, located in New York.

Like the textile industry, leather producers use trade shows to market their products and present fashion trends. The Tanner's Apparel and Garment Show is held each October in New York City. Internationally the Hong Kong International fair takes place in June, and the oldest trade show—Semaine du Cuir—is presented each September in Paris.

Efforts are being made by the Leather Industries of America and its members to enlist public support for the leather products of the United States through educating the consumer concerning the virtues of American-made leather and its qualities. Those efforts include pressuring the federal government for help in resolving many of the industry's foreign trade problems.

The leather industry, in turn, has been affected by public pressure and government regulations as far as the types of hides and skins it processes. Under the Endangered Species Conservation Act of 1969, the sale and use of such heretofore popular skins such as crocodile are prohibited.

Though the past few years have shown a marked decrease in the size of America's leather industry and an increase in its many problems, many within the industry feel that effective marketing decisions, the help of the federal government, and consumer support can minimize, if not completely solve, these problems.

THE FUR INDUSTRY

No sector of the primary markets has undergone such redirection as the fur industry. Years ago, its principal contribution to fashion was singular: *mink*. Women, mainly those over 40, considered this fur the prized status symbol of the upper- and upper-middle-class elite; mink was for those who had "made it" financially.

Then, during the early 1960s, the fur market began to undergo tremendous change. It was the time of the "youth quake" in fashion when new styling concepts were introduced. Off-beat, less expensive, unusual pelts were worked into coats and all types of apparel, even pants. Heavy promotion of the new "fun" and "sport" furs by the fur industry and retailers succeeded in making customers "fur conscious" rather than "mink conscious."

Today, the fur industry continues to reflect those changes. The present fur market target is a much younger, more casual—though still financially secure—individual. Men are included in that target, and "furs for the man" are also heavily promoted (see Figure 9–5). All manner of fur is now accepted and demanded by the consumer, so that mink constitutes only 50 percent of all fur sales. The old, staid, stuffy "mink stole" industry is gone. In its place stands an industry of fur producers who, even when they "think mink," present original and exciting fashion concepts. It is the market reorientation and strong fashion image that have pushed fur sales over the billion dollar mark.

Courtesy: The American Fur Industry

•••••••• **FIGURE 9-5 Finally, equal rights for men.**

The Product

Basically, there are 100 different kinds of furs on the market today. These include such domestic ones as beaver, muskrat, rabbit, raccoon, fox, and seal; and imported ones such as sable, marten, Persian lamb, and lynx.

Furs are differentiated from hides and skins by the fact that hair, fleece, fur fibers, or guard hairs are not removed from the animal skins. These unshorn skins are referred to as *pelts*. Pelts are obtained either by *trapping* or by *breeding* the animals. Today the ratio is approximately 60 percent breeding (fur farming) to 40 percent trapping. Once the pelts are removed from the animals, they are brought to central locations to be sorted in terms of size and quality. The furs are then bundled and sold at auctions to processors.

The fur *processors* then *dress* and *color* the pelts. *Dressing* is a process that, like the curing done in the leather industry, prevents the decomposition of the pelts. *Coloring* is optional, but may include bleaching, darkening, or altering the natural color of the fur completely. Finally, the pelts are *glazed*—adding beauty, luster, and shine to the fur.

At this point, the pelts are ready to be made into garments or used as trim. The *fur goods manufacturer* takes over this role. It is a highly specialized skill and nearly all the steps used in the construction of a fur garment are intricately performed by hand.

It is because of the intricate, time-consuming nature of all these processes, from breeding to sewing, that the retail prices of fur items are always relatively high and their methods of production relatively slow.

Characteristics of the Industry

The fur industry is worldwide in scope. Among the many major fur-producing countries are Russia and the other CIS countries, Canada, France, Germany, Scandinavia, and, of course, the United States.

Fur trapping and trading are credited with opening up and developing this country from the early days of New World colonization. In fact, cities such as Detroit, Chicago, and St. Louis had their start as major fur trading centers. Even the seal of the state of New York contains two beavers, indicating the animal's importance in the development of the state.

Today, America's fur trapping is done in virtually every state, but most pelts are obtained from the Northwest and Northeast. Fur farming is also principally located in these two areas.

Since the industry is an international one, fur auction centers exist in countries throughout the world, with each country specializing in selling its native pelts. New York, Seattle, St. Louis, and several Canadian cities handle pelts native to North America. Other auction centers are located in Russia, Scandinavia, England, and Germany.

New York is the heart of this country's fur processing and manufacturing; it does over 90 percent of the country's business. Most operations are small, independent businesses employing fewer than 20 people. In late May of each year, New York City's fur district hosts "fur week," when new fur collections are presented to the retail trade over a period of about three weeks.

Nationwide, there are approximately 350 small establishments employing nearly 3,000 workers in the fur industry, many of whom are represented by the Fur Department of the Amalgamated Meat Cutters and Butchers Workers of the United States and Canada Union.

The retail distribution of the fur is varied. Fur manufacturers can sell their products to small, independent fur salons; to leased departments in retail stores; or directly to the store-owned department of a retail store. There are approximately 4,000 fur retailers in the United States. In the past, most furs were given to the retailer on a consignment basis. The term *consignment* applies to an arrangement between manufacturer and retailer whereby unsold furs can be returned to the manufacturer along with payment for sold ones. Consignment selling is rarely available to retailers nowadays. Most retailers must pay for deliveries from fur manufacturers as they pay other producers in the fashion industry.

Like the textile and leather industries, the fur industry is confronted by several major problems. The most pressing is its need to maintain an abundant supply of high-quality pelts. The industry is a strong advocate of conservation and tries to keep a proper ecological balance between supply and demand. To do so, it encourages only prudent and selective methods for the trapping and breeding of fur-supplying animals.

As in other industries that use highly skilled artisans, the industry also faces the problem of a decrease in its skilled labor supply. Traditionally, the fur industry's labor was supplied by immigrants who arrived equipped with skills obtained in their native countries. Today, with the decline in immigration, this supply is fast dwindling. However, with the help of federal funds and industry contributions, programs have been launched to attract career students into fur manufacturing. Working with schools like the High School of Fashion Industries in New York City, the fur manufacturers hope to obtain the necessary supply of highly skilled artisans.

Also, as in other fashion industries, imports have hurt. Less than 20 years ago, imports accounted for just over 5 percent of industry sales. Today, imports have reached 50 percent. Coats and apparel come from the Far East and cater to the lower price points of the fur market. Using less skilled workers and lower quality furs, imported products have caused a deflation in prices.

Some environmental groups have waged a war on the fur industry. Claiming cruelty to animals, these groups have boycotted and protested against stores selling fur products. They have been known to attack fur wearers with verbal abuses and have even thrown red paint at those wearing fur. This kind of publicity has negatively affected fur sales.

Marketing Activities of the Fur Industry

The major marketing thrust for the fur industry has not come from individual trappers, processors, or manufacturing firms. Most of these enterprises are too small to undertake specialized marketing activities. Therefore, this job has been left to the various trade associations and organizations representing all or a segment of the fur industry.

The American Fur Information and Industry Council acts on behalf of all its members to research and develop new markets, stimulate consumer interest, assist other members of the fashion industry, research new production methods, and collect and disseminate fur information. This is the organization most responsible for the fur industry's exciting new fashion image, picking up on young fashion trends in the early 1960s and reorienting the fur industry toward a new crop of younger customers.

Furs are also promoted on an individual basis by several industry groups. One that heavily promotes mink to both the industry and the consumers is EMBA—Eastern Mink Breeders Association. The GLMA (Great Lakes Mink Association) and the ECBC (Empress Chinchilla Breeders Cooperative) are two groups that perform the same functions, promoting their respective furs.

Efforts to unite the many segmented fur groups for the purpose of coping with the major industry problems have been made by the Council of American Fur Organizations. One priority of this group is to maintain and, if necessary, upgrade a positive fur industry image among conservationists, the federal government, and the general public. In doing so it hopes to counter the rising amount of imported furs and, at the same time, promote the sale of U.S. fur products to countries throughout the world.

The industry must and does strictly adhere to various federal laws that govern it in terms of consumer protection. For instance, the Fur Products and Labeling Act, enacted in 1952 and amended in 1961 and 1969, prevents false advertising and mislabeling practices by insisting that the label include (in English) the name of the animal from which the fur was obtained and the country of its origin. Furthermore, if an item contains fur that has been used before or is made from left-over pieces (waste fur), it must be so labeled.

The Endangered Species Act of 1969, aimed at the preservation of rare animals, also applies to the fur industry. Domestic pelts from the Texas red wolf, Eastern timber wolf, and Florida panther—to name a few—cannot be used or sold. Foreign pelts from the jaguar, leopard, tiger, and cheetah—once highly valued by the industry—are also on the list of endangered species and cannot be imported into the United States in any form.

The reduction in the variety of furs and the introduction of synthetic "fake furs" could have very easily hurt American fur producers. However, due to the foresight and marketing efforts of the various trade associations, both these threats were successfully overcome.

Finally, for added consumer appeal and status, designer labels have been added to fur garments. Via licensing agreements, names such as Geoffrey Beene, Bill Blass, Adolfo, Fendi, Hubert de Givenchy, and Yves Saint Laurent are now found on prestige furs. This, combined with fur's increasingly affordable prices, makes today's fur industry one of the most profitable sectors of the fashion industry despite its problems.

Sources of Market Information

Listed below are some trade associations, groups, and representative companies that may be contacted for specific information on their particular area of the primary markets.

Trade Associations

American Fabric Manufacturers
   Association
1150 17th Street
Washington, DC 20026

American Fur Industry
363 7th Avenue
New York, NY 10001

American Printed Fabrics Council
1040 Avenue of the Americas
New York, NY 10019

American Textile Manufacturers
   Institute
1801 K Street, N.W.
Washington, DC 22037

American Wool Council
200 Clayton Street
Denver, CO 80206

Color Association of the United
   States
24 East 38th Street
New York, NY 10016

Cotton, Inc.
1370 Avenue of the Americas
New York, NY 10019

Eastern Mink Breeders
   Association
151 West 30th Street
New York, NY 10001

Fur Information and Fashion
   Industry Council
101 East 30th Street
New York, NY 10016

Great Lakes Mink Association
151 West 30th Street
New York, NY 10001

International Silk Association
200 Madison Avenue
New York, NY 10017

Knitted Textile Association
386 Park Avenue South
New York, NY 10010

Leather Industry of America
2501 M Street N.W.
Suite 350
Washington, DC 20037

Mohair Council of America
1412 Broadway
New York, NY 10036

National Cotton Council of
   America
Market Research Service
1918 North Parkway
Box 12285
Memphis, TN 38112

Textile Distributors Association,
   Inc.
45 West 36th Street
New York, NY 10018

Textile Fabric Association
36 East 31st Street
New York, NY 10013

Wool Bureau
360 Lexington Avenue
New York, NY 10017

Textile, Fiber, and Fabric Manufacturers

Allied Chemical Corporation
Box 1087
Morristown, NJ 07960

Burlington Industries
1345 Avenue of the Americas
New York, NY 10021

Celanese Inc.
Consumer Education Department
522 Fifth Avenue
New York, NY 10036

Chemstrand Company
Public Relations Department
350 Fifth Avenue
New York, NY 10001

Dan River Inc.
111 West Fortieth Street
New York, NY 10036

Milliken Inc.
1045 Avenue of the Americas
New York, NY 10018

Eastman Kodak Chemicals
Products Inc.
Education Department
Fiber Division
260 Madison Avenue
New York, NY 10016

Firestone Tire and Rubber
Company
45 Rockefeller Plaza
New York, NY 10036

E.I. Du Pont de Nemours & Co.
Textile Fibers Department
Production Information Section
Centre Road Building
Wilmington, DE 19898

Monsanto Company
1114 Avenue of the Americas
New York, NY 10036

Springmaid Fabrics
104 West Fortieth Street
New York, NY 10018

Union Carbide Chemicals
Textile Fibers Department
Advertising Manager
270 Park Avenue
New York, NY 10017

.... TERMS TO REMEMBER

**primary markets   natural fibers   synthetic fibers   greige goods
converter   vertical integration   derived demand   fabric library   Première
Vision   Interstoff   CAD   CAM**

.... HIGHLIGHTS OF THE CHAPTER

- The primary markets of the fashion business include textile, leather, and fur producers.

- The largest segment, the textile industry, is composed of four sectors: fiber pro-

duction, yarn production, fabric construction, and fabric finishing.

- Major problems facing the textile industry include rising costs of labor and competition from imported goods.

- The industry has become increasingly vertically integrated and is dependent on derived demand for its production output.

- Leather production is a slow process that takes about four weeks to complete. Therefore, leather producers work far in advance of the rest of the fashion industry.

- A major problem for the U.S. industry is the rapid increase in imports of hides and skins as well as finished products made from leather.

- The fur industry has undergone a change in emphasis from being mink oriented to being fur oriented.

- Over 90 percent of the fur processors and fur product manufacturers are located in New York City.

- Because the industry has many small enterprises, major trade associations like the American Fur Information and Industry Council carry out most marketing activities for the industry.

.... REVIEW QUESTIONS

1. Name four natural fibers. Which ones are produced in the United States?

2. What are the two types of synthetic fibers? Which fiber was the first to be produced synthetically?

3. Define *greige goods*.

4. What kinds of qualities are given to fabrics in the finishing process?

5. What geographic changes have occurred in the location of U.S. textile production?

6. Define vertical integration.

7. What is derived demand? How does it affect the production of textiles?

8. What are the major competitive sources for the U.S. leather industry?

9. Explain the change in customer focus undertaken by the fur industry.

10. How does the Endangered Species Act affect the fur and leather industries?

.... RESEARCH AND PROJECTS

1. Even with extensive competition from fake furs and endangered species laws enacted in the past years, the fur industry has been able to grow tremendously. Explain why this is so.

2. Outline the collective problems facing all the sectors of the primary markets with regard to foreign competition. What countries are the major competitors for the U.S. primary markets?

3. Using information obtained from the various trade associations and examples located in magazines and newspapers, demonstrate derived demand as it is used by the segments of the primary markets.

4. Research the future of each of the segments of the primary markets as described in the current edition of the *U.S. Industrial Outlook* manual. Cite changes in production figures within the last five years. Based on the data you have collected, make recommendations for improving domestic sales.

5. Select one of the many primary market trade associations listed in the second Industry Feature section in this chapter. Write for information about the organization and ask for examples of their fashion forecasts.

6. Reading various fashion magazines, locate examples of furs other than mink that are popular. Show how, through fashion design, fur has truly become "fun" to wear.

Part Four

· ·

TODAY'S FASHION INDUSTRIES

· · · · · · · · In Part Three we learned about the development of marketing strategies from the earliest production of apparel in the United States and how social, political, and economic forces contributed to the growth of the great clothing industries. Part Four details the specific industries and provides insight into the production and marketing of the garments and accessories we wear.

CHAPTER 10

•••

Creating and Marketing Womenswear

•••••••• LEARNING OBJECTIVES

After reading this chapter, you should be able to:

- Describe the characteristics, methods of designing, operation, and marketing activities of womenswear manufacturers.
- Discuss the problems facing New York's Garment Center and locate other centers of production and sales.
- Identify the six fashion seasons, define market weeks, and cite when they occur.
- Outline the steps used in the design and production of clothing.

•••••••• PERFORMANCE OUTCOME

After reading this chapter, you should be able to:

- Navigate through New York's Garment Center to locate various showrooms for different categories of fashion goods.
- Speak the industry jargon.
- Identify various departments and specialty stores in terms of price line, size, and type of apparel in the retail fashion marketplace.

In the United States, producing fashion merchandise is big business. The fashion industry ranks among the top ten industries in the United States. It manufactures a vast array of products, generating annual sales of nearly $120 billion.

It is an industry made up of more than 20,000 firms. Located throughout all 50 states, these operations provide jobs for nearly 1 million workers. There is an unusual mix of giant and small firms, with huge corporations and conglomerates existing alongside small family-owned operations and partnerships. The industry is highly volatile—sudden style changes and customer fashion whims occur overnight, and success or failure is governed by the ability of a producer to accurately predict those changes and whims and to satisfy them.

In all areas—men's, women's, and children's wear and accessories—the nature of the industry is changing. Most of the changes can be observed in its largest and most influential sector: women's wear.

CHARACTERISTICS OF THE WOMENSWEAR INDUSTRY

The production of womenswear is the very heart of this country's garment industry. It accounts for nearly two-thirds of all the clothes made and generates over $115 billion in revenues each year. Besides being the largest segment of the ready-to-wear business, it is also the most dynamic, fast-paced, and aggressively competitive portion of the "rag" business.

Womenswear also provides fashion direction for the entire industry. Colors, silhouettes, and themes all begin here. No matter what kind of apparel or accessories one makes or sells, one must continuously monitor the fashion happenings in the womenswear market.

Location

Over 3,000 firms are engaged in the production of womenswear. Most of them are located in the Middle Atlantic region, with New York, Pennsylvania, and New Jersey as the leading states.

New York City is considered the "fashion capital" of the United States. The New York metropolitan area is responsible for 60 to 70 percent of the country's annual production of womenswear, and the apparel industry is the city's primary private employer.

The Garment Center and world famous Seventh Avenue are located in midtown Manhattan (see Figure 10–1 and Industry Feature entitled "New York's Fashion Markets"). Although it is a relatively small geographic area, it contains the headquarters and/or showrooms for nearly every manufacturer of fashion apparel.

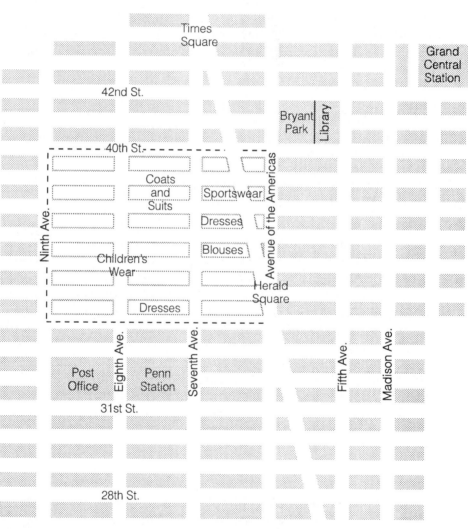

FIGURE 10-1 New York City's Garment Center

New York's Fashion Markets

To an unfamiliar visitor, New York City seems chaotic, unorganized, and unmaneuverable. This is not so for those who are visiting New York's Garment Center and related fashion markets. When buyers come to town, they discover that all of their particular resources may be found in a few short blocks or even in a few clustered buildings. Below is a partial listing of the most representative locations for each of the specialized areas of New York's fashion markets.

New York City is also endowed with a heavy concentration of allied industries that are essential to apparel manufacturing. These allied trades are primarily located in and around the Garment Center, and include producers of belts, buttons, needles, pins, hooks and eyes, and other notions; and also embroidery, tucking, pleating, and trimming firms.

Women's and Children's Apparel

Couture and higher-priced lines	500, 512, 530, and 550 Seventh Avenue
Moderate and budget-priced lines	Located in Chinatown district of the Garment Center, mostly in 1400, 1407, 1410, 1411, 1441 Broadway
Sportswear	1407 Broadway
Bridal	1375 Broadway
Furs	Seventh Avenue mostly between Thirtieth and Thirty-fourth Streets
Underwear and intimate apparel	Madison Avenue between Twenty-eighth and Thirty-fourth Streets
Children's wear	112 W. 34th Street

Men's and Boys' Apparel

Men's clothing and outerwear	Seventh Avenue, mostly between Fourteenth and Twenty-fourth Streets
Men's furnishings	The Empire State Building
Boys' clothing and outerwear	Madison to Eighth Avenue between Fourteenth and Thirty-fourth Streets

Fashion Accessories

Shoes	Thirty-fourth and Broadway; also the Empire State Building

Handbags	Madison Avenue and Broadway between Thirtieth and Thirty-fourth Streets
Costume jewelry	Fifth Avenue between Thirtieth and Fortieth Streets
Fine jewelry	Fifth and Sixth Avenues between Forty-eighth and Fifty-third Streets; also Nassau and Fulton Streets in downtown Manhattan
Gloves	Madison and Fifth Avenues between Thirty-fourth and Forty-second Streets
Millinery	Fifth and Sixth Avenue between Thirty-eighth and Thirty-ninth Streets; also upper Fifties.

Although, in terms of fashion, New York City is "where it's at," an ever-increasing number of firms are shifting part of their operations—primarily that of garment construction—outside of the New York area.

Apparel production has shifted to other areas of New York State, as well as to locations in Pennsylvania, Massachusetts, New Jersey, and Connecticut. The most recent trend, however, has been to leave the Northeast completely. Many firms have gone to the South or the West, while many, because of the savings involved, have moved their production operations entirely out of the United States.

Some New York firms have also moved or expanded their *sales* and/or *distribution* operations. Most have gone to Los Angeles, Chicago, Dallas, St. Louis, Cleveland, Kansas City, or Miami, cities long established as secondary apparel centers, housing many of the nation's leading manufacturers. Los Angeles, for instance, serves as the home of all the top swimwear makers. Although they do not have as great a concentration of resources as New York, these centers draw an impressive number of buyers who welcome the "close-to-home" accessibility of these regional markets. The increasing acceptance of these markets by retailers is but one of many reasons given by New York firms for shifting all or part of their operations to other areas. Here are some others:

- First and foremost is *cost*. Labor, overhead, taxes, and plant construction costs are all cheaper out of town.

- New York space is both expensive and severely limited. The space that is available is old and in need of renovation. Construction of new facilities is virtually nonexistent.

- New York's readily available supply of skilled and semiskilled immigrant labor—traditionally attracted to the needle trades—is dwindling. The simple styling of many of today's garments, especially moderate- and budget-priced goods, can be handled adequately by the less skilled, cheaper labor found outside of New York. And, should detailed work be necessary, it can often be done less expensively by foreign labor.

- Improved *transportation*, particularly trucking, makes it easier and more reasonable to distribute from out-of-town production locations. The Garment Center is not designed to accommodate the easy loading and unloading of trucks; and furthermore, shipping costs within the Metropolitan Area are exorbitant.

- Finally, since the garment industry has traditionally separated the design, marketing, and production aspects of the business, geographic separation is plausible and in many ways facilitates rather than hinders the garment-making process.

Although New York remains the country's unquestioned design center and nearly two-thirds of all women's apparel is still produced there, these reasons make it apparent that New York may some day have to share the title of "America's apparel center" with other geographic locations.

Structure

Today, the bulk of the 3,000 firms producing womenswear are small, privately owned corporations or partnerships employing fewer than 20 people. They are highly specialized in terms of their product lines. Most have sales of under $100 million.

At the other end of the spectrum are the giants with their many divisions. For example, the VF Corporation produces a wide variety of apparel in its four divisions. Its most famous division and brand name is Vanity Fair intimate apparel. VF also markets Jantzen sportswear and Lee and Wrangler jeans. In total, VF's annual sales volume is over $2 billion. Other giant apparel makers include Levi-Strauss, Liz Claiborne, and Murjani International.

The industry is still fertile territory for the aspiring entrepreneur with limited capital; easy entry has long been a characteristic of this industry.

Unfortunately, because of the fickleness of fashion, the industry is plagued with an unusually high bankruptcy rate. It averages about 18 percent a year. The recent increase in imports has added to the industry's high mortality rate, and each year there are fewer firms in operation than there were the year before.

The industry is also undergoing a change in its method of production—shifting from "inside" to "outside" shops. The concept of separating the various manufacturing processes is not new. These trade terms refer to firms that are specifically classified as manufacturers, jobbers, or contractors. *Manufacturers* that handle all phases of production are known as *inside shops*. In recent years, the number of these firms has declined, to be replaced by **jobbers** or *outside shops*, firms that handle all activities but the actual sewing, and by contractors hired to do the sewing.

The reasons for these changes are simple: First, the jobber and contractor are specialists, each handling the aspects of apparel production they know best. Because their operations are separate, they are naturally smaller, requiring less capital and labor to operate. Their smaller labor force minimizes personnel training, expenses, and problems. Second, the jobber makes use of the contractor's services only when those services are needed, thus increasing efficiency. The contractor, meanwhile, is free to receive work from more than one jobber, fully utilizing its capacities. All these features turn into advantages that reduce the operating and labor costs of all concerned. These reduced costs result in higher profits and lower retail prices, benefiting producer and consumer alike.

In both inside and outside shops, either the *task* or *piecework* system of operations is used. Under the task system, a team of workers—a baster, sewing machine operator, finisher, and presser—is responsible for one complete garment. This system is generally used for higher priced merchandise. Under the piecework system, also known as *specialization,* an operator works on just one part of the garment. For instance, one operator makes buttonholes, one sews on collars, and another sets in sleeves.

Although the primary advantage of the piecework method is its low cost and simple training requirements, critics charge it causes a decline in quality and craftsmanship, resulting in inferior merchandise. Still, the pressure to reduce costs in order to remain competitive makes this method an attractive alternative and the one most widely used today.

Labor

Finding good, inexpensive labor is difficult in any business. For the garment industry this is a special concern because labor costs can and do run as high as 50 to 55 percent of the final cost of a garment. The industry has heavily relied on women and on immigrant labor; these groups represent nearly 80 percent of the employees in the industry. The scarcity and the rising cost of good labor have spurred research into new and faster production techniques, particularly among the giants in the field. Such devices as laser beam cutting instruments and computer-assisted manufacturing (CAM) and computer-assisted design (CAD) are already in use. Unfortunately, in spite of intense research, apparel production is still a mechanized but nonautomated industry because so many firms are too small to bear the expense of upgrading.

Efficient, affordable labor is not only a concern of management; it is a concern of the industry's union as well. The International Ladies' Garment Workers' Union, which represents nearly 90 percent of the workers in both women's and children's wear, has long recognized the importance of working with—rather than against—management for industry growth.

Both management and labor groups have established learning programs and scholarships to encourage young people to enter the field of fashion. Working through apprenticeship programs and with various educational institutions on the secondary and postsecondary levels, both are hoping to increase and improve the supply of labor the industry needs to survive.

METHODS OF OPERATION

In the "rag" business, the start of every season represents a new challenge, a new beginning. To manufacturers, most of the styles, fabrics, and colors that sold well a few short months, weeks, or even days ago are ancient history. They are well aware that, to stay in business, at least two, but more often four or five separate times a year they must produce something new and exciting. These times correspond to the industry's six fashion seasons.

Fashion Seasons

In essence, **fashion seasons** are selling seasons. Each season brings some change in the styling details of fashion merchandise, and by having so many seasons, both manufacturers and retailers hope to profitably entice consumers into increasing the frequency of their fashion purchases.

Although manufacturers are constantly updating their collections or lines and retailers may receive new merchandise weekly or even daily, the fanfare of "out with the old, in with the new" corresponds basically to the following demarcations:

- *Fall (Fall II)/Back to School.* Most important fashion season. Most major style innovations and a major transformation in color and fabric occur at this time.
- *Holiday.* A minor season. The most successful of the fall fashion trends are refined and interpreted in dressier, more formal wear.
- *Resort.*[1] Also a minor season. Primarily a preview for summer lines and especially important to certain sportswear manufacturers such as swimwear makers. Some high-priced manufacturers present their Holiday and Resort lines together.
- *Spring.* Second most important fashion season. Of particular importance to designer houses and dress manufacturers. Many volume and medium-priced manufacturers combine their spring and summer lines.
- *Summer.* Designer, dress, and sportswear manufacturers—especially swimwear makers—are usually those presenting separate summer lines. Silhouette trends are often tested at this time, and successful ones are carried into fall merchandise.
- *Transitional/Early Fall*[1] *(Fall I).* A minor season. Early fall trends are tested as a preview for Fall II.

Specialization of Product

All apparel manufacturers specialize according to *size, type of apparel,* and *price.* Even the giants follow this formula, maintaining separate divisions for each type of merchandise they produce. By maintaining these divisions or—as in the case of the small firm—by concentrating on a narrow product line, producers can more effectively service and cater to their immediate and primary customer: the retailer.

Retailers have organized their operations *departmentally.* They have done so to meet the special needs of a wide array of people. For instance, a woman who is looking for a medium-priced dress in a reg-

---

[1]These two seasons are sometimes referred to as checkout seasons. *Checkout* is the industry term used for testing market reactions to styling changes by monitoring which styles consumers buy.

ular size will go to the department featuring moderately priced misses dresses, bypassing higher priced departments or those with junior sizes.

In terms of *size specialization* for women's wear, the following categories are used by manufacturers. Unfortunately, there is no industrywide standardization of sizes. This means that the dimensions of a size vary from one manufacturer to another, and it explains why a customer may have to buy a size larger or smaller, depending on which manufacturer made the garment.

> *Misses* (even numbered sizes from 2 to 14). Garments in this category are cut for the mature, fuller figure types.
> *Juniors* (odd numbered sizes from 3 to 15). These garments are designed for the slender figure type and younger customer.
> *Petites/Junior Petites*. These sizes are aimed at the smaller framed woman under 5'4" tall.
> *Women's* (even numbered sizes from 16 to 20 and 36 to 52). These are apparel sizes for the larger sized women.
> *Half sizes* (sizes 12½ to 26½). These sizes are for women who are short waisted.

Of the categories listed, misses is the most significant in terms of sales volume. It represents the majority of women's apparel sold. The petite category has over 45 million customers, making it the second most important category. However, the fastest growing size category in terms of sales volume is women's sizes.

Today, demographically speaking, nearly 25 percent of all adult females in the United States wear size 14 or larger, a fact that the fashion industry discovered in the mid-1980s. Prior to that, large-sized customers found it impossible to find fashionable clothing in the marketplace. Only a few specialty stores such as Lane Bryant carried these sizes. Most of the styles offered were without much fashion savvy.

When it was discovered that these women represented such an important market segment in terms of demand and purchasing power, manufacturers began to produce garments that fit the business and social lifestyles of these women. At the same time, mainstream retailers began devoting floor space and creating departments to cater to this clientele. Liz Claiborne introduced the Elizabeth line. Spiegel included a separate section in their mail-order catalog, and the Forgotten Women specialty chain began opening outlets throughout the country.

Specialization by type of apparel refers to the classification of goods in terms of their appearance and/or function. There are nine categories, each representing a manufacturing specialty:

- *Dresses.* Either one- or two-piece. Dress manufacturers also make two- and three-piece ensembles that include a dress with a jacket or coat.
- *Sportswear.* Pants, shorts, tops, jackets, sweaters, blouses, active sportswear, and coordinated separates.
- *Swimwear and beachwear.*
- *Maternity.*
- *Intimate Apparel.* Undergarments, lingerie, and robes.
- *Outerwear.* Coats, suits, pantsuits, jackets, and rainwear.
- *Evening wear.*
- *Bridal.* Also includes bridesmaids and mother-of-the-bride dresses.
- *Uniforms.* For workers in medicine, dentistry, airlines, restaurants, and other commercial sectors.

Finally, manufacturers *specialize by price lines,* producing merchandise that is expected to retail to the consumer in one of four price ranges:

- *Designer.* The industry's most expensive apparel, this category features prestige name manufacturers and designer labels such as Galanos, Donna Karan, Ralph Lauren, Geoffrey Beene, and Calvin Klein.
- *Bridge.* Less expensive but fashion forward apparel, which includes designer secondary lines. Examples are DKNY (Donna Karan), Anne Klein II, Ellen Tracy, and Adrienne Vittadini.
- *Better.* Medium prices, classic designs. Lines such as Liz Claiborne, Evan Picone, Jones New York, and J. H. Collectibles are included in this category.
- *Moderate.* Refers to medium-priced goods and includes well-known manufacturer brands such as Koret, White Stag, and Russ Togs.
- *Budget.* The least expensively priced, but most widely offered merchandise. No major designer or manufacturer brand name identification. Includes private label and house brand items.

Specializing in a *type,* a *size,* or a *price range* of apparel offers a manufacturer several advantages. To begin with, it gives the firm's name and its product fast and easy recognition from store buyers and consumers alike. The firm of Levi Strauss, for instance, became famous for specializing in blue denim jeans—a *type* of merchandise.

Other manufacturers like White Stag (makers of good but well-*priced* sportswear) and Junior Sophisticates (known for their specially *sized* junior clothes) made their reputations by being "priced right" or because they "fit right."

Specialization also helps a manufacturer service the customer. By specializing and concentrating solely on the needs of a particular market, it can more effectively service that market.

THE DESIGNING PROCESS

The first process in the production of women's wear is the *designing process*. A person who conceives or interprets styles of wearing apparel for men, women, and children is called a *fashion designer*. Designers translate creative thoughts into visible forms by using the basic elements of design: silhouette, texture, color, detail, and trim.

Because of its creative aspects, an aura of mystery and eccentricity often—and erroneously—surrounds the profession of fashion design. In truth there is little mystery in how designers perform their jobs. Whether seeking sources of design inspiration or performing the highly skilled techniques of sketching, cutting, or draping, most designers develop a methodic, almost scientific approach to the art of fashion design.

In order to continuously develop and create new designs, a designer requires a great deal of stimulation or inspiration. Past styles that were successful are updated; past trends that are still important are repeated. Designers also review the work of other designers and keep tabs on what's happening in the industry by reviewing domestic and foreign publications, such as *Women's Wear Daily* and *L'Officiel,* and by visiting trade shows and international fairs.

The textile industry can also help to stimulate creativity. Well before creating a collection, designers familiarize themselves with the new fabrics of the season. They not only look for new colors and textures but new technological developments as well.

Designers also draw from the events that surround them. In Part One we learned how such things as political, social, and economic events, as well as changing lifestyles, influence fashion. A good designer watches these developments, understands how these forces can govern fashion changes, and then designs accordingly.

Perhaps the single, most important source of inspiration for a designer is the customer. Top designers like Ralph Lauren and Calvin Klein freely admit that they are inspired by their clients. Calvin Klein, whose forte is designing clothes that are typically American in look,

·········· TABLE 10-1   Typical Timetable for Producing Seasonal Lines

Season	Designing Begins in	Market Week for Buyers	Delivery to Retailer Completed by
Fall I	January	March	Early August
Fall II	January	April/May	October
Holiday*	January		Mid-October
Cruise/Resort	June	August	January
Spring	September	November	Mid-April
Summer	November	Late January	Mid-May

*NOTE: No separate market week for holiday lines

remarked that he was mainly "interested in the young American woman and I *watch her*."[2]

Designers must create three to five collections a year, depending upon the firm they work with. The work on each collection begins at least three months before the collection is presented to store buyers, and 12 to 18 months before it is bought by the consumer (see Table 10–1 and Industry Feature on producing the fall line). For example, a fall collection, which is shown to buyers in May and shipped sometime between July and August, is begun no later than January. Some firms start to plan and order fabric requirements as much as 1½ years before the merchandise is presented to the consumer.

Once designers have availed themselves of all the information that contributes toward the creating of a design—fabrics, trends, and prior failures and successes—they then proceed to the job of designing a collection or line.

Designers who produce original work, the innovators of the business, begin by draping or sketching a design. Those who work with fabric, drape and cut on a dressmaker form until their ideas are formalized. Those who prefer to set their ideas down on paper make many rough sketches before settling on a final choice.

When an idea is finalized, the designer passes a swatched rough sketch to a sketcher for a final drawing. The sketch is then given to the assistant designer, who cuts a muslin pattern of the design. Once the muslin pattern is approved by the designer, the assistant uses the pattern to cut out the fabric chosen for the design. The final garment is then sewed by a sample hand, who returns it to the designer and the heads of the firm for approval. Once a sample is completed and

[2]Reprinted by permission from *Time*, The Weekly Newsmagazine; Copyright, Time Inc. (March 22, 1976), p. 67.

approved by the heads of the firm, it is passed on to the production department and becomes part of the new line.

Types of Designers

There are four types of designers in the American fashion industry. The couture or high-fashion designer, the moderate or popular-price market designer, the stylist, and the freelance designer.

Couture or High-Fashion Designer
Couturier is a French word referring to a person involved in *couture*, the business of designing, making, and selling the finest *custom-made*, *custom-fitted* clothes for individual clients. This type of operation has been the backbone of the French fashion industry for over 100 years, but in America there is no custom-made clothing industry to speak of and, therefore, no true "couture." All American designers are in the business of creating ready-to-wear. There are those, however, who produce high-fashion merchandise and whose originality has raised their status to the level of the French couture. To emphasize their distinctive position of leadership within the industry, the wearing apparel created by these designers is referred to as *couture ready-to-wear*.

The Moderate and Popular-Priced Market Designer
Most designers work in the moderately priced markets. The majority of the firms in these markets produce new but "safe" fashion apparel rather than trend-setting high fashion. Though couture designers gain wider recognition and fame, designers at this level receive much satisfaction from their work. Their job is constantly challenging, as they try to produce new fashion with mass appeal.

Stylists
Many firms that produce popular-priced or budget-priced apparel base their collections on styles that have already met with success. To choose and adapt these styles to the new season, they use the talents of a **stylist** instead of a designer. These fashion experts look inside and outside their firms for styles that catch on immediately with the public and sell in great quantity. They then incorporate new versions of these styles into their lines. Stylists primarily copy and adapt more expensive designs to their price range. These versions are referred to as **knockoffs.** Because designs are not copyrighted, this copying or **style piracy** is a perfectly acceptable way of doing business among lower priced manufacturers on Seventh Avenue.

Freelance Designer

Freelance designers sell sketches of their designs to manufacturers. They design either high-fashion originals or adaptations of current styles. The choice depends entirely upon their ability and the requirements of their manufacturer clients. Once a freelance designer sells a sketch to a manufacturer, the designer's responsibility for that particular design is complete.

Other Careers in Design

The four basic types of designers are described in this chapter. There are, however, other career opportunities available in fashion design. The Industry Feature entitled "Career Opportunities in Fashion Design" lists positions that often serve as an apprenticeship for beginning designers, but in many firms they are important enough to merit consideration as ultimate career goals.

THE MANUFACTURING PROCESS

The second process in the production of womenswear is the *manufacturing process.* In most cases, the manufacturing process does not begin until prospective buyers have seen a line and have placed orders for specific styles. Only the "hot numbers"—those styles that receive enough orders—go into production.

In this respect, the garment industry is different from most others. Very little, if any, inventory is stockpiled. The rule of thumb for most firms is "don't cut the goods until you have the paper," which simply means that you don't begin the production of any style until a written order has been received from a buyer. This rule gives the manufacturer tremendous flexibility to produce only those styles that it intends to sell. On the other hand, this policy makes the production period very short: Goods have to be produced and shipped within three to eight weeks.

The actual production process begins with the patternmaker, who takes the paper pattern pieces used in construction of the sample and *grades* them into other sizes. That is, the sample pattern (usually an average size) is mathematically reduced and enlarged into each of the sizes that the style will be made in.

The pattern pieces are then arranged on a large piece of paper called a *marker.* This is a very important step because it determines fabric costs. The closer the pieces are fitted together, the less fabric is used. The pieces, however, must follow a careful arrangement. The

Career Opportunities in Fashion Design

Fashion Design On-the-Job Training

When entering the field, it is essential to choose firms that produce the type of fashion you are interested in. This initial choice is most important since experience usually dictates future jobs. For example, a young assistant designer who has held a few jobs with a popular-priced sportswear firm might find it difficult to enter a coat and suit house; and that same assistant might find it equally difficult to "trade up" to a job with a better (or designer) sportswear firm.

Assistant Designer. This position requires top technical knowledge and skill. An assistant interprets the ideas of the designer by making the first muslin pattern of the design and then cutting out the original fabric sample.

Patternmaker. When a sample of a design is acceptable in terms of appearance and fit, a patternmaker "grades" the pattern, making a separate pattern for each of the sizes in which the design is to be manufactured.

Sample Maker. The sample maker is the top dressmaker of a firm. He or she constructs the first sample of a design. Coat and suit houses employ tailors instead of dressmakers, while firms producing a wide range of apparel employ both.

Sketcher. Working from the rough sketches of the designer, the sketcher makes the final drawing of a design. These drawings are used for reference by the assistant designer and the sample maker during the process of making the sample. The swatched drawings are then placed in a binder for a showroom book, providing the firm and its clients with a complete record of each style in the designer's current collection.

Formal Training

Training for any of these jobs is available at both the secondary and college levels. Not all high schools, of course, offer vocational training in patternmaking, draping, and similar subjects, but there are quite a few that do. Those schools often equip students with enough training and knowledge to make it possible for them to enter the industry directly from high school. But for those whose ultimate goal is a career in design, we recommend the marvelous education and training offered by many specialized college courses throughout the United States.

Month	Dec.	Jan.	Feb.	March	April	May	June	July	Aug.	Sept.	Oct.	Nov.
Step 1	Fabric Preview and Selection											
Step 2		Begin to Design and Sketch										
Step 3			Swatch and Begin to Make Samples									
Step 4				Continue Making Samples; Key Styles Selected								
Step 5					Prepare for Openings; Early Production Begins							
Step 6						Openings and Market Week; Retail Orders Placed						
Step 7							Major Production Begins					
Step 8								Production Continues; Begin In-Store Promotions				
Step 9									Major Shipping Period; More In-Store Promotion			
Step 10										Shipping Continues; Reorders Period		
Step 11											Delivery Complete	
Step 12												Begin Preparation for Summer Line

arrangement must take the fabric grain (the lengthwise thread of the fabric), the matching of stripes, plaids, and other pattern characteristics of the fabric into consideration. Several copies of each original marker are made, and then each is placed on top of fabric that has been *laid up.*

Laying up the fabric is also a critical step. It involves rolling out the fabric on long cutting tables—one layer on top of another. The fabric must be perfectly straight, directly in line with the piece underneath and—in the case of patterned fabrics such as plaids—each layer must be identical to the one below.

After laying up anywhere from 50 to 150 layers of fabric, the marker is placed on top and the *cutting* begins. This step is done by skilled craftspeople using an electric cutting knife. Cutters who work quickly and accurately mean a great deal to the manufacturer and are often the highest paid of the firm's production staff.

The next step involves *assembling* the necessary pieces of the garment. The cut pieces are *bundled* according to size and shipped to sewing operators. After the garment is sewn together, it is *finished,* that is, all of the small and final construction details such as hems and buttonholes are completed. Then it is *pressed, inspected,* and *bagged* (placed on hangers and covered in plastic). The completed garments are then sent to the firm's shipping facilities where orders are *packed* and made ready for shipping.

The entire process is repeated for styles that become "runners," the term applied to reordered goods.

THE MARKETING PROCESS

Designing and producing salable merchandise are only part of a manufacturer's job. The other part is marketing it profitably. Because the *marketing process* is required of all manufacturers, regardless of the type of product involved, many marketing procedures are standard. But certain marketing techniques used by apparel producers are unique. These include their methods of selling goods to retailers, their financial arrangements, and certain aspects of their advertising and promotion.

Selling Goods to Retailers

One of the sales methods manufacturers employ to sell their products to retailers is road or territorial sales personnel, who visit retail establishments showing the manufacturer's line. This method is quite expensive and, more important, time-consuming. Its use, therefore, is limited to very large firms that desire and can afford national distribution and to manufacturers of "basic" merchandise, such as undergarments and hosiery, which does not experience fast fashion changes.

The majority of garment manufacturers find it easier and decidedly less expensive to maintain showrooms in New York or in the various regional merchandise marts and have the retailers send buyers to them. This method has several advantages. It gives the manufacturer the flexibility to add and delete styles from a collection because of instant and direct buyer feedback; and it maintains the tradition of presenting the new lines to all retailers at the same time during certain specified periods of the year called **market weeks.** Market weeks are held for each of the fashion seasons and are timed for the convenience of both the manufacturers and retailers. Table 10–2 lists the approximate times of the market weeks held in New York.

Buyers whose operations are located some distance from the markets visit manufacturers only during market weeks. Buyers who are located close to the market can visit their resources on a monthly or even weekly basis. Very large retailers such as Sears or J. C. Penney, whose orders are in the thousands of units, plan their upcoming market week purchases by working with their resources much earlier than the scheduled market weeks.

Traditionally, sending the buyers "to the market" meant going to New York City. But since apparel markets with permanent manufacturer showrooms have emerged in other parts of the country, buyers may now opt to go to more than one market (see Table 10–3).

Visiting manufacturer showrooms, particularly those of designer and high-priced lines, may mean seeing an elaborate fashion show

· · · · · · · · **TABLE 10-2   New York Market Weeks**

Fashion Season	General Timing*
Summer	Late January
Early Fall (Fall I)	March
Fall/Back to school (Fall II)	Late April or Early May
Holiday**	
Cruise/Resort	August
Spring	Late October or early November

*Dates vary each year

**No separate market week for holiday lines.

Part Four   Today's Fashion Industries

•••••••• TABLE 10-3   Regional Markets for Womenswear

City	Facility	Number of Showrooms
Atlanta, Ga.	Atlanta Apparel Mart	600
Birmingham, Ala.	Civic Center	200
Boston, Mass.	Bayside Expo Center	300
Charlotte, Va.	Carolina Trade Mart	225
Chicago, Ill.	Chicago Market Apparel Center	800
Dallas, Tex.	Dallas Apparel Center	1500
Denver, Colo.	Denver Merchandise Mart	300
Kansas City, Kans.	Kansas City Market Center	200
Los Angeles, Calif.	California Mart	2000
Miami, Fla.	Miami International Merchandise Mart	300
Minneapolis, Minn.	Hyatt Merchandise Mart	350
Pittsburgh, Pa.	Greater Pittsburgh Merchandise Expo Center	300
Portland, Wash.	The Galleria	—
San Francisco, Calif.	Trade Show Center	800
Seattle, Wash.	Seattle Trade Center	370

complete with music, models, and much fanfare. The more typical buyer's visit, however, involves a private "off-the-rack" (on hangers) presentation of a line by a specialist—the showroom salesperson.

Usually, a salesperson is assigned to a buyer, and after several seasons, the salesperson develops a knowledge of the type of merchandise and services that buyer needs. Specifically, a salesperson's job consists of "showing the line," providing buyers with information on trends, and helping to plan and coordinate any joint advertising and promotional ventures.

Good salespeople are essential to the manufacturer. In addition to their important selling role, they also provide invaluable feedback. This information can help a manufacturer refine a line and anticipate the future demand of a style or a trend. Showroom personnel, therefore, are usually well paid, working on a salary plus commission basis.

Financial Arrangements

Garment manufacturers rely heavily on a technique known as *factoring* to obtain the necessary cash for operational expenses. Factoring involves a third party—a factor—who enters into the sales agreement between a retail buyer and a manufacturer. It may be simply described as follows: When a buyer writes up an order for merchandise and gives it to the manufacturer, the manufacturer needs cash for materials and labor to begin production. The manufacturer obtains the cash by "selling" the order to a factor, who pays the manufacturer a *discounted* amount of the total sum of the order. When payment is due, the retailer sends the full amount to the factor.

This system is most suitable for the garment industry. It gives maximum flexibility to the manufacturer and reduces the investment requirements, allowing it to produce up-to-the-minute styles at a reasonable price.

Advertising and Promotion

Until several years ago, the advertising and promotional activities of manufacturers were minimal. These activities were primarily the responsibility of the retailers. Now, large and small manufacturers alike engage in several kinds of advertising and promotion.

There has been a considerable increase in *direct* advertising to the consumer; some manufacturer brand names such as Jordache have become as famous as those of leading designers. As a result consumers place less importance on store labels. But the de-emphasis of the store label does not imply that manufacturers and retailers do not work together to promote fashion. *Cooperative* advertising, where each shares the limelight and the advertising costs, remains especially important for both.

A manufacturer may also supply *promotional aids* to the retailer. These include display materials and fixtures, mailing pieces for charge customers, hang tags for garments, photographs and mats for newspaper advertising, and selling aids such as training sessions for salespeople on current fashion trends. Finally, some manufacturers provide merchandise; props; scripts; and, in some cases, even a commentator for presenting in-store fashion shows.

Some of the larger firms also maintain aggressive public relations departments. These publicists use many techniques to bring a firm's name to the attention of the consumer; probably one of the most familiar is that of supplying television personalities with a wardrobe in exchange for an airwave mention or "plug" of the firm's name.

**fashion seasons   knockoff   style piracy   marker   hot number   runners
market weeks   factoring   jobber   contractor   piece rate   couture
designer   stylist   freelance designer**

.... HIGHLIGHTS OF THE CHAPTER

- The majority of womenswear manufacturers are located in New York City's Garment Center. But Los Angeles, Chicago, Dallas, St. Louis, Cleveland, Kansas City, and Miami are growing secondary apparel markets.

- To service the similarly defined departments of retailers, apparel manufacturing is categorized by price, size, or type of apparel. Large firms often produce merchandise in several of these categories, but most apparel manufacturers specialize in one.

- The production process of apparel involves almost a dozen technical steps, which include patternmaking, cutting, machine and hand sewing, pressing, and packing operations.

- Apparel manufacturers use standard marketing procedures to sell their products, but a few of their procedures are indigenous to the apparel industry. These include the methods apparel producers use to sell to retailers; the arrangements they make to finance their business; and some of the techniques they use to promote and advertise their products.

- Buyers of fashion merchandise visit manufacturers several times a year during designated market weeks. At that time, expert showroom salespeople present the season's new lines, selling and advising buyers of the type of merchandise that will be most salable for their stores.

- Due to an increase in the advertising and sales promotion activities of manufacturers, consumer recognition and demand of manufacturer brand names have markedly increased.

.... REVIEW QUESTIONS

1. Where is the fashion capital of the United States? What is this area called, and how is it organized?

2. Where are some of the secondary apparel centers located?

3. Mention the reasons why these regional markets have become important.

4. Describe the structure of the womenswear industry.

5. Name the six fashion seasons found in women's wear. Which are major and which are minor seasons?

6. How do womenswear manufacturers specialize in marketing their products?

7. What are the three processes in the production of womenswear?

8. What are the four types of designers who work in womenswear? How do they differ from one another?

9. What are market weeks? When approximately does each occur for the various fashion seasons?

10. Define factoring. What are its advantages to womenswear producers?

.... RESEARCH AND PROJECTS

1. Describe the activities involved in each of the three phases of garment production.

2. Procedures for marketing womenswear are very different from those used in other industries. Describe how and why this is so.

3. There are problems facing the Garment Center and the industry in general. List the major ones and offer some possible solutions.

4. Using the latest editions of the *U.S. Industrial Outlook* manual, research the future of the women's wear industry in terms of New York's Garment Center and changing national geography.[3]

5. If you were a womenswear garment manufacturer, explain how you would specialize your product in terms of size, price line, and type of garment. What kind of shop would you operate?

6. From Table 10–3, locate the nearest regional market to your hometown. Write to them asking for literature, and request a tour of the facility.

7. Arrange an interview with a buyer who goes to regional markets and to New York. Discuss the differences of each location in terms of the buying trips. Prepare a written summary of your conversation.

[3]Industry and Trade Association, U.S. Department of Commerce, *U.S. Industrial Outlook* (Washington, D.C.: U.S. Government Printing Office, current year).

CHAPTER 11

....

Creating and Marketing Men's Apparel

.... LEARNING OBJECTIVES

After reading this chapter, you should be able to:

- Outline the circumstances that led to the rise of American menswear design as we know it today.
- Describe the characteristics, methods of production, designing, operation, and marketing activities of menswear manufacturers.
- Identify the fashion seasons in menswear, and cite when they occur.
- Be familiar with how menswear is distributed and promoted.

.... PERFORMANCE OUTCOME

After reading this chapter, you should be able to:

- Contrast and compare the men's apparel industry and the women's apparel industry in terms of structure, methods of operation, fashion seasons, and promotional methods.
- Know when and where major menswear trade shows are held and be able to contact trade associations and publications for fashion information.
- Identify major menswear brand names, designer labels, and licensed merchandise in the marketplace.

• •

In 1789, when George Washington took the oath of office as the first president of our new nation, he was considered to be in the height of fashion. He wore a silk brocade coat, velvet britches, silk stockings, a shirt with handmade lace, a wig, and diamond-buckled high-heeled shoes. As was the case for womenswear, Washington's wardrobe was inspired by the latest French fashions being worn at the Court of Versailles.

After the French Revolution, it was no longer acceptable to wear such elaborate garb. Menswear took on a simple, tailored look and fashion inspiration shifted from France to England. Beau Brummel and the tailors of Savile Row set the fashion standards.

As lifestyles became more mobile, comfortable, practical clothing replaced the stiff, padded styles of the Victorian period. Now menswear was concerned with function and practicality rather than glamour. The English influence remained strong during the 1920s in the United States. Items such as the polo coat and button-down collars came right off the playing fields and into men's everyday wardrobes. Fit and tailoring replaced bold colors as important elements of design.

This trend continued into the 1930s and 1940s with Hollywood setting the fashion pace. Stars such as Fred Astaire, Cary Grant, and Clark Gable fostered looks of elegance and sophistication. By this time, there were definite sartorial rules governing attire. Occasion dressing meant separate outfits for separate social events such as golfing or cocktails and dinner. Thus, the tuxedo, smoking jacket, and sportswear were born.

By the 1950s, most men conformed to the dress code of the gray flannel suit for business. It was the ubiquitous male uniform. However, as in womenswear, sportswear continued to grow in importance. Suburban lifestyles generated a need for a more casual leisure time wardrobe.

The 1960s brought about a major transformation in menswear. There was a revolt against the established dress code of the 1950s. Dubbed the "Peacock Revolution" by *Esquire* magazine, men rebelled against conformity and, like the male peacock, began to show their plumage. Instead of the English look from Savile Row, it was the English look from Carnaby Street. Bell bottoms, Nehru jackets, and leisure suits in bright colors were worn by young and old.

The spirit of self-expression and a heightened interest in fashion gave opportunities to many womenswear designers to enter the menswear field in the early 1970s. American (Bill Blass and Oleg Cassini) and French (Pierre Cardin and Yves Saint Laurent) designers began producing menswear collections. Soon after, Ralph Lauren and Calvin Klein began promoting an elegant yet relaxed, truly American look. At the same time, Italian designers, including Giorgio Armani, Gianni Versace, and Basile, invaded the U.S. shores. Men now became familiar with designer labels and licensed merchandise.

As the baby-boomers aged into their thirties and forties and became the yuppy generation of the 1980s, menswear was once again affected. Men greatly increased their consumption of wearing apparel. They became more fashion conscious in terms of quality and design. They were willing to experiment with patterns and colors unlike any previous generation.

Sportswear continues to grow in importance as a major category of menswear. Changing demographics, casual lifestyles, and even relaxed dress codes at the office have contributed to this phenomenon. Today, sportswear is equal to tailored clothing in terms of retail sales.

The menswear industry accounts for 26 percent of total U.S. apparel sales each year. This makes menswear an integral part of today's fashion picture.

CHARACTERISTICS OF THE MENSWEAR INDUSTRY

Size

Because of the manner in which the industry is organized, separate statistical facts about menswear are usually not given. Instead, they are combined with those of boyswear. For example, according to the U.S. Department of Commerce, there are nearly 3,000 firms employing approximately 266,000 workers that produce men's and boys' apparel. Some make clothing for men, others make clothing for boys, and still others make apparel for both. Industry output is estimated to be over $19 billion at the wholesale level. Consumer expenditures are approximately $56 billion at retail for men's and boys' clothing and accessories, including imported goods. Men's and boys' wear is the leading category of exports for the U.S. apparel industry.

Location

The production of menswear is carried on in all sections of the country. However, the heaviest concentration of manufacturers is found in the Middle Atlantic region. Three states—New York, New Jersey, and Pennsylvania—are responsible for over 45 percent of the entire industry's output. In the rest of the country, California, Georgia, Texas, and Missouri are the top menswear- and boyswear-producing states. (See Industry Feature entitled "Important Menswear Markets.")

New York City serves as the design and marketing headquarters for the nation's industry. All major manufacturers have showrooms in or around the Garment Center from Fifth to Seventh Avenues between 51st and 53rd Streets. The Empire State Building and 1290 Avenue of the Americas (6th Avenue) are two other major showroom locations.

The New York metropolitan area also houses a very large share of the industry's present production facilities. But, as in women's

··········
INDUSTRY FEATURE
··········

Important Menswear Markets

The following cities and their apparel specialties are established production and marketing centers for menswear:

New York. Largest and most important menswear center. All grades of apparel are produced and sold. Important for formal wear. Leader in terms of high fashion, and trend-setter for industry.

Philadelphia. Known principally for medium- to better-priced tailored clothing and formal wear.

Chicago. Home of several very large manufacturers of separates and medium- to better-priced, excellent quality tailored clothing.

Rochester. Recognized for its high-quality tailored clothing.

Baltimore. Noted for rainwear. Important also for medium- and better-priced tailored clothing and specialized summer merchandise.

Cincinnati. Center for medium- to better-priced tailored clothing and separates. Also produces summer merchandise.

Boston. Primarily noted for outerwear and rainwear.

Los Angeles. Dominates in sportswear production. Becoming increasingly important as a trend-setting center for all of menswear, especially medium to top-grade high-fashion garments.

Dallas. Tailored clothing, trousers, slacks, and sportswear.

Miami. Sportswear and swimwear.

wear, the number of manufacturing operations doing business in the area continues to decline as firms move to other areas of the country and off shore.

Manufacturers tend to congregate together according to the type of apparel they produce, and there seem to be several very definite geographical distinctions. For instance, tailored clothing (with the exception of separate trousers) is produced, almost exclusively, in the Middle Atlantic region, where highly skilled labor is available. California is an important sportswear producing state. Trousers, work clothes, and furnishings are made in the South and Southwest. There, less expensive—although less skilled—labor is found. Several manufacturers have found ideal plant locations outside of the continental United States in Puerto Rico, Mexico, some South American countries, and the Far East.

Structure

The majority of the 3,000 firms producing men's and boys' apparel are small; most employ fewer than 250 workers. Over 80 percent employ fewer than 50 employees. Each firm specializes in some particular type or category of merchandise such as tailored clothing or shirts. These categories correspond to standard industrial codes (SIC numbers), which is the way data is classified by the industry and the government for reporting purposes.

Tailored Clothing. Suits, jackets, slacks, formalwear, overcoats, and uniforms.

Trousers and Slacks. Includes jeans and casualwear.

Work Clothes. Work shirts, overalls, and washable apparel.

Shirts. Knit and woven, casual and dress.

Underwear and Nightwear.

NEC (not elsewhere classified). Ties, outerwear, swimwear, and socks.

Although these categories have been used by the industry for product classification since 1987, there is confusion over the fact that many retailers and manufacturers still describe the various categories in the following jargon:

Tailored Clothing. Suits, sports coats, dress trousers.

Outerwear. Overcoats and topcoats.

Sportswear. Casual pants, shirts, and sweaters.

Formal Wear. Tuxedos and morning coats/tails.

Furnishings. Shirts, socks, neckwear, nightwear, and underwear.

Work Clothes. Jeans, overalls, and work shirts.

Miscellaneous. Hats, belts, small leather goods, and cosmetics.

These categories most often correspond to the layout of the men's departments in specialty and department stores.

Like womenswear, manufacturers of menswear are highly specialized in terms of their product lines. Also like womenswear, some firms have diversified and crossed over by operating several different divisions. For example, Levi Strauss, the jeans maker, also produces casual sportswear in its Dockers division. Liz Claiborne operates a separate division for its Claiborne menswear line (see Figure 11–1).

Although the majority of the firms producing menswear are small, a few large companies dominate the market in terms of sales volume. To illustrate, nearly 30 percent of the total sales of menswear

Courtesy: Liz Claiborne, Inc.

•••••••• **FIGURE 11-1 Claiborne Menswear. (See Color Plate 7)**

is done by just six major companies: Levi Strauss, Hartmarx, Phillips-Van Heusen, Russell, Oxford Industries, and Farah. Other large firms producing menswear include Cluett-Peabody (owned by Biderman Industries), McGregor-Doniger, Manhattan Industries, Blue Bell, Haggar, and Palm Beach.

Labor

Contributing greatly to the nature of the men's and boys' wear industry is its union: the Amalgamated Clothing and Textile Workers Union. Known simply as the "Amalgamated," this union—with over 400,000 members—has long been regarded as one of the most progressive and successful trade unions in the country.

Since its inception in 1914, the Amalgamated has consistently sought to meet the needs of its members by bargaining for decent wages and extensive fringe benefits. It is considered a pioneer in America's labor movement for its introduction and operation of a broad range of services for its union members. These innovative features include housing facilities, a bank, a life insurance company, health and day care centers, and college tuition assistance programs for members' children.

Well over 95 percent of the workers who produce tailored clothing are represented by the Amalgamated. However, many segments of the industry, including producers of sportswear located in the South and Southwest, remain unorganized.

As in womenswear, the composition of the labor force in menswear has changed. Immigrant tailors, mostly male, have all but been replaced by women who now hold jobs as sewing machine operators and finishers. In fact, the custom tailor, once so indispensable to the production of menswear is but a tiny minority of the menswear work force of today. Tailors who operate their own retail stores number a scant 1,000 or so; and tailors to-the-trade—those who work in firms that specialize in individual made-to-measure garments—produce less than 5 percent of the industry's output.

METHODS OF OPERATION

The steps used in producing a line of menswear are basically the same as those used for womenswear, with two notable differences. First, most tailored menswear is produced by "inside" shops. The use of "outside" contractors and jobbers is limited to inexpensive lines and to sportswear items. The extreme flexibility needed by womenswear producers to keep up with style changes is not essential in most menswear. Furthermore, menswear producers must maintain direct control over production to maintain quality.

Second, the construction of men's clothing is more difficult and complicated than that of women's clothing, requiring a great deal of hand sewing and tailoring. For example, a man's jacket is a "structured" (firmly shaped) garment. To achieve its shape, portions of its interfacings, facings, and lining must be applied and sewn by hand, slowing down the entire manufacturing process. Of course, when the styles of garments change to a more casual, unstructured look, the production process time is reduced. But today, the majority of men's clothing continues to be "structured," requiring some type of time-consuming handwork.

Producing Tailored Clothing

As already mentioned, the menswear industry is divided into six categories for statistical and reporting purposes. Individual manufacturers within each category either limit their lines to one specific type of garment within a category such as suits, or they produce a variety of items within a classification.

Clothing within the tailored category is classified even further. It is graded from 1 through 6 +: The higher the number, the more hand-tailored the operations and the more expensive the item. Some companies build their reputations on this grading system, boasting of a large amount of hand-tailored operations in their production process to sell their product. They also use the grade of their product to determine its price, and, subsequently, these firms are classified by price.

At the top of the 6 + list are firms like Hickey Freeman and Oxxford. These companies specialize in hand-tailored clothing, that is, the manufacturing process must have a minimum of 25 separate hand operations. For example, in an Oxxford suit, the majority of the 160 construction steps of the jacket and 65 steps of the trousers are done by hand, bringing the minimum cost of any of the firm's suits to at least $1,000. At the other end of the spectrum are firms that produce suits to retail for $150 and under with obviously few, if any, hand-done manufacturing operations.

Generally speaking, there are four distinct price lines in tailored clothing. The highest priced category is referred to as "Savile Row," and suits in this range can cost as much as $3,000. Next is the "designer" or "status" level; these suits retail between $500 and $900. The "average" price range includes suits costing between $150 and $500. Finally, the "budget" category has suits priced below $150.

Figure 11–2 is an advertisement sponsored by the trade organization, Tailored Menswear Council of America, promoting tailored clothing.

Sizing Tailored Clothing

Compared with womenswear, the number of sizes in tailored clothing is mind-boggling. First, five basic figure types are used by suit manufacturers for sizing purposes. These include:

- Regular, for men with average proportions with a height of 5'7" to 5'10"
- Short, for men with shorter arms and legs with a height of 5'5" to 5'7"
- Long, for taller men with longer arms and legs with a height of 5'11" to 6'3"
- Portly, for men of average height but heavy in stomach and waist areas with a height of 5'8" to 5'10"
- Stout, for heavier men with a height of 5'7" to 5'10"
- Young mens/Active, for men who have smaller waists in comparison to jacket size.

Additionally, there are various combinations of these sizes, such as portly long or portly short, which may be included in a manufacturer's size offerings. Within each of these figure type classifications are numerical sizes. Some examples are as follows:

- Regular sizes, 35 to 48
- Short sizes, 36 to 44
- Long sizes, 37 to 48

In separate trousers, sizing is doubly defined. For instance, men's pants are cut in waist sizes 27 to 42 and, if hemmed, inseam lengths of 29 to 36 inches.

Shirt manufacturers also use two measurements. They cut a shirt with neck sizes ranging from 14 to 17½ inches, and sleeve lengths between 30 to 36 inches.

Because of changing demographics, some manufacturers are adding additional size categories such as Big and Tall (also known as BATMAN) to their lines. This is due to the fact that more than 10 percent of the U.S. adult male population is 6'3" inches tall and 230 pounds or over, making this category a viable and profitable market.

Why should you wear
tailored clothing?

It doesn't squeak when you walk in it.

When negotiating you can ask for a larger fee
because they'll think that's what you're getting.

A crisp white handkerchief isn't quite the
same in the breast pocket of overalls.

If you dress like your boss, he'll be more
likely to appreciate your company.

Boutonnieres just don't make it on flannel shirts.

It doesn't hurt to look like you're on the
way to something more important.

Hostile strangers will be less likely to punch you,
thinking you might be a lawyer.

Through member donations,
the Tailored Menswear Council of America
supports the Pediatric AIDS Foundation.

American Tailored Clothing.
Required Wearing.

Tailored Menswear Council of America

© 1993 Clothing Manufacturers Association, 1290 Avenue of the Americas, New York, NY 10104. Photographer: Steven Klein; model: Adam Stanger; ad agency: Calman & Stefenoor; clothing: Pincus Brothers.

• • • • • • • • **FIGURE 11-2 Tailored Menswear Council of America**

Producing Sportswear

Although this category of men's apparel was introduced in the 1930s, it did not become a major component of men's retail sales until the 1950s. Clothing for leisure activities, casual living, and more relaxed business attire requirements has continued to grow in importance and now represents over 45 percent of all menswear sold. U.S. consumers spend over $22 billion a year on men's sportswear. Unfortunately, this category of menswear has been the hardest hit by imports. For example, nearly 66 percent of all sport shirts were imported last year.

The sportswear business is based on separates that are presented as a coordinated line much as in women's sportswear. The customer can "mix and match" and create an individual look. Retailers have reorganized their departments and changed their visual presentations to reflect this new collection concept. No longer are all shirts grouped together; rather, they are displayed with other items to target a particular type of consumer. Or merchandise is presented using the boutique concept where each designer has his or her own selling area for the entire collection.

Most men's sportswear manufacturers rely on outside contractors for sewing, just as is done in womenswear. Since there is little or no hand sewing and styling is simplified and cheaper, less skilled labor can be used. Even sizing is less complicated than tailored clothing with S, M, L, XL replacing exact neck, sleeve, or waist size. Often length of pants is expressed as 29/30 or 32/33 or pants are shipped unhemmed so that the customer can adjust the hem himself.

FASHION SEASONS

Traditionally, menswear had just two fashion seasons: Fall/Winter and Spring/Summer. This is still the case for tailored clothing. The Fall/Winter lines are presented to buyers in January and the Spring/Summer line is shown in late July or early August.

Because of simpler production methods and increased consumer demand for updated styling, men's sportswear manufacturers now have four fashion seasons. Fall I is presented to the buyers in March. Fall II/Holiday is shown in June. The Spring line opens in October and Summer is offered in January. Some of the larger companies like Claiborne have begun to separate Fall II from Holiday and hold a separate Holiday market week in August.

Like womenswear, the two most important collections in terms of fashion direction are the Fall and Spring lines. Both the Winter and the late Spring-Summer collections follow the styling trends of the previous season, making modifications in the weight and in the colors of the fabrics.

In spite of the constantly increasing speed in modern production methods, fashion evolves rather slowly in menswear. Silhouette changes take about 20 years to complete their fashion life cycle. Style changes such as the widening of a lapel or trouser leg generally change ever so slightly each year, so that a jacket or a pair of pants may not appear outdated until two to four years after the change is introduced.

THE MARKETING PROCESS

Menswear manufacturers hold market weeks, use cooperative advertising, rely heavily on factoring, and use many of the same marketing techniques found in the rest of the apparel industry. However, there are three aspects to marketing menswear that are unusual and, therefore, worth mentioning. The first involves its methods of distribution; the second is the importance of national brands and the origins of designer label merchandise; and third is fashion promotion.

Distribution

The traditional method of selling and distributing menswear at retail was almost exclusively through men's specialty shops and specialty chains. As in the days of the "slop shops" (see Chapter 7), these stores were intended for a quick in-and-out visit by their male customers. Even when department stores expanded into menswear, that department was almost always located on the main floor, separate from the rest of the selling area, and often with an entrance and exit door close by if not right within the department.

Since the 1970s, there has been a major change in how and where menswear is marketed. Perhaps the biggest shift is to discount chain stores such as Wal-Mart, Kmart and Caldor. These kinds of outlets now account for approximately 25 percent of all menswear sales. Department stores, specialty stores and specialty chains are nearly equal in terms of distribution share, each accounting for 21 percent, 20 percent, and 18 percent, respectively.

Another change is the fact that menswear and womenswear are being merchandised in much the same way by the same retailers. For example, many specialty stores are no longer exclusively male. Barneys, Brooks Brothers, and Wallachs have added womenswear to their merchandise mix. Conversely, more and more department stores are expanding the floor space devoted to their menswear lines with much success.

Although mail order sales account for only 4 percent of the total volume of menswear sales now, this method of distribution will continue to grow strongly throughout the decade. Companies such as Victoria's Secret are already featuring menswear in their catalogs.

In addition, shop-at-home TV networks and other nontraditional outlets, that is, supermarkets, discount membership warehouses, and sporting goods stores, are responsible for nearly 12 percent of men's apparel sales. As in the case for mail order sales, these methods of distribution are expected to gain in importance in the coming years.

Although an overwhelming majority of today's menswear manufacturers sell their merchandise to independent retailers, some still sell their goods exclusively through their own retail outlets. This *exclusive method of distribution* is also a holdover from the "slop shop" days when retail tailors found it profitable to manufacture an inventory of menswear, thus performing both the manufacturing and retailing functions themselves.

Another method of distribution that originated in earlier days is a process known as *dual distribution.* Through this method, a manufacturer sells goods directly to the consumer through its own manufacturer-owned retail outlets. It also sells merchandise wholesale to independent retailers. In a sense, this makes the manufacturer supplier *and* competitor to the independent retailer. This unusual relationship has been successfully maintained by an exceptional few of the very large and very well known manufacturers in the industry. Some of these dual distributors include Botany Industries, Phillips-Van Heusen, Cluett-Peabody, and the king of dual distribution in menswear—Hartmarx Corporation (see Table 11–1).

As in womenswear, both dual distribution and vertical integration have increased in popularity especially among designers. One of the first designers to successfully attempt these combined techniques was Ralph Lauren. Not only does he design and manufacture menswear, but his lines are available for sale in Ralph Lauren Boutiques and other fine department and specialty stores.

National Brands

Because of the dominance of large corporations, menswear has been traditionally marketed with the major emphasis on manufacturer brand names. Hart, Schaffner & Marx, Arrow, Levi Strauss, Lee, McGregor, and even Fruit of the Loom have been well known labels for menswear for many years. Some newer brands—Nike, Champion, Haggar, and Dockers—have been added to the list of successful na-

TABLE 11-1 Dual Distribution by Hartmarx

468 retail stores owned (partial listing)	Kuppenheimer
Hartmarx Specialty stores	Henry Grethel Studio
Baskin	F. R. Tripler
Silverwood	Graham & Gunn
Sansabelt Shops	Wallachs

32 manufacturer brands and licensed label merchandise sold to company-owned and independent stores (partial listing)

Austin Reed	Sansabelt
Nino Cerruti	Jack Nicklaus
Christian Dior (rainwear)	Hickey Freeman
Pierre Cardin (tailored clothing)	Jaymar

tional brands that appeal to specific target markets within certain menswear categories.

Brand names play a much more significant role in menswear than in womenswear. This is because until the early 1970s, no known designers produced and marketed menswear lines. Up until that time, menswear was considered by most people to be functional, not fashionable. All that changed after the radical 1960s. Not only were women and minorities demanding equality in society, but many men felt the time had come for individual expression and fashion equality. Men started their own revolt, the "Peacock Revolution," which gave them freedom of expression in the fashion marketplace regarding styling and color. It was only natural that womenswear designers saw an opportunity and began offering designer label goods to men on a large scale.

Many of these designers have entered the menswear business through licensing agreements. Bill Blass, an early pioneer, has licensing agreements for menswear products with such firms as Revlon, After Six, and Buxton. Hartmarx, producer of the Hart, Schaffner & Marx label, also markets tailored clothing under the licensed labels of Christian Dior and Pierre Cardin. Ralph Lauren (who began in menswear and then added womenswear) has Chaps as one of his most successfully licensed labels.

Menswear Designer Labels

One of the most valuable tools for improving the fashion image of menswear has been the use of designer labels. The designer first credited with offering menswear under his label was Pierre Cardin. The time was the late 1950s, a period in which his type of European continental styling became important in men's clothing. Cardin's success inspired other well-known womenswear designers to successfully enter the menswear field. Some of these designers are:

Adolfo	Givenchy
Geoffrey Beene	Calvin Klein
Bill Blass	Oscar de la Renta
Oleg Cassini	Yves Saint Laurent
Liz Claiborne	John Weitz
Christian Dior	Donna Karan
Perry Ellis	

Besides American and French designers, another major group of designers are the Italians. The menswear shows held in Florence, Italy, are extremely trend-setting to the entire industry because of the beautifully tailored and imaginatively styled clothing presented there. Leading Italian designers and fashion houses include Giorgio Armani, Gianni Versace, Gianfranco Basile, Gianfranco Ferré, and Valentino. Collectively, their work, along with others who show their lines in Florence, has made Italy a major menswear fashion center. In turn, these designers have also added prestige to designer-name merchandise in menswear.

As is the case in womenswear, some designers gear their collections to specific target markets. They have introduced "knockoff" sequel collections aimed at different price points to complement their designer and higher priced lines. An excellent example is Giorgio Armani's A/X line which features less expensive sportswear.

Fashion Promotion

Traditionally, menswear manufacturers have been a conservative group, hesitating to introduce unusual or extreme fashion and building their lines around quality and price. When exciting fashion changes began to occur in menswear during the 1960s and 1970s, progressive industry members welcomed the opportunity to generate increased interest in menswear. Every leading trade group and organization began to place a stronger emphasis on fashion, hoping to encourage all members of the industry to move in that direction.

There are several trade associations in the menswear industry and, in one way or another, all help to develop, stimulate, and promote menswear fashion. One of the oldest is the Clothing Manufacturers Association (CMA), which represents manufacturers of tailored clothing. It was initially formed to bargain for manufacturers with the Amalgamated union. But as the importance of fashion grew and style changes increased, manufacturers also began to turn to the CMA for fashion direction. The association then expanded its activities, developing a very successful fashion program that coordinates and presents styling and fashion trends to its members.

In 1953, another trade association—the National Association of Men's Sportswear Buyers (NAMSB)—was formed to give identity to a then new line of menswear. As its name implies, the NAMSB is made up of store buyers, and its purpose is to keep its membership informed of the industry's fashion trends. This is primarily accomplished by staging the world's largest menswear trade shows held four times a year in New York. Approximately 1,000 manufacturers offer 37 categories of merchandise to the more than 30,000 retail buyers who attend these shows.

The Designers' Collective, founded in 1979, serves as a showcase for designer-labeled tailored clothing, sportswear, shirts, trousers, outerwear, fur, shoes, furnishings, and accessories. Both the press and members of the retail trade attend the semiannual shows in New York held prior to the spring and fall market weeks to gain an overall view of upcoming fashion trends in menswear. It is sponsored by the Men's Fashion Association (MFA), the public relations organization for the industry. The MFA, in cooperation with the makers of Cutty Sark Scotch, has created the Cutty Sark Men's Fashion Awards. These awards recognize those who have made outstanding contributions to the field of menswear design. Other major menswear trade organizations and the trade shows they sponsor are listed in Table 11–2.

In addition to trade associations, a growing number of trade and consumer publications promote men's and boys' wear. Table 11–3 lists some major publications and their addresses.

Through its own concerted efforts, the menswear industry has been able to radically change its fashion attitude and image. This industry, once rigidly conservative, has—in less than 20 years—transformed itself into one of the most creative contributors to the fashion business.

TABLE 11-2   Major Menwear Associations, Trade Shows, and Regional Markets

National Association of Men's Sportswear Buyers (NAMSB), New York—January, March, June, and October

Designer Collective (sponsored by Men's Fashion Association), New York—January and July

Atlanta Men's and Boys' Market—January

Pitti Uomo, Florence, Italy—January

Uomomoda, New York—January

Short Men's Apparel Association (SMAA), New York—January and July

Surf Expo, Orlando, Florida—January

Action Sports Retailer, San Diego—January

Salon International de l'Habillement Masculin (SEHM), Paris—February

International Menswear Fair, Cologne, Germany—March

Men's Apparel Guild (MAGIC), Las Vegas—March and September

Los Angeles Men's Market—March and July

Dallas Men's and Boys' Market—April

Men's Fashion Association (press preview), Ryebrook, New York—June

Big and Tall Apparel Needs (BATMAN), Minneapolis—July

Salon International Mode Masculine, Montreal—July

••••••• TERMS TO REMEMBER

tailored clothing   sportswear   Amalgamated   fashion seasons   exclusive distribution   dual distribution   CMA   NAMSB   Designers' Collective   MFA   Cutty Sark Men's Fashion Awards

••••••• HIGHLIGHTS OF THE CHAPTER

- Menswear production is geographically concentrated in the Northeast with New York City serving as the design and marketing headquarters.

- Tailored clothing and sportswear are the most important of the six categories of menswear.

- Unlike womenswear, menswear is dominated by large corporations and conglomerates in terms of sales volume.

- The primary labor union for workers in the men's and boys' clothing industry is the Amalgamated Clothing and Textile Workers Union, simply referred to as the Amalgamated.

- Many of the steps involved in the production and specialization in womenswear are the same in menswear. Two major differences are in methods of distribution and promotion.

TABLE 11-3 Important Trade and Consumer Publications for Men's and Boys' Wear

DNR (Daily News Record) 7 East 12th Street New York, NY 10003	*The Licensing Book* 264 West 40th Street New York, NY 10018
Children's Business 7 East 12th Street New York, NY 10003	*M Inc.* 7 East 12th Street New York, NY 10003
Apparel Merchandising 425 Park Avenue New York, NY 10022	*Mr Magazine* Box 5550 Norwalk, CT 06856
Details 632 Broadway New York, NY 10012	*Rolling Stone* 745 Fifth Avenue New York, NY 10151
Esquire Magazine 1790 Broadway New York, NY 10019	*Sportswear International* 29 West 38th Street New York, NY 10018
GQ (Gentlemen's Quarterly) 350 Madison Avenue New York, NY 10019	*Surfer Magazine* Box 1028 Dana Point, CA 92629
In Fashion 29 West 38th Street New York, NY 10018	

- Designer names and licensing are now important aspects of the successful marketing of menswear.

••••••• REVIEW QUESTIONS

1. What was the "Peacock Revolution"? Was it successful? What impact did it have on the men's fashion industry?

2. Which region of the country produces the most menswear? Where is the marketing and design center for menswear?

3. List the six categories of menswear. Which are the most dominant?

4. In terms of structure, describe the differences between the menswear industry and the womenswear industry.

5. What is the Amalgamated?

6. What are the four price lines in tailored clothing?

7. Define and give examples of men's furnishings.

8. Explain dual distribution. Explain exclusive distribution.

9. What are the CMA and NAMSB? What function does the Designers' Collective perform?

10. What is the Cutty Sark Award and to whom is it given?

.... RESEARCH AND PROJECTS

1. The "Peacock Revolution" did not take place in menswear until the 1960s. Why didn't it occur before? What facts about the 1960s have you learned in other chapters to explain this?

2. Compare the menswear industry with womenswear industry in terms of the following: structure of the industry, methods of operation, fashion seasons, and marketing activities.

3. Research the clothing styles in menswear most popular in each decade of this century.

4. By using fashion publications such as *Daily News Record*, *M*, *GQ*, and *Esquire* magazine, prepare a fashion forecast for the upcoming fashion season. Describe the look in terms of the elements of design and the language of fashion as discussed in Chapter 1.

5. Assume that you are the menswear buyer for a major department store in your area. Define your menswear customer in terms of demographics and psychographics. Then determine what kinds of apparel and which designers would best serve your target customer. (A personal visit to a store would be most helpful in doing this project.)

6. Visit a large chain store, a department store, and a specialty store. Compare a line of menswear or men's furnishings in each store in terms of quality, price variety, and choice of size and color. Explain why there are such differences among stores.

CHAPTER 12

· ·

Creating and Marketing Children's Apparel

· · · · · · · · LEARNING OBJECTIVES

After reading this chapter, you should be able to:

- Describe the characteristics of the children's wear industry: the design, the operation, and the marketing activities.
- Discuss the importance of the calendar in children's wear.
- Identify the major children's apparel labels.
- Enumerate the ways in which the computer has affected the children's clothing industry.
- Outline the reasons for tension on the part of the store buyer and the special skills required for the showroom sales staff to deal with them.

· · · · · · · · PERFORMANCE OUTCOME

After reading this chapter, you should be able to:

- Find your way to the office buildings in Manhattan that contain most of the showrooms offering children's wear.
- Know how to find the largest trade shows that offer children's wear and the dates for the shows in trade journals.
- Offer new and tested ideas for promoting children's clothing.
- Know how to locate the factories that produce children's apparel in the United States.

Great splashes of primary colors set against the irridescents, perhaps with a black background, characterize the children's wear industry today. Comfort is the keynote for the industry, as is ease of care. Those producers of children's clothing that conformed to traditional styling have left the scene, and the current social movements proclaim their messages on the sportswear being worn by boys and girls: SAY NO TO DRUGS!! SAVE THE RAIN FORESTS!! RECYCLE!! Children are aware of the serious problems of the 1990s and proclaim that awareness to the world. Shod in sneakers, kids are free to run and jump their way into any activity.

Even infants have benefited from kids' liberation. Disposable diapers designed to conform to the sex and stage of growth of the infant provide comfort for the youngest members of our society. Knits created to stretch and flow with each movement of the young child make exercise and development possible at earlier stages than before. Special occasions call for special costumes for the festivities of life, with young girls looking something like wrapped gifts and young boys like Wall Street brokers. Infant girls wear an elastic around their heads emblazoned with an artificial flower or a satin bow, and infant boys often wear a baseball or football uniform to mark a special event.

As in the past, the children's wear industry continues to market aggressively. **Demographic figures** show that children continue to be an important percentage of the population. The dream of ZPG or zero population growth faded as the United States opened its doors to refugees from the Hispanic countries where large families have been the way of life. It is estimated that an even larger number of illegal refugees have found their way into this country as well, creating a need for easily cared for and wearable low-cost clothing.

CHARACTERISTICS OF THE CHILDREN'S WEAR INDUSTRY

The production of apparel takes its cue from the needs of the consumer. The $19 billion children's clothing market is a growing segment of the retail industry which has seriously stagnated in recent years. As reported in *Kids Fashions*,[1] there were more babies born in 1990 than in any year since 1961. This 4.2 million addition to the population may be the start of a trend that may continue for the next several years. If this birth rate continues, there will be more than 20.2 million pre-school children by 1996. With the estimated cost of raising a child from birth to age 17 between $150,000 and $300,000, we can easily predict a boom in the children's wear market for the next few years. The buyers of children's clothing can be the parents, the grandparents, other relatives, and the children themselves. Teenagers earned an estimated $94.7 billion in 1991, an increase of 6.5 percent over the previous year.

Families with both parents in the work force are having fewer children and are having them at an older age. This kind of family has more money to spend on children's clothing. However, there is an increase of single-parent families, and the impact of two-parent families is declining. What kind of merchandise does the family of today demand from the industry? Today's family perceives value in national brands. Large volume retailers, such as Sears, are moving away from **private-label** merchandise in the children's wear departments. Today, a shopper can find many **national brands** in Sears. Children's boutiques are growing in popularity as are discount retailers with their promotionally priced merchandise. For families that are looking for a classical, higher priced garment, Gap Infants and Gap Kids have exploded onto the scene. Here sportswear is retailed in strong colors that never change from year to year and that inspire parents to buy with the idea that clothing can be passed down to siblings with some updated separates that will always look well with items purchased for older brothers and sisters.

No longer is the old idea of pink for girls and blue for boys a byword of children's apparel design. Young boys wear hot pink prints and irridescent colors. Many of the sportswear items for girls are unisex in nature, and girls identify with famous sports heroes or heroines. Children like to be a part of the main scene and identify with every popular movement, be it environmental, antidrug, or cartoon character that has catapulted into favor.

Some retailers have designed environments that are entertaining and exciting for youngsters. The Disney children's stores are bright with flashing lights. Cartoons run on a continuous basis on a full screen, and there are comfortable places for children to sit. Gymboree stores, with their newborn to toddler clothing, feature bold, primary colors in stores that often have exercise areas for parents and children and always have a comfortable corner with tiny seats and television screens displaying colorful cartoons. In many of its stores, J. C. Pen-

[1] *Kids Fashions*, April 1992, p. 28.

ney features a corner within the department where children may sit and play, thus creating a nook that is pleasing to youngsters.

Location of Showrooms

The heart of the children's apparel industry is in the **showroom.** This is where buyers come to see the offerings for the season and talk over their needs with the salespeople who represent the manufacturer. The planning for production and marketing strategies takes place here. Sometimes the clothing is also designed and cost-estimated in the showroom. At other times, lower rental facilities are provided for the design, the **costing** of the garments, and the production of the designer and showroom samples. The major showrooms for the children's apparel industry are in Manhattan in New York City, the heart of the Garment District. The most important location for showrooms continues to be 112 West 34th Street, with the best secondary location at 1333 Broadway. Locations at 350 Fifth Avenue, 1411 Broadway, and 1441 Broadway are among many in which manufacturers have their showrooms. Figure 12–1 shows clearly the locations where these office buildings may be found. Here buyers can easily make their selections for the coming season without venturing far.

The major **trade shows** of new merchandise in New York City are presented four times a year in the Jacob Javits Convention Center by International Kids Fashion Show (see Figure 12–2). The Larkin Group, which is the parent company of the International Kids Fashion Show, is also the publisher of a monthly children's wear **trade journal,** *Kids Fashions.* Important shows are also presented by the Florida Children's Wear Manufacturers' Guild in Miami, where many children's wear manufacturers are located. There are **regional markets** in Dallas, Chicago, and Atlanta, and many manufacturers maintain showrooms in these cities, but they are more likely to rent space for the children's markets held there. Children's clothing manufacturers' showrooms are located in the San Francisco and Los Angeles areas, as well as in other states of the Union and in Canada. Dates for all trade shows are announced in the trade journals.

Many small manufacturers who do not have the expertise or budget to maintain showrooms with sales staffs use the services of manufacturers' representatives. These people are independent agents who perform the duties of a selling staff and who work on a commission basis. Sometimes the **manufacturers' reps** handle the line for a single manufacturer, and sometimes they handle the lines of several non-competing manufacturers.

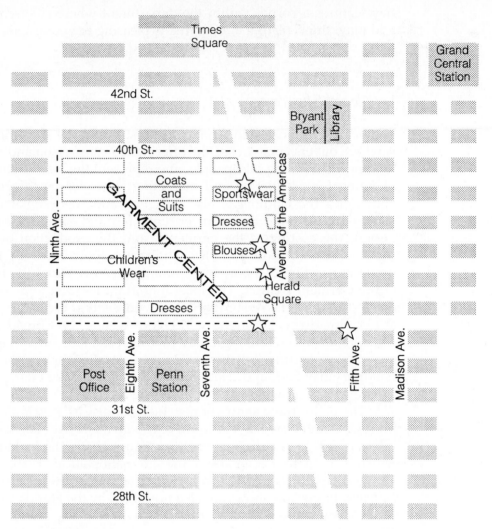

FIGURE 12-1 The stars indicate the children's apparel showroom locations in New York City.

Location of Manufacturing Facilities

There has been a major change as to the actual place of manufacture of children's garments. Many of the old landmark factory buildings of Manhattan where the union shops in the Garment District were located have unoccupied floors. Secret locations in the boroughs of New York where illegal immigrants work for low wages have sprung up. Factories have opened in the South which can attract workers who are willing to work for less money. Some of the labor on children's wear

¡GO!

to the **48**th

INTERNATIONAL
KIDS FASHION
S H O W

OCTOBER 17-18-19-20, 1993

Sunday 9am to 7pm; Monday & Tuesday 9am to 6pm
Wednesday 9am to 4pm

JAVITS CONVENTION CENTER
NEW YORK CITY
Spring Market

If you were to compile a list of the items critical to your Spring buying efforts, it would most assuredly include ... **contact with new and established children's wear designers and manufacturers from across the globe, a comprehensive overview of the latest kids' fashions, a marketplace designed to make your shopping easy and convenient** and an **unparalleled mix of fashion excitement**. In essence, your choice for increased contacts and striking merchandise would be the **48th International Kids Fashion Show, October 17-20, at the Javits Center in New York City.** Simply put, there is no other single shopping and exhibition forum that provides you with more of what you need to increase your sales and replenish your after-summer inventories.

Start your season off right with the *freshest* selection of Spring fashions at the world's largest children's wear trade show. Discover **over 1,600 lines** of traditional and contemporary apparel, accessories, footwear and juvenile products all under one roof. When it comes to providing the nation's retailers with everything they need to remain on top, the Kids Show has it all and more: **more of the industry's hottest designers and manufacturers, more fashions** and **more ways to shop and stay out in front of the competition!**

See why many of the country's biggest & best specialty, chain and department stores shop the Kids Show ...

Courtesy: Stanley Kaye, the Larkin Group

FIGURE 12-2   The major children's wear trade show, International Kids Fashion Show, is held four times a year.

today is performed outside of the United States. The Schwab Company, which produces Little Me and Mufflings and employs 600 people, uses the Caribbean Basin Initiative, ruling 807. This lowers the duty costs by having the garment cut in the United States and assembled in the Caribbean. This company maintains 25 showrooms in the United States and Canada as well as sales agents in Europe and the Middle East.

Sometimes children's garments are completely manufactured on other continents such as Asia and Europe. The major children's wear manufacturers, Health-Tex, Carter, and Oshkosh B'Gosh, produce their apparel in this country. The majority of private-label merchandise in the children's clothing industry is manufactured overseas. The key areas for low-priced manufacture of apparel are in China and Sri Lanka. Private label can be a designer name that is leased out for production or one in which the retailer with its own design facilities acts as manufacturer, but contracts out the production of the apparel. A good example would be Small Creations, the Lord & Taylor private label for infants. In this case, the corporate central office either hires an established manufacturer to produce its line or develops its own design department and contracts out the manufacture of the garments. **Contractors** are becoming increasingly important as they produce whole garments or components of garments in **outside shops. Inside shops,** on the other hand, are on the premises of the manufacturer.

Structure of the Industry in the United States

It is difficult to obtain reliable data on the manufacture of children's wear in this country. This is because the U.S. Department of Commerce in its Business Census, published every five years, reports an aggregate amount for the apparel produced for men and boys. However, data from *County Business Patterns 1990*, published by the U.S. Department of Commerce, Bureau of the Census are available for girls', children's, and infants' dresses, blouses, shirts, and outerwear. There are 672 of these manufacturing establishments in the United States which employ 61,070 people. If we compare these figures with the data from the 1987 Business Census, we learn that there was a loss of 163 of these manufacturing establishments in this three-year period and 10,630 jobs. The states that lead in the production of these products are New York, Pennsylvania, and California.

The Unions in the Children's Wear Industry

The major unions that organize the workers and negotiate wages and practices for people who work in manufacturing facilities in the United

States are the International Ladies' Garment Workers' Union, more familiarly known as the **ILGWU,** and the Amalgamated Union, known as the **ACTWUA.** In addition, there is a smaller union known as the United Garment Workers, which was at one time a part of the Amalgamated. If a person is employed in a union shop and is doing a job covered by one of these unions, that person is entitled to become a member. As a general rule, infants' wear, girls' wear, and womenswear are under the jurisdiction of the ILGWU; boys' wear and menswear are under the jurisdiction of the Amalgamated. However, if the manufacturer that produced jeans for men expanded its operation to include infants', children's, boys', girls', and women's jeans, the whole operation would probably be Amalgamated.

METHODS OF OPERATION

As in the other apparel industries, children's wear production and design is based upon the seasons as the calendar changes. Even in the subtropical regions of the southern parts of the United States, there is a subtle difference in the clothing worn by children and a more apparent difference in the clothing worn by adults from season to season.

The New Collections

All production starts with a calendar. Each year the major manufacturers decide on a structure and time frame for the four seasons. Not every manufacturer produces for all four seasons. The most important fashion season of the year is Back to School, when most of the purchases are made. Next in importance comes Spring, then the Holiday line, and finally the smallest line, Summer. Some manufacturers combine their Spring and Summer collections.

Specialization

The largest manufacturers produce merchandise that is considered high end, moderate, and budget. Some limit themselves to a particular price line or a particular type of merchandise, such as dressy wear or sportswear. The largest manufacturers will produce special goods for their best customers—special designs, special fabrics, and special prices. They make garments that are unique and top quality as well as garments that have been changed to meet the price needs of buyers whose stores or catalogs target budget-minded customers. Some manufacturers of adult apparel, such as Levi-Strauss, Lee, and Danskins, have separate divisions that specialize in children's wear.

Some producers specialize by manufacturing only a specific size range. Because children at different stages of development have different bodily proportions, garments are cut to fit the growth stage of a child rather than the weight of the child. When children are very young, the sizes are the same for boys and girls: sizes 3 months to 24 months and toddler 2 to toddler 4. Girls' sizes then range from children's 4 to 6X, girls' 7 to 14, and preteen 6 to 14. Boys' sizes are children's 4 to 7 and 8 to 12. The manufacture of boys' sizes 14 to 20 is considered a part of the menswear industry and is called young men or student wear.

Some manufacturers, such as Carter, also produce undergarments and sleepwear for children.

THE DESIGNING PROCESS

The process of creating children's wear is similar to that of adult clothing. All clothing starts with a design. The designers usually specialize in a particular price range or category of clothing as in the other apparel industries. The designers may be employed by the manufacturers on a full-time basis or may be **freelance** designers. A designer is constantly looking for new ideas in order to create original and exciting new items for the collection. Sometimes the designer gets his or her ideas from a trade journal, from seeing what other companies are doing in the trade shows, or by utilizing the services of a fashion forecaster. Ideas sometimes come from the offerings of the textile companies, retailers who buy from the manufacturer, or from other designers.

From Idea to Sample

The designer selects the fabric and sketches the proposed design. Either the designer or the assistant, who is usually a designer in training just out of school, cuts the fabric and gives it to the sample hand to assemble. This kind of process is called **cut and sew.** Sometimes manufacturers choose to reconsider best-sellers from the previous year. They ask their designers to select new fabrics or to make some changes in an item that alter the appearance but that are actually minor. Different designs are created for each different size range. More than 300 cut-and-sew samples may be created for a season. Trimmings, buttons, and belts are applied. The samples are then hung in price categories and looked at from a sales potential. The head of sales has the important task of determining how many styles are needed in each price category and what the manufacturer has the capacity and ability to produce for a particular season.

Knit Goods

In creating knitted sportswear for children, the designer sketches the idea, selects the fabric, and brings it to the factory where the special machines that sew the overloop seams are located. In the New York City area, these facilities are in the lowest rent districts in the outlying boroughs. Here the samples are produced in the same location where the final garments are manufactured.

THE MANUFACTURING PROCESS

In order to make a decision as to which items should be produced, meetings are held on a regular basis with the design, sales, and production staffs. A moderately large company may make the decision to produce from 100 to 130 styles (item numbers) for a particular season. The fabrics are purchased and patterns are made for the samples the selling staff will use. These are called the *showroom sample lines.* In the creation of the showroom samples, yardages are checked again and mistakes are caught and corrected. The manufacturer's best customers are invited in for a preview of the line. The buyers critique the models with the designers and changes are made based on their suggestions. Buyers also make additional suggestions for items to fill out the line according to their own needs in their own stores. Early orders are placed.

Holding Down the Cost

Costing the garments is an important part of the manufacturing process. The production people make suggestions for changes that would keep the price down without altering the designs in any appreciable way. Notes are written to the pattern maker for the most cost-effective way of producing the garments. Today many manufacturers use the computer to help them grade the garments. The screen enables the grader to produce the patterns in all of the size ranges quickly and accurately. The person who arranges the pattern pieces on a huge sheet used by the cutter is called the *marker.* The sheet that has the arranged pattern pieces on it placed to maximize the use of the fabric is also called the *marker.* The computer is also utilized in the preparation of the markers.

The Four Seasons

As we mentioned earlier, all manufacturing is based on a calendar. Each year the major manufacturers decide upon a structure and time frame for the seasons. The showings are held during a period known as **market week.** The first showings for a season are held during this period in New York City. Thereafter, market weeks are held in each of the regional markets around the country.

Production Begins

With early orders in hand, the manufacturing process rolls into gear. Manufacturers estimate that each sewing machine can produce approximately ten dozen garments a week, and they generally work on a three-week turnover. The first group of items to be cut consists of about 50 percent of the anticipated line, based upon early orders and anticipated sales. Schedules are set for the projected cuttings for the new styles for the coming season. Cutting tickets are now prepared with the style numbers, the dozens to be cut, and the sizes to be cut.

Buttons, lace, and other components are carried in stock in the factory. Made-to-order embroideries are ordered at the same time as the **piece goods,** and appliqués are shipped out to be prepared as well. Finished belts are ordered after the fabric is cut. When the ordered piece goods and trimmings arrive, the pattern making, grading, marking, and cutting take place in the same manner as in the womenswear industry. The garments are then finished with appliqués, lace, and buttons. Hats are sometimes an important part of a finished design. They are then pressed. The garments are placed over a form that shoots out steam and final touch-ups are done by hand. The apparel is pinned, often to tissue paper within, which helps keep the shape of the garment, and is hung in the stockroom. After the apparel is inspected, it is packed for shipping according to the order, on hangers or without hangers in cartons.

Bread and Butter and Gravy

The **bread-and-butter customers** are the large-order retailers who maintain a loyalty to the manufacturer. These retailers depend upon the manufacturer to supply them with the kind of merchandise that creates and maintains the store image and the size needs of their customers. The small-order retailers are the **gravy customers.** Their orders are the ones over and above those the manufacturer has counted on to get through the season. Frequently, in children's apparel, the smaller orders are shipped out in **pre-packs,** which have predetermined sizes. Small order customers who need specific sizes may find it necessary to purchase sizes that are unnecessary in order to get the ones that are needed.

The Production Calendar

The entire process from beginning to end takes approximately 13 weeks, with overlap as one season's reorders end and the next season's new items go into production. The calendar schedules the cutoff dates for:

1. Design
2. Showroom sample line
3. Piece goods to be received for cutting
4. Cutting completed
5. Sewing and finishing
6. Shipping

Reorders

When items are **hot,** reorders come in early in the season. Manufacturers must be able to anticipate the crunch of reorders that will make or break the season. Reorders must be shipped out quickly in order to be salable by the retailer, who often specifies that if not received by a particular date, the order is cancelled.

Cash Flow Problems

The **dogs,** or items that have not had a sufficient number of sales by the manufacturer, are sold almost at cost to **discounters** or flea market vendors at midseason to give the manufacturers some **cash flow** to continue cutting the popular items that have caught on. Sometimes manufacturers use **factors** in order to help them with the problem of cash flow. A factor is similar to a banker who advances a percentage of the value of the order directly to the manufacturer. This enables the manufacturer to purchase additional fabric and cover the costs of labor and overhead as the season progresses. The factor then takes responsibility for collecting the money due from the stores.

THE MARKETING PROCESS

All marketing starts with need, so it is not surprising that fashion marketers of children's apparel look first to the latest demographic figures supplied by the U.S. Department of Commerce and the Bureau of the Census to see if there will be a growing market or a diminishing market for this type of goods. At the present time, children ranging from newborn to 14 years of age comprise more than 21 percent of the population.[2] This figure is expected to remain constant in the next few years and to diminish to a small extent as we approach the year 2000. People 55 years of age and older, the grandparent generation, comprise 22 percent of the population. (See Figure 12–3.) Many older people in this market segment have money to spend on their grandchildren.

Demographics

The Census Bureau projects that the number of children from birth to age 8 will decline in the year 2000, and the number of children ages 10 to 16 will increase. At the present time, the highest percentage of children under 18 years of age live in the South, the Midwest, the West, and the Northeast regions of our country. The projections for the years 2000 to 2010 show a steady increase in the number of children living

Newborn to age 14
21%
of population

Adult
57%
of population

+55 years in age
22%
of population

FIGURE 12-3 Demographic figures show that there will be a growing market for children's apparel.

[2]Standard and Poor's Industry Surveys, March 5, 1992.

in the West and the South. The Midwest and Northeast regions of the country will decline in number (*Fairchild Fact Files*).

Marketers also will look at trends in family income to see how family income is distributed in the United States.

Trends in Family Income
Percentage of Families in Each Income Bracket

Income	1970	1980	1990
$0–$24,999	33.8	35.4	33.3
$25,000–$49,999	43.4	39.8	36.3
$50,000–$74,999	16.2	16.6	18.2
over $75,000	6.5	7.9	12.3

We can learn from this chart, prepared from information supplied by the U.S. Bureau of the Census and reported in Standard and Poor's Industrial Surveys, March 5, 1992, that the poorest families in this nation, earning less than $25,000 a year, still comprise about one-third of the families. Each year, the United States receives as new residents about 100,000 immigrants. Because of language problems and lack of skills in the areas where employment may be found, these families are often found in the lowest income categories. The next category of families, however, is growing smaller. The group of families that earned between $25,000 and $49,999 has diminished in size, and some of these families have moved into the higher earning brackets. The same applies to the percentage of families that earned between $50,000 and $74,999. We know that there are more two-person earners in families today than there were in the past. This provides families with more disposable income which may be spent on children's clothing.

Focus Groups

A technique that is being used increasingly in getting information about an upcoming line is the **focus group.** Children and their parents are invited in to test their reactions to the new offerings. The children are given crafts to play with while the group of mothers is interviewed. Then the children are asked for their reactions. Everything is videotaped, and these tapes are distributed to the showroom, the manufacturer's reps, and to the bread-and-butter retailers.

Lee Apparel also uses focus groups to gain insight into what children like. In 1989 they organized Youthwear Fashion Boards groups. Children are asked to name products and offer their opinions on the merchandise offerings. Lee products have a greater visibility in children's departments since the onset of these groups.

Giving the Marketing Message

Information and merchandise are channeled through the industry. Following the practices of the womenswear apparel industry, children's clothing utilizes trade journals such as *Women's Wear Daily, Children's Business, Discount Store News, Daily News Record, Kids Fashions* (see Figure 12–4), and *California Apparel News,* as well as market weeks, regional showrooms, cooperative advertising, and trade shows to get the message to its customers about its offerings. While this is not a fashion forward industry, it does take its cues from the successes of the fashions of the women's and men's apparel leaders.

Specialized Skills

Showroom selling to buyers requires sensitivity to the needs of the buyer and a clear understanding of the kind of store image the buyer must live up to. Children's wear is a part of a cohesive whole and must fit into the store's mystique. Showroom personnel must be attuned to their customers and must make the buying decision an easy one for the store buyer. When the store buyer comes to shop, he or she is often accompanied by a divisional merchandise manager or a senior counselor as well as an assistant buyer. The process must be made a pleasant one since a lot must be accomplished during market week. Lunch is offered to the representatives of the store, but eating is hurried; and the salesperson continues to show the line during this period. Sometimes the buying decision is not made in one visit, but rather in two or three, with consideration given to the lines of other manufacturers. A skilled salesperson must be adept with figures, must know when merchandise can be shipped, must know the pricing policies of his or her company, and must be an able negotiator.

Distribution Channels

There is a decided change taking place in the way children's wear is being distributed today. In the past, the most widely used channel for children's clothing was manufacturer to retailer to consumer for the larger retailer or boutique. Mom-and-pop stores used **wholesalers** because of the great variety of merchandise they offered. With the acceptance of chain operations such as Kids Gap, Baby Gap, and Gymboree and of private-label merchandise by retailers, we see a greater percentage of **direct channeling** being used. Wholesalers are diminishing in importance and are used primarily by mom-and-pop dry goods operations that are becoming less important, for staple retail merchan-

Courtesy: D.A.Y. Kids Sportswear, Inc., New York

• • • • • • • • FIGURE 12-4 Advertisement by D.A.Y. Kids Sportswear which appeared in *Kids Fashions*, a trade journal of the children's wear industry, April 1992. (See Color Plate 8)

dise such as underwear, and by institutional purchasers who require the submission of bids by middlemen.

Computerized Response

In an attempt to reduce the amount of merchandise stored in its distribution centers, Wal-Mart has instituted a computerized direct access system with many of its suppliers. Automatic orders are generated whenever supplies of stock reach a predetermined level. Manufacturers themselves are computerizing their operations in order to be able to fill these orders quickly. **Optical scanners** are used within store systems in order to quickly identify items that are becoming hot so that reorders can be issued quickly. Wal-Mart is not the first of the large retailers to use this system.

Retailers

Traditional and upscale department stores and specialty stores have not increased their percentage of floor space for children's apparel. In fact, some chains such as Saks Fifth Avenue have no children's apparel in some of their branches such as Town Center in Boca Raton, Florida. Burdines, a Southeast traditional department store chain owned by Federated Department Stores, has about 12.5 percent of the floor space devoted to children's apparel. First Impressions, the private label, constitutes about 25 percent of the children's wear. Other labels that can be seen on the floor are Carter, Buster Brown, and OshKosh. Byron's, a large specialty chain, has about 10 percent of its merchandise in private label, Little Lambs. The owner of Byron's is Ancina Holding Company. National labels that may be seen frequently on the floor are HealthTex, Buster Brown, Carter, Levi, and Cherokee. Twenty-five percent of the merchandise in the store is children's apparel. The store believes in **promotional pricing** and is sale driven. The merchandise price lines are budget and moderate. In a typical department at Sears, one of the largest department store chains in the country, the private-label merchandise, Sears and Kids and More, constitutes 25 percent of the merchandise in the departments. The floor space is about 15 percent of the store. Labels that can be readily seen in the department are OshKosh, Levi, Lee, Duck Head, Dockers, and Bugle Boy. At Sears, about 60 percent of the children's merchandise is imported. Sears has the added advantage of two groups of clothing not often seen in department stores. For large boys there is a Husky label and for large girls a Pretty Plus label. In addition, they carry up to size 16 for girls and 20 for boys. A special offering by Sears is a program called Kid Vantage. Clothing that is worn out before it is outgrown is replaced.

Retail Trends in Children's Wear

The *Fairchild Fact Files,* Children's Market 1990, published the trends in sales of children's clothing based on the type of retail establishment. Retail stores were categorized into seven different groups: department stores, chain stores (including Sears, J. C. Penney, and Montgomery

Ward), discount stores (including Kmart and Wal-Mart), specialty stores, mail order, factory outlets, and other outlets. The clothing was also divided into three categories: infants' wear, girls' wear, and boys' wear.

In the infants' wear category, discount stores, which accounted for 58.4 percent of the numbers of items sold, showed a growth of 2.7 percent from 1989 to 1990. There was also a corresponding increase in dollar sales. The additional kinds of retail outlets that showed clear increases were mail order and other outlets. In girls' wear, the only retail category that showed a substantial growth was the discount store. In the boys' wear category, the increases were under 1 percent.

Mail Order

The increase in growth in mail order for infants' wear can probably be attributed to the proliferation of upscale catalogs targeted to families where both parents work and shopping time for clothing is limited. Glossy and beautiful catalogs are (see Figure 12–5) distributed by Maggie Moore, Biobottoms, Talbots Kids, and Patagonia. Hanna Andersson offers a 20 percent deduction from the original cost of merchandise returned that has been outgrown, but not outworn. The company contributes this merchandise to charity. Spiegel Shops offers a 300-page catalog featuring merchandise from 13 different children's specialty boutiques. Shoppers can have their purchases gift wrapped and can send flowers to the new mothers through this catalog as well. Land's End and L. L. Bean also offer substantial sections devoted to children's apparel in their catalog offerings.

Catalogs continue to be successful with retailers such as J. C. Penney and conglomerates such as Sara Lee, parent company for L'Eggs and Hanes (among others), which issues its *Outlet Catalog.* This successful apparel catalog, which originally started with irregular pantyhose and expanded to underwear and sportswear for men and women, always offers several pages of irregular toddler and children's sportswear and underwear.

Leased Departments

It is not often that a **leased department** offering children's apparel can be found in stores, but Lee Apparel has opened Lee Concept Shops which carry menswear, womenswear, and boys' wear in some of the J. C. Penney stores. Lee is also opening a Concept Shop in Jones, a Kansas City store. It is planning to introduce girls' wear in a year or so in these shops.

FRESH AIR WEAR FOR KIDS

FALL 1993

Courtesy: Biobottoms, Petaluma, California

• • • • • • • • **FIGURE 12-5 A successful, ecology-minded mail order catolog, Biobottoms, offers infants', children's, and boys' and girls' wear. (See Color Plate 9)**

Promoting Children's Wear

Most of the advertising dollars spent for children's wear are spent by retailers using the print medium. Newspapers are the most successful way of drawing people into the stores. Pennysavers, which are newspapers distributed without cost to consumers, are successfully used by small retailers to announce sales events. **Cooperative advertising** will most frequently be found in special issues of *The New York Times* that feature children's fashions.

Many stores successfully utilize the broadcast medium to get the message to their customers. Local radio and television stations offer information on sales events. There is a growing tendency to sell merchandise via shopping channel television. However, children's apparel is a small fraction of these offerings.

Mall Promotions

Children's specialty shops and boutiques which are located in malls often participate in joint promotions with other shops in these locations. Malls sponsor promotional events to herald the onset of the Christmas season, and during this period, tiny train rides or gifts from Santa may be a draw for the smallest shoppers.

New Marketing Ideas

According to *Kids Fashions,* some aggressive retailers have started the promotion of children's apparel prenatally. Expectant mothers in childbirth classes are given 25 percent off coupons and offered an enrollment in a baby shower registry. Other stores use birth announcements in local newspapers as a source for new customers and send out coupons in this way. Some stores visit the homes of regular customers when additional children are born, and the parents are urged to come in and show off the new baby. The parents are given a gift for the new baby when they come into the store. To increase the volume of infants' wear, one boutique offers, without cost to the customer, a better quality gift wrap which is beautifully displayed. Boutiques freely use toys to enhance the attractiveness of the apparel they sell and usually manage to increase the amount of the sale as well by the add-on of the toy that is displayed with the garment.

Retail Selling Environments

Successful stores that target older children make shopping fun for them. The use of lots of visual and verbal humor and comfortable music makes children feel a part of something new that is going on. The selling atmosphere is especially important for this market. These stores, which have a distinctive image, know that they must promote all the time. Some stores make the mistake of advertising only sales events.

Other stores use oversize props to help create a fun image. They use large crayons, oversize blocks and animals, and large dolls on the wall to identify the various departments in the children's area. The OshKosh B'Gosh store in Wisconsin makes shopping for the parents easy. It offers wide aisles for strollers, shopping carts with seat belts, and bathrooms with diaper-changing areas. OshKosh B'Gosh uses different channels of distribution for its merchandise. It uses a direct channel by selling its own merchandise in its own store and uses the manufacturer to retailer channel as well. OshKosh also may use a manufacturer to wholesaler to retailer channel for small stores that want to offer their merchandise.

The use of incandescent lighting rather than fluorescent lighting in children's wear departments creates an atmosphere of warmth. Additional spotlights add drama and interest to the merchandise offerings. Attractive floors delineate the area of the department and set it off as a special island.

Children's Attic in Philadelphia uses **consignment merchandise,** both worn and new, for part of its offerings and buys **closeouts** from manufacturers in order to position itself between the mass-marketers and the expensive boutiques.

Production Schedule for Girls' Dresses

It is important that the industry adhere to a strict schedule during the course of a year in order to best utilize the plant facilities and provide work for the employees on a year round basis. Assuming that a company has the capability of producing approximately 75,000 dozen dresses during the course of a year, the dresses would be allocated as follows by season:

Fall	25,000 dozen
Holiday	18,500 dozen
Summer	7,500 dozen
Spring	24,000 dozen

This allows a company to produce approximately 1,500 dozen dresses each week.

To express this on a monthly basis, the industry assumes 4.25 weeks in every month, which accounts for 51 weeks during the course of the year. The additional week in a 52-week year is the allowance for national or state holidays. Personal vacation time is rotated in so that the flow of production never stops.

Month	Weeks	Season	
January	3.5	Summer	6.00 weeks
February	2.5	Summer	

Month	Weeks	Season	
February	1.75	Fall	16.5 weeks
March	4.25	Fall	
April	4.25	Fall	
May	4.25	Fall	
June	2	Fall	
June	2.25	Holiday	13.25 weeks
July	4.25	Holiday	
August	4.25	Holiday	
September	2.5	Holiday	
September	1.75	Spring	15.25 weeks
October	4.25	Spring	
November	4.25	Spring	
December	4.25	Spring	
January	.75	Spring	

In addition to adhering to the above schedule, meetings of all heads of the departments take place on a weekly basis in order to review the current line. During these meetings, decisions are made as to whether to adopt or discard a style number after retail buyers have reviewed the samples and placed their orders. The orders are journalized and decisions are made as to which items should be cut. A list is prepared that stipulates the styles to be cut and the order in which the styles are cut. This is called *putting down* the cuttings. An important consideration is the date the garments are to be shipped.

Cutting tickets are prepared that also list the piece goods and trim that must be ordered. One ticket remains with the journal. The other ticket flows from the piece goods buyer to the trim buyer to the production department, where the following steps are taken:

1. The patterns are finalized—sometimes changes are made to meet the needs of the retail buyer.
2. The patterns are sent to the grader.
3. The graded patterns are sent to the marker. Markers are prepared when the piece goods arrive in the production department.
4. Styles are cut and assembled with all the trim and sent to the outside shops for sewing and finishing along with the date to be completed for shipment.

If the sewing and assembling of garments is to be completed off shore, the whole process is advanced three months.

1. Each industry has its own set of traditions. The producers of fabric close their mills the first two weeks in July for vacation. How do you suppose the garment makers cope with their own tradition of rotating vacations during the summer and keep their facilities operating on a full-time basis when no fabric is produced or shipped the first two weeks in July? Why must a fabric buyer be a good negotiator?

2. What part does marketing play in the above example of production?

.... TERMS TO REMEMBER

national brand   private label   discount retailer   showroom   trade show trade journal   regional markets   manufacturer's representative contractor   outside shop   inside shop   ILGWU   ACTWUA   freelance designer   cut and sew   costing   market week   piece goods   appliqués bread-and-butter cutomers   gravy customers   pre-packs   hot items   the dogs   cash flow   factors   demographic figures   focus groups   direct channel   wholesalers   optical scanners   promotional pricing   leased department   selling environments   consignment merchandise   closeouts *Fairchild Fact Files*   cooperative advertising

.... HIGHLIGHTS OF THE CHAPTER

- New York City is the most important market for the children's apparel industry. However, regional markets in Dallas, Chicago, Atlanta, Miami, and California are growing in importance.

- Children's clothing sizes are based on the growth stage of a child rather than on the weight or height of a child.

- The production of cut-and-sew children's wear is similar to that of the women's wear industry.

- Vital statistics must be monitored in order to be able to predict accurately the market needs for children of today, tomorrow, and the year 2000.

- Each job in the children's apparel industry requires its own specialized skills.

- Merchandise that is not properly promoted is not sold.

- The atmosphere of a children's department in a retail establishment is crucial to successful selling.

.... REVIEW QUESTIONS

1. Why are the showrooms for children's apparel located in the same or nearby buildings? What building contains more children's apparel showrooms than any other?

2. Why does the children's wear industry expect increasing sales in the next few years?

3. How have the colors and fashions of children's clothing changed over the years?

4. What makes a retail environment successful in children's wear?

5. What is the impact of trade shows and trade journals on the children's wear industry?

6. What are manufacturers' reps? What are foreign sales agents?

7. How are focus groups used?

8. Why are catalog sales growing in the children's wear industry?

9. Why are discount store sales growing in the children's wear industry?

10. Why is the print medium used most frequently to get the advertising message across?

.... RESEARCH AND PROJECTS

1. If you are located in the New York Metropolitan area, visit a showroom where children's apparel is sold. Look at the directory of one of the buildings where the showrooms are located and see if you can recognize a familiar label. Go up to the showroom and introduce yourself and ask if you can interview showroom personnel. Explain that you are a student writing an article about the industry. Write up the interview. If it's good, submit it to *Women's Wear Daily* or *Kids Fashions.*

2. Try to sketch a child's play outfit that you have seen. Now sketch five different variations of the same outfit. If they're good, submit them to a children's wear manufacturer.

3. Describe in an article the underlying tensions during the selling process in a showroom. What can the salesperson do to alleviate those tensions and still close the sale successfully?

4. Try to think of five new ways to bring people into a children's store. Why do you think your ideas will be successful? Go to a children's boutique and sell your ideas.

5. Analyze a children's apparel department in a discount store. How is the department organized? What are the size ranges? What prices do you see most frequently in each of the size ranges? What labels are on the merchandise? Is the merchandise imported or is it domestically made? How can you tell? Name the brands that you see. Tell if each brand is a national brand or a private label.

6. What are some reasons for you to enter the children's apparel industry? What kind of additional training do you think you will need? How would you look for a job in the industry? Why would anyone want to hire you?

CHAPTER 13

· ·

Creating and Marketing Fashion Accessories

· · · · · · · LEARNING OBJECTIVES

After reading this chapter, you should be able to:

- Describe the characteristics of the various accessories industries: the manufacturing processes, the location of the industries, and the marketing activities of the industries.
- Discuss the importance of accessories in the fashion world.
- Identify the major accessories labels.
- Enumerate the ways in which accessories complement major items of apparel.
- Outline the development of franchising operations within the industry.

· · · · · · · PERFORMANCE OUTCOME

After reading this chapter, you should be able to:

- Know how to locate trade shows and showrooms in New York City.
- Recognize the names of the important trade journals of the accessories industries.
- Determine the quality of a well-made leather glove.
- Purchase cosmetics products with discernment in flea markets.

The great variety of accessories that we buy reflects the changing needs of the American market. Just as the leaves and needles complete the beauty of trees, so do the handbags, wallets, jewelry, fragrances, cosmetics, activewear, shoes, and intimate apparel complete the beauty of the apparel that is worn by the American man and woman. Accessories make us feel good, and because of that we are willing to spend billions of dollars every year for items that reflect the lifestyle we would like to experience and the lifestyle in which we would like to be perceived.

In times of economic downturn, the purchases of accessories outperform those of apparel. We use the accessories to make a new statement, to update our garments of yesteryear, and to reflect the changes that are taking place in our lives. In times of economic growth, we buy upscale, unique items that speak to us of good times and the prosperity that lies before us.

While it is difficult to discuss the myriad of items we buy to make our lives pleasant and lovely, we will analyze the most important of the industries that manufacture and distribute these products.

PERSONAL CARE PRODUCTS

According to an estimate by the U.S. Department of Commerce in 1990, more than $18.5 billion a year are spent by the American man and woman for fragrances, cosmetics, and toiletries. The most recent changes in the industry reflect a shift away from **high-end lines** and toward products that are **mass-merchandised.** Supermarkets and discount stores are including many more products of this nature, as are the large drug store chains that have become ubiquitous throughout our nation.

In the same report, hair care products represented 25 percent of the money spent on personal care products, skin care 15 percent, fragrances 13 percent, color cosmetics 9 percent, deodorants 6 percent, men's toiletries 5 percent, sun care products 2 percent, and all other products which include dentifrices and shaving preparations, 25 percent (see Figure 13–1). These figures do not include soaps and detergents, nor do they include household scents and potpourris.

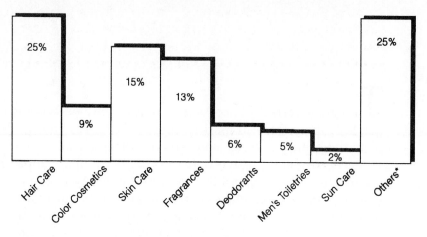

*Products such as soaps, detergents, and household scents are not included in "Others."

•••••••• FIGURE 13-1 **Where the money goes for personal care.**

The Industry

There has been a dramatic shift in the nature of the personal care industry. Once a mix of large, medium, and small independent companies, recent mergers and acquisitions are creating giant companies that dominate production and sales. In the past, the giant companies had large research and development departments, always creating new products to please the consumer. Today, the large companies are merging with other large companies and acquiring smaller ones in order to increase their **market share** and their profits. These companies now see themselves as giant **multinational companies** with brand recognition all over the world. Further, the industry categorizes its products as prestige and mass-market cosmetics and fragrances. The prestige products are found in department stores and specialty shops, whereas the mass-market products are usually found in the large chain drug stores, supermarkets, and discount stores.

The Leading Manufacturers

According to *Business Week* (July 31, 1989), Estée Lauder, with its four leading brands—Estée Lauder, Clinique, Aramis, and Prescriptives—is the leading manufacturer of prestige cosmetics and fragrances and has more than one-third of the market share. Cosmair, a French firm, with its lines of L'Oreal, Lancôme, Biotherm, and designer fragrances is next in importance and has about a 13 percent share of the market. Unilever is controlled by English and French interests and is next in importance. It offers such lines as Calvin Klein, Fabergé, and Elizabeth Arden. The Elizabeth Taylor fragrances, Passion and White Diamonds, and her newest Fragrant Jewels collection, which includes Diamonds and Rubies, Diamonds and Emeralds, Diamonds and Sapphires, and Rough Diamonds, are a growing element of the Elizabeth Arden lines. Rough Diamonds is a men's fragrance line that is about to be introduced in prestige stores. The Avon company, with its lines of Giorgio and Oscar de La Renta, among others, is next in importance. The privately owned Revlon lines are in the process of reorganization in preparation for a public offering of stock. However, two of its major divisions, Max Factor and Betrix, have been acquired by Procter and Gamble. Revlon has been changing its market strategies and is using different and younger models to promote its lines. Chanel, Christian Dior, and Clarins are Paris-based companies with strong lines of their own.

The greatest change that has taken place among the fragrance and cosmetics companies has been the expansion of Procter and Gamble, the largest producer of detergents and soaps and the developer of disposable diapers, into the field of personal care. The company has, however, had successful lines of hair care products such as Pert Plus and Head & Shoulders. Procter and Gamble products are, for the most part, **positioned** as middle- and mass-market products. The most important merger into P&G includes the products of Noxell Corporation: Cover Girl, and its 23 percent of the United States mass market; Clarion; and Noxzema. As mentioned above, Max Factor, with its important 5 percent share of the mass market, has also been purchased. Max Factor is a leading brand in Japan. Betrix, the second acquisition from Revlon, is a popular brand in Germany and the Eastern European countries and is expected to provide P&G with handsome profits. Included in this acquisition from Revlon was the Mary Quant line and the fragrances California and Le Jardin.

To meet the challenge of the growing market for fragrances and cosmetics in the mass market, prestige manufacturers are developing new products to improve their growth and profits. A number of new products are also being introduced to meet the needs of the environment-conscious consumer. These products are free of animal byproducts and chemicals and are packaged with biodegradable and recyclable materials. One such new product is being developed in a new division by Estée Lauder, Origins Natural Resources.

Location of Manufacturers

The states with the greatest number of establishments that produce toilet preparations are California, New York, and New Jersey. This does not include soaps or detergents. In the United States, as a whole, there are 682 manufacturing establishments that employ 63,637 people, according to *County Business Patterns 1990,* published by the U.S. Department of Commerce, Bureau of the Census.

The most important source of information about industries in the United States is the Economic Census which is undertaken every five years by the Department of Commerce during the second and seventh year of every decade. The 1992 census reporting data compiled from individual establishments is so encompassing that final data is not scheduled for publication until the second half of 1994. These data are released on a flow basis, as printed, to major university libraries and research companies, as well as the Library of Congress. Each industry is assigned a special number called a Standard Industrial Classification Code, or SIC number, which contains four digits. Information is compiled that reflects the growth or decline of each industry in comparison to the previous censuses, the location by state of the industries, the number of employees, and the payroll figures.

The source that is used in this textbook is compiled on an annual basis and offers similar information. However, the information is derived from administrative records and current surveys as reported by counties in the United States, thus providing great geographical detail on the industries. This information is also not immediately released as the data require careful study before publication.

Communication Within the Industry

The most important trade association is the **Cosmetic, Toiletry, and Fragrance Association (CTFA)** which keeps its members informed about all changes in the industry. It helps its members understand the laws that pertain to cosmetics products. By law, cosmetics may not alter the body's structure or functions. For example, wrinkle cream may not remove wrinkles on any kind of permanent basis, but may only mask them on a temporary basis. The Food and Drug Administration (FDA) is the branch of the government that regulates the cosmetics industry. The FDA makes sure that manufacturers do not use any ingredients in their products that may be harmful. The 1966 Fair Packing and Labeling Act requires companies to list the ingredients in their products in order of weight.

In addition to its regular coverage of events within the industry, *Women's Wear Daily,* the largest trade journal in the country, also offers a special edition several times a year devoted to cosmetics. Here people can learn about new products to be introduced, people or stores in the industry doing a terrific job, and items that are moving best in different major stores in different regions of the country.

Production of Fragrances

The fragrance industry is probably the most secretive of all the accessory industries. The perfumer may select many elements from thousands of animal, vegetable, mineral, and synthetic products in order to develop a unique and salable scent. Most cosmetics contain fragrances, some so mild that the consumers are unaware of their presence in the product. Some manufacturers are even applying scent to tissues and to air conditioning systems in some establishments to improve production and sales. The most expensive ingredient in fragrances is the essential oil. This oil is extracted from a variety of vegetable substances that may include flower petals, barks of trees, leaves, and many other materials. Synthetic products may replace the vegetable products or be used in conjunction with the vegetable products in order to manufacture a less expensive fragrance. In order to have a scent that lasts, a fixative is added. The most traditional and expensive fixative used is prepared from the scent glands of skunks or other animals. All but the most expensive fragrances have synthetic fixatives either combined with the animal products or used alone. Coloring matter, alcohol, and water, among other ingredients are also added to the product. The value of the fragrance is determined by the amount of essential oils it contains and by its packaging. The product with the largest percentage of essential oils is called *perfume* or *parfum.* Next in value comes perfume water or eau de parfum, toilet water or eau de toilette, cologne water or eau de cologne, and cologne.

The package of a fragrance greatly enhances the value of the product and adds a considerable cost to it. Many beautiful handblown lead crystal flacons have become collectors' items and can be found in museums around the world. The Baccarat Museum in Paris has a glorious collection of perfume bottles. Among the artifacts recovered and displayed from the earliest civilizations can always be found interesting glass and pottery containers for fragrances that were used by both men and women.

Skin Care Products

The value of skin care products has been increasing at an annual rate of 12 percent. This impressive growth rate is due to the demographic changes taking place within the population and to the distressing, harmful effects of the sun which have been causing skin cancer as well as premature wrinkling, spotting, and aging of the skin. The most popular brands of skin care products sold in department stores are Clinique, Estée Lauder, and Lancôme. Mass-marketed products in order of sales are Oil of Olay, Vaseline Intensive Care Lotion, Pond's, and Noxzema.

Skin care products include face creams, cleansers, astringents, masks and lighteners, hand and body lotions, acne products, suntan products, and lip protectors. We are beginning to see an increase in private-label products offered and sold to the public by supermarkets and large chain drug stores.

Changing Demographics

Ethnic products designed for the multiplicity of races that make up the population of the United States have been successfully developed and are selling at unprecedented rates. Revlon's ColorStyle for African-American women, and Revlon's Almay cosmetics for customers with darker complexions are examples of these products. Ethnic cosmetics are not only found in stores but also are being successfully marketed directly by catalog. Gold Medal Products of Freeport, New York, does a particularly good job in marketing hair cosmetics for African-Americans. Thirty percent of the people in the United States will be non-Causasian by the year 2000, as reported in *Fairchild Fact Files*, 1990, Toiletries, Cosmetics, Fragrances, and Beauty Aids. In addition, demographic projections show that more than half of the population will be over the age of 35 in the twenty-first century, prompting companies to develop new lines of products that will diminish the effects of the aging process on the skin. Cosmetics companies will be introducing intensive treatment products such as firming and anticellulite creams designed for specific body areas that may be more prone to problems.

The depletion of the ozone layer is considered by most scientists to be the cause of the great increase in skin cancer as well as precancerous skin conditions that people are experiencing today. Many of the cosmetics companies have responded to the need and are developing lines of sun-block products to filter out the harmful effects of the sun's rays. In fact, sun-blocking ingredients are being added in small amounts to lipsticks and other color products used on the skin. Blocks designed to protect the delicate skin of infants are readily available and recommended by pediatricians. Manufacturers are also beginning to target men with new sport lotion sun-care products containing block. Self-tanning creams that make the skin appear to be tanned are gaining acceptance as people become more aware of the dangers of the sun and tanning salons.

While the latest findings on sun-blocks have shown them to be ineffective in protecting a person from melanoma, the most serious form of skin cancer, they have been most effective in preventing wrinkling and aging of the skin. Since the sun-blocks do change the chemistry of the skin, there is a growing sentiment among dermatologists to have these products reclassified as drugs rather than cosmetics.

Hair Care

According to the U.S. Department of Commerce, shampoos represent about one-third of the hair care market. Another 15 percent is made up of conditioners, rinses, and tonics. The rest of the products consist of hair coloring, permanents, mousses, and special ethnic products. These ethnic products are indicative of the growth in number of professional African-American women and of the response by the manufacturers to the need for specially designed products for African Americans, Hispanics, and Asian Americans.

Another factor in the growth of sales of hair care products is the popularity of professional hair care items sold only in salons. The five most important products in this category are Nexus, Redken, Paul Mitchell, Matrix, and Sebastian (*Advertising Age*, April 16, 1990). As of this writing, these products are all individually owned and are one segment of the market that has not been acquired by the giants. These products are designed to correct hair problems such as thinning hair. New products include hair masks, hair regulating jellies, and pre-shampoo conditioners.

Procter and Gamble's Pert Plus, which combines shampoo and conditioner in one product, is the leading shampoo, according to *Advertising Age* (March 19, 1990). A dandruff-control version is being introduced as well. P&G's Head & Shoulders is next in sales, with Helene Curtis products, Suave and Finesse, following next in rank.

Color Cosmetics

The sale of color cosmetics is continuing to grow. The fastest rate of growth is evidenced by the increasing sales in national drug chains and supermarkets which account for more than half of the sales. In a study done of discount stores in *Discount Store News* (October 16, 1989), the best-selling brands are Maybelline, Cover Girl, Revlon, and Max Factor. Beauty supply outlets and specialty stores are also increasing their sales of color cosmetics. A smaller growth is being experienced in department stores with the greatest increase of sales due to the popularity of custom blending foundation, eyeshadow, lipstick, and blush to the skin type and taste of the customer. Customers enjoy the personalized attention given to them and become repeat purchasers. The four major custom blenders are Luminique, Prescriptives, Charles of the Ritz, and Visage.

Nail care continues to grow as an industry, and consumers are spending more money on these professional services. More companies are developing nail care products and expanding their lines. The top-selling nail care companies are Revlon and Cover Girl.

Men's Products

Two out of every three purchases of men's fragrances are made by women, and sales of these products continue to grow as more and more new scents are being introduced. Grecian Formula is the top-selling hair coloring product, but new products will be introduced that will incorporate hair thickening with hair color. Aramis will focus on skin problems caused by shaving and will be introducing clinics for men to promote its skin products.

The Marketing Process

Cosmetics and fragrance companies have strong ties with department stores. Prestige product manufacturers often train their own demonstrators and share the payment of salaries of these employees with the department stores. Most of these products are impulse purchases and require a great deal of skill in selling techniques. A system of rubber-banding, where unsold merchandise is returned to the manufacturer for fresh merchandise, insures that the stores carry only the best quality products. Cosmetics areas are usually given the best locations by department stores to capture the greatest traffic. In some cases, the product is completely controlled by the manufacturer. Not only does it train, but also pays the salary of, the employee, who is considered a line representative. In this case, the company also pays for the counter space used. Sometimes cosmetics companies, including Adrien Arpel, offer private salon treatment such as facials within the store.

Mass-marketed products are usually sold to supermarkets, chain drug stores, and discount stores by middlemen. The lower the cost of the product, the more likely several middlemen will be used. In some cases, displays are replenished and maintained by **rack jobbers.**

Some personal care products are channeled directly to the consumer by the manufacturer. The largest and most successful of these companies is Avon, followed by Mary Kay. Some retailers position themselves as beauty supply stores which sell to salons and consumers. These stores may offer private-label merchandise. Products sold to salons are sold at wholesale prices. Beauty supply stores are not alone in offering private labels. Prestige stores such as Bergdorf Goodman and Neiman Marcus also carry such lines. Salons usually use middlemen to purchase the items they use and the items they sell to consumers.

Personal Care Retailers

Discount operations such as Caldor and Kmart carry mass-marketed brands that are packaged for self-service. Wal-Mart also carries some prestige products, which are kept in locked cases. The prices are similar to those in prestige department and specialty stores. Walgreens, a large drug store chain, has been unique in obtaining two prestige products on a direct basis. The stores also carry a number of others that are supplied by middlemen. Stores such as Saks Fifth Avenue, Lord & Taylor, and Macy's allocate a large percentage of first-floor space to all the prestige products offered. Macy's also has kiosks of specific products near departments such as intimate apparel and dresses.

Flea markets do a brisk business in fragrances and color cosmetics. Some of the merchandise offered there is outdated. In addition to selling private-label products that imitate the popular prestige items, vendors may offer purchasers gray market goods which are legitimately produced overseas, but offered here by unauthorized distributors. Counterfeit fragrances may also be found in the stalls.

Promoting Personal Care Products

Manufacturers of personal care products have been unique in the promotion of their offerings. They maintain control of their message and do not leave it in the hands of the retailers who sell the products. In addition to creative advertising on television, producers prepare mail order brochures for the store to send to their customers. They also give the stores envelope stuffers that are scented or have special offerings to enclose in monthly bills. They have special promotions with low-cost premiums offered with a purchase. Frequently, the premiums are unique status symbols such as the Aramis umbrellas offered to men with a purchase of cologne. Sometimes they are a chest of color cosmetics for a customer to sample. Magazine advertising is unusual as well. Many fragrance companies offer strips of the scent in the magazine as part of the advertisement. Color cosmetics in tiny packages may be sampled in the magazines as well.

FOOTWEAR

Once a thriving industry in the United States, most footwear worn in this country is imported. From high fashion items designed and imported from Italy to low-cost products found in discount operations that are imported from China, the footwear industry has seen a major change in the past two decades. Some American shoe operations have closed their domestic factories and laid off many workers and have expanded into foreign countries where labor is cheap. However, the news is not all bad. There was a 1 percent increase in sales of American-made footwear in 1992 after five years of losses. This is because of the growth of U.S. brands such as Timberland, producer of sturdy, comfortable footwear.

Comfort is the key word in shoe design for today's shoppers. It has become more important for a purchaser to feel good wearing shoes than for the purchaser to like the styling, the construction, and the price. An important second factor is the feeling of power a person has when the shoe is just right. More than any other article of apparel, the shoe becomes a part of a person's body as it takes on the configuration of the foot. Once a person has worn a shoe, it will never feel completely comfortable on anyone else's foot.

Infants walk earlier and more comfortably with the softer shoes and rubber soles now on the market, and women have a new freedom to stride purposefully and comfortably in the home and in the workplace. Shoes were once used as a restrictive means to keep women enslaved to a home. Beginning in the tenth century and continuing into the early twentieth century in China, women's feet were bound when they were children. This distorted the foot, forcing women to hobble at a slow pace. In the 1830s in Europe, shoes were made so flimsily that women could not venture far outside their homes. A decade or so later, women had to have one or two toes removed in order to wear the narrow shoes that were then fashionable.

The Leading Manufacturers

According to Footwear Industries of America, the top seller of footwear in this country in 1992 was Nike with sales of $3.4 billion. Having surpassed all other companies with its sales of athletic footwear, Nike is expanding its efforts at staying on top with its new lines, Cole Haan and i.e., footwear that combines the comfort of athletic shoes with a casual look. Reebok, the second largest producer of footwear in the United States with $3 billion in sales, is the parent company of Rockport, Metaphors, Weebok Casuals, Avia, and Ellesse U.S.A., as well as its lines of athletic footwear. U.S. Shoe Corp is the third largest seller with $2.7 billion in sales. This company encompasses such brands as Bandolino, Capezio, Cobbie Cuddlers, Easy Spirit, J. Chisolm Boots, Joyce Shoes, Pappagallo, Selby, and Texas Boots. The fourth and fifth biggest sellers of footwear are Stride Rite Corporation ($586 million) with its additional lines of Sperry Top-Sider and Keds, and L.A. Gear ($430 million). The final big seller was the up and coming Timberland with $291 million worth of sales.

Location of Manufacturers

There are 421 establishments that manufacture nonrubber footwear in the United States. This includes nonathletic shoes for men and women as well as house slippers. The industry employs 62,768 people according to *County Business Patterns 1990*, published by the U.S. Department of Commerce, Bureau of the Census. The states that lead in the production of footwear are Missouri, Maine, and Pennsylvania.

Imports and Exports

It would be remiss for students not to have a comparison figure for the quantity of nonrubber footwear imports in 1990. This information comes from the U.S. Department of Commerce, working with the International Trade Commission. We imported 897,500,000 pairs of shoes and produced during the same period in the United States 198,445,000 pairs of shoes. We imported 267,400,000 pairs of shoes from China during this same period, and sizeable quantities from countries such as Taiwan, South Korea, Brazil, and Italy. Most of the shoes that we import are retailed in discount stores at low prices. Prestige lines of shoes are imported from Italy, France, and Spain.

Canada, Japan, and Mexico are the chief countries that buy shoes from us. During this same period, they purchased 9,200,000 pairs of shoes from the United States. Many shoe manufacturers are discovering that there is a market in Europe for the kind of quality shoes that we produce here, and companies such as Timberland, Sebago, and Cole Haan are leading the way in developing a European market.

Marketing Shoes

There are several important trade associations in the footwear industry. The Fashion Footwear Association of New York, popularly known as FFANY (see Figure 13–2), represents manufacturers of men's, women's, and children's shoes. Each year it holds four trade shows at the Plaza Hotel in New York City. The National Shoe Retailers Association (NSRA) represents the shoe retailers and is based in Columbia, Maryland. The Western Shoe Association (WSA) holds two large annual trade shows each year in Las Vegas. Another important trade association is the Sporting Goods Manufacturers Association (SGMS).

Worldwide the largest trade show is the GDS, the International Shoe Fair held in March and September in Dusseldorf, Germany, where footwear of 1,400 manufacturers from 45 countries is exhibited. The other major show is the Shoe Fair in Bologna, Italy. Store buyers, manufacturers, and shoe designers are sure to attend both trade shows for information on trends and stock purchases.

The trade publications read by people in the industry are *Footwear News* and *Footwear Plus*. Information about fashion trends in the footwear industry, features about retailers, interviews of successful people in the industry, photographs, and manufacturers' advertisements regularly appear in these publications.

Each year FFANY presents the Fashion Medal of Honor to the designer or retail establishment that has achieved great success in the footwear industry. Recent winners are Calvin Klein for fashion design, Ferragamo for his footwear design, and Nordstrom for its fashion leadership in retailing.

Distribution

In the shoe industry there are many examples of manufacturers retailing their own products. Melville Corporation manufactures and retails Thom McAnn shoes in its own stores, as does U.S. Shoe and the Brown Group. In addition, they may sell their products to other retailers. When they do so, it is known as *dual distribution*. These companies may also lease departments in large department store chains and offer bargain prices in manufacturers' outlets for close-out items that they do not plan to manufacture anymore. At the present time, we are seeing a growth in the development of franchised operations in the shoe industry. In addition to owning and operating their own stores, manufacturers are offering franchisees opportunities all over the country. In athletic shoes, consumers can find franchised operations, such as Athletic Attic, in malls and shopping centers.

Hard-to-find sizes may also be ordered from catalogs such as

(a) Surprisingly modern is this example of seventeenth-century shoes from the Vivegane Museum in Italy.

(b) From the Museum of Footwear in Elda, Spain, are two winning entries in a competition for young designers to create shoes in the tradition of Spain.

(c) Intershoe, owned by Italian makers and tanners and managed by an American staff, exports these shoes to the United States. These are examples of Via Spiga, Studio Paolo, Nickels, Jazz, Glacee, and Paloma brands.

Courtesy: Fashion Footwear Association of New York. From the FFANY Special Edition 1993.

•••••••• FIGURE 13-2 Yesterday, today, and tomorrow. (See Color Plate 2)

Masseys, in Lynchburg, Virginia. This company offers selections from major shoe companies such as U.S. Shoe and Reebok as well as private-label merchandise and merchandise from their own factory. The shoes are both American made and imported. Consumers may wear the shoes for 31 days before deciding to keep them. Masseys also offers discounted shoes on site in a 20,000-square-foot facility.

Promotion

Shoes are generally promoted by the retailer. However, there are many examples of cooperative advertising on television, and in the newspapers and magazines.

INTIMATE APPAREL

No other apparel products have changed as much in recent years as those that constitute the intimate apparel industry. Once considered the private domain of the very wealthiest and of the motion picture industry, the satins and laces and sexually explicit nightwear and undergarments are affordable and are demanded by the whole spectrum of shoppers in this country. Credited by the entire industry for the new direction and new popularity of intimate apparel, Victoria's Secret started as a single boutique in Palo Alto, California, and quickly expanded to more than 500 stores all over the country.

Retailers quickly adopted the lingerie boutique concept within their stores with products that were imitative and settings that tried to emulate the boudoir look of the new intimate fashion leader. Now owned by The Limited, the concept has developed to include the introduction of products such as men's silk undershorts, fragrances, and romantic music. Indeed, people spurred by the beauty of many of these fashions began to wear some of them as outerwear.

There are three categories of intimate apparel. **Foundations** include body shapers such as bras, girdles, and garter belts. **Lingerie** includes slips, panties, and sleepwear. **Loungewear** includes nightwear such as robes and negligees and daywear such as long and short housecoats.

The Leading Manufacturers

As in other industries, there has been a consolidation of the many small independent firms that once made up the industry into the large corporations. During 1987, which is the last available year reported on by the U.S. Bureau of the Census, retailers reported the sale of more than $6.6 billion worth of intimate apparel. The leading manufacturer is Playtex (part of the Sara Lee conglomerate), which also includes Body Views and Jean Cacharel foundations. Next comes Maidenform, followed by Vanity Fair. The latter company has improved its position in the market by means of the adoption of the Quick Response System, which allows the manufacturer to communicate with the stores by computer in order to ship quickly those items needed to maintain a proper inventory level. Vanity Fair also acquired Eileen West Sleeplines, Vassarette, and Form-O-Uthe. Warnaco is fourth in importance and includes the Warner's and Olga labels as well as the **licensed** Valentino Intimo, Arnold Scaasi, Bob Mackie, Blanche sleepwear lines, and Ungaro. Carole Hochman Designs include the licensed Dior sleepwear, Prima Donna Sleepwear, and Sara Beth. Jockey International continues to grow with its Jockey for Her line which is imitative of men's jockey undershorts, yet is comfortable and sexy at the same time. Wacoal Corporation is a giant Japanese innerwear giant which is an important presence in department stores all over the United States and produces the Donna Karan line.

The newest acquisition in intimate apparel is the sale of the Calvin Klein men's underwear, men's accessories, and women's intimate apparel to the Warnaco Group.

Location of Manufacturers

The states that produce the greatest value of women's and children's underwear and nightwear are New York, North Carolina, and California. There are 564 establishments that manufacture these products and employ 68,264 people in the United States according to *County Business Patterns 1990*, published by the U.S. Department of Commerce, Bureau of the Census.

Marketing Intimate Apparel

The intimate apparel industry is unusual in that it offers preticketing services to its customers. This is especially useful to small stores since merchandise can be immediately placed on the sales floor and the tickets provide POS (Point of Sale) information to the retailer. This enables the retailer to fill in the needed sizes and products. Manufacturers also train salespeople to sell their products properly.

Brand names are very important in the intimate apparel industry, and manufacturers spend a lot of money advertising their products in the media individually as well as on a co-op basis. They also provide **stitch-ins** for store catalog offerings and brochures for special promotions providing a premium of a free bra with the purchase of two. Coordinated sets of underclothing have been well received by consumers. There has been a marked increase in designer influence in the industry. Foundations and loungewear are being combined as a result of the comfort of lycra garments and the use of innerwear as outerwear. Donna Karan has been pioneering these new products for entertaining at home. Her products are featured in stores such as Saks Fifth Avenue, Bergdorf Goodman, and Neiman Marcus. New lines with Christian Dior, Ralph Lauren, Fernando Sanchez, Josie Natori, Eileen West, and Calvin Klein labels will also be offered.

There are three trade associations in the industry: the Associated Corset and Brassiere Manufacturers, the Intimate Apparel Council of the American Apparel Manufacturers Association, and the Lingerie Manufacturers Association. New York City is the center of marketing activities and the manufacturers maintain showrooms between 28th Street and 38th Street on Fifth and Madison Avenues. Market weeks are held twice a year in New York and in the regional markets.

Catalogs

There is an increase in the number of folios being offered to the consumer. The Spiegel catalog has page numbers that are color-coded and named, which makes each section easier to find. The index, also color tabbed, gives a small synopsis of the merchandise to be found in each section. The intimate apparel section is called Private Lives.

The Sara Lee Outlet Catalog, which features slightly imperfect merchandise at reduced prices, regularly offers Bali, Henson Kickernick, Playtex, and Hanes intimate apparel. All of these products are under the **conglomerate** umbrella.

HOSIERY

The one accessory that is truly close to meeting the fashion marketing ideal is hosiery. Using the latest computer technology, both retailers and manufacturers are able to provide consumers with the colors, shapes, sizes, sheerness, and patterns most desired by utilizing both POS information and Quick Response to produce and ship exactly what is being purchased and needed. This is an industry that does not feel threatened by imports from countries that pay their workers very little. Although there are some imports, the cost of producing hosiery is not severely dependent upon the cost of labor since the mills that produce this knitwear do not require many workers. Instead, the mills depend upon the latest technology and the chemical development of new and better fibers.

Most hosiery is produced in North Carolina. Many other states in the Southeast are developing their industries but have not managed to produce appreciable amounts of hose in comparison.

Production

Most hosiery is knitted in a circular fashion and hence does not have seams. The machinery is able to change designs and sizes with the turn of a knob. The product is produced in the **greige** so that the colors needed can be applied at the last moment. Some of the mills dye and finish the hose directly; others ship the **greige goods** to finishers who complete the product as needed by the market. Finishing also includes a blocking process that sets the shape with heat.

Hosiery is made from cotton, nylon, acrylic, and spandex. Cotton is used primarily for sports socks and knee-high socks, nylon for pantyhose, with the latest fashions combining spandex with nylon for better fit, appearance, and durability. Spandex is the growth fiber in the industry and is outpacing the growth of nylon. Designers are experimenting with this fiber by combining it with silk (Calvin Klein) and using it for novelty legwear. Acrylic is the primary fiber used for men's hose, other than athletic socks.

There is a great variety of products on the market today geared to different needs of men, women, and children. Stockings are produced in ankle, calf, and full lengths. Full-length stockings may be *full-fashioned*. This means that the hose is knitted flat rather than round with stitches reduced to conform to the shape of the leg. The stocking is then seamed and finished. Control-top hosiery is also produced with elastomer (spandex) in the top of the pantyhose. Support hosiery with greater amounts of elastomer combined with nylon can be purchased as stockings or as pantyhose. Maternity hose meets the needs of still another market, as does hosiery produced for infants and children. Tights are produced for men, women, and children active in dance or sport or just to keep out the cold. Socks for men can be ankle high, calf high, or executive length. They can be sheerer for dress wear, bulkier for winter wear, or cottony for sports. Interesting patterns can be knitted into knee-length multicolored socks using yarns of different colors.

The Leading Manufacturers

The industry leader is a conglomerate, Sara Lee, with its Hanes lines of Underalls, Slenderalls, L'eggs, Sheer Energy, Sheer Elegance, Fitting Pretty, Hanes Too, Hanes Alive, Just My Size, Silk Reflections, and Bill Blass. Sara Lee also produces the new Donna Karan hose which is sold in department stores. Kayser-Roth, the producer of No Nonsense and Calvin Klein pantyhose, is another giant in the hosiery industry, as are Round-the-Clock (Givenchy), Bonnie Doone (Geoffrey Beene), and Hot Sox (Ralph Lauren).

Marketing Hosiery

The major producers advertise their hosiery products on television and in the print media. Most of the money spent promotes the national brands. Cooperative dollars are also offered to retailers who choose to advertise the products. There is a trend toward special self-service packaging for discount stores, chain drug stores, and supermarkets. Displays and in-store selling aids are also offered. Many stores offer their customers private-label hose, which has a following among loyal patrons. The Sara Lee slightly imperfect catalog mentioned earlier devotes about one-third of the space to its hosiery products (See Figure 13–3). The National Wholesale Company in Lexington, North Carolina, offers a retail and wholesale catalog at the same time. Customers purchasing three dozen of any item are offered special prices in a price list that can be requested. The items offered are a combination of national brands and private-label merchandise. The catalog includes intimate apparel and sportswear.

• •

JEWELRY

Since the beginning of recorded time, people have had a love affair with jewelry. From the magical tale of Ali Baba to the stories of pirates on the seas, the star of the show has always been jewels. Jewels have withstood the test of time and have tended to grow in value over the years, even outpacing the inflationary cycles.

What is it about jewels that make them so wonderful? Precious stones can be rare and unique and are called *gems*. They require the skilled hands of well-trained craftsmen called **lapidaries** to fashion them into objects of beauty. The metals that are used to create lovely brooches, earrings, rings, bracelets, and necklaces are rare as well and

Courtesy: Sara Lee Products

Thigh Highs—a fashionable *and* comfortable alternative to pantyhose!

Style Description	Style No.	Size†	Color No.	3 PAIRS	6 PAIRS	12 PAIRS
Hanes* Silk Reflections* Silky Thigh Highs Sandalfoot (Reg. $5.50 pr.)*	3048D	AB, CD and EF	Pearl (05) Jet Black (71) Barely Black (74) Soft Taupe (50) White (02) Little Color (89) Barely There (14)	$8.25 SAVE $8.25	$16.50 SAVE $16.50	$33.00 SAVE $33.00
Hanes* Thigh-Hi Sandalfoot (Reg. $4.50 pr.)*	3608L	P. MD, MT, and T	Pearl (05) Jet Black (71) Barely Black (74) Town Taupe (16) South Pacific (64) Little Color (89) Barely There (14)	$6.75 SAVE $6.75	$13.50 SAVE $13.50	$27.00 SAVE $27.00

*First quality suggested retail price. One style, size and color per pack.
**These colors not available in all styles. †See Hanes HI size chart and Thigh High size chart on B5 in center of catalog. Made in USA.

FIGURE 13-3 Off-price hosiery is directly marketed to the consumer via catalog. This is a page from a recent L'eggs, Hanes, Bali, Playtex Outlet Catalog.

require creativity and training in order to enhance the beauty of the stones in their proper settings.

Not everyone can afford to own precious jewelry, but certainly the purchase of costume jewelry, called *fashion jewelry* in the industry, is within everyone's budget. For a few cents or a few dollars, there is a choice of different kinds of costume jewelry made of plastic, wood, metal, shells, glass, other imitation stones, and papier mâché that can enliven any outfit worn and give the wearer a feeling of confidence. Costume jewelry was invented by the famous French designer Coco Chanel, who also taught us that beauty can be found in simple designs made of simple fabrics. Some of the best jewelry designers today work in the costume jewelry industry. Their names are unknown to the general public, but their designs are often copied by creators of fine jewelry. This is a change from the clothing industry where couturiers' designs are quickly copied by the manufacturers of budget clothing.

Today there is a new category of jewelry called **bridge jewelry,** which can retail from $200 to $2,000 and is made with **semiprecious stones, synthetic stones, karat gold,** and **sterling silver.**

Location of the Industry

According to *Jewelers' Circular-Keystone,* a trade periodical for the jewelry industry, in 1990 sales of precious metal jewelry, bridge jewelry, costume jewelry, and watches reached $24.8 billion. Sales and production levels are expected to be increased by 1.5 percent for precious jewelry and 1 percent for costume jewelry annually through 1995, according to the International Trade Administration.

In the United States, there are 2,147 plants that produce precious metal jewelry, 768 plants that produce costume jewelry, and 179 plants that produce watches and clocks. These three industries employ 67,414 people according to *County Business Patterns 1990,* published by the U.S. Department of Commerce, Bureau of the Census. The states with the most establishments that produce precious metal jewelry are New York, Rhode Island, and New Jersey, while costume jewelry is produced in greatest number in Rhode Island, New York, and Florida. Watches and clocks are produced in the leading states of Washington, Maine, and Pennsylvania.

The Manufacturers

Fine jewelry is designer driven. Companies such as Cartier and Tiffany have always had unknown designers on their staffs. Today, however, pieces by Elsa Peretti and Paloma Picasso, who work exclusively for Tiffany, have an éclat and following of their own. In addition, independent designers such as Angela Cummings sell their pieces at a number of fine jewelry establishments. Judith Leiber, famous for her fine quality and unusual handbags, offers a line of jewelry that is being produced by Harry Winston. Eddie LeVian designs for A. LeVian and Company, which sells to many fine jewelry stores.

The costume jewelry leader is Crystal Brands, the parent company for Monet, Trifari, and Marvella Pearls. The Napier Company, the Artra Group, the Lori Corporation, the 1928 Jewelry Company, and Carolee Fashion Jewelry are other leaders in the field. Liz Claiborne has recently introduced a successful line of jewelry that generated more than $8 million in retail sales in 1990. The manufacture of costume jewelry is concentrated in fewer firms that are substantially larger than those that produce fine jewelry. They use techniques, such as CAD/CAM, that are more suited for mass production in order to be able to manufacture inexpensively.

In addition to the jewelry lines offered by Crystal Brands, the conglomerate offers sportswear lines under the labels of Izod, Gant, Salty Dog, and U.S. Open. The company is presently reorganizing under Chapter 11 and hopes to emerge from bankruptcy soon.

Imports and Exports

Imports of jewelry are not a serious threat to the U.S. jewelry industry. More than one-third of the jewelry the United States imports comes from Italy,and more than 10 percent comes from Hong Kong. At one time, 18 Karat gold was manufactured primarily in Italy, 10K gold in England, and 14K gold in the United States. Today these three countries produce gold alloy products in all three popular karats. The value of precious jewelry imports for 1990 was more than $2.6 billion, whereas exports amounted to more than $400 million. Most of the mechanical watches that we import come from Switzerland, while quartz watches come primarily from Japan, Hong Kong, and Switzerland, according to the U.S. International Trade Commission in its 1990 report.

Marketing Jewelry

Approximately one-fourth of the jewelry sold comes from retailers who specialize in this product. According to the Bureau of the Census in its *1987 Report of Retail Trade*, this represented about $11 billion in sales and more than 50 percent of the value of jewelry purchased. The Census Bureau also predicts that since the 35 to 54 age group will increase by such a significant number and that this will be the highest income years, that sales of luxury products such as jewelry will increase. In recent years we have also seen a growth in the number of fine jewelry chain establishments.

There has also been a trend toward fewer leased departments of fine jewelry in department stores. A major reason for this is that the primary leasee of space, Zales, is having financial difficulties. Many of the estate jewelry departments, however, continue to be leased by Marcus, Incorporated. Customers purchasing fashion jewelry will notice that there is an increase of famous designers' licensing lines. Among these can be seen jewelry with Dior, Donna Karan, and Anne Klein II labels.

The trade associations for the industry are the Jewelry Showroom Associates, which specializes in costume jewelry, the Manufacturing

Rose Levitt—Buyer of Fine Jewelry

"If your goal is to be a buyer of fine jewelry in a store that specializes in this exciting product, you have to decide very early in life that you're willing to work very hard. This is the most important requisite in becoming a success in the field," states Rose Levitt, for many years fine jewelry buyer for Fortunoff's, a specialty store whose flagship is located in Westbury, New York. "The second is to love what you are doing so much that you'd be willing to do it for nothing."

Now retired and living in Florida, Rose spends her days performing services for other retirees and for the elderly and infirm with the same energy and drive that she had during her days working under Helene Fortunoff, whom she describes as "tough, but fair, and the smartest and most brilliant person in the field."

"To be successful in retailing, you have to start getting your training at an early age." Rose worked on Saturdays in a department store while she was still in high school. She was moved around into different departments and began to get a feel for the merchandise and for the people who were her customers. After spending a year in college, she was offered a position she couldn't refuse working on a full-time basis in the same store. Soon after she was offered a position as assistant jewelry buyer for Goldsmith Brothers on Nassau Street in the financial district of New York City. From there she became a jewelry buyer for Balch-Price, an organization that leased space in department stores, and moved on to Lambs and Hubbard of Boston which had a similar operation. Rose feels that contrary to practices in most retail stores today, a person should specialize early in a specific area. "She should really train herself to be an authority in a particular field."

After taking time off for motherhood and child raising, Rose decided that she wanted to work at Fortunoff's, which was not far from home and which was noted for its jewelry offerings. She was interviewed by Helene Fortunoff who wanted to know what kind of position she was seeking. Without hesitation, Rose responded, "Jewelry buyer." She was informed by Helene Fortunoff that there was only one jewelry buyer in the store and Rose was looking at her. When offered the job of sales associate, Rose accepted without hesitation. During the first year and a half, Rose was the best washer and trimmer of cases in the department, and a short time later was appointed buyer of fine jewelry and assistant to Helene Fortunoff.

When asked what her job entailed, Rose answered, "I cataloged the merchandise. Each piece is photographed and entered in a log with the manufacturer's name and the style number. It is important with fine jewelry to have accurate records of your stock. I checked the merchandise when it came in to see if it was what I ordered and if the quality was perfect. Good stores such as Fortunoff's send its people to the Gemological Institute to learn as much as possible about jewelry. There are courses at different levels, and the Institute offers certification at different levels.

"It's important to be close to your customer. I always spent part of one day a week behind the counter in the Westbury store. The computer tells you the sales made, not the sales lost. The only way you can tell that is with direct contact. Wednesday was my day to be behind the counter in the Fifth Avenue store. Sometimes I had to run down to the market to buy pieces to fill in the stock. Alternate Saturdays were spent in the stores in Wayne and Paramus, New Jersey. It is very difficult to work for an organization that has many stores around the country, because the needs of the customers are so different everywhere. For example, some sections of the country have customers without pierced ears, some sections of the country prefer pearls with a pink cast, others with a white cast."

"I went to trade shows in New York City two times a year to get a feel for what was being shown and to look at the offerings from new vendors. The trade shows were held the last week in July and the first week in February. Whenever a company called to say that they had something to show us, we set up appointments in the Westbury store. Our offices were in the basement and that was where we saw the vendors. We looked for quality merchandise at good prices. Occasionally we used the vendors' catalogs to fill in stock. There were some manufacturers who refused to sell to us at the beginning, but they changed their minds when they saw how successful we were. I was always on the lookout for unique items for our retail catalogs which were published and distributed several times a year as well as for merchandise for special newspaper promotions. I was careful about the placement of the jewelry when it was being photographed for the catalogs and newspaper advertisements and made sure that the presentation was perfect. Our stock turned four times a year as compared with 2.2 average turns in other specialty stores. Because of this, we were able to offer our jewelry at lower markups than other stores, and we also had very few markdowns. I sometimes went along to the European trade shows with Helene and her husband Alan. They were then held concurrently in Basle and Milan. First we went to one and then the other. My own preference was to give the business to American jewelers rather than European ones."

"There's one more quality a jewelry buyer has to have—chutzpah! She has to know what she's doing, take risks, be aggressive, and stand up for what she thinks is right and best for the department and the store. My experiences as a buyer were among the happiest in my life, and I wouldn't trade them for anything!"

Problem Solving

1. Why is the number of times the stock turns such an important aspect of a successful department and store? How did Helene Fortunoff and Rose Levitt manage to achieve their success with stock turn?

2. What marketing skills did Rose Levitt have that enabled her to become so successful?

Jewelers and Silversmiths of America (MJSA), the United Jewelry Show Organization (UJSO), and the Silver Trust International, all based in Providence, Rhode Island. The JSA holds trade shows in Providence as does the MJSA, which holds them jointly with UJSO. The Jewelry Industry Council is the trade association based in New York City.

The Larkin Group holds the International Fashion and Boutique Show at the Javits Center in New York City four times a year. This group publishes *Accent*, a trade publication that specializes in costume jewelry and watches. The Fashion Accessories Expo (FAE) is also held four times a year, usually at the Javits Center. The name of the FAE trade publication is *Accessories*, which features a variety of products including hosiery and hair adornment products in addition to jewelry. The trade publication that specializes in fine jewelry is the *National Jeweler*, while the oldest and most famous of the trade publications is the *Jewelers' Circular-Keystone*. Two other trade shows, the Accessories Circuit and the International Trade Fair, are regularly held in New York City in different locations such as hotels and piers. In addition, manufacturers of fine, bridge, and costume jewelry offer their customers catalogs for fill-in ordering whenever needed.

Internationally, there are two important fairs held two times each year, usually in January and June. In Paris, there is the Bijorhca, and in Milan, Italy, the Chibidue.

In recent years there has been a proliferation of consumer catalogs offering fine, bridge, and fashion jewelry. Among these are Ross-Simons (See Figure 13–4), Lewis and Roberts, Ciro, Adco, and Nature's Jewelry. Some even offer clearance merchandise on specific pages in the folio.

3A. Rope-Knot Pin of 18kt gold with lustrous cultured pearls capping the ends. $995.00

3B. Fabulous Band of square-cut emeralds, rubies and sapphires with 36 diamonds. 2.60cts tot. gem wt. 18kt gold. Our best selling band. $2500.00

3C. Diamond-Swirled Earrings of 18kt gold. .70ct tot. wt. of diamonds. Clip/post. from Italy. $2650.00

3D. Swirled Choker outlined in diamonds, 2.75cts tot. wt., and accented with roping. A superb piece of 18kt gold, of substantial weight. From Italy. 16" Length. $8495.00

3E. Hinged Hoop Earrings of 18kt gold sleeked with a line of diamonds. .64ct tot. wt. From Italy. $1250.00

3F. Wide Band of ridged 18kt gold bordered with 10 bezel-set diamonds, .88ct tot. wt. $1995.00

3G.-H. Glowing Mobé Pearls accented with black onyx latticed in 14kt gold and sparked with diamonds.

3G. The 14kt Ring with .15ct of diamonds. $795.00

3H. The 14kt Earrings with .25ct of diamonds. Clip/post. $1150.00

3K. Fabulous Fish Pin of white and yellow 14kt gold, brilliant with diamonds and a ruby eye. $450.00

3L. Mobé Pearl Ring rimmed with cabochon sapphires, emeralds and rubies between diamonds, on a ribbed band of 18kt gold. 2.25cts tot. gem wt. From Italy. $1550.00

3M. Mobé Pearl Earrings swirled with cabochon sapphires, emeralds and rubies, sparked with diamonds. .48ct tot. wt. 2.40cts tot. gem wt. 18kt gold. Clip/post. From Italy. $2500.00

3N. Tennis Bracelet with 44 diamonds between S bars of 14kt white gold. 3cts tot. wt. of diamonds $1995.00*

3P. Tennis Bracelet as above, with 3cts tot. wt.of diamonds set in 14kt yellow gold. $1995.00*

3Q. Set of 2 Diamond Tennis Bracelets above. $3950.00*
*Our diamond tennis bracelets are also available in lengths longer than the standard 7". Call for information.

3J. Glistening 14kt Gold Mesh Bracelet from Italy. Rigid when clasped. Superb value at this Ross-Simons' price. 7" Length. $795.00 8" Length. $895.00

Three

Courtesy: Ross-Simons, Cranston, Rhode Island

• • • • • • • • **FIGURE 13-4 Consumers may purchase fine, bridge, and costume jewelry by means of a catalog or store visit. This is an example of private-label fine jewelry from a recent catalog. (See Color Plate 4)**

ACTIVEWEAR

Probably the fastest growing segment of fashion apparel, activewear has entered the fashion scene with different kinds of clothing for every conceivable athletic activity. One has only to look at the product patches worn by the tennis stars in the U.S. Open to be aware of the proliferation of brands of tennis clothing available to enthusiasts of this sport. Producers of sports equipment have expanded horizontally to encompass the growing demand for the right thing to wear for each participant.

There is no question that the growth of interest in these products reflects the change that has taken place in the society of the nineties. Ever mindful of the importance of healthy bodies, men, women, and children are exercising more and eating better foods. According to the 1989 survey by the National Sporting Goods Association, the top ten activities participated in by people seven years of age and older are swimming, exercise walking, bicycle riding, fishing, camping, bowling, exercising with equipment, billiards or pool, boating, and basketball. The next group of ten include aerobics, volleyball, running or jogging, hiking, golf, softball, roller-skating, tennis, hunting with firearms, and dart throwing. Some of these activities are **gender correlated.** Women represent about 83 percent of the aerobics participants and 65 percent of the exercise walkers. They are in the majority among the swimmers and bicycle riders and are more likely to work out at a club. However, only 9 percent of those people who hunt with firearms are women.

Age is another factor in the kind of activity chosen. The 55 plus age group is more likely to participate in exercise walking, golf, fishing, exercising with equipment, hiking, bowling, camping, swimming, and bicycle riding. Those baby-boomers entering the middle years of 35 to 54 and representing the greatest percentage of the population are shifting to less strenuous activities such as golf, walking, and biking and are putting away their racquetball equipment and clothing and their long-distance running garb.

Among the younger generation can be seen many participants in the sport of roller-blading. However, manufacturers have not as yet provided special clothing for this activity.

Activewear is also reflective of the economic condition of the nation. Families do not invest in leisurewear when they are having trouble putting food on the table. The families that are more likely to invest in apparel of this nature are those that have both parents in the labor market. This kind of family is also more likely to participate in bowling as a family activity.

The Leading Manufacturers

SportStyle, in its issues of June 11, 1990, and July 30, 1990, reported on the leading manufacturers of activewear according to category. Danskin, Jacques Moret, and Weekend Exercise Co. were the leading producers of performancewear, while bicycle riders were more likely to buy products manufactured by Descente, Bellwether, and Nike. Swimwear was divided into three categories: beachwear, junior swimwear, and competition swimwear. The first-category manufacturers were Ocean Pacific, Gotcha, and Body Glove; the second were OP Juniors, Sunset Beach, and Sassafras. The competition swimmers were more likely to be wearing suits made by Speedo, The Finals, and Arena.

Rugged outerwear leaders were Woolrich, Pacific Trail, and Patagonia. Ski apparel was most likely to be manufactured by Columbia, Head, and Sport Obermeyer. The most popular tennis apparel producers were Le Coq Sportif, Head, and Sergio Tacchini. Others kinds of activewear apparel were produced by Russell, Tultex, and Ocean Pacific.

The leading producers of team apparel, other than swimwear, were Russell, Champion, and Delong. Golfers were more likely to wear Izod, Aureus, and La Mode. The leading hunting and fishing apparel manufacturers were Woolrich, Walls, and Columbia.

Location of Manufacturers

The three states that lead in the number of establishments producing activewear are California, Florida, and Texas, with California the location for more than one-third of the number of plants of all the states combined that produce this product. There are 1,784 establishments that employ 58,415 people in this industry according to *County Business Patterns 1990,* published by the U.S. Department of Commerce, Bureau of the Census.

Marketing Activewear

Activewear is marketed along with other traditional sportswear apparel. However, we are beginning to see some consumer catalog growth and a growth in the numbers of specialty retailers of this category of merchandise.

OTHER FASHION ACCESSORIES

Fashion accessories provide comfort and convenience as well as styling to a man or woman's look. This category includes items such as gloves, hats, hair adornments, umbrellas, pocketbooks, small leather goods, belts, eyeglasses, and neckwear. Many of these products are part of a collection of several, each to complement a special use, a special color, or a special size. There is no single industry for these many different kinds of products as each is unique in its production.

Fashion accessories are, perhaps, more **cyclical** in nature than other kinds of apparel. Each season brings in new fashions, and the items purchased to complement those fashions must harmonize and be effective for their purpose. Scarves may be brilliant in color for one season, subdued for another, and barely worn for a third season. Although an intrinsic part of designer fashions in their showings, hats have never returned to the popularity they experienced years ago when men and women were never seen in public without them. Today, people buy hats for very special uses: to provide a striking adjunct to a costume, to shield the tennis player or fisherman from the sun, to provide warmth, or simply to make a statement.

As a general rule, accessories sell better than other kinds of apparel. Even in times of economic downturn, when dresses and suits may experience a decline in sales, accessories will show a gain. A basic item of apparel can be changed dramatically with the addition of the correct accessory. Licensing is on the increase in this area as well. Many apparel designers and sportswear firms are entering into agreements to have accessories manufactured with their labels. This is especially true in handbags, belts, and small leather goods.

Retail sales of accessory items are estimated to range between $14 and $17 billion annually, with the largest share of the women's market attributed to purses and wallets, followed by hats and scarves. The largest share of the men's market is attributed to ties, followed by belts. Stores credit their success with accessories to more effective tracking of sales through POS information, thus enabling them to always have the proper assortments of the demanded styles and colors. Another important characteristic of accessories is that many do not come in size ranges. One pocketbook can be carried by any size woman or man, and scarves and mufflers can be purchased with impunity regardless of the size and shape of the person. Even fabric gloves now come in one-size-fits-all, making them an easy purchase for a child to present to a parent. It is for this reason that accessories make such wonderful gift items for holidays and life-cycle events.

Accessories showrooms are generally clustered near or in the Empire State Building in Manhattan on 34th Street. In recent years, however, some luxury leather goods firms have relocated to the 57th Street and Madison Avenue area where they maintain retail as well as wholesale facilities.

Gloves

There are actually two different glove industries—fabric gloves and leather gloves—and each operates in different ways. The fabric glove industry is located in the mill areas of North Carolina and Georgia since this kind of glove is knitted to provide comfort and elasticity. Knitted gloves are usually a part of a large company that manufactures many different kinds of knitted products. Isotoner gloves, for example, is under the Sara Lee umbrella, which includes Hanes underwear, socks, and hosiery. Kayser-Roth, another producer of intimate apparel and hosiery, also produces fabric gloves. Gloves may also be insulated or lined, for cold weather; they may be mittens for additional warmth or for skiing, and may include plastic or leathers for better grip or decorative effect.

Leather gloves are labor intensive. The best gloves are table cut, with each of the tiny parts carefully measured and cut by hand to match and make the best use of the leather. A properly cut leather glove gives the wearer comfort and warmth and fits attractively whether the hand is open or closed. A well-made leather glove has a separate thumb piece; a trank that covers the top and bottom of the hand; fourchettes, which are small rectangular pieces and provide width to the fingers; and quirks, the tiny triangular pieces at the base of the second, third, and fourth fingers and which allow the fingers to be flexible. Less expensive leather gloves are clicker cut. Here the pieces are stamped out with a die. Very inexpensive gloves, called sandwich gloves, merely have the front and back sewn together.

New York State is the leading producer of leather gloves with Gloversville the center of the industry. This is where the National Glove Manufacturers Association is located and is the home of Grandoe, a leading manufacturer of gloves. The other leading states where quality leather gloves are produced are Wisconsin and Illinois. Fownes is another important producer of quality leather gloves.

Hats

Hats, caps, and millinery are manufactured by many small firms that specialize in just one product. Missouri has the most firms, with Texas and Pennsylvania following. Hats and caps can be made by hand or by machine. Millinery is more labor intensive and requires a lot of handwork. Much of the millinery industry is located on West 37th Street between Fifth and Sixth Avenues in New York City. Since the millinery companies are small, they can be very responsive to change and are not limited to their usual four seasons a year. New colors, fabrics, felts, or straws can be introduced on a continuing basis if their customers demand it.

Hair Adornments

This fashion accessory is presently on a cyclical upswing. Generally found within ladies' accessories departments near jewelry and neckwear, displays include ribbons, clips, elastics covered with metallic fabrics and satins, combs adorned with colored stones, and wooden and plastic items in many shapes and colors. Most of these items are manufactured in the United States, and company showrooms are found in New York City's Fashion District. Many hair adornments are products of individual people who display them in craft fairs for purchasers who seek a unique look. In the new mall shops that specialize in accessories, perhaps one-fifth of the items displayed fall into this category.

Umbrellas

Although the primary purpose of the umbrella is to provide protection from the rain or snow, today's umbrellas have become a fashion accessory. They are signed by designers, printed in the latest fabric patterns, and coordinated with fashion raincoats and rainwear.

This fashion concept has been the only noticeable change in the design and construction of umbrellas in recent years. The canopy is primarily made from nylon, cotton, or plastic. The shank and ribs are often metal, and the handle is either wood or plastic. Two basic styles of umbrellas are sold—regular and folding. Prices vary widely, depending on materials, methods of construction, and, of course, fashion impact. Isotoner has recently introduced an umbrella which has a Teflon-coated canopy. Called "the dry umbrella," it quickly sheds the rain.

Handbags

Once a healthy and thriving industry in the United States, the handbag industry has been losing ground to imports from China, which provides the United States with 59 percent of the handbags that are imported. These low-cost products are ubiquitous throughout discount stores and national chains that promote low prices. Almost $1 billion worth of handbags at cost value are imported into the United States as compared with $536 million produced in this country. New York State is the leading producer of domestic handbags, followed by Florida and California.

The industry has been spurred by licensing agreements offered by major designers and sportswear apparel firms. J. H. Collectibles, J. G. Hook, Ellen Tracy, Jones New York, Adolpho, and Leslie Fay are the newest signature lines being offered. There is also a great demand for quality domestic handbags, including Coach (see Figure 13–5) and Dooney & Bourke, as well as the imported products from France and Italy. Louis Vuitton, Hermes, and Gucci frequently have their own boutiques within department stores. Judith Leiber is famous for her top-of-the line evening bags in beads and metals.

While a number of men in the United States carry handsomely crafted handbags, the fashion has not quite caught on as it has in the fashion cities of Europe.

Women and children generally own a number of handbags in different colors and shapes. Handbags may be made of leather, cloth, or plastic and may have fittings of metal or plastic. They come in many different styles, including **pouch, envelope, clutch, box,** and **tote.** They are carried by a handle, by a shoulder strap or, in the case of the

COACH

AN AMERICAN LEGACY

Courtesy: Coach Leatherware Company, New York

• • • • • • • • **FIGURE 13-5 Quality leather handbags by companies such as Coach are manufactured in the United States. (See Color Plate 3)**

envelope handbag, in the hand or under the arm. There are generally four showings a year to coincide with the apparel markets.

Small Leather Goods

This category includes wallets, coin purses, calendar organizers, and cases for credit cards, makeup, eyeglasses, jewelry, calculators, and keys. Prince Gardner, Buxton, and Swank are easily recognized brands in the industry. Designers are licensing their ideas to producers, and an influx of interesting products will appear on the market because of their creativity. New York, California, and Massachusetts lead in the production of these products.

Belts

Generally made of woven and knitted fabrics, as well as leather, plastic, and metal, belts are needed on an ongoing basis for men and on a fluctuating basis for women, depending upon the fashion trend of the season. In the United States, the leading producers are New York, California, and Pennsylvania. Belts may be offered as a component of a product such as sportswear in the men's and women's apparel industry as well as individually purchased by the consumer to update an ensemble or to wear with a man's suit.

Eyewear

Ever since Jacqueline Kennedy Onassis began wearing oversized sunglasses, eyewear has become a fashion industry. Frames for corrective lenses have been licensed by designers through eyewear stores, and sunglasses are offered with designer frames in all kinds of department and specialty shops. Because of the increasing consumer awareness of the dangerous effects of the sun's rays, manufacturers have begun producing lenses that filter out the harmful ultraviolet rays.

Neckwear

Both men and women are accustomed to wearing clothing around their necks for warmth as well as fashion. There are a myriad of products included in this category, encompassing ties, scarves, and shawls. Echo scarves are well known in the industry as are many products that are licensed by well-known designers.

MARKETING ACCESSORIES

The primary trade journal for the accessories industry is *Women's Wear Daily*, which offers special issues of *A* as well as its usual coverage. *Accessories* is another important publication. Trade shows held in New York are the National Fashion Boutique and Fashion Accessories Expo. Regional shows are held as well. The trade association representing manufacturers is the National Fashion Accessories Association. However, most of the member firms produce handbags. Retailers usually offer accessories lines in counters adjacent to cosmetics in high-traffic areas, since so many are impulse purchases.

There has been a growth in recent years of accessories stores in the malls. One such store, Accessory Lady, was recently acquired by Woolworth from the Melville Corporation, the parent company of Thom McAnn. There are currently 119 Accessory Lady stores in the United States and the numbers are growing. One of the reasons for the great success of these stores is their ability to **target market** their products. The stores are brightly lit with a combination of fluorescent and incandescent lighting. Most of the merchandise offered is made in the United States and includes a mix of designer label, national brands, and private label. The price points are low and affordable. Smaller and more expensive pieces are behind counters and require service, but most of the merchandise is attractively displayed and reachable. Lively music surrounds the occupants of the store. The selling staff is young and friendly. It is no wonder that one can find ten customers in a small store, half of them in line waiting to pay for the merchandise they have selected.

TERMS TO REMEMBER

high end lines mass-merchandised market share multinational companies positioned value added Cosmetic, Toiletry, and Fragrance Association (CFTA) rack jobbers gray market counterfeit fragrances premiums franchised operations foundations lingerie loungewear Quick Response licensed POS stitch-ins greige full-fashioned conglomerate lapidaries bridge jewelry semiprecious stones synthetic stones karat gold sterling silver CAD/CAM gender correlated cyclical labor intensive table-cut thumb piece trank fourchettes quirks clicker-cut caps millinery canopy shank ribs signature lines clutch tote envelope box pouch target marketing

...... HIGHLIGHTS OF THE CHAPTER

- American consumers spend billions of dollars on accessories every year.

- There is a tendency for consolidation of small companies into large ones in the accessories industries. Some of these companies are multinational.

- The U.S. Bureau of the Census gives us an accurate picture of earnings of employees, locations of plants, and value of products produced and shipped in its Census of Manufactures done every five years.

- Demographics are always changing. We can expect that 30 percent of the population will be non-Caucasian, our life expectancy will increase, and the middle-

year group of 35 to 54 years of age will be the largest segment of the population by the year 2000.

- The intimate apparel industry has seen a change in direction in recent years.

- Many trade shows are held in the Jacob Javits Convention Center in New York City.

- The U.S. population is becoming more health conscious. Designers and manufacturers must be aware of the needs of men, women, and children when they pursue active sports, and provide them with the most attractive and comfortable activewear possible.

...... REVIEW QUESTIONS

1. Define prestige personal care products? Name three stores where they may be found. Name three brands.

2. Where can you find mass-marketed personal care products? Are they packaged the same way as prestige products? Name three brands.

3. In spite of the increase of skin cancer, why do people continue to go to tanning salons and bask in the sun? What alternatives are there that are better for the skin?

4. According to projections from the 1990 U.S. Census, the Hispanic population will be the largest minority group in the country by the year 2015. What long- and short-range plans should marketers of fashion accessories be making to capture this important segment of the market?

5. What are three ways that a U.S. producer might improve its market share of footwear without contracting the production of the shoes overseas?

6. In walking through a regional mall, it is easy to see four different stores each carrying a different label of a U.S. Shoe product. Why would one corporation want its products to compete with each other in the mall?

7. What influence did Madonna have on the intimate apparel industry?

8. Name five products that use lycra in the fabric.

9. How does the computer help the retailer do a better job selling accessories?

10. Why will there always be a demand for good quality leather gloves? What makes them so expensive?

...... RESEARCH AND PROJECTS

1. Analyze a line of prestige personal care products. Name the products and their uses.

How many sizes does each product come in? What is the price of each item sold in the line? Are the products displayed attractively? Does the packaging enhance the items? What products could be added to the line to increase its market share? Where would you find the address of the manufacturer or distributor? Write a letter to the manufacturer or distributor outlining your suggestions for more successful marketing of the product.

2. Describe five different advertisements for personal care products for men. The ads may be on television or in the newspapers or magazines. What is the underlying message of the advertisement? Since most of the purchasers of men's fragrances are women, are the ads properly targeted? Write a brief description of an advertisement for a man's fragrance that better reaches the target buyer. Why is your ad better than the others? Send your idea to the agency that handles the product. Ask your professor how to get that information.

3. You are talented in creating hair ornaments that are unusual and inexpensive to make.

What are five different ways that you might market your product?

4. You have been asked to create special clothing for men and women to use while rollerblading. What features would you incorporate in this clothing? Can you sketch the apparel? If so, and if you like what you are doing, submit your ideas to an activewear manufacturer.

5. Do a study of five different trade publications. What does each have to offer? Rank them in order as to how well they cover the market. What was particularly good about the best publication? What was particularly poor about the worst?

6. If you were going to open a small mall specialty store dealing in accessories, which would you select? Why did you select those accessories? How would you design your store? How would you reach your customer?

Part Five

···

MERCHANDISING TODAY'S FASHION

········· In Part Four we learned about the industries that are the backbone of the apparel and accessories world in the United States. Part Five takes us to the final and most important step in marketing—getting these products into the hands of the ultimate consumer. We will learn about the techniques used by the retailers, in an ever-changing retail environment, to purchase and merchandise their products, and the media through which these products are promoted.

CHAPTER 14

Fashion Retailers

After reading this chapter, you should be able to:

- Trace the birth and growth of fashion retailing in the United States.
- Identify and give an example of the various types of retailing operations existing today.
- Explain the five types of retail organizations.
- Be familiar with the various career opportunities in retailing.

.... PERFORMANCE OUTCOME

After reading this chapter, you should be able to:

- Assess which types of retail organizations might be your choice for a future career because of their success in using the latest technology profitably.
- Visit local branches or chain operations and determine which qualities they have that make them unique.
- Recognize different specialty units in a mall that belong to the same parent organization.
- Know what to expect when participating in executive training.

L ike the rest of the fashion industry in the United States, fashion retailing evolved in response to the changing social and economic climate of the developing nation. As this country grew and changed, various types of retail institutions emerged to meet an ever increasing consumer demand for goods and services.

Fashion retailers are the most direct link between the fashion industry and the consumer. As merchant intermediaries, they buy an assortment of fashion merchandise from various manufacturers and wholesalers with the express purpose of reselling that merchandise to their clientele at a profit.

In this chapter we shall trace the historical development of the institution of retailing to modern day. We will speak about the various forms of operations that are successful, and we will discuss the contributions of innovative fashion retailers to the industry. We will also discuss the dramatic changes that are yet unfolding in response to current economic and social conditions.

THE DEVELOPMENT OF FASHION RETAILING

The Early American Retailers

The exact origin of fashion retailing in this country is obscure. However, it was the desire for luxurious furs, skins, and hides for fashionable wearing apparel that prompted the European exploration of North America and the eventual establishment of America's first retail outlet—the **trading post.**

The European fur trading companies dotted the landscape of Canada and the northeastern United States with these trading posts. The Hudson Bay Company of Canada originated as a trading post and was chartered by the Queen of England in 1670. Settlers and trappers exchanged their fur bounty for necessary foodstuffs and tools at the posts, making the tiny outlets the first type of retail store in the New World. The fur pelts were the medium of exchange. Although trading posts were generally located on navigable rivers and convenient crossroads, many were in outlying areas.

To meet the needs of people who lived in port cities such as Boston and New York, another type of retail establishment emerged during the 1600s—the **specialty shop.** The name arose from the fact that the merchants specialized in one type of goods. These outlets were often located in the homes of the shopkeepers. Sometimes the products were made in the shops, and sometimes the merchandise was imported from Europe. The products sold were classified as either foodstuffs or dry goods. Wearing apparel such as capes, shoes, millinery, wigs, fabrics, thread, and trimmings were dry goods. Although the little shops usually began by carrying one of these items, in time many expanded their assortments to include several or all types of dry goods. Known as **dry goods stores,** this type of retail establishment eventually gave rise to the modern day **department store.**

As the population of the United States grew and expanded westward, the peddler became an important retailer. Loading a backpack or wagon with an assortment of goods purchased in the port cities, this enterprising merchant would travel inland, selling wares from house to house. Sometimes this original door-to-door salesperson would decide to settle down permanently but would continue in the retail trade by opening a general store in a suitable location. This type of retail operation carried a variety of whatever items could be obtained by the shopkeeper and might be needed by surrounding settlers. The founders of Goldwater's, Saks Fifth Avenue, and the May Company all started as itinerant peddlers.

The First Department Stores

By the middle of the 1800s, eastern cities were flourishing, and retailers dramatically increased the quantity, quality, and variety of their fashion merchandise. During this period, several of the country's most famous dry goods stores were founded, including John Wanamaker's in Philadelphia (see Figure 14–1). The original building as well as the existing flagship store were hailed as architectural wonders. The whole central area of today's Wanamaker's is a beautiful dome with mosaic glass and marble columns. The upper floors of the store are circular, and customers can look down upon the main floor. The **flagship store** of Galleries Lafayette in Paris has a similar structure with a beautiful glass dome. The original Marshall Field's in Chicago and A. T. Stewart's Marble and Cast Iron Palace in New York were grand emporiums as well, with elaborate facades, statues, and chandeliers.

Avenue of the Americas, then called Sixth Avenue, was the site of many beautiful stores in Lower Manhattan and came to be called the Ladies' Mile. The most beautiful of these stores was called Siegel-Cooper Dry Goods Store, and the building between 18th and 19th Streets is still in existence today. When it was built in 1896, it had a telegraph office, dentist, stock trading service, and advertising agency.

Courtesy: John Wanamaker, Inc.

• • • • • • • • **FIGURE 14-1 John Wanamaker's Grand Depot.**

Traces of the beautiful marble floor and fountain that graced the main floor can still be seen in the building which houses a number of factories on its six floors. The Sixth Avenue Elevated line had an entrance from the platform directly into the second floor of the building. People visiting or working in the factory building who are unaware of its glorious history are often surprised by the elaborate and lovely windows that look down upon the street. The second floor was exquisitely decorated with elegant furnishings and full-length mirrors and became known as the ladies' parlor. All the early stores maintained elaborate custom-made dress operations for those women who could afford hand-tailored apparel.

ZCMI, Zion's Cooperative Mercantile Institution in Salt Lake City, Utah, was the first department store to be incorporated. The early Mormon settlers felt they were being charged exorbitant prices for things they needed such as cloth and foodstuffs, and they established a community store that supported the home industries and enabled them to purchase large amounts of goods at lower prices and resell these items as inexpensively as possible to the people. When it was incorporated in 1870, each person bought whatever shares of stock he or she could afford. Today, the Mormon church owns one-third interest in the store, and many ancestors of the original stockholders are still collecting dividends. The original façade adorns the new building, which is a landmark in Salt Lake City (see Figure 14–2).

Courtesy: Zion Cooperative Mercantile Institution, Salt Lake City, Utah

•••••••• **FIGURE 14-2 Top: The main entrance of ZCMI at the turn of the century. Bottom: The main entrance of ZCMI retains its beautiful façade today.**

The great merchants of the 1800s did much to influence the retail business that exists today. From the beginning, they emphasized the importance of attractive physical surroundings and tastefully planned merchandise displays. They introduced such merchandising policies as nonnegotiable prices on goods, free delivery service, the training of sales personnel, and full money-back guarantees. These merchants recognized the importance of catering to their customers.

In time, the merchandise assortment of these clothing stores grew and diversified to include housewares and home furnishings. For greater efficiency, the merchandise was offered for sale and records were kept on a departmental basis—hence, the name department stores.

Today's Department Stores

Department stores today are characterized by having a minimum of 50 employees, home furnishings, apparel for the family, and household linens. Similar stores with fewer employees are called *miscellaneous general merchandise stores.*

Department stores may have a catalog ordering service and provide assistance and check-out service within each department. These stores are called *conventional department stores.* If the stores are affiliated with a company that operates multiple similar outlets nationally, they are known as *national chain department stores.* Stores that meet all these criteria but have centralized check-out, little, if any, service in a department, and an image of fast turnover at low prices are called *discount or mass-merchandising department stores.*

Some large national chain department stores maintain a *flagship* store which serves as a central office and is, as well, the largest store among a group of satellite stores carrying similar merchandise. In some cases, as the stores grow in size and number, additional offices are opened in other buildings where some of the activities such as public relations and buying are located. The satellite stores are known as *branches* and may be suburban locations for the urban flagship. In other cases, the branches may be located all over the country, as in the case of Neiman Marcus. In addition, department stores also offer specialty operations that carry a specific line of goods. These smaller operations are known as **twigs.** A good example is Bloomie's at JFK Airport, a twig of Bloomingdale's. Macy's East branches extend from Albany, New York, to New Orleans, Louisiana, and include the original Bamberger chain of department stores. Macy's West includes the I. Magnin and Bullocks chains in the western part of the country. Macy's West has an unusual organization in its San Francisco store on Union Square. It has a completely separate store offering only men's and boys' wear right near the original San Francisco store. This cannot be called a twig, as it is larger than many department stores in the United States and complements the merchandise of the original store; rather it is a department store housed in two separate buildings. (Strawbridge and Clothier in Philadelphia is housed in several adjacent stores.) Macy's East, West, and South each maintain separate offices and function independently. The corporate offices of the parent organization are located within the largest store in the world, Macy's Herald Square in New York City (see Figure 14–3). Here, corporate decisions are made for the other members of the group, which also includes small specialty chains offering Italian-style menswear and womenswear. In addition, the corporate area houses the designers, buyers, and executives of the private-label facilities which provide the member stores with merchandise bearing the myriad labels produced by Macy's.

There are no flagship stores among the original large department store chains. The headquarters of J. C. Penney, for example, serves as the control center and houses the administrative offices, computer center, buying offices, testing and research laboratories, and visual display center. Everything emanates from the **central headquarters.** Many of today's chain department stores maintain regional offices to better meet the needs of the consumers living in a particular section of

Courtesy: Macy's East

• • • • • • • • **FIGURE 14-3 Macy's Herald Square store, New York City.**

the country and to provide personnel services to the stores in the region.

Early Mail-Order Retailers

The department store was an urban phenomenon. For those who lived in the rural areas and were unable to travel to the cities, another form of retailing was devised—mail-order selling.

In the late 1800s, the United States Postal System introduced the postal money order and rural free delivery. These two features made it possible for mail-order catalog companies such as Montgomery Ward (the catalog division was phased out in 1985), J. C. Penney, Spiegel, and Sears, Roebuck and Company (catalog now discontinued) to profitably service rural America with a variety of merchandise including wearing apparel. Children who were raised in rural farm areas had the advantage of using the catalogs as toys and would cut out the pictures and play with them. During the 1920s, the automobile improved transportation to the towns and cities, and mail-order merchants added retail outlets to their operations.

Today's Mail-Order Retailers

Mail-order firms can be either general merchandisers or specialty-type operations. The two largest and most famous—J. C. Penney and Spiegel—fall under the general merchandiser classification. As mentioned earlier, Montgomery Ward has discontinued its mail-order division and is concentrating its efforts on its store operations. Sears has eliminated its mail-order division as well because of the huge expense of producing and distributing its voluminous catalog. In addition, the rise of Wal-Mart in localities previously serviced by mail-order firms has provided severe competition for the Sears catalog. The Spiegel catalog, on the other hand, has been innovative and successful. It is arranged in specialty format with apparel at one end and home furnishings and domestics reversed at the other end. The catalogs are in full color and printed on glossy paper. Color coding for each type of apparel or furnishing enables the consumer to find exactly what he or she wants with a minimum of effort. Each color-coded section has the look of a boutique and highlights designer and national label products, with financial participation from these sources welcomed by Spiegel. Another reason for the great success of the Spiegel catalog is that they carefully track consumer purchases and customize their catalogs to fit past customer purchase patterns.

Specialty mail-order firms are those that offer a unique line of

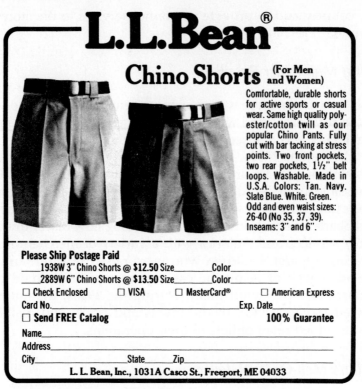

Courtesy: L.L. Bean, Freeport, Maine.

•••••• **FIGURE 14-4 Merchandise from an L.L. Bean catalog.**

merchandise. A good example of this type of operation is L. L. Bean of Freeport, Maine, which has become highly successful by offering the best in sporting goods and sports apparel to its mail order customers (see Figure 14-4). In fact, they have become so successful that they had to open a 24-hour store on Route 1 in Freeport, its home base of operations.

Sears has not completely disowned the mail-order aspect of its retail business as they will be licensing specialty apparel catalogs in the near future.

The more specialized the catalog is, the more successful it seems to become. Victoria's Secret, a lingerie catalog, and the Outlet Catalog, published by Sara Lee and featuring slightly imperfect merchandise produced by its conglomerate divisions of L'Eggs, Hanes, Bali, and Playtex at outlet prices, are both highly profitable ventures. It would be remiss not to mention successful catalogs produced by conventional retailers. Fortunoff's, a specialty retailer of domestics, home furnishings, jewelry, and cosmetics, with its flagship in Westbury, New York, produces a highly successful catalog that is distributed to regional homes. Bloomingdale's produces and distributes specialty catalogs utilizing demographic information on age, income, and car and home ownership to target its products successfully. And the most famous retail catalog of all, the Neiman Marcus Christmas catalog with its assemblage of unique gifts, is collected throughout the world.

Figure 14–5(a) shows just two unusual articles for sale in the 1993 Christmas Book offered by Neiman Marcus. These His and Hers automated dinosaurs, the baby tyrannosaurus rex and the adolescent triceratops, feature moving heads and tails, darting eyes, and sound effects. They are 6'1" high and 8'4" long, and 6'8" high and 12'10" long respectively and are produced by the same company that manufactures similar exhibits for museums. Figure 14–5(b) shows a cashmere ensemble by Donna Karan in oatmeal from the same edition. A percentage of the selling price of each article featured in the 1993 catalog is contributed to United Earth. This worthwhile organization works to inspire young people into action for a better society and environment.

Selling through the mail is a unique operation. The preparation of catalogs is a lengthy and expensive process. To get them to the customer at the beginning of a selling season, mail-order houses must begin producing their catalogs far in advance. For instance, the planning of a fall-winter catalog, which is made available to customers about July, begins at least one year before its distribution. Most manufacturers do not have their regular lines ready that far in advance, but they supply the mail-order houses with early samples of forthcoming styles for illustration and photographic purposes. The styles are kept simple so that they will not become outdated by the time the catalog is distributed. As a result, the catalog offerings of a large general merchandiser mail-order house are usually classic and conservatively styled. They offer all types of fashion apparel for men, women, and children.

The First Discounters

Until the 1950s, most fashion retailers followed the service-oriented philosophy of the first retailers: providing customers with attention and atmosphere as well as fine merchandise. The cost of these extras was automatically incorporated into the retail price tags of the merchandise. But when the post-World War II buying boom began, some young, enterprising "revolutionary" retailers felt it was an opportune time to introduce a different selling approach, one that had the following features: few, if any, customer services; outlets devoid of atmosphere but high in sales volume; check-out centers centralized to ac-

Courtesy: Neiman Marcus, Dallas, Texas

• • • • • • • • **FIGURE 14-5 Unusual articles from the Neiman Marcus 1993 Christmas catalog include his and hers life-size, automated dinosaurs and a cashmere ensemble by Donna Karan (see Color Plate 1).**

commodate many departments; and, most important to the customers, low prices. These early **discount** operations, such as E. J. Korvette's (now defunct), specialized in **hard goods** such as appliances, tableware, and domestics. Apparel was gradually introduced and, at first, operated as a **leased department** to enable the suburban consumer to shop for all of his or her family needs in one place. A leased department is one that is run by an independent merchant who pays the store owner a rental fee and a percentage of sales for the use of the store's space and services. In some cases, supermarkets were added.

However, the discount selling approach was not entirely new. Wearing apparel had long been discounted by stores such as Ohrbach's, Alexander's, S. Klein's, and Mays. Ohrbach's was opened in 1923 and was located on Union Square in New York City, easily reached by subways, buses, and tubes. It operated on an **average markup** of 21 percent in the women's dress department and was a magnet for quality clothing at low prices. In order to make a profit, higher markups were applied to the other merchandise Ohrbach's carried, but the feeling that the customer was getting excellent value for money spent pervaded the atmosphere of these stores. The conventional retailers in the Herald Square area and along Fifth Avenue were largely unaffected by these early discounters. The period of mass migration to the suburbs following World War II changed the retailing scene, and the discounters started to expand exponentially.

Today's Discount Store

It is interesting that all of the stores mentioned above are no longer in existence. Many of the traditional stores found ways of cutting their services and their expenses and were able to compete aggressively with a barrage of advertising and promotions. In other cases, the descendants of the founders of the early discounters did not have the genius and drive to maintain the discount concept. And, at this point, we began to see the rise of a new kind of retail ownership: real estate developers who were without knowledge of retail operations, but who were able to borrow large amounts of money and to mount take-overs of the discounters. In order to satisfy the debts that were contracted, the discount stores were squeezed and mismanaged until they eventually closed.

Today's discounters are a different breed. They may run a specialty operation, or they may be general merchandisers that carry both **hard** and **soft goods.** However, the original concept of limited help within departments, few services, and stark decor with neon lighting still exists. The new discounters have instituted better control of shoplifting by having checkouts at the exits and limited entry into and exit from the store. Most importantly, they have pioneered electronic techniques that enable them to reduce inventory, utilizing the latest computer technology and to reorder merchandise electronically as it is needed, bypassing the wholesaler, and thus reducing their sales costs. They are also able to warehouse as little merchandise as possible through the use of this technology and have been known to change the destination of merchandise en route if it is needed in other locations.

Wal-Mart stores has the distinction of being the number-one retail store in the United States. It is also the largest discount department store operation, followed by Kmart, Target (a division of Dayton Hudson Corp.), and Caldor. These stores are also referred to as mass-merchandisers because they offer many items of hard goods and soft goods with high stock turnover rates and lower markups. T. H. Mandy is a successful women's apparel discount specialty chain and is one of the many specialty operations owned by U.S. Shoe Corporation.

Today's Specialty Stores

Specialty stores are either **single-** or **limited-line operations.** For example, if the store sells only hosiery, it is a single-line operation. If the store sells an assortment of items such as outerwear, suits, sportswear, and accessories, it is then referred to as a limited-line operation.

Some limited-line specialty stores such as Saks Fifth Avenue, Barney's of New York, and Bergdorf Goodman of New York are so large that they have separate departments for each of their merchandise categories. Their size and the variety of merchandise they carry often cause them to be mistakenly identified as department stores. However, since they do not carry a full complement of hard goods, they must be considered specialty stores.

Specialty operations may carry high-end merchandise, discount merchandise, or off-price merchandise. They may be part of a national chain, or units of corporate groups. The Limited, based in Columbus, Ohio, is an example of a specialty chain that has grown and successfully absorbed other retail operations such as Henri Bendel in New York City, Lerner's, and Lane Bryant. They have their own staff of designers who create their private-label collections, which are contracted out to manufacturers in Asia. Instead of the usual six months from order to delivery, merchandise is received in one month. This enables The Limited to be on top of the trends and responsive to changes in market demand. Another successful specialty operation is The Gap, based in San Francisco, which has expanded its target market to children's clothing. Gap Kids and Baby Gap are two of its successful ventures. Banana Republic and American Eagle Outfitters are also owned by this parent organization. The Gap continually freshens its merchandise with new collections every two months.

Today's Boutique

The word **boutique** means little shop, but in today's retail environment, it means more than that. The boutiques emphasize off-beat and unusual merchandise and displays. Frequently, boutiques offer an unusual mix of accessories and apparel, and each boutique tries to make a statement with its offerings. The setting might be in an old brownstone building in a gentrified urban area, as seen in Boston, Massachusetts. Or the setting might be that of a parlor with comfortable couches and antique furnishings. Henri Bendel's was the first large retailer to offer a series of boutiques on its main level and the concept was quickly imitated by other large retail stores. Today, designer boutiques can be found in upscale department and specialty stores. The Ralph Lauren shops are the most notable. Recently, French designer Claude Montana opened a shop with its own entrance in Henri Bendel's.

Today's Off-Price Retailers

An **off-price retailer** is one who buys merchandise for less and thus can sell it for less to the consumer. The merchandise purchased usually consists of the overstocks and returns that the vendor cannot offer to other retailers at traditional prices. Sometimes a vendor has many bolts of fabric that have not been used because the expected number of orders were not received. In this case, an off-price retailer can contract with the vendor to produce the merchandise for him or her at reduced cost. This is a great advantage to the vendor as it provides him or her with the necessary **cash flow** to purchase fabric for the forthcoming season. The original off-pricers advertised that all of their merchandise was brand name and designer label. This is no longer true. As the off-pricers developed and grew, they became chain operations and had to resort to private-label merchandise in order to offer a balanced and **deeper stock assortment.** In some cases, it is difficult to see the difference between specialty operations that are off-price and those that are discount.

In order to compete with the off-price fashion retailers, regular-priced merchants have had many more sales and markdowns than before and have increased their percentage of private-label merchandise. In addition, they have acquired some of the off-price retailers to avoid losing their share of the consumer fashion dollar.

Some of the notable off-price organizations are Marshall's, owned by Melville Shoe Company; Loehmann's, owned by a group of corporate investors; T. J. Maxx and Hit or Miss, owned by TJX (formerly called Zayres); Filene's Basement, owned by the May Company; and T.H. Mandy, owned by U.S. Shoe Corporation. Sym's Incorporated and Dress Barn are independently owned.

Today's Other Fashion Retailers

Flea Markets

In some areas of the country, there has been a growth of **flea markets** offering fashion apparel. On the southeast coast of Florida are many large offerings of this sort which may cover several acres of land (see Figure 14–6). During the high shopping season, these flea markets may be open seven days a week, but usually they are open from Wednesday to Sunday. Some of these markets are housed in climate-controlled buildings and offer merchandise that is designed and manufactured by the booth operators or purchased from manufacturers and wholesalers. Usually, the flea markets have eating facilities and sometimes valet parking. Sales taxes are absorbed and paid for by the flea market vendors so that the apparel shopper feels that he or she is getting an especially good value. Rentals are low for the space occupied, and flea market vendors can afford to sell their merchandise at low markup prices.

Courtesy: Festival Flea Market

FIGURE 14-6 Interior of Festival Flea Market, Pompano Beach, Florida.

Courtesy: Sawgrass Mills, Sunrise, Florida

•••••••• **FIGURE 14-7   Interior of Sawgrass Mills, Sunrise, Florida—a unique enclosed factory and retail outlet mall (see Color Plate II).**

Factory Outlets

Another phenomenon that is achieving unique popularity is a new kind of mall that features manufacturers' outlets. The Storehouse Shops in Reading, Pennsylvania, contains retail outlets that are operated by manufacturers. Another highly popular complex is one in Lawrence, Kansas, a beautifully designed river-front facility.

Sawgrass Mills in southeast Florida (see Figure 14–7) contains a combination of manufacturers' outlets and specialty and department store markdown outlets offering low-price merchandise that has been left over from the previous season or overstocked. Stores such as Ann Taylor and Saks Fifth Avenue have outlets there, as do many shoe and lingerie manufacturers. The attractive mall also offers a food court with numerous fast-food booths and comfortable tables and chairs for lunchers.

Warehouse Stores

Fashion apparel is a very small percentage of the merchandise offered in warehouse stores. However, because of the tremendous growth of this kind of operation, it is important to make note of them. The apparel offered is generally sportswear, and there is no place to try on any of the merchandise. The assortments are **deep** and **narrow.** In order to be able to shop in a warehouse store, a consumer must belong to a "club." This means that a $25 to $35 yearly membership must be paid, and shoppers must carry identification cards with photographs. Some of the important warehouse stores are Price Club, Costco, Pace Membership Club (a division of Kmart), Sam's (a division of Wal-Mart), and BJ's (a division of TJX). Price Club and Costco have recently merged.

The Megamall
Situated on 78 acres in Bloomington, Minnesota, is the Mall of America, a new concept for recreation and shopping (see Figure 14–8). The four floors take up the equivalent of 88 football fields worth of space. Less than half of those football fields are used for shopping, but those that are include 400 specialty stores anchored by Bloomingdale's, Nordstrom, Macy's and Sears.

The center of the complex is adorned with 400 trees, 30,000 plants, a mountain, and a four-story waterfall. This area is called Camp Snoopy and is one of the world's largest amusement parks, offering a myriad of rides, dozens of restaurants, and a 14-screen movie house.

The retail complex has four different sections each with a different theme, such as North Garden, which is lined with gazebos and wooden trellises. Even the music is targeted to please shoppers in dif-

FIGURE 14-8   The Mall of America in Bloomington, Minnesota.

ferent areas, with Billy Joel and James Taylor piped into the common areas and current rock hits heard in stores where the shoppers are from 12 to 20 years of age. The Mall of America is somewhat based on the world's largest mall in West Edmonton, Canada, which also contains hotels and a swimming pool with waves.

Other Notable Retailing Locations

Rodeo Drive
Rodeo Drive, in Beverly Hills, California, is a unique area of the United States. The stores on this and neighboring streets gross probably the highest dollar sales per square foot in the country. Rental costs are equally high for the retailer. Among the shops can be found Giorgio Armani, Ralph Lauren Polo, Vidal Sassoon, Frette, Prada, Mark Cross, and Guess. There is valet parking, which provides the famous movie stars and foreign dignitaries who shop on Rodeo Drive more discreet access to the stores.

Fashion Valley Mall
Fashion Valley Mall in San Diego, California, is unique because of its beauty and eclectic mix of stores and kiosks. It is a multilevel mall that is not enclosed, but which offers enclosed bridges from one store to another on the second level. The anchors are J.C. Penney, Firestone Automotive, Nordstrom, Neiman Marcus, I. Magnin, Robinson's, and Broadway. There are approximately 150 units in the mall, including many apparel specialty shops such as Victoria's Secret, as well as restaurants, fast-food outlets, cafés, and bakeries.

A short, half-mile away is the Mission Valley Mall, **anchored** by Bullock's, May Company, Saks Fifth Avenue, and Brooks Brothers. There are many specialty shops here as well. This mall is also adjacent to a large Montgomery Ward department store and Focus.

For people who enjoy shopping, this area of the world is a little bit of heaven.

Shopping District
Located in the heart of Nassau County, New York, is probably, outside of Manhattan, the largest shopping district in the United States. It is comprised of numerous shopping centers and free-standing stores, and from the air probably looks like two arms radiating out of Roosevelt Field Shopping Center, which is a three-story mall anchored by Macy's, J.C. Penney's, Stern's, and A & S. Starting in the Northwest in the area that was near the original Nassau County location of E.J. Korvette's, are three strip discount centers perpendicular to Voice

Road. Manufacturers' outlets and discount operations abound on Voice Road. Traveling south are Macy's, Bloomingdale's, and A & S furniture outlets and three more shopping centers; Country Glen, which offers Filene's Basement and many other retail stores; and, across the street, two other shopping centers offering discount clothing stores of every conceivable kind as well as Toys R Us. As you travel eastward from Roosevelt Field, you can see the Fur Vault, a large fur retailer, and soon you come to the newest collection of stores, Kmart, Marshall's, and Price Club Warehouse. Just east of this shopping center is Fortunoff's, famous for its fine, bridge, and costume jewelry collection. It is worth mentioning that a mile or two away are free-standing branches of Saks Fifth Avenue, Lord & Taylor, and Bloomingdale's. To visit every store in this shopping district would probably take an intrepid consumer two weeks.

Trump Tower

Anchored by Galeries Lafayette is another unusual mall. This **vertical mall,** called Trump Tower, is located at Fifth Avenue and 57th Street in New York City. It consists of the lower seven levels of a multipurpose building. The upper levels contain offices and luxury condominium apartments. The focal point of the mall is a four- or five-story waterfall cascading over a wall of Italian marble. Escalators and elevators bring shoppers to all the levels of specialty shops that cater to the wealthy, fashion-conscious American shopper as well as to tourists.

Your Television Set

One of the fastest growing locations for a retail store is the customer's own television screen. Cable services often provide their subscribers with several channels that are exclusively devoted to retail offerings. Most of the merchandise seen is fashion apparel. The watcher may make instant choices of the merchandise offerings by telephoning the retailer and offering a credit card for payment. The shopping channels can be fun to watch and are a special boon for those people who are unable to reach traditional retailers by car or by public transportation. Shut-ins or people who work at night find this kind of shopping convenient. It is no wonder that television screen retail stores are growing at such a rapid pace!

Innovative Fashion Retailers

Every type of fashion retail organization has its own leaders, the people or teams that really made a difference and designed a new form of institution that changed the way retailing functioned. These leaders have offered something extra, something that made the stores unique in this highly competitive field. The stores that have been selected are all functioning successfully today and have shown that they are not only innovative but also able to change with the times and remain retailing leaders.

Loehmann's

Freida Loehmann transformed an automobile showroom in Brooklyn, New York, into a virtual "dress palace" with elaborate furnishings and marble in 1921. But it was not the decor that attracted shoppers to Loehmann's. It was the merchandise: prestigious designer clothes at low, low prices.

Before her name became synonymous with high fashion at bargain prices, Mrs. Loehmann had been a well-known buyer for a Fifth Avenue store. With access to many manufacturers' showrooms, she was able to buy their samples, overstock, and closeouts. She always used the service elevators, paid cash which she kept hidden in her stockings, and carted the merchandise away in a truck. The labels were always removed before selling the items at reduced prices. Freida Loehmann took her best customers to her apartment above the store where she kept her designer offerings. Today these special garments can be found in the Back Room where shoppers can still find great bargains in designer and bridge merchandise.

The Loehmann's tradition for innovative retailing was continued by her son Charles, who opened the store in the Bronx near Fordham Road and who established firm merchandising and advertising policies: no credit, no refunds, no exchanges, no alterations, no delivery service, a communal dressing room, and no featured merchandise in store ads. The Bronx store is now located in Riverdale. These merchandising policies were extremely successful, and Charles Loehmann was able to expand the operation. Loehmann's is now an 86-store operation in 26 states, owned and managed by a private investment group that is attempting to change their direction to make their stores more competitive with other off-pricers. Reorganizing under Chapter 11, they are redesigning many of their stores to give shoppers privacy while trying on garments and are accepting returns for credit. Customers may now use credit cards, and designer and manufacturer labels are left on the clothing.

Neiman Marcus

What store would feature a rare antique secretary and desk, fabulous furs, and original uniform buttons from the Republic of Texas Army

Courtesy: Neiman Marcus, Dallas, Texas

• • • • • • • • **FIGURE 14-9   Exterior of Neiman Marcus store in Beverly Hills, California**

for sale in a mail-order catalog? Only a store that bases its operation on "complete customer satisfaction"—Neiman Marcus. In fact, today's entire Neiman Marcus operation of 27 stores has, from the beginning, been like no other. (See Figure 14-9.)

Neiman Marcus was founded in Dallas, Texas, in 1907 by Carrie Neiman and her brother, Herbert Marcus. Young and ambitious, they dreamt of bringing high fashion apparel to the Southwest. They attracted the patronage of the oil-rich millionaires of Texas, but word of their exquisite merchandise and extraordinary personal service soon spread nationwide.

In 1926, Stanley Marcus, Herbert's son, joined the store. Although the merchandising policies of the store were legendary, young Marcus was intensely interested in expanding the sales promotion activities of the store. To supplement the work of the store's advertising staff, he created a public relations department. That department was responsible for instituting the annual "Fortnight" promotion. This is a month-long storewide celebration featuring the merchandise from one country. Today, many retailers have copied this idea.

When people buy merchandise from Neiman Marcus, they not only buy the product, but they buy the mystique of the store and the many services offered, including personal shoppers and fashion shows with food graciously served. The fashion shows have become social events for its customers. There are now many N-M branches all over the United States, from California to Florida.

The parent company of Neiman Marcus is called the Neiman Marcus Group. The NMG includes Bergdorf Goodman, another important trend-setter in the United States, and Contempo Casuals. During the December 1992 season, sales outperformed many of the largest discount operations. This seems to prove that low price is not the only motivation for the purchase of fashion merchandise. A beautiful environment, caring service, carefully purchased merchandise offerings, and a unique image seem to be the key factors in the success of this store.

Wal-Mart

The largest retailer, the fastest growing retailer, and the greatest profit-making retailer in the United States—this is what evolved from an idea of Sam Walton, who felt that there was a need for discount department stores on the outskirts of small towns in the Midwest. The stores drew customers like magnets from the surrounding areas and were an instantaneous success. Sam Walton was always visiting the stores in order to talk to customers and find out what they were buying. He was also a genius in organization and set up 15 territories for the 1,800 plus and growing discount store chain. Each territory is headed by a regional vice president who heads a staff of 11 to 15 district managers. Each district manager is in charge of 8 to 12 stores that each have their own managers.

Sam Walton died in 1992, but because of his insight and ability, the institution is still growing successfully. The regional vice presidents spend about 200 days of the year visiting stores in their territories to speak with the customers and look for trends in merchandise that they should be responsive to. They communicate with employees and check the shelves for gaps. Merchandise that isn't on the floor doesn't get sold. Records of sales by store and department can be compared via computer with other stores in any district, regionally, or nationally. And if anything needs attention, it gets attended to immediately, even if it means flying a team from a successful store to the laggard one to do retraining.

Good store managers get moved from store to store as they are needed—to inspire the employees of a new store or to help redirect the sales activities of stores that are not meeting appropriate levels of performance. A good store manager can earn more than $100,000 a year, while assistant managers earn from $20,000 to $30,000 annually. All employees of Wal-Mart are encouraged to buy Wal-Mart stock, which has risen from about $15 a share to $60 in the past five years.

The store is now headed by Rob Walton, Sam's eldest son. Every Friday there is a meeting at the store's headquarters in Bentonville, Arkansas, which is attended by all Wal-Mart officers. Here the news is heard about the success of the new ventures in urban areas where Wal-Mart is challenging its closest competitors, Kmart and Target.

The success of Wal-Mart is due not only to excellent communication among the staff and with the customers, but also to excellent computer systems which provide information regarding the distribution of merchandise to stores, stock within the stores, sales, and communication with vendors. All ordering is computer to computer. Agreements have been worked out with suppliers such as Gitano to have jeans stored in Wal-Mart's warehouses so that the merchandise can move quickly into the stores. The title changes as the merchandise moves out of the warehouses, and at that point Wal-Mart is responsible for payment to its vendors. Another way that Wal-Mart is containing its distribution costs is by means of vertical integration. This means that a new unit of the **channel of distribution** has been incorporated into the retail organization. The recent purchase of the McLane Company, one of America's best specialty distributors of cigarettes, candy, and perishables, will enable Wal-Mart to lower its overall costs. With distribution savings of this nature, Wal-Mart can afford to offer lower prices to its customers and to have a greater number of sales associates on the floor as well as greeters in each store who welcome customers and direct them to the areas in which they want to shop.

Wal-Mart is not a trend-setter in innovative fashion apparel, but it provides services that make shopping for clothing pleasant, inexpensive, and appropriate for a great many American shoppers. In the soon to come Mexican Wal-Marts, our neighbors to the south will experience this American shopping concept.

Barneys, New York

One of the most famous addresses in fashion retailing is the "corner of Seventh Avenue and Seventeenth Street, the only store of its kind in New York"—the location of the flagship store, Barneys. This 70-year-old men's specialty shop has an inventory of nearly 30,000 suits on hand, making it the largest store of its kind in the world.

The store was opened in 1923 by Barney Pressman. The story is told that in order to have enough money for the rent and for merchandise, Barney had to pawn his wife's engagement ring. Once in business, he became known as a discounter of fine quality menswear. Barney bought merchandise at bankruptcy sales and from overstocked merchants and sold it at tremendous savings to his customers.

After World War II, Barney's son Fred took over the business. He

Courtesy: Barneys, New York

• • • • • • • • **FIGURE 14-10 Sketch of Barneys new Madison Avenue store in New York City, designed by Peter Marino and Assoc. Architects.**

transformed it from a fashion discount operation to a world leader in men's fashion. He introduced several unique merchandising concepts, all of which are still in effect today. First, Barneys stopped buying merchandise to sell at a discount. Rather, Barneys was the first men's retailer to feature fine quality designer merchandise from Europe. Names such as Pierre Cardin, Hubert de Givenchy, and later Giorgio Armani became known to American men because of Barneys. Also, Barneys began to deal with high-quality menswear manufacturers such as Oxxford. Suits are custom-made to Barneys specifications.

In terms of customer service, the staff is polite and fully knowledgeable about merchandise and coordination. Customers each have a salesperson who, if they choose, will accompany them from department to department. If a customer wishes to browse, he is provided with a "Just Looking" button. If a customer is too busy to shop, he can call for an appointment and will be provided with a salesperson and fitter for instant service. In some cases, if a client is unable to come to the store, a salesperson and fitter will go to that person's New York office or hotel with merchandise for the customer's approval.

There is never a charge for any alterations done by Barneys staff of 40 to 50 tailors in the flagship store alone. Further, if a customer wants custom-made clothing, Barneys is happy to oblige.

Today, Fred Pressman and his wife Phyllis have been joined in the business by their two sons, Gene and Robert, and their wives as well as Fred and Phyllis' daughter, Nancy Pressman-Dressler. Two floors of clothing for women can be found in the flagship store. Barneys has embarked upon an expansion of their concept from the new 11-floor store on Madison Avenue in New York City (see Figure 14-10) to a chain of satellite stores in shopping malls from Long Island to Texas to California to Tokyo, together with a new partner, the Isetan Company of Japan. Isetan is Japan's sixth largest retailing operation. Barneys, New York, is a private corporation and is therefore not required to submit sales information. With a new mix of men's fashion forward clothing as well as its conservative lines, and new lines for women, Barneys hopes to become an international chain of at least 25 stores.

Types of Retail Organizations

All retail establishments operate under one of the following forms of ownership: as **independents,** as part of a **franchise,** as part of a **chain,** as part of a **corporate group,** or as part of a **conglomerate.** It is sometimes difficult to categorize some of the retail organizations because of the great changes that have been taking place recently. As you will see, sometimes an organization falls under more than one category, or organizations change to become more competitive and to better meet the needs of their markets. Sometimes totally new retailing concepts are attempted where a retailer sees an opportunity for market share, as in the case of Macy's and its variety of new specialty stores. Divestiture of a chain may take place after an unfortunate bout with bankruptcy and reorganization under Chapter 11.

Independents

The majority of retailers are independently owned. This means that their businesses are either family run, a partnership, or a closed corporation. In a closed corporation, the public does not have the option to buy stock in the business, nor is the corporation obligated to publish information about its business as traditional corporations are. A good example of an independent that is a closed corporation is Barneys, New York, which we have just discussed. Another might be a children's apparel shop or boutique in your town. Perhaps you know of a clothing store that has two or more owners that is not incorporated. This is known as a partnership and functions in the same way as a similar store with one owner.

Franchises

Under this arrangement, a company provides its name, merchandise, management, and marketing knowledge to a merchant in return for the merchant's capital investment and a share of the profits. The merchant is a co-owner of the store and is responsible for its operation. Good examples of successfully franchised fashion apparel shops are the Saint Laurent Rive Gauche and Bennetton stores. However, some of the units of these shops belong to a different category—chain stores.

Chain Stores

A chain operation is one of multiple stores that are similar in physical appearance, carry the same merchandise, and are centrally owned and operated. Sears, Nordstrom's, J.C. Penney's, and Dillards are general merchandise chains, and Merry-Go-Round, Ann Taylor, and Loehmann's are specialty chains. Leased departments in department and specialty stores may also be part of a chain organization.

Wal-Mart, a chain mentioned previously, now operates a chain of warehouse stores called Sam's because it saw an opportunity for growth in the retail market for this fast-developing operation. It must now be considered a corporate group.

Corporate Groups

Through mergers and acquisitions, the corporate group has become another type of retail owner-management organization. These companies are made up of large department and specialty stores that were once independently owned. The stores continue to operate under their original names and—assuming their original method of operation has been successful—continue to maintain their own merchandising policies. As a result, most stores in a corporate group are quite different from one another, with each functioning under policies that are most profitable for its store. However, corporate group headquarters maintains close contact with each store, supplying management advice and fashion direction as well as absorbing the profits and losses of each member store. Another important reason for the establishment of corporate groups is the proliferation of private labels among retailers. Many corporate groups have now become manufacturers with their own design facilities and overseas operations and they oversee the contracting for manufacture of their products. In this way, they can absorb the profits earned by private manufacturers and offer lower priced merchandise to their customers. A good example of a corporate group that maintains these facilities is Macy's, which is the owner of Macy's East, South, and West, Bullock's, and I. Magnin. However, this is a group that is in transition because of its reorganization under Chapter 11. By the time this book goes to press, Macy's will probably have merged with Federated, making it the largest department store company in the United States.

Table 14–1 lists some of the important corporate groups not mentioned above and the stores under their umbrellas.

TABLE 14-1   Some Corporate Retail Groups and Their Subsidiaries

Dayton Hudson	Allied Stores	Federated Stores
Mervyn's		Bloomingdale's
Marshall Field	Stern's	Abraham & Straus
Target	Bon Marché	Burdine's
	Jordan Marsh	Rich's/Goldsmith's
		Lazarus

The Gap	The Limited	TJX
Baby Gap	Limited Too	T.J. Maxx
Gap Kids	Henri Bendel	Hit or Miss
Banana Republic	Victoria's Secret	BJ's Wholesale Club
	Lane Bryant	Chadwick's
	Lerner's	
	Express	
	Structure	

May Dept. Stores	Woolworth	Neiman Marcus
Volume Shoe	Kinney Shoes	Bergdorf Goodman
Filene's	World Foot Locker	Contempo Casuals
Robinson's	Lady Foot Locker	
G. Fox	Foot Locker	
Lord & Taylor	Afterthoughts	
	Northern Reflections	
	Accessory Lady	

Conglomerates

A conglomerate is an organization that includes a multiplicity of organizations that frequently have no relationship at all to one another. The parent organization operates in a similar manner to corporate groups and differs only in its diversity of interests.

Sara Lee is one such organization. Not only does it include its bakery products divisions, but it also includes manufacturing companies such as Bali, L'eggs, Hanes, Playtex, and Henson, as well as its retail catalog operation. The Melville Corporation is another conglomerate. It owns and operates shoe manufacturing facilities as well as fashion retail establishments, including Marshall's, Thom McAnn, Foot Action, and Kay-Bee. U.S. Shoe Corporation is a third such conglomerate. In addition to owning shoe manufacturing facilities, it is the parent of apparel retailers Casual Corner, Ups 'N Downs, Caren Charles, August Max, T.H. Mandy, Career Image, and Petite Sophisticates. Genesco and Manhattan Industries are conglomerates with interests in textiles, footwear, and retail operations.

Sears, Roebuck & Company is a conglomerate in transition. It is in the process of spinning off its financial service division, Dean Witter Reynolds, and its real estate division, Coldwell Banker. The structure of Allstate Insurance will also be changing in the near future. Sears plans to change some of its smaller units into specialty operations and to close other units that are not profitable.

The National Retail Federation

The retailing industry, as well as all the industries in the United States, has its own trade association and publications which are geared to the type of retail store in operation. The trade association, the National Retail Federation, with its annual trade show each January, is based in New York City and has evolved from its earliest beginnings as the National Retail Dry Goods Association to the National Retail Merchants Association to its present organization of worldwide membership.

- -

FINDING A CAREER IN FASHION RETAILING

Many students who wish to become a part of the fashion business can do so by taking advantage of the many career opportunities that are available in all types of fashion retail stores. Those who are drawn to the excitement of buying and selling can enter into the merchandising or promotion of merchandise, while those who have an interest in finance can work in store operations.

Careers in Fashion Merchandising

Many large retailers offer executive training programs that prepare qualified young people for fashion merchandising positions. In order to be accepted into these excellent programs, the applicant is usually expected to have a college background, some selling experience, and a keen fashion sense. Upon completion of the program, the career path of the trainee would probably progress in this order: assistant department manager, department manager, assistant buyer, and buyer.

Assistant Department Manager

This position offers the novice an excellent opportunity to learn the basic day-to-day merchandising techniques of retailing. An assistant manager is required to help the manager with all phases of running a department, particularly with inventory control, sales personnel supervision, and merchandise display.

Department Manager

The key role of a department manager is to maintain an efficiently run, profitable department. The two major responsibilities of this position are (1) to supervise and train a well-informed and cooperative sales staff, and (2) to supply the department's buyer with accurate, up-to-date information on the sales performance of the department's merchandise.

Assistant Buyer

As the buyer's "helping hand," an assistant buyer has the excellent opportunity to learn the intricate but exciting technique of buying fashion merchandise. Under the buyer's guidance, the assistant covers the market, does the majority of the department's "paperwork," assists the buyer in evaluating the department manager's merchandise reports, places reorders, and contacts manufacturers (or "follows-up") about the on-time delivery of goods. Because the assistant performs so many of the buying functions for a department (although none of the actual buying), this position usually serves as an "understudy role" for the position of buyer.

Buyer

All ultimate buying decisions on the merchandise that is purchased for a department rest with the buyer. Since these decisions determine the success of a department, all good buyers carefully analyze their customers, their market, and all current and incoming fashion trends before coming to their conclusions. Most of their information is obtained through their coverage of the market by visiting manufacturers, fabric houses, and fashion editors. But they also consult with some of the other fashion executives of their organization, particularly their merchandise manager and the store's fashion director. Other information and guidance for the buyer is available from the various ancillary merchandising organizations most retailers subscribe to. These include buying offices and fashion consultants; their advisory role is discussed fully in the following chapter.

The position of buyer is exciting and well paying. Buyers are among a store's most highly respected executives, and buying is a challenging career goal for the talented and aggressive student. Although the backgrounds of many present-day buyers vary in terms of academic and professional experience, almost all have been assistants before moving up to the buyer's position. This type of on-the-job training as an assistant is invaluable and is a "must" for almost all buying positions.

Careers in Promotion

For people who are interested in using their creativity within the fashion industry, retailers offer enormous opportunities through their sales promotion divisions. The fashion advertising, display, and publicity departments of these divisions employ artists, writers, and other creative people to sell and publicize the merchandise and name of a store. All aspects of sales promotion, including the many exciting careers found in this field, are discussed in detail in Chapter 15.

Careers in Finance, Store Operations, and Personnel

There are many career opportunities in the finance, operations management, and personnel divisions of a retail store. For instance, some of the country's top retail executives began in finance, rising through the ranks to become comptroller and eventually president of major retail organizations. Those who have an interest in any of these three areas will find that the retail field is a lucrative and creatively rewarding one.

Executive Training

FASHION FEATURE

While the career paths of some people in retailing are through the ranks starting as sales associates, and some are lucky enough to be the son or daughter of a founder of a large retailing empire, most of the people who would like to have a career in fashion merchandising start as executive trainees of large department and specialty stores. Most colleges and community colleges provide large organizations with recruitment time on the campuses and schedule students for interviews. Sometimes, applicants are tested during the interview or are asked to come back for testing at a later time. Frequently, the skills required include competency in mathematics, retail problem solving, or creativity. Writing skills are important in communicating ideas.

Students who are fortunate in having internship programs in retailing as part of their studies are frequently asked to become executive trainees upon graduation. Four-year colleges provide most of the executive trainees for the largest department and specialty stores. However, special programs have been devised for students of community colleges with strong retailing and fashion merchandising programs. This has been true for Nassau Community College graduates at Macy's branch stores on Long Island in New York State. In addition, large conglomerates such as the Melville Corporation actively recruit on the campuses of community colleges.

Training takes place in a large classroom in central headquarters or the flagship store, and there are usually about 25 trainees in a class. These classes start at different times of the year, and the members of the class are graduates from colleges all over the country, some with little experience in fashion retailing. A coordinator is responsible for teaching some of the classes and for scheduling lectures by key company personnel.

Students are given a textbook with information about the history of the store, a table of organization, a schedule of classes, and the information necessary to function in the retail environment of that particular organization. The course outline usually includes mathematics; understanding computer printouts; public relations; entering different transactions on the point-of-sale registers; handling markdowns, markups, and transfers; and receiving merchandise. Time is spent in the classes on the various ways to control shoplifting. Different department managers speak to the trainees about their departments, and trainees are given a tour of the flagship store.

One of the interesting projects trainees are asked to do is to study a particular department in depth and then compare the merchandise, its presentation, and the prices with a number of different stores with similar or disparate images. The trainee is then assigned to a department for several days to familiarize himself or herself with selling techniques, the recording of sales transactions, and the attractive arrangement of stock.

Several buyers are then invited to make presentations about their duties, and trainees are assigned to buyers for about a month to learn about the buying end of the fashion retailing business. Trainees accompany the buyer to vendor offerings and to the corporate offices where the private-label designers and buyers are located. If trainees are lucky enough, they are permitted to sit in at market week at the corporate office when the buyers of the different divisions make their selections for private-label offerings. Among the duties of the trainee is the tracking of incoming foreign merchandise from the time it arrives at the port until it arrives at the store. Merchandise needed for an advertised promotion needs special attention. Trainees also act as liaisons with department managers of the branch stores and call them every day to get information and to give information as to changes in retail pricing and movement of merchandise.

During the last month, trainees are assigned to a department manager and act as his or her assistant. Here they are fully prepared to run a department efficiently and effectively. Then comes graduation and a party. The trainees are assigned to their own departments, but a special bonding always remains with the members of a training class, who by now have become great friends.

Problem Solving

1. In what way could you prepare yourself for acceptance in an executive training program? What special skills should you hone? What should you do in order to feel comfortable during an interview? How should you dress for an interview? How should you dress as an executive trainee?

2. Prepare a list of large fashion retail department and specialty stores. Organize the list as to preference. What criteria should you use in the selection of a store training program? How could you get information about training programs in stores?

.... TERMS TO REMEMBER

mail-order firm   dry goods store   specialty store   hard goods   soft goods
department store   twig   discounter   off-price retailer   leased department
boutique   independent store   franchise   chain store   corporate group
conglomerate   trading post   flagship store   central headquarters   average
markup   stock turnover   single line   limited line   cash flow   flea
market   anchor   vertical mall   channel of distribution   narrow and deep
stock assortments

.... HIGHLIGHTS OF THE CHAPTER

- The first retailers in early America were small trading posts, specialty shops, general stores, and mail-order houses. These grew and evolved into the large retail institutions of today.

- Specialty stores deal in one kind or a limited line of merchandise, whereas department stores sell all kinds of goods (hard and soft), presenting them "departmentalized."

- Post-World War II was a time for much innovation on the part of retailers and discounters; branch stores and boutiques emerged during that period.

- The discount store is identifiable by its merchandising policy, which encourages cut-rate prices, large volume, and a limited amount of service. Branch stores are retail outlets that are usually built in the suburbs by inner-city stores to accommodate the growing suburban populations. The boutique is a small shop that carries unique fashion merchandise not ordinarily found in traditional stores.

- Stores are owned and managed by five types of retailers: the independent, the franchiser, the chain store operation, the corporate group, and the conglomerate.

- The activities of people who work in a retail store fall under five categories: merchandising, promotion, finance, personnel, and store operations.

- The majority of executive positions in retailing are those in merchandising where talented people can become department managers and buyers, usually beginning as their assistants.

- The off-price retailer is a significant force in the fashion apparel scene today.

- The growth of the mall in America has changed the way people shop for fashion apparel.

- Retailing is always in a state of change. It reflects the economic condition of the United States and the needs of its customers.

.... REVIEW QUESTIONS

1. Describe how America's first retail stores were founded and the course of their development into today's great retail institutions.

2. What is the difference between a *single* and a *limited-line* specialty store? Give an example of each in your home town.

3. How have discount and branch stores changed since they were introduced?

4. Describe the five types of ownership for retail establishments.

5. If you had the opportunity to open a store, what type would you choose and what kind of merchandise would you sell? Why?

6. Would you be interested in any of the careers offered in retailing? Explain why.

7. Describe the events of the "retail revolution."

8. What is a leased department?

9. What is an off-price retailer? Mention some major retailers who operate off-price establishments.

10. Give the backgrounds of two innovative fashion retailers.

1. Fashion retailing is quite different today from its early pioneer days and the late 1800s. What are some major contrasts?

2. The discounter has had a profound effect on fashion merchandising and retailing in general. Describe this impact. What do you see as the future for fashion discounting?

3. Research the future of retailing in the United States. What major changes will impact the rest of the fashion business?

4. There are many career opportunities in fashion retailing. Select a position that you are most interested in and research it by using the current edition of the *Dictionary of Occupational Titles*, by interviewing a person already in the position, and using the help-wanted advertisements to see how plentiful jobs for the position are in your area.[1] Include in your report the job description, which includes the actual tasks and responsibilities of the position, and the job specifications, which describe the attributes, qualifications, and any necessary skills required to perform the job.

5. Select one of the five corporate groups featured in Table 14–1. Using reference materials and stockholder reports, prepare a profile of the organization, including financial data, a history, and any future plans the company may have for expansion.

6. Prepare a list of questions that may be asked during a job interview by the interviewer regarding your knowledge about the firm from which you are seeking employment. Ask your reference librarian to assist you with locating books and materials that provide background information about companies. The many books published by Moody's Investor's Service in New York may be helpful to you.

[1] U.S. Department of Labor, *Dictionary of Occupational Titles* (Washington, D.C.: U.S. Government Printing Office).

CHAPTER 15

....

Ancillary Merchandising Operations/Promoting Fashion

...... LEARNING OBJECTIVES

After reading this chapter you should be able to:

- Identify the types of ancillary firms that are available to the fashion industry to assist them in merchandising and promoting fashion merchandise.
- Define the specific functions of those firms.
- Understand how these firms gather, analyze, and define fashion information for incorporation into a store's merchandising, promotion, and advertising plans.
- Understand the importance of sales promotion in the retailing of merchandise.
- Know the importance of sales promotion in the development and projection of a store's fashion image.

...... PERFORMANCE OUTCOME

After reading this chapter, you should be able to:

- Differentiate between the types of resident buying offices and identify the store clientele each type of office services.
- Know how to use the services of fashion consultants, consumer and trade publications, and other sources of market information to project future fashion trends.
- Select from the various types of promotional activities a store or fashion office can use to promote its merchandise and fashion image in an effective and economical manner.

To help retailers have the "right merchandise, in the right amount, at the right price, at the right time," the fashion industry offers many specialized services. Resident buying offices, fashion consultants, magazines, trade organizations, trade publications, and textile and clothing manufacturers are just some of the many people and operations that assist stores in the buying and selling of fashion goods. But, in the retailing business, getting the right merchandise into a store is only half the job; convincing the customer to buy that merchandise is the other half. The advertising, display, publicity, and other techniques used to induce those sales is called *promotion.*

All medium to large size retail stores that advertise, display, and otherwise promote their fashion merchandise have a sales promotion division. Typically, most stores have a sales division that is headed by one sales promotion director and have other key people managing the various promotional activities of the store. Usually an advertising director runs the advertising department, and a visual merchandising director handles a store's display efforts. Stores that receive or seek a large amount of publicity generally have a publicity or public relations director. And, unless store policy places its fashion office in the merchandising division, the store's fashion director is also included as part of the sales promotion executive staff.

Together, these experts imaginatively communicate with the public, relaying a store's fashion message and persuading its customers to buy.

RESIDENT BUYING OFFICES

Definition and Background

In an industry where today's "ford" (a popular style) may be tomorrow's markdown, stores must keep constant tabs on all the changes and developments occurring in the wholesale marketplace. Since out-of-town store buyers and executives do not have daily access to the country's wholesale market centers, stores can learn what is happening in the market by using the services of a resident buying office.

A **resident buying office** is an organization that serves as advisor and buying representative for one, several, or many noncompetitive retail stores. (Stores are considered "noncompetitive" when they are situated a comfortable distance away in different towns or cities, giving each other little or no competition.) Resident buying offices do not replace store buyers. They do not have a budget to spend or an "open-to-buy". Rather, resident buyers assist store buyers. They serve in an advisory capacity, keeping a pulse on the day-to-day happenings in the Garment Center and important fashion locations around the globe. Resident buyers seek out new resources, forecast hot new trends, and do follow-up work that the store buyer is unable to do because of being removed from the fashion marketplace.

Resident buying offices are located in the country's top fashion market centers. The majority are in New York City, with others in Los Angeles, Chicago, Dallas, and Miami. Some of those outside New York are branches of the larger New York buying firms. Some also maintain foreign branches in the important fashion market centers abroad.

An updated listing of resident buying offices can be found in *Sheldon's Retail Directory of the United States*, which is published annually. The directory also organizes information by listing stores and the resident buying offices used by each. It should be noted that one store may utilize the services of several buying offices, depending on its special product needs.

Resident buying offices have been in existence since before the turn of the century. In those days, the typical "office" consisted of one person who worked and lived in New York City, buying and covering the market for a single out-of-town store. During the 1920s—a period of rapid growth for New York's ready-to-wear industry—the number and size of buying offices multiplied. They enlarged their staffs, took on more clients, and, as a result, began to exert a new and powerful influence in the market.

Types of Resident Buying Offices

There are four types of resident buying offices: the independent or paid office, the corporate office, the cooperative or associated office, and the private office. The first is independently owned; the last three are store or corporation owned.

The Independent Buying Office
The majority of resident buying offices are independent enterprises that are run for a profit. These *independent resident buying offices* charge

their member stores—their clients—a fee for services. The fee varies; generally it is based on the store's sales volume and on the amount and types of services used by a store.

The size of an independent office can also vary. Some are small, servicing as few as under a dozen stores. Others—like the Doneger Group which operates 11 divisions and represents over 560 stores—are huge, complex businesses. Other well-known independent buying offices include Certified Fashion Guild, VBW Associates, and Atlas Buying Corporation.

Independent offices strive to create a particular image and reputation. For instance, one successful office, Betty Cohen, caters to fine specialty and department stores and has developed a reputation as a buying office with fashion "savvy." Other offices have built their image or reputation on specialization. For instance, some offices—such as Good Buys, Price Breakers and Jerri Pollack—expertly cover the "promotional" or low end of the market for stores that sell inexpensive goods. Others are even more specialized. These offices cover only one segment of the market, for instance, servicing retailers that deal exclusively in furs, children's wear, menswear, or any other large single market category.

The Corporate Buying Office

The second type of office is the *corporate resident buying office*, maintained and owned by a parent company or its stores. The parent company is usually a large corporation that has built a syndicate or chain simply by acquiring independent stores.

Many of the stores acquired by the large chains are very different from one another. Usually they vary in size. Almost all keep their original name and—assuming they are successful—their retailing policies. Consequently, a corporate buying office may find itself in the position of having to fulfill a broad variety of needs for dissimilar stores.

The corporate office is a well-staffed organization that is deeply involved in the welfare of its stores and intent on providing almost unlimited service, making no profit on its own. As part of the parent firm, the corporate office has the power to buy and distribute merchandise for its stores. Because of this power, it carries great authority in the marketplace. Typical of the large corporate buying offices are May Department Stores, Carter Hawley Hale, and R. H. Macy & Company.

The Cooperative Office

A *cooperative resident buying office* is owned by a group of nonrelated, noncompeting, privately owned stores. It is also referred to as an "associated" office. Its stores support it on a joint basis. Fees vary for each member depending on the store's sales volume and the services it requires.

When a cooperative office is organized, it limits its membership to stores with similar characteristics. The merchandising policies, sales volume, and clientele of stores belonging to a cooperative office are usually alike. To maintain this similarity, new memberships in a cooperative office are by invitation only.

The best known office of this type is Associated Merchandising Corporation (AMC). Founded in 1918 and located in New York City's Garment Center, it represents such retailers as F. & R. Lazarus of Cincinnati, J. L. Hudson of Detroit and Foley's of Houston. Until 1985, it also represented the Federated Department Stores, including Bloomingdale's, Abraham & Straus, and Filene's. (Federated decided to open its own corporate office for domestic operations.)

One of the major services provided by AMC is assistance with import goods. AMC has 32 offices outside the United States in such places as London, Paris, Australia, the Far East, and South America. It assists with the rigors of import buying, global sourcing and new product development for its members. Stores such as Saks Fifth Avenue (Investcorps) and Sears use the services of AMC's international division.

The other major cooperative office is Frederick Atkins. Like AMC, it is global in nature, scanning the world's fashion markets for its clients. Member stores include Dillards, McCurdys, Hess Brothers, and Trimingham's of Bermuda.

The Private Office

A *private resident buying office* is owned by a single retailing firm and services that firm exclusively. The cost of maintaining a private office is high, and only giant chain, department, or specialty stores can afford to do so.

Two famous, but very different, retailers with private resident buying offices are Montgomery Ward and Neiman Marcus. Ward's has buying offices in New York, Los Angeles, Dallas, Miami, and Chicago—its home base—to help it expedite the enormous volume of its 500 stores and huge mail-order business. Neiman Marcus maintains its own New York buying office to support the kind of unique high-fashion, top-quality operation that made the Texas specialty store world famous. Although their needs are quite different, each of these retailing giants finds that the services of a private resident buying office are necessary to run its business.

Organization of the Resident Buying Office

In essence, a resident buying office duplicates the buying and other executive staff of a retail store. Every department of a large store is represented in a buying office. Vice-presidents head up the apparel, home furnishings, sales promotion, and financial divisions of a buying office. The fashion director, divisional merchandise managers, resident buyers, and assistants work directly under the merchandising vice presidents; the art, display, advertising, and direct-mail departments fall under the jurisdiction of the sales promotion vice president. By duplicating the organization of a store and having one or more specialists to represent each department, a buying office is able to give all members of a store the help and guidance they need.

Services of the Resident Buying Office

To advise—that is the main function of a buying office. To fulfill that function, each day resident buyers, merchandise managers, and fashion office personnel thoroughly scour the market looking for new fashion trends and market conditions. During market weeks, when store buyers are in town, resident buying offices have the opportunity to present their findings to the stores personally. During the rest of the year, the buying office communicates with the stores via telephone and by sending bulletins, brochures, and other written communications.

Resident Buyer

A specific area of the market is assigned to the **resident buyer.** Sometimes that market is limited, but by no means small. For instance, there are so many dress manufacturers in New York that a large office like Federated divides the dress market among six resident buyers, separating it by size and price. Each buyer covers one of the following classifications: junior dresses; pacesetter and budget career dresses; daytime dresses; bridal, better, and designer dresses; moderate and casual dresses; and women's world.

The typical day of a resident buyer is long, full of hard work, sometimes exciting, and always interesting. The morning may include meetings with visiting store buyers, meetings with manufacturers' representatives, receiving and making cross-country telephone calls, reading and answering mail, sorting orders, writing and proofreading bulletins, and setting up a day's schedule. By noon, the resident buyer is in the market where new lines are covered and older lines reviewed. Store orders and reorders are placed. In the late afternoon, the buyer rushes back to the office and, between phone calls and meetings with merchandise managers and fashion coordinators, gets bulletins off to the stores on the new market developments of the day.

This pace becomes even more hectic during the market weeks. In order to supply store people with a preview of the season's new fashion trends, prices, and market conditions, the buying office may hold meetings, fashion shows, and "clinics" in which each resident buyer participates.

These separate full-day meetings are held just prior to, or at the start of, the market openings. They are organized on a divisional basis. For instance, there are dress meetings, sportswear meetings, menswear meetings, and so on. To illustrate their recommendations, the buyers gather sample merchandise from their manufacturers and present it visually. Sometimes, they invite a manufacturer who has a special line or a new marketing or sales promotion program to speak before the stores. These sessions present a wealth of information to stores, making it much easier for them to organize the new season's buying plans.

In addition to informing stores on market developments, resident buyers also have the power to "buy." However, in most resident offices, buyers cannot place orders except when asked to do so by store buyers. Only buyers who work for a private or corporate resident office—where the buying office and store belong to one parent firm—have the money and authority to place orders. These resident buyers are allocated an amount of money called an "open-to-buy," which gives them the option to ship merchandise they feel is right for their member stores without waiting for the approval of those stores.

It must be emphasized, however, that resident buyers are not substitutes for store buyers. It is their function to *supplement* rather than to replace the work of a store buyer. Because they serve as representatives for a store buyer, resident buyers are also called *market representatives*. Regardless of his or her title, the resident buyer has one of the most challenging jobs in a buying office.

The Fashion Office

The responsibility of the fashion office in a resident buying office is to research, analyze, and then define current and future fashion trends. The purpose of this is to incorporate these trends into a store's merchandising, promotion, and advertising plans.

The fashion office is headed by a fashion director or coordinator, who is assisted by one or several people. To determine the trends for a given season, the staff starts compiling information more than six months before manufacturers present their lines to the retailers.

A Fashion Office Calendar

JANUARY	Analyze the swatched predictions of fall color and fabric trends from the editorial offices of fashion magazines, major mills, leather manufacturers, and fashion consultant firms like Color Association.
FEBRUARY-MARCH	Visit stylists at leading leather houses for their opinion on the direction of fall color.
MARCH-APRIL	Visit fabric houses. Begin with large mills like Burlington, Klopman, and Milliken for popular, overall color and fabric trends. Continue with the "pacesetters"—the small but high-fashion fabric houses like Anglo Woolens, Concord Fabrics, and Eininger. Visit Wool Bureau, Cotton Council, and other similar fiber organizations. Visit and get forecasts from fabric editors of leading fashion magazines. As complementary leather and fabric swatches come in from these sources, set up swatch boards in fashion office of each color and fabric in thematic fashion groupings for referral by staff members of buying office and store personnel.
JANUARY-MAY	Analyze ready-to-wear trends. Begin by studying European spring couture and ready-to-wear lines for new silhouette, color, and texture directions. Before the May openings, visit a few key ready-to-wear manufacturers for a "hint" of the direction they are taking.
EARLY MAY	Revisit magazines to see the merchandise editors for fall promotions they are offering to stores and for their analyses of the fall fashion trends.
MAY	Visit accessory market. Coverage of the accessory market will not only supply the new accessory trends, it will offer a confirmation of the top ready-to-wear trends as well.
MAY	Consult with resident office buyers and merchandisers to get opinions on trends and coordinate themes. For instance, if the fashion office endorses a new trend of "skirts that are soft and wide," store people will be much more receptive toward promoting that trend if it is also endorsed by buyers.

To better understand the timing of market coverage by a fashion office, assume the staff is working on a forthcoming fall season. The high-priced manufacturers present fall lines in April. The bulk of the market opens the first week in May. It is necessary for the fashion staff to have full knowledge of those fall trends *weeks* before the openings in order to prepare written material and the meeting agenda it will present to the stores. To obtain that information, a working schedule is prepared for that particular fall season. The Industry Feature entitled "A Fashion Office Calendar" presents a sample of a typical schedule for a fashion office staff working in New York City. By following such a schedule, a fashion office obtains a *total* fashion picture to present to the fashion directors, executives, merchandisers, and buyers of its member stores. It does so through (1) an illustrated and swatched fashion brochure or book, (2) a fashion promotion calendar with correct timing for presenting each theme, and (3) a seminar or large meeting run by the fashion director.

Through the rest of the season, the fashion office *follows through*. It sends daily bulletins, continually feeding the stores information on current and forthcoming fashion trends. To help train store salespeople, it may also provide stores with slides and taped commentary giving a seasonal fashion report. The quality and amount of material produced by a fashion office vary among the buying offices and depend on the size, writing ability of its staff, and the production budget of the office.

Import Buying

Another important function that the resident buying office performs is in acquiring import goods. Offices known as *commissionaires* are located overseas and serve stores by finding resources, doing product development, assisting with buyer visits and meetings, and doing the necessary follow-up work to insure the merchandise is shipped and billed correctly.

Private-Label Programs

One of the most important newer services being offered by resident buying offices today is the development of private-label merchandise for its client stores. Working closely with manufacturers, buying offices are able to oversee custom designing and custom labeling of goods that become unique products for their stores.

Group Purchasing

Purchase of identical merchandise from a manufacturer at one time by a group of stores is called *group purchasing*. Because of the large volume of the purchase, the manufacturer will sell the goods at a special reduced price. Through group purchasing, a resident buyer may also develop an item with a manufacturer for exclusive distribution to a group of stores. It may be a new fashion item not yet available in the market or an item for the Christmas, back-to-school, or seasonal catalog that buying offices produce for their stores. Stores also have the opportunity to take advantage of group purchasing when a resident buyer purchases closeout merchandise at the end of a season from a manufacturer who wants to clear out its inventory.

Centralized Buying

A centralized buying operation is one that buys for a specific department of its member stores. Each department supplies the office with a dollar budget and information on the colors, fabrics, and styles that sell well in its department. Equipped with these monetary and style guidelines, the resident office buyer selects and orders stock.

Most resident buying offices have a centralized buying operation. It is used primarily in low-priced or budget dress, sportswear, and accessory departments.

There are several advantages to a centralized buying operation, particularly for a smaller store. First, it eliminates the expense of maintaining a department buyer in the store. Instead, it offers the advantage of having a resident buyer who is in the market continually, supplying a department with a flow of fresh, new merchandise. And, because the resident buyer is buying for more than one store, it also gives the individual store price benefits that can only come from group purchasing.

Other Fashion Services of the Buying Office

Although its prime function is to provide buying and fashion advice, a buying office also offers stores a variety of sales promotion services. Most of the larger offices maintain sales promotion staffs with visual merchandising (display), advertising, and direct-mail departments.

A visual merchandising department in a New York buying office services the office's stores by providing fresh information on the new materials and price conditions appearing in the New York display market. The advertising staff of an office is responsible for preparing suggested ad layouts and copy for new fashion themes; the direct-mail department prepares a variety of brochures, catalogs, and many other mailing pieces a store sends to its charge customers.

As mentioned earlier, the degree and quality of service offered by resident buying offices vary. A store, however, considers its buying office—regardless of the office's size and type—"special." During market weeks, it represents a home away from home; a friendly, supportive place to check in and get an all-important sense of direction before going into the market. During the rest of the year, it maintains a necessary physical and psychological link between the store and the marketplace.

Listed below is a summary of some of the services offered to stores by a buying office.

- Cover and report on fashion trends and market conditions on a day-to-day basis through written and telephone communication.
- Supply preview of new market trends at the beginning of a season through meetings, fashion shows, and "clinics."
- Help stores organize seasonal buying and sales promotion plans.
- Provide efficient and economical buying services through centralized buying and group purchasing.
- Provide direct-mail, advertising, display, and other sales promotion advice and material.

FASHION CONSULTANTS AND REPORTING SERVICES

Another important merchandising aid for the retailer is the **fashion consultant** or reporting service. A fashion consultant is a person or independent firm retained by retailing firms to help them merchandise the fashion areas of their businesses. A consultant researches and evaluates the fashion markets, submitting evaluations and recommendations to client firms. Perhaps the most well known and respected of these firms is Tobé Associates (see Industry Feature entitled "Tobé Associates"). Other fashion consultants and reporting services providing varied sources of information are listed in Table 15–1. All these organizations have offices in New York City.

CONSUMER FASHION MAGAZINES

Another help for the retailer is *consumer fashion magazines. Vogue, Harper's Bazaar, Glamour, Mademoiselle, Seventeen,* and *GQ (Gentlemen's*

TABLE 15-1   Important Fashion Consultants and Reporting Services

Color Box	Promostyl
Color Projections	Stylists Information Service (SIS)
Fashion Works, Inc.	The Fashion Service (TFS)
Here and There	
IM International	
Merchandising Motivation Inc. (MMI)	
Nigel French Enterprises, U.S.A., Ltd.	
Pat Tunsky	
Prism	

Quarterly) are the fashion magazines most widely read by the American public. Other important publications include *Elle, Vanity Fair, Mirabella, Savvy, Details,* and *Esquire.* Naturally, the fashions they choose to present on their pages greatly influence the fashion preferences of their readers.

Retailers recognize the strong influence of these fashion periodicals; their customers often come into their stores to find a dress, an accessory, or even a "look" that they saw in the latest issue of *Vogue* or *Mademoiselle.* To anticipate those requests, retailers work very closely with the staffs of these fashion publications.

In addition to fashion editors, promotion editors, and fabric editors, magazines employ *merchandise editors.* It is their function to inform retailers of the merchandise, trends, and fashion themes that will appear in forthcoming issues. Throughout the year, retailers visit magazine editorial offices to meet with merchandise editors. There, they are shown "dummies"—rough paste-up replicas—of forthcoming issues. The dummies contain photographs and accompanying editorial copy of the fashions chosen from the wholesale market that, in the opinion of the fashion editors, represent fashion news.

At the same time, the retailers meet with the *fabric editors.* They are responsible for covering and evaluating the textile market and for providing an analysis of future fabric and color trends.

To help them choose the type of merchandise that will be most appealing to their readers, magazines maintain research departments. These departments survey their readership, compiling data on age, lifestyle, occupation, buying power, and buying habits. The magazines send the results of their surveys to retailers, who also find it extremely helpful in servicing their markets.

Tobé Associates

One of the oldest and most prestigious fashion consulting firms is Tobé Associates, the *doyen* of fashion forecasting. It was founded in 1927 by Tobé Coller Davis, a celebrated fashion personality with an uncanny ability to analyze fashion and predict trends. Hiring several young but capable reporters, Tobé and her staff scoured the market for fashion "news." Tobé died in 1962, but the company continues to publish the highly successful weekly *Tobé Report*.

Today the staff of twelve editors extensively covers all the major fashion markets and happenings both here and abroad. Their evaluations and interpretations are compiled along with data on prices, manufacturers, and sketches of recommended merchandise, organized by classification and presented to the subscribers of Tobé Associates.

Over 500 clients, including all major retail stores, subscribe to the *Tobé Report*. A relatively new service called *Tobé on Tape* is now available to clients. It is a video presentation of fashion forecasts for various merchandise lines and has been received extremely well by the industry.

Fees for the services provided by Tobé Associates are based on the dollar volume of the subscriber store. In some cases, the fees can be in the $25,000 range and up. Because of the consistent accuracy of the reporting by this widely acclaimed firm, stores consider the services as being very valuable.

TRADE PUBLICATIONS

A number of newspapers, magazines, and journals are published that supply information on fashion and market developments for those in the industry. The most famous of these **trade periodicals** is *Women's Wear Daily*, the trade paper for the wholesale and retail women's garment industries. Everyone in the industry—designers, manufacturers, salespeople, fashion editors, and retailers—reads *Women's Wear Daily*. The paper is published every weekday by Fairchild Publications, a publishing firm that was founded in 1890.

At the present time, Fairchild also publishes *W, Footwear News, Fur Age Weekly, Homefurnishings Daily*, and *Daily News Record*. The latter publication is considered the "bible" of the men's and boys' wear industries. There are many other trade publications to help retailers in their merchandising activities. Most specialize in one area of the industry. Typical examples are listed in Table 15–2.

········ TABLE 15-2   Fashion Industry Trade Publications

American Fabrics	*Fashion Week*
Apparel Manufacturer	*Footwear News*
Body Fashions	*Fur Age Weekly*
Boot and Shoe Recorder	*Masculines*
Boutique Magazine	*Men's Wear*
California Apparel	*Modern Retailer*
News	*Modern Textiles*
California Men's Stylist	*Stores*
Chain Store Age	*Style for Men*
Clothes	*Visual Merchandising*
Daily News Record	*Women's Wear Daily*
Fabric News	

Finally, a discussion of important trade publications would be incomplete without mentioning the **Fashion Calendar.** Although it neither advises nor reports on fashion, it is the one publication considered indispensable. Published monthly, it offers a daily listing of upcoming events, market weeks, manufacturers' showings, trade shows, and all the other important happenings of the market. The time, place, number, and name of the person to call for information are conveniently included with each listing.

··

OTHER SOURCES OF MARKET INFORMATION

There are so many sources providing pertinent market and fashion information that a buyer, merchandiser, or fashion director of a store would find it impossible to take advantage of them all. Most retailers pick and choose, extracting reading material and covering areas of the market that best help them.

Trade Organizations

There are several large organizations within the industry composed of manufacturers, retailers, or members of the press that provide helpful fashion and trade information. The most specialized are the retail buyers' groups such as the **National Association of Men's Sportswear**

The Fashion Group, Inc.

A unique and exciting trade organization is The Fashion Group, Inc. It was formed in 1931 by 17 women; among them were fashion giants such as Dorothy Shaver, president of Lord & Taylor; Edna Woolman Chase, editor-in-chief of *Vogue;* Carmel Snow, editor-in-chief of *Harper's Bazaar;* Tobé of Tobé Associates; and Estelle Hamburger, vice president of Jay Thorpe.

The original purpose of The Fashion Group was to increase the opportunities for women at the executive levels of the fashion industry. But since its inception nearly a half century ago, The Fashion Group has expanded its goals. It now offers a wide range of services, some of which are available to those outside the organization.

The group's most famous activity is its exciting fashion presentations. Through lavish fashion shows and fabric displays, the group offers all in the fashion industry its expert analysis and evaluation of upcoming seasonal fashion trends. For its members, The Fashion Group offers career counseling workshops, fashion-career literature, and the automatic prestige that comes from membership in the organization.

To be accepted for membership in The Fashion Group, an applicant must have at least five years of executive-level experience in the fashion industry, plus the sponsorship and recommendation of Fashion Group members.

The original New York Group has multiplied many times over. The Fashion Group is now an international organization with 42 chapters, 31 in the United States, and over 6,000 members. They are located in Mexico City, Paris, Tokyo, and many other cities throughout the world. Its main chapter, however, continues to operate in New York City, the international headquarters of The Fashion Group, Inc.

Buyers (NAMSB), which is discussed in Chapter 11. Other associations have a much less specialized area of interest, dealing with problems in every area of retailing and providing information on all important areas of the industry. One example is the **National Retail Federation,** a dynamic organization to which most department and apparel specialty stores belong. Another specialized organization is **Fashion Press Week, Inc.,** which organizes press showings for high-priced womenswear firms. Probably the most prestigious trade organization for women in the fashion business is **The Fashion Group, Inc.** (see Fashion Feature describing the Fashion Group).

FASHION PROMOTION

Fashion promotion has two functions. One is to sell merchandise; the other is to project what is now commonly called a store's "image." In retailing, the word image refers to the mental impression the public has of a store's fashion expertise.

Advertising, publicity, and display can help to project a store's fashion image as tools of sales promotion. But these sales promotion activities cannot, by themselves, create that image. To develop a fashion image, a store must (1) decide on who it wants as customers; (2) offer fashion merchandise that will appeal to that group of customers; and (3) promote that merchandise with sales promotion techniques that will be most effective with that clientele.

When choosing the type of people it wants as customers, a store simply looks for that portion of the public that it feels it can service most profitably. The type of merchandise a store sells is determined by the tastes of those customers. For instance, if a store has customers who prefer expensive, high-fashion clothes, then its merchandising policies will be based on obtaining the best available selection of high-styled, quality clothes.

Once a store has established its clientele and merchandised its inventory accordingly, the store promotes and presents that merchandise in a manner that will most appeal to that clientele.

ADVERTISING

Buying space or time in the print or broadcast media such as newspapers, magazines, radio, and television is known as *advertising*. It is the most important means of communication between a retail store and its potential customers. Almost every major store that advertises has a director who heads an advertising staff of copywriters and artists. Together they produce or help produce the ads a store places in both the printed and broadcasting media.

The Printed Media

Newspapers
Retailers spend more money on advertising than on any other form of sales promotion. And the majority of their advertising budget goes toward buying newspaper space.

Men's clothiers were the first to use newspaper advertising as a sales promotion tool. During the early 1800s, they discovered that it was better to advertise in newspapers than to hire "hawkers" to stand outside their doors and announce or "hawk" their merchandise to the passing public.

Originally, the ads were composed solely of copy. Joseph Schaffner, a founder of the Hart Schaffner & Marx menswear firm, is credited with introducing illustrations into advertising, when, in the late 1890s, he began to use a "copy plus pictures" advertising technique. The ads immediately increased his business and were widely copied by retailers and manufacturers alike.

Hartmarx, as the firm is called today, also pioneered "nonadvertising" *institutional* advertising. An **institutional ad** does not sell merchandise. Instead, it publicizes or "sells" the store. Ads of this type may present a general fashion message, announce a community event, or even salute an unusually famous personality. Figure 15–1 is an example of this type of advertising done by Wallachs, a Hartmarx Corporation retail division.

Although most advertising costs come out of the retailers' pocket, a good portion of their ads is subsidized through "co-op" advertising. **Co-operative advertising** is the arrangement where manufacturers and retailers share the cost of featuring the manufacturer's merchandise in the store's ads (see Figure 15–2).

Retailers now consider newspaper advertising their greatest business builder. The Newspaper Advertising Bureau sponsored a research study that confirmed the value of this medium as a sales booster. The study indicated that consumers who were pulled into a store by an advertised item went on to buy additional merchandise elsewhere in the store. On the average, it was found that for each dollar people spent on an advertised item, another dollar was spent throughout the store.

Retailers generally advertise in local newspapers, choosing the one that most appeals to their customers. In New York, for instance, the stores that sell better high-fashion merchandise advertise in *The New York Times,* a newspaper that has an affluent, fashion-conscious readership.

Fashion Magazines

Godey's Lady's Book was the first fashion magazine in America to gain nationwide recognition. It was published between 1830 and 1879 and, as the only source of fashion information available to most women, was known as the "Victorian bible of the parlor." Along with illustrations of the latest fashions, the magazine presented poetry, fiction, recipes, and assorted bits of advice on fashion and social graces. Sara

MAN ON A HORSE

 *There was a tremendous change in the appearance of American advertising in the years just before and after the first World War. Instead of being non-descript in appearance, the best of it began to be "designed." Such men as Cooper, Dwiggins, Goudy, Penfield and Rogers raised the standards of commercial art with their new typefaces, hand-lettering, trademark designs and layouts.*

Edward Penfield was one of the best of them, an American disciple of Toulouse-Lautrec and the other great French poster designers. In 1911 he did several booklet covers for Hart Schaffner & Marx. And in 1914 he designed the famous HS & M trumpeter trademark which appeared for the first time in print on February 15, 1915.

So for over half a century now, this horseman-on-a-label has been a guarantee of superiority and satisfaction in clothes. It has always been "a small thing to look for, a big thing to find."

wallachs

You'll like our style as well as our clothes

Wallachs—Service, Quality and Dedication to the communities we serve. This copy excerpted from a Wallachs ad originally run on October 17, 1968.

A HARTMARX Company

Courtesy: Wallachs, Inc., New York

•••••••• **FIGURE 15-1 Wallachs' famous institutional ads are still being used for special promotions.**

Josepha Hale became famous as *Godey's* talented editor, but because of her influential editorials on the acceptance of women in the medical, teaching, and missionary professions, she is also remembered as one of the first exponents of women's rights.

Although the slick fashion magazines of today are much more sophisticated, *Godey's* was responsible for developing the format all present-day magazines follow: fashion plus interesting reading matter. *Vogue, Harper's Bazaar, Glamour, Mademoiselle,* and *Seventeen* are the "big five." Except for some fiction or a timely article, all devote their

The mark of the lion.

On lineen! Anne Klein's new essentials for spring. Linear, leather-trimmed shapes in a treated nylon fabric that retards grime and grit, as well as repels the rain. These, in smart spring-thru-summer colors of coffee, with coffee or camel leather trim; or bone with bone leather trim. By Anne Klein for Calderon. Find them in Handbag Collections, Fourth Floor—where we are all the things you are.

Our first class envelope is flapped, with an outside back zipper, an inside zippered compartment, and adjustable shoulder straps, $65.

As flat as all that...is the sleekest little clutch, with back entry, and wrist-strapped for carrying. $29.

A large, roomy, impeccably contoured hobo, with easy entry. And an outside back zipper, an inside zippered compartment, and adjustable shoulder straps, $65.

Going places? Get a grip...on our large, roomy double-handled satchel—top-zipped—with an outside pocket, back zippered compartment, and an inside zippered compartment, as well. $95.

Saks Fifth Avenue

We are all the things you are

Courtesy: Saks Fifth Avenue, New York

• • • • • • • • **FIGURE 15-2 This ad illustrates designer and store participation in co-op advertising.**

pages to the subject of fashion. Each, however, has its own fashion philosophy and image that are tailored to appeal to different segments of the population. *Vogue* and *Harper's Bazaar* cater to the woman who is interested in expensive high fashion. *Glamour* and *Mademoiselle* gear their fashion presentations to the sophisticated, well-educated college, career, or young married women. And *Seventeen* edits its magazine to please the tastes of the American teen-aged girl. Although there are some fashion editorials and a good deal of fashion advertisements in *Playboy*, *Esquire*, and *Details*, *Gentlemen's Quarterly (GQ)* is the only magazine exclusively devoted to fashion for men.

When magazines feature an item on their editorial pages, the magazine supplies its readers with the name of one or more stores throughout the country that will carry the featured item. This free bit of publicity for the store is known as an *editorial credit*.

In terms of sales, magazine advertising is not as important for a store as newspaper advertising. Most of a store's business comes from its local customers; retailers do not expect to get unusual sales results from a nationally or regionally distributed magazine ad. They do feel, however, that national exposure in one of the country's leading fashion magazines adds valuable prestige to their store and, for that reason, are willing to give part of their advertising dollar to magazines.

Direct Mail

Advertisements that retailers mail directly to the consumer are known as **direct mail.** Direct mail comes in many forms—from simple postcards, leaflets, and brochures to elaborate catalogs. When a piece of direct mail is inserted with the customer's monthly financial statement, it is known as a *statement enclosure*. These enclosures are provided to the retailer by the manufacturer. Eager to publicize their products, manufacturers swamp retailers with offerings of enclosures, but mailing costs prohibit stores from taking advantage of many of their offers.

Brochures, catalogs, and any other mailing pieces that feature items from more than one manufacturer are produced by the retailer. Manufacturers, however, are agreeable to contributing toward most or all of a store's production costs for the privilege of having their merchandise included in these mailing pieces.

The first mail-order catalogs were introduced during the 1800s by city retailers who wanted to service customers who were unable to travel to their stores. However, these retailers did not extend their offerings to people living in the rural areas. To reach that untapped market, in 1872, Aaron Montgomery Ward produced a one-page "catalog" that introduced the concept of selling exclusively by mail.

That concept was copied by others, including Sears, Roebuck and Company. As the country expanded to the west and demand for ready-made clothing grew, the mail-order business flourished. But in the 1920s, the introduction of the automobile improved rural transportation, and small independent stores began to spring up close to the rural areas. To meet this new competitive threat, Sears opened its first retail store in 1925, and other mail-order firms then followed suit.

The huge success of these direct-mail efforts has prompted stores to continue with those efforts. In addition to the traditional back-to-school and Christmas catalogs, stores are now sending their customers exquisitely prepared "magazine" type mailings called *folios* that feature each season's newest merchandise.

The Broadcasting Media

Radio

In order to appreciate fashion, it must be seen. Newspapers, magazines, and direct mail are appropriate for fashion advertising because each presents fashion visually. Radio cannot. And because it cannot, stores have used a limited amount of radio advertising to promote fashion.

Cosmetics such as shampoos, face creams, and so on—which need not be seen to be appreciated—are the only fashion products that are heavily promoted on radio, and then usually by their manufacturers. Retailers reserve their radio fashion advertising for the announcement of special fashion sales and promotions, which, like cosmetics, do not require a visual presentation.

Television

Television is, of course, a visual medium. But it was not automatically accepted by retailers for fashion advertising. To most, television represented an unfamiliar advertising medium whose ads took too much time and money to prepare. Until recently, stores still preferred to sell their fashion in print.

Bloomingdale's, and many other leading fashion stores have increased their fashion advertising on television. These retailers have preferred to launch short television campaigns for the purpose of upgrading their image or announcing an important sale. Unfortunately, most of these one- to three-week campaigns cannot be used to measure accurately the effectiveness of television advertising. However, it is reasonable to assume that retailers will continue to expand their use of the television medium to reach their "target" customers if their advertising budgets allow.

PUBLICITY

When a person, product, or firm receives free and voluntary mention in any media, that mention is known as **publicity.** In order to obtain publicity, retailers must provide the media with information that will be considered "news." In most cases, the "news" pertains to special events that are taking place in a store. These may include the opening of a new branch store, the visit of an important designer or fashion editor, the opening of a new fashion department within the store, or any other "happening" that might be of interest to the local reading and listening public.

Large stores employ a staff publicity director who has contact with the local media. It is his or her function to publicize a store's name and—in the case of a fashion store—the store's fashion leadership. Publicists use several methods to pass "news" along to the printed and broadcasting media. The most popular method is to use press releases. A *press release* is a written description of a product, personality, or event. Press releases are written by a store's publicity department, but they are also made available to a store by manufacturers who wish to publicize their merchandise. Often, manufacturers will include accompanying photographs with their press releases. Many local newspaper fashion editors rely on these press releases and photographs to provide them with most of the news they print on their fashion pages, and give editorial credit.

Although a store does not pay the media for publicity, publicity is not cheap. It is expensive to maintain an expert publicity department to produce the fashion events that bring a store publicity. But leading retailers justify their publicity expenditures by insisting that these efforts invariably improve their businesses.

A major exponent of this theory is Stanley Marcus, son of the founder of Neiman Marcus in Dallas, Texas. One of the great modern pioneers of sales promotion in retailing, Marcus displayed his flair for sales promotion early in his career when he created two retailing classics: the luncheon fashion show in 1926 and the bridal fashion show in the 1930s. The success of these ventures prompted Marcus to introduce many other fashion promotions. One of the most successful has been the famous *Fortnight in Dallas,* which, in its two-week celebration, annually honors a foreign nation. Publicity from this event has enhanced the store's national and international reputation. But, according to Marcus, "the fundamental purpose of the *Fortnight* was to help us overcome a historical business lag of mid-October."[1] The event turned October into a peak traffic month, even surpassing Christmas, and netted the largest sales increases for that month in the store's history. Publicity, Marcus has proven, does pay.

· ·

VISUAL MERCHANDISING

The presentation of merchandise in a store is known as **visual merchandising.** Until recently, the activity was simply called *display.* But as window and interior store presentations become extremely effective in *selling* merchandise and fashion ideas to the public, the industry felt

[1]Stanley Marcus, *Minding the Store* (Boston: Little, Brown, 1974), p. 210.

that "visual merchandising" was a much more accurate description of this activity.

Merchants did not always consider presentation of their merchandise to be important. In fact, until the 1890s, stores were bare and unattractive, not at all like the stores of today. Merchandise was never "displayed"; stock was simply piled high on tables. At the turn of the century, retailers entered into their "plate glass period," replacing the large old barnlike stores with places that were faced with huge plate glass windows. Store interiors displayed new stock cabinets, while women's tea rooms, men's barber shops, shoe-polishing facilities, and restrooms were added as conveniences.

The first mannequins were primitive dolls when compared with today's lifelike creations. They were made of wax, extremely delicate, and posed a special problem in hot weather. As the temperature rose, window trimmers had to periodically pour cold water into the heads and hands of the mannequins to prevent them from melting. Over the years, the quality of display materials rapidly improved; and by the 1930s, store display—fashion and otherwise—had become firmly established as a creative art.

CREATING A TOTAL FASHION IMAGE

Since the fashion image of a store is determined by the type of merchandise it sells and the characteristics of its sales promotion activities, stores that sell little or poorly styled fashion apparel and employ unimaginative sales promotion techniques automatically project a "poor" fashion image. As the American consumer becomes increasingly fashion oriented, retailers are consciously trying to maintain or upgrade their image. Changing an image, however, is a huge and difficult task, and successful transformations are few and far between. Bloomingdale's is one of the few and probably the most impressive example of how a store can systematically change and improve that very important ingredient known as a store's fashion image (see the Industry Feature entitled "From Bloomingdale's to 'Bloomie's'").

TERMS TO REMEMBER

resident buyer   resident buying office   fashion consultant   trade
publication   Fashion Calendar   National Association of Men's Sportswear
Buyers (NAMSB)   Fashion Press Weeks, Inc.   The Fashion Group
institutional ad   editorial credit   direct mail   publicity   press release
visual merchandising   institutional ad   co-op advertising   fashion image

From Bloomingdale's to "Bloomie's"

As stated in its advertising copy, "Bloomingdale's—no other store like it in the world"—is one of the country's most exciting fashion trendsetters. It draws people from all over the world, and it is not unusual to see international film, television, and political celebrities mingling with the public as each looks at and buys one of the thousands of exciting items alluringly displayed throughout the store.

Although it has been in business over 100 years, Bloomingdale's did not always enjoy its current reputation as an international fashion pacesetter.

The original store is located at Fifty-ninth Street and Lexington Avenue in what is now an affluent area of high-rise apartments and office buildings. At the end of World War II, however, it was surrounded by tenements and small shops, and a lot of its business was in low-end, low-priced merchandise.

When the post-war building boom began to upgrade other parts of the city, Bloomingdale's realized that, in time, its neighborhood would also be upgraded to a district of affluent residents and high-income career people. To attract these two groups, the store began to alter its image, introducing three ingredients into its merchandising policies: quality, fashion, excitement.

The change involved every aspect of the store—merchandise, advertising, publicity, display, and service. The transformation took place in stages, department by department. As the quality of the merchandise in one department was improved, attention was directed to the next. Once a department's merchandise was upgraded, it was imaginatively displayed and advertised to the public. Displays became "showcases." Ads stressed fashion. Even the store logo was changed. The "new" Bloomingdale's was aggressively and expertly promoted to the public.

Although the changes began as early as the late 1940s, it was not until the 1960s that Bloomingdale's new image wholly crystalized. The revolutionary fashion of that period provided the store with just the type of material it needed. Fashion was young and avant garde; lifestyles were unrestricted. Immediately, Bloomingdale's aligned itself with these trends, and soon every department in the store—from designer dresses to stationery—was successfully catering to its upper-income target market with the newest, trendy merchandise. By the 1970s, the store had become "Bloomie's"—the "in place" to shop.

Today, Bloomingdale's reputation as a fashion leader is firmly established. It draws customers from the city's outlying suburban areas as well as from its own posh neighborhood. The store's fame as a trendsetter also attracts Seventh Avenue manufacturers and the country's retailing executives who "shop" the store religiously for trends that are usually six months ahead of the rest of the country.

The store itself has become a sort of "social gathering place." An after-hours charity fashion show or an afternoon wine-tasting party promoting a $45 book on *The Joys of Wine* are daily rather than rare occurrences. Many of these activities take place on Saturdays, and "Bloomie's" has become a Saturday social meeting place for the young and affluent New Yorker, a place to meet old acquaintances or develop new ones.

Although Bloomingdale's has won fame because of its fashion leadership, the store's success in changing and upgrading its image to cater to a changing clientele has also made retailing history. Its methods are now known as the Bloomingdale's formula: Identify your customer and then woo that customer by presenting distinctive merchandise in imaginative displays, with a great deal of showmanship.

······· HIGHLIGHTS OF THE CHAPTER

- There are many people, organizations and publications that help the retailer in the buying and selling of goods. The most valuable assistance comes from resident buying offices, which serve as advisors and buying representatives for stores.

- A fashion consultant is a person or independent firm retained by retailers who want supplementary expert help in merchandising the fashion areas of their businesses.

- The fabric and merchandise editors of consumer fashion magazines help retailers formulate their merchandising plans by presenting their viewpoint on fashion and market trends. Similar information is available to retailers in the pages of *Women's Wear Daily, Daily News Record*, and other trade publications.

- The advertising, display, publicity, and other techniques used by retailers to induce sales is called *promotion*. All medium to large stores employ promotion activities to sell fashion merchandise, but these activities vary depending on the promotion policies of a store.

- Buying space or time in newspapers, magazines, radio, and television is known as *advertising*. Fashion retailers use all media for advertising, but retailers consider newspapers their greatest business builders.

- Free and voluntary mention in the media is known as *publicity*. To obtain publicity, retailers maintain expert publicity departments, which supply the media with interesting information or "news" about their stores.

- Visual merchandising is also known as *display* and refers to the presentation of merchandise in a store.

- The fashion image of a store refers to the impression the public has of a store's fashion expertise. Most present-day retailers spend an enormous amount of time and money to maintain a favorable fashion image for their store.

.... REVIEW QUESTIONS

1. Describe the organization and basic function of a resident buying office.

2. Name the four types of buying offices and describe the differences in terms of ownership of each.

3. What is the main function of a fashion office in a resident buying office?

4. In addition to providing buying and fashion advisory services, buying offices provide stores with other services. What are they?

5. What methods do fashion consultants, fashion magazines, trade publications, and trade organizations use to provide fashion information to retailers?

6. What is The Fashion Group, Inc.? What services does it provide?

7. What kinds of services are provided to the trade by consumer fashion publications?

8. How and when did newspaper fashion advertising originate in this country? Define institutional ad.

9. How do stores pay their direct-mail production costs? Obtain several pieces of direct mail sent to your home and discuss the sales-provoking qualities of each.

10. Is the fashion advertising that retailers are presenting on television effective? Explain.

11. How do local retailers transmit information or "news" of their store to the media for the purposes of publicity?

12. Visit several large stores in your area and "shop" their windows and interiors, looking for the fashion themes each store is trying to project through its displays. Rate the efforts of the stores, and explain your ratings.

13. Rate the fashion image of one of your local stores. How do you think that image could be improved?

.... RESEARCH AND PROJECTS

1. A resident buying office does not replace the buyer, rather it assists the buyer with doing his or her job. Explain how this is accomplished.

2. Specifically, how does a fashion office in a resident buying office function? What services does it provide to the buyer?

3. Contact your local chapter of The Fashion Group, Inc. and request specific information about the chapter and exactly how it serves the fashion industry in your area.

4. Visit a small fashion specialty store. Interview the owner or buyer to see if he or she uses the services of a resident buying office. If so, ask about the kinds of services received, the type of office used, how the services are paid for. If they do not use a resident buying office, find out why, if possible.

5. Advertising means buying time or space in a medium. Which media forms are the most important? Which are the most and least expensive?

6. By using current fashion magazines, find two examples of each of the following types of advertising: institutional ads; co-op ads between retailers and manufacturers; co-op ads featuring a primary market source, a manufacturer and a retailer; and a regular retail ad.

7. Select a particular department in a department store, and evaluate it in terms of visual merchandising effectiveness. Next visit the same department in a chain store and in a discount operation. Describe the similarities and differences, and decide which store was better at merchandise presentation. Give your reasons why.

Accent, Various Articles. Newton, MA: Larkin-Pluznick-Larkin Inc.

Arnold, Pauline, and White, Percival. *Clothes and Cloth: America's Apparel Business.* New York: Holiday, 1961.

Anspach, Karlene. *The Why of Fashion.* Ames, IA: Iowa State University Press, 1967.

Beaton, Cecil. *The Glass of Fashion.* New York: Doubleday, 1954.

Beckman, R. "Clothes Make the Person," *Psychology Today* (April 1974).

Bell, Quenton. *On Human Finery.* New York: Schocken Books, 1976.

Bender, Marylyn. *The Beautiful People.* New York: Coward-McCann & Geoghegan, 1967.

Bennett-England, Rodney. *Dress Optional.* London: Dufour, 1968.

Boyer, G. Bruce. *Eminently Suitable.* New York: W. W. Norton, 1990.

Bradley, Martha Sontag. *ZCMI: America's First Department Store.* Salt Lake City, UT: ZCMI, 1991.

Calasibetta, Charlotte. *Essential Terms of Fashion.* New York: Fairchild Publications, 1986.

Calasibetta, Charlotte. *Fairchild's Dictionary of Fashion.* New York: Fairchild Publications, 1975.

Charles-Roux, Edmonde. *Chanel, Her Life—Her World—and the Woman Behind the Legend She Herself Created.* New York: Knopf, 1975.

Cobrin, A. Harry. *The Men's Clothing Industry—Colonial Through Modern Times.* New York: Fairchild Publications, 1970.

Corbman, B. *Textiles: Fiber to Fabric.* New York: McGraw-Hill, 1982.

Daily News Record, Various Articles. New York: Fairchild Publications.

Dior, Christian. *Christian Dior and I,* trans. Antonia Fraser. New York: Dutton, 1957.

Dorner, Jane. *Fashion.* London: Octopus Books, 1974.

Evans, Helen M. *Man the Designer.* New York: Macmillan, 1973.

Fairchild Fact Files, Various Articles. New York: Fairchild Publications, Market Research Division.

Fairchild's Textile and Apparel Financial Directory. New York: Fairchild Publications, Annual.

Fashion, Art and Beauty (Bulletin). New York: Metropolitan Museum of Art. Vol. XXVI, No. 3 (November 1967).

Flugel, J. C. *The Psychology of Clothes.* London: Hogarth Press, 1930.

Flusser, Alan. *Clothes and the Man.* New York: Willard Books, 1985.

Footwear Plus, Various Articles. New York.

Frings, Gini Stephens. *Fashion from Concept to Consumer.* Englewood Cliffs, NJ: Prentice Hall, 1991.

Garland, Marge. *Fashion.* Baltimore MD: Penguin, 1962.

Hall, Max, ed. *Made in New York.* Cambridge, MA: Harvard University Press, 1959.

Hamburger, Estelle. *The Fashion Business—It's All Yours.* San Francisco: Canfield Press, 1976.

Hawes, Elizabeth. *Fashion Is Spinach.* New York: Random House, 1938.

History of the Menswear Industry 1890–1950, Men's Wear 60th Anniversary Issue. New York: Fairchild Publications, 1950.

Hyde, Jack. *Esquire's Encyclopedia of 20th Century Men's Fashion.* New York: Abrams Publications, 1990.

Johnson, Laurence A. *Over the Counter and on the Shelf: Country Storekeeping in America, 1620–1920.* New York: Bonanza Books, 1961.

Joseph, Marjory L. *Essentials of Textiles.* New York: Holt, Rinehart, and Winston, 1984.

Kaplan, David G. *World of Furs.* New York: Fairchild Publications, 1974.

Kelly, Katie. *The Wonderful World of Women's Wear Daily.* New York: Saturday Review Press, 1972.

Kids' Fashions, Various Articles. Newton, MA: The Larkin Group.

Kidwell, Claudia B., and Christman, Margaret C. *Suiting Everyone: The Democratization of Clothing in America.* Washington, DC: Smithsonian Institution Press, 1974.

Lambert, Eleanor. *World of Fashion.* New York and London: R. R. Bowker, 1976.

Latzke, Alpha, and Hostetter, Helen P. *The Wide World of Clothing.* New York: Ronald Press, 1968.

Laver, James. *Costume*. New York: Hawthorn, 1963.

Laver, James. *Modesty in Dress*. Boston: Houghton Mifflin, 1969.

Levin, Phyllis. *Wheels of Fashion*. New York: Doubleday, 1965.

Levine, Louis. *The Women's Garment Workers*. New York: B.W. Heubsch, 1924.

Lynam, Ruth, ed. *Couture*. New York: Doubleday, 1972.

Mahoney, Tom, and Sloan, Leonard. *The Great Merchants*. New York: Harper & Row, 1966.

Marcus, Stanley. *Minding the Store*. Boston: Little, Brown, 1976.

Martin, Richard, and Koda, Harold. *Men's Styles in the Twentieth Century*. New York: Rizzoli International Publishers Inc., 1989.

McCardell, Claire. *What Shall I Wear?* New York: Simon & Schuster, 1956.

McJimsey, Harriet T. *Art and Fashion in Clothing Selection*. Ames, IA: Iowa State University Press, 1973.

Morgenstein, Melvin, and Strongin, Harriet. *Modern Retailing: Management Principles and Practices*. Englewood Cliffs, NJ: Regents/Prentice Hall, 1992.

Murray, Maggie Pexton. *Changing Styles in Fashion: Who, What, Why*. New York: Fairchild Books, 1990.

Nystrom, Paul H. *Economics of Fashion*. New York: Ronald Press, 1928.

Ocko, Judy Young, and Rosenbaum, M. L. *Advertising Handbook for Retail Merchants*. New York: NRMA, 1976.

Packard, Sidney. *The Fashion Business Dynamics and Careers*. New York: Holt, Rinehart, and Winston, 1983.

Peglar, Martin, M. *Visual Merchandising and Display*. New York: Fairchild Publications, 1983.

Pintel, Gerald, and Diamond, Jay, *Retailing*. Englewood Cliffs, NJ: Prentice Hall, 1983.

Pizzuto, Joseph J., Price, Arthur and Cohen, Allen C. *Fabric Science*. New York: Fairchild Publications, 1984.

Roach, Mary Ellen, and Eicher, Joanne B. *The Visible Self: Perspective on Dress*. Englewood Cliffs, NJ: Prentice Hall, 1973.

Robinson, Dwight. "Style Changes: Cyclical, Inexorable and Foreseeable." *Harvard Business Review* (November-December 1975).

Rogers, Dorothy, S. and Gamans, Linda R. *Fashion: A Marketing Approach*. New York: Holt, Rinehart, and Winston, 1983.

Roshco, Bernard. *The Rag Race*. New York: Funk & Wagnalls, 1963.

Rudofsky, Bernard. *The Unfashionable Human Body*. New York: Doubleday, 1971.

Ryan, Mary. *Clothing: A Study in Human Behavior*. New York: Holt, Rinehart & Winston, 1966.

Standard and Poor's Industrial Surveys. Retailing Basic Analysis, Various Articles. New York.

Stevens, Mark. *The Inside Story of Bloomingdale's*. New York: Ballantine, 1979.

Tolman, Ruth. *Selling Men's Fashion*. New York: Fairchild Publications, 1982.

Tortora, Phyllis. *Understanding Textiles*. New York: Macmillan, 1982.

U.S. Congress, Office of Technology Assessment. *The U.S. Textile and Apparel Industry: A Revolution in Progress—Special Report*, OTA-TET-332. Washington, DC: USGPO, 1987.

U.S. Department of Commerce. *U.S. Industrial Outlook*. Washington, DC: 1992.

U.S. Department of Commerce, Bureau of the Census. *1987, 1992 Census of Manufactures*. Washington, DC: USGPO.

Veblen, Thorstein. *The Theory of the Leisure Class*, Mentor ed. New York: New American Library of World Literature, 1963.

Vecchio, Walter, and Riley, Robert. *The Fashion Makers—A Photographic Record*. New York: Crown Publishers, 1968.

White, Palmer. *Poiret*. New York: Clarkson N. Potter, Inc., 1973.

Wilcox, Ruth, and Wilcox, Roy. *Dictionary of Costume*. New York: Scribner's, 1969.

Wilson, Kay. *A History of Textiles*. Boulder, CO: Westview Press, 1979.

Wingate, Isabel B. *Fairchild's Dictionary of Textiles*. New York: Fairchild Publications, 1979.

Winters, Arthur A. and Goodman, Stanley. *Fashion Advertising and Promotion*. New York: Fairchild Publications, 1984.

Women's Wear Daily, Various Articles. New York: Fairchild Publications.

Young, Agnes. *Recurring Cycles of Fashion*. New York: Cooper Square Publishers, 1966.

ACTWUA—The Amalgamated Clothing Workers and Textile Union (commonly known as the Amalgamated) is the major union representing workers in the boys' and men's wear industries.

Adoption Process—This refers to the flow of fashion from one class or group to another.

Adornment Theory—A theory that contends that clothing originated as a result of the human desire to enhance one's self-concept and sexual image among peers and the opposite sex.

Advertising—The paid-for mention in any medium of a person, product, or firm.

Alta Costura—Represents the designers who produce couture apparel in Spain. The organization is responsible for the shows, which are held in Madrid.

Arkwright Cotton Spinning Machine—This was the first successful English spinning machine which was copied from memory by Samuel Slater in Rhode Island.

Art Deco—A style of art popular in the early 1900s, mostly in architecture, but also in clothing by Paul Poiret, and in furniture. Early *Vogue* covers by Erté exemplified this art movement.

Bias Cut—Fabric cut on the diagonal rather than along the straight warp or woof.

Bottom-Up Fashion—Fashion that originates with the masses and then moves to the upper classes.

Boutique—A small shop selling unusual and eclectic merchandise. Also refers to an innovative method of merchandising and displaying merchandise within a large retail organization.

Branch Store—A retail outlet under the direction of a main store. Often carries a modified line of merchandise.

CAD/CAM—Computer-aided design and computer-aided manufacture are techniques employed to further automate industry and produce better designed and manufactured products.

Cámara de la Moda Española—An organization, headquartered in Madrid, of women's and children's ready-to-wear producers which assists its members in marketing their goods and organizes trade shows.

Caribbean Basin Initiative (Section 807)—Tariffs are applied only to the value added to merchandise during the manufacturing process in the countries of the Caribbean.

Caution—French term for an advance fee that is sometimes required of those attending a couture showing.

Chain Store—Eleven or more stores that are centrally owned and operated that have similar physical appearance and the same merchandise.

Chambre Syndicale de la Couture Parisienne—An organization that represents the French *haute couture*.

Channel of Distribution—The route that a product follows from the raw material stage until it reaches the ultimate consumer or industrial user.

Chemise—This style of dress has no waistline and hangs straight. It recurs frequently in American fashion.

Classic—Style or design that remains in fashion year after year.

Collection—The output of a designer or manufacturer for a particular season.

Color—A phenomenon of light that, in a visual sense, distinguishes one object from another.

Combined-Need Theory—This theory contends that the origin of clothing was multidimensional, filling several human needs at the same time.

Consignment—An arrangement between a manufacturer or individual and a retailer where title does not pass to the retailer. Rather, the retailer acts as an agent in the sale of the apparel.

Conspicuous Consumption—The purchase of apparel and other objects in order to improve one's status in the eyes of others.

Contractor—This is a kind of apparel manufacturer who is paid by the primary manufacturer for specific work done on a garment, such as sewing.

Converter—A firm that changes unfinished or greige goods into finished fabric.

Cooperative Advertising—Where more than one entity in the channel of distribution shares in the cost of an advertisement for consumer goods.

Coty American Fashion Critics' Award—These awards were given to American designers for excellence in women's wear and men's wear fashion design.

Council of American Fashion Designer Awards—These annual awards are presented to the best American designers for their achievements during the year.

Couturier (male) or Couturière (female)—French words for *dressmaker*; in the fashion business they are used to identify designers who make and sell the finest high-fashion, custom made apparel. Sometimes called *haute couturier* or *haute couturière*.

Daily News Record—The fashion industry's major men's wear and textile trade publication.

Dandy—Upper-class Englishman whose main occupation was dressing to perfection. The leader was Beau Brummel, who was a powerful influence on English society from 1796 to 1816.

Demography—Statistics describing the characteristics of people such as age, income, marital status, educational level, etc. This information is used by marketers to define and reach a target market.

Department Store—A large retail institution that carries apparel for the family, hard goods, and domestics, and is organized on a departmental basis, with similar goods offered in each department.

Derived Demand—A need for primary products, such as raw materials, that originates with the ultimate consumer demand for the final manufactured product.

Design—A unique version of a style. Design consists of the elements of silhouette, texture, color, detail, and trim.

Detail—Various components or parts of a garment. Examples include collars, cuffs, and sleeve types.

Discount Store—A retailer that sells its merchandise at a lower markup and makes its profit by means of high volume, limited service, and simple store decor.

Display—See Visual Merchandising.

Domestics—Household linens sold in retail stores.

Dry Goods Stores—Stores that carried wearing apparel and accessories for women as well as sewing supplies. Forerunner of today's department store.

Dual Distribution—This is the term applied to goods sold at both the wholesale and retail level by a manufacturer.

Editorial Credit—Getting free mention as the retailer or manufacturer of an item that is featured editorially in a newspaper.

Empire Look—A low-cut, small puffed sleeved, high-waisted sheer white dress worn by women during the rule of Napoleon in France. It was worn over a flesh covered maillot and was reminiscent of the clothing worn by women in classical Greece.

European Union—An organization of 14 European nations that provides for free trade and economic unity among its members. Often referred to as the Common Market, the European Economic Community, or the European Community. Many new nations have applied for membership and the EU expects substantial growth in the near future.

Fabric Libraries—Places where swatches of historic textile prints and woven goods are maintained for manufacturers and designers to refer to in the creation of up-coming fashions. The term may also be used by manufacturers and retailers for their location where current or up-coming fabrics used in apparel are displayed.

Factoring—A process used by manufacturers to improve their cash flow by selling title to their invoices for a discount of their value. The factor now has full responsibility for the collection of money owed by the retailer.

Factory Outlet—Retail operation where manufacturers offer their merchandise at a low price to consumers. May be a free standing store such as the Coach Outlet in Amagansett, in New York, or may be a unit in a mall which specializes in this kind of operation.

Fad—Styles or items that gain and lose their popularity within a short period of time.

Fashion—The acceptance and purchase by consumers of artistically designed apparel and accessories that are mass produced and marketed by the fashion industry in a timely manner in order to satisfy consumer wants and needs. May also refer to nonapparel industries.

Fashion Consultant—A person or firm who is retained by other firms in the fashion industry to help merchandise and promote fashion items.

Fashion Director (or Fashion Coordinator)—One who researches, analyzes, defines, and presents current and future fashion trends. May also assist in the merchandising of apparel and accessories from different departments as well as work in public relations for a retailer.

Fashion Elite—The creators, reporters, and wearers of high fashion.

Fashion Forecasting—The ability to recognize or predict current and future fashion trends.

Fashion Life Cycle—A graphic presentation of the four stages of the acceptance and decline of a fashion.

Fashion Marketing—Directing the flow of fashion goods from producer to consumer in order to profitably satisfy consumer wants and needs.

Fashion Season—A term used by manufacturers and retailers to designate a particular selling period during the year.

Fiber—A natural or synthetic hairlike filament from which yarn is made.

Finishing—A process that dyes, bleaches, prints, or otherwise treats unfinished or greige goods to convert them into useable fabrics.

Flea Market—Usually outdoor place with booths where vendors offer merchandise to consumers at low prices. Vendors may be independent, offering their own attic merchandise or goods they have purchased from a wholesaler or retailer, or may be manufacturers offering overstocks and returns at a low price.

Focus Group—A small representation of a target market that is invited to a manufacturer to react to new products.

Fords—Styles that catch on immediately with the public and sell in great quantities.

Franchise—A store in which a parent company (franchisor) provides its name and merchandise, as well as management and marketing expertise in return for an initial payment from the merchant (franchisee) and a share of the profits. This term is also used interchangeably with licensing agreement, a contract between a manufacturer and designer or owner of the rights of a cartoon figure. In this case, the manufacturer is permitted to produce merchandise bearing the likeness of the cartoon or label of the designer in exchange for a royalty.

Garment Center—This is the wholesale fashion district located in midtown New York City.

General Agreement on Tariffs and Trade (GATT)—A world trade body which adjudicates trade disputes in the best interest of world relations. An historic agreement reached on December 16, 1993, provides for the phasing out of some tariffs and the elimination of some others by 117 nations.

Greige Goods—Fabric that has not been dyed, bleached, printed, or otherwise treated. Also known as unfinished fabric.

Hard Goods—Nonapparel merchandise such as appliances, furniture, and luggage.

Haute Couture—The finest, custom-made, high-fashion clothing.

High Fashion—New, expensive fashions marketed to a small elite group of consumers.

Hobble Skirts—A style of clothing designed by Paul Poiret which was narrow at the bottom and prevented women from walking comfortably.

Homecloth Period—These were the years just prior to the American Revolution when the colonists learned to spin, weave, and sew in order to produce their attire.

Hot Number or Hot Item—A style that has caught on and is being reordered by retailers.

ILGWU—The International Ladies' Garment Workers' Union is the major organization representing workers in the women's and children's wear industries.

Inside Shop—This refers to a manufacturer that performs all the steps involved in designing, producing, and selling apparel.

Institutional Ad—An advertisement that "sells" a firm's name by presenting a general message instead of merchandise.

Jobber—This is a manufacturer who farms out some of the manufacturing operations. Term is also used for a kind of wholesaler.

Knockoff—A copy of a garment that is expected to be a hot item.

Leased Department—A store department that is operated by an outside independent firm.

License—This contract between a designer and manufacturer pays the designer a royalty or fee for the use of the designer's name on a product. (See Franchise)

Maillot—French term for a suit which wraps the torso. Used in the United States to describe a one piece bathing suit with straps and no skirt.

Mannequin—The woman who wears the creations of designers of high-quality, custom-made clothing during fashion shows in Paris. In the United States the term refers to the artificial figure used to display merchandise.

Marker—A large piece of paper on which pattern pieces are arranged in order to enable the cutter to cut the fabric properly and cost effectively. Today, markers are computer generated. The term also is used to denote the person who prepares the marker.

Market Weeks—Periods of times when manufacturers show and sell their lines.

Marketing Oriented—Refers to a firm that plans most or all of its entire operation around the idea of satisfying consumer wants and needs.

Mass Fashions—Adapted from high fashions marketed to the middle class at lower prices than high fashions.

Mass Merchandiser—A large volume retailer that sells a wide variety of goods.

Media—Methods of communication such as newspaper, magazines, radio, and television.

Minimum—French term used to indicate the smallest purchase required of a customer who wishes to attend a couture showing.

Model—In France, the term for the design item. In the United States, the person who wears and displays the apparel.

Modesty Theory—A theory that contends that clothing originated as a result of human shame over the naked body.

Multifiber Textile Agreements (MFA)—Bilateral pacts between the United States and foreign countries which control the amount of textile goods and clothing that may be imported into the U.S. Many of these pacts are now superseded by the new GATT agreements.

New Look—A design introduced by Christian Dior in 1947 with a cinched waist, a wide and long skirt, and absence of shoulder pads.

North American Free Trade Agreement (NAFTA)—A pact among the United States, Canada, and Mexico which provides for open borders and economic cooperation. The pact is expected to phase out tariffs over a period of time to protect the industries of the United States. NAFTA is similar to the agreements of the European Union.

Off-Price Store—A retailer that buys for less from manufacturers by purchasing overstocks and past season merchandise. The decor of the store is sparse and simple.

Outside Shop—A term used to identify a firm that does sewing and pressing for a manufacturer on a contract basis. Since the work is done outside the manufacturer's premises, the contractor's firm is called an outside shop.

Paste—Imitation jewelry.

Piece Rate—The amount paid to a worker for each item of completed work.

Planned Obsolescence—The deliberate outmoding of merchandise by the subsequent introduction of newer products.

Prêt-à-Porter—The French word for ready-to-wear.

Primary Data—Information that is collected from scratch and not previously available to a researcher from any other source.

Primary Market—Those markets which provide the fashion industry with raw materials for fashion goods. They are the textile, leather, and fur producers.

Private Label Merchandise—Merchandise which is designed and produced by a retailer for distribution within its own organization. Frequently an outside agent is utilized for the production of the merchandise, but the full responsibility for it rests with the retailer.

Protection Theory—A theory that contends that the basis for the origin of clothing is the human need for shelter and the care and comfort of the body.

Psychographics—Statistical data on one's attitudes, values, and beliefs. May be used to target a particular market.

Publicity—The free and voluntary mention of a person, product, or firm.

Purchasing Power—The amount of money a consumer can spend. Consists of three factors: personal income, accumulated net worth, and available consumer credit.

Quick Response—A computerized system which enables the retailer and manufacturer or wholesale supplier to communicate instant need for a product by means of point of sale electronic devices. Relieves the retailer of warehousing unneeded merchandise.

Resident Buying Office—An organization that serves as an advisor and buying representative for one or many noncompetitive retail firms.

Runners—Items that are heavily reordered.

Sartorial Rule—Synonymous with sumptuary law.

Savile Row—Street in London whose tailors have provided high quality custom-made clothing for men for more than two hundred years.

Scandinavian Clothing Council—Trade organization of the Scandinavian countries. Oversees the trade shows, which are held in Copenhagen, for the apparel and accessories industries.

Secondary Data—Readily available information that has been gathered and published by others.

Seventh Avenue—Main thoroughfare of New York City's Garment Center. Also called Fashion Avenue.

Silhouette—The general outline or shape of a costume. In fashion there are three silhouettes: the bell; the tube; and the bustle.

Slop Shop—Because of the poor quality of the clothing, this was the name applied to the stores selling the earliest ready-made attire for sailors.

Soft Goods—Merchandise that is classified as wearing apparel.

Specialization (or Piece Work)—A worker produces only one part of a garment such as a sleeve or collar.

Specialty Store—Carries a single or limited line of goods.

Style—A basic characteristic of clothing such as a shirtwaist dress. Also refers to a characteristic inherent in a person, place or thing such as Early American furniture.

Style Piracy—Copying another's design.

Stylist—In France, used to identify ready-to-wear designers. In the United States, a person who adapts current fashions into new ones.

Sumptuary Law—Law that prohibits lavish dress by regulating personal expenditures on extravagant and luxurious items.

Sweatshops—Factories with unsanitary working conditions, long hours, and low pay, were given this appellation in the early 1900s.

Target Market—A market segment consisting of potential users of a product or service.

Task System—A team of workers (a baster, operator, finisher, and presser) who cooperate to produce each garment.

Texture—The feel of fabric and the appearance of its structural quality.

The Fashion Group—Professional organization of the fashion industry's top women executives.

Toile—French term for muslin replica of a design. Also sheer linen cloth.

Trade Association—Organization of members of a particular industry which keeps its participants informed about changes, new techniques, and other relevant industrial matters by means of conventions, workshops, and journals. Some organize trade shows for their members.

Trade Show—Place where many manufacturers and retail store buyers meet to order merchandise for an upcoming season.

Trading Post—Place where early American settlers and trappers exchanged furs for supplies. Earliest form of American retailing.

Trend—The direction fashion is taking. Trends are either incoming or outgoing.

Trickle-Down Fashions—Fashion that originates with the upper class of a society and then moves to the classes below.

Trim—Decorative additions to a garment that are not part of its general construction. Examples include buttons, belts, and lace.

Vertically Integrated Company—A company that handles more than one aspect of the channel of distribution. For example, a company that manufactures hosiery, then retails it through consumer catalogs, or Coach Handbags with its specialty store operation.

Visual Merchandising—The attractive presentation of merchandise in a store. Also referred to as display.

Warp—Yarns that are placed on the loom before weaving.

Women's Wear Daily—The fashion industry's major women's, children's, and accessory trade publication.

Woof—Yarns that interlace the warp in order to form a textile. Also called filling.

.... INDEX

Abraham & Strauss (A & S), 345
ABS USA, 135
Accessories stores, 323
Acrylic, 307
Activewear, 316–317
Adolfo, 196, 321
Adoption process, 46–48
Adornment theory, 38
Adrian, 177–179, 181
Adrien Arpel, 298
Advertising
  broadcast media, 382
  cooperative, 244, 280, 284, 304, 306, 308, 378
  direct mail, 381
  fashion magazines, 378–381
  institutional, 378
  newspapers, 377–378
Alexander's, 339
A. LeVian and Co., 310
Alfaro, Victor, 193
Allard, Linda, 195
Almay, 296
Alta Costura, 124
Amalgamated Clothing Workers Union of America (ACWUA), 166–167, 253, 273
American look, 193
Ann Taylor, 343, 353
Anne Klein II jewelry, 311
Arena, 317
Arkwright cotton spinning machine, 150
Armani, Giorgio, 117, 129, 190, 249, 261, 345
  fragrance, 293
Art Deco, 86
Average markup, 339
Avia, 301
Avon, 293, 299

Baby boomers, 184, 316
Baby Gap, 280, 268, 340
Back-to-school line, 273
Balenciaga, Cristobal, 92–93, 95
Bally Shoe Company, 125
Balmain, Pierre, 94, 192
Bamberger's, 333
Bandolino, 301
Barneys New York, 340, 350–352
Basile, 249, 261
Bathing suits, 181
Bean, L. L., 283
Beauty supply store, 297, 299
Beene, Geoffrey, 191, 196
Beged-Or, 126
Bella Centret, 124
Bellwether, 317
Belts, 318, 322
Benneton, 353
Bergdorf Goodman, 299, 306, 340, 349
Bertin, Rose, 74–76

Bias-cut tent dress, 181
Bijorhca, 314
Bikini, 94
Biobottoms, 283
Biotherm, 293
Blanche sleepwear, 305
Blass, Bill, 128, 185, 191, 192, 196, 249, 260, 308
Blocking, 307
Bloomer, Amelia Jenkins, 179
Bloomingdale's, 333, 337, 344, 346, 385–386
Blue jeans, 155
Boarding house system, 151
Body Glove, 317
Body Views, 305
Bohan, Marc, 91
Bonnie Doone hosiery, 308
Bottom-up adoption process, 46
Bottom-up fashion, 74, 155, 185
Boutiques, 90, 104, 268, 280, 284, 285–286, 341
Brassiere, 85
Bread-and-butter customers, 276, 279
Bridge jewelry, 310, 314
Brooks Brothers, 156–157, 258, 345
Brown Group, 302
Brummel, Beau, 78–82
Burlington Industries, 205
Burrows, Stephen, 189
Bustle, 85
Butterick Pattern Company, 161

CAD (computer-aided design), 135
Caldor, 299, 340
Calico, 181
CAM (computer-aided manufacture), 135, 311
Cámara de la Moda Espanola, 124
Canopy, 320
Capezio, 301
Caps, 319–320
Cardin, Pierre, 109, 186, 191, 249, 260–261
Career Image, 355
Careers
  fashion merchandising, 356
  finance, 357
  operations, 357
  personnel, 357
  promotion, 357
Caren Charles, 355
Caribbean Basin Initiative (Section 807), 131, 139, 272
Carnegie, Hattie, 184, 192
Carter, Inc., 272, 282
Cartier, 310
Casual Corner, 355
Catalog, 176, 273, 283, 296, 302, 306, 308, 313, 314, 317
Central headquarters, 334, 358
Centralized buying, 371